THIEVES IN THE NIGHT

A Brief History of Supernatural Child Abductions

BY JOSHUA CUTCHIN

ANOMALIST BOOKS

*San Antonio * Charlottesville*

An Original Publication of ANOMALIST BOOKS
THIEVES IN THE NIGHT:
A Brief History of Supernatural Child Abductions
Copyright 2018 by Joshua Cutchin
ISBN: 978-1-938398-95-7

Cover Art by Mister Sam Shearon, mistersamshearon.bigcartel.com
Book Design: Seale Studios

For information about the publisher, go to AnomalistBooks.com, or write to:
Anomalist Books, 5150 Broadway #108, San Antonio, TX 78209

Contents

Author's Note vii

1. "THIEVES IN THE NIGHT"
An Introduction 1

2. "TOO BAD FOR HEAVEN & TOO GOOD FOR HELL"
A Primer on the Fae Folk and Faerie Abduction 11

3. "CHIEF VICTIMS OF THE FAIRY STROKE"
Risks, Methods of Abduction, & Destinations..................................23

4. "NOT YOUR CHILD, NOR IS HE A CHILD"
Changelings..41

5. "FRESH BLOOD AND HUMAN VIGOR"
Motivations Behind Faerie Abduction 57

6. "MASTERY BEYOND THE LIGHT OF THE CAMPFIRE"
Preventing and Thwarting Child Faerie Abduction...........................71

7. "THE ACORN BEFORE THE OAK"
Changeling Confirmation & Resolution 91

8. "MARVELOUS OR DIRE"
Restoration or Resignation...111

9. "HORRIFYING TO TRAGIC"
Medical & Psychological Perspectives on Changelings 119

10. "NOTHING MORE FAMILIAR"
Paranormal Child Abduction Worldwide..133

11. "GOING BUT NEVER GONE—COMING BUT NEVER HERE"
Modern Modalities of Paranormal Child Abduction: An Introduction 159

12. "A 'TAGGED ANIMAL'"
Child Alien Abduction...165

13. "CHILDREN OF THE NORTHERN PEOPLES"
Risks, Methods of Abduction, & Destinations................................179

14. "IT'S TIME TO TAKE IT"
Missing Fetuses 195

15. "WE NEED BABIES"
Motivation & the Hybridization Theory 211

16. "YOU ARE NOT WANTED HERE!"
Preventing, Thwarting, Confirming, & Resolving Child Alien Abduction...227

17. "JUST OUT-OF-FRAME"
UFOlogy, Hybrids, Faeries, & Changelings: An Intersection 237

18. "COME OUT TOWARDS THE WOODS"
Child Sasquatch Abduction 265

19. "AS A BABY IN MY CRIB"
The Crib Creepers 289

20. "STORM CHILD"
Missing 411...297

21. "WE NEED SHAMANS"
Seeking Answers 309

Acknowledgements 329
Endnotes 331
Bibliography 393
Index..435
About the Author..461

... my eye caught a picture... It was that of an ancient Puritan interior—a heavily beamed room with lattice windows, a settle, and clumsy seventeenth-century furniture, with the family sitting about while the father read from the Scriptures. Every face but one showed nobility and reverence, but that one reflected the mockery of the pit. It was that of a young man in years, and no doubt belonged to a supposed son of that pious father, but in essence it was the kin of the unclean things.

— H.P. Lovecraft, "Pickman's Model"

Author's Note

Thieves in the Night deals with complex and delicate issues pertaining to human sexuality, reproduction, mental health, and gender. Because many of these topics can be quite sensitive, every effort has been taken to handle their discussion in an intellectual, respectful manner.

The views herein—particularly the final thesis—should be treated as thought experiments and launching points for further discussion and debate of the paranormal, rather than objective truths.

Chapter 1
"Thieves in the Night"
An Introduction

Of my young Harry. O that it could be proved
That some night-tripping fairy had exchanged
In cradle-clothes our children where they lay,
And call'd mine Percy, his Plantagenet!
Then would I have his Harry, and he mine.

— William Shakespeare, *Henry IV*, Part 1

"Those are my persons!"

Until this moment, the California mother and her two-year-old son had lived a relatively uncomplicated life. It all changed when the boy found the book splayed on the floor, eliciting kisses and affection.

It was his mother's copy of Budd Hopkins' *Intruders*, the seminal 1987 work that further popularized the alleged "alien abduction" phenomenon. The objects of the child's affection were illustrations of spindly, large headed, black-eyed alien "Greys," a depiction now deeply engrained in popular culture.

Suffice to say, this outpouring of emotion alarmed his mother. She listened, disturbed, as her son described a "woman and man" who took him aboard some type of craft for regular physical examinations.

Further details emerged when the mother and son spoke to

John P. Timmerman, who interviewed them on behalf of the Center for UFO Studies in 1988. Each encounter began with being "flown out the window" into a multicolored "spaceship" where the entities told the boy to remain calm while they "hurt" his eyes, forehead, and mouth. Chillingly, the interview concluded when he whispered to his mother that the beings would "get mad at him" for speaking with Timmerman.

"They're my friends."[1]

Regardless of the account's veracity, the boy's story suggests an unsettling trend: are children, for whatever reason, more prone to paranormal activity?

Perhaps such encounters are simply "tall tales," as we all invented in our youth. But to the Fortean—someone studying the subjects popularized by anomalist Charles Fort—these stories carry more weight, neatly fitting into a historical continuum of interaction with the supernatural realm. The remarkable consistency of such accounts, recorded since mankind's earliest days, suggests something more objective than mere storytelling is at work.

If—admittedly "if"—such accounts are true, perhaps children are subject to paranormal encounters because their souls, freshly minted, are not so far removed from Otherworld. In animistic cultures, children are more susceptible to spirit-borne illnesses than adults, their souls weaker and not fully attached to the physical form.[2] From another perspective, perhaps paranormal-prone youth possess greater innate psychic aptitude; research conducted in the 1960s by famed English ghost investigator Andrew Green suggested psychic intuition peaks in the general population around age seven before taking a backseat to the adult values of logic and intellect.[3]

"What fascinates me is why so many children have recently been witness to UFO experiences," researcher David Rees wrote of the trend in 1979, which has shown little sign of abating since. Rees also noted how some sightings over densely populated areas are exclusively witnessed by children, who also prove steadfast in their accounts. "Is it that the children are 'tuned in' to see something—

and if so, what?"[4]

Today's children continue to encounter a robust spectrum of alleged paranormalia. They recall past lives with greater ease, serve as the focus for poltergeist activity, entertain imaginary friends, and witness entities, apparitions, UFOs, and cryptids with an apparent frequency far greater than adults.

They are also abducted more often.

"Children vanish more frequently than any other group," wrote noted author and paranormal researcher John Keel in 1971's *Our Haunted Planet*. "We're not talking about ordinary runaways. In August, 1869, thirteen children vanished in Cork, Ireland. No sign of kidnapping or foul play. The same month there was a wave of disappearing children in Brussels, Belgium. Another group of youngsters melted away in Belfast in August, 1895. And again in August 1920, eight girls (all under 12 years of age) disappeared forever in Belfast... Children have been disappearing in large numbers for centuries all over the world, and most of these cases have remained unsolved."[5]

For millennia, parents worldwide have tightly clutched their babies in the fear that *something* from the darkness will steal them away: madmen, spirits, faeries, demons, beasts, monsters, or—in the case of our technology-obsessed, materialist society—extraterrestrials from another galaxy.

One of the earliest documented examples of paranormal child abduction comes from a nearly 1,600-year-old Turkish account following a cataclysmic earthquake. According to the historian Nicephorus, the people of Constantinople had gathered in the countryside to pray when a child was abruptly pulled into the air by some unseen force, then quickly returned to Earth. It was deemed the work of angels.[6] The case bears a striking resemblance to the poltergeist plaguing the East German village of Sandfeldt where, for three months in 1722, children would be dangled in mid-air in front of numerous witnesses—or even vanished altogether, reappearing only after much fuss and worry from their parents.[7]

By some reports, as many as 800,000 children are reported

missing each year in the United States alone, and it is shocking to consider that some of those who vanish for good may be victims of unearthly kidnappers.[8] Such speculation should not detract from the unfortunate criminal reality of these tragedies—but if a mere fraction of a percent of these disappearances results from supernatural predation, it warrants attention.

THIEVES IN THE NIGHT

This book marks the first interdisciplinary attempt to compare paranormal child abduction from antiquity through the modern era. Predominantly, this means focusing upon Western interpretations of faerie folklore and the pernicious alien abduction phenomenon, particularly the means and motivations behind kidnapping, but multiple detours cover global traditions, Sasquatch abductions, and the recently popularized subject of disappearances in national parks. The book concludes with a look at tangentially related modern phenomena, followed by an attempt to incorporate all previous topics. Forteans are familiar with many of the topics covered; any reader well versed in one subject but less so in another is encouraged to reexamine their area of expertise, as they will likely discover connections previously unnoticed between these phenomena.

One obliquely related topic is worthy of a bit more coverage than others. To the well-read Fortean, tales of child abduction are reflective of a more salacious trend: the preoccupation supernatural forces have with human reproduction and hybridity. It is one of the field's most consistent themes and predates the formation of modern religion. In antiquity, gods and spirits regularly crossbred with human beings. Genesis 6:4 describes the pairing of supernal beings with human women: "The Nephilim were in the earth in those days, and also after that, when the sons of God came in unto the daughters of men, and they bore children to them; the same were the mighty men that were of old, the men of renown."

Mankind's crossbreeding with the alien Other appears in

folklore across the globe. The faeries of yesteryear abducted young ladies for lovers from the British Isles, hairy hominids stole and bred with America's First Nations women, today's aliens snatch us out of bed to collect our gametes—the list is practically endless. Even less-celebrated entities seem interested. West Virginia's Mothman displayed "a penchant for scaring females who were menstruating" during its 1966-1967 reign of terror, according Keel.[9] (Much more can be said about this trend, and anyone seeking to explore this reproductive obsession in even greater depth is encouraged to read Graham Hancock's *Supernatural*.)

Readers are encouraged to make liberal use of their mental filing system's "interesting if true" basket. There may be an objective reality to these phenomena; it is also possible they are mere expressions of every parent's shared fears. The healthiest way to approach the data is as a comparativist.

"What the bad comparativist will do is say, 'Oh, well the Virgin Mary was really a space alien,' or, 'The extraterrestrials were really the Virgin Mary,'" said religious scholar Jeffrey Kripal when discussing the similarities between the 1917 Our Lady of Fátima apparitions and modern UFO sightings. "He or she will privilege one worldview and shove everything into it. What the good comparativist will do is say, 'It looks to me like something similar is going on in those two contexts, but I don't have the slightest idea what it is. But it obviously takes on different mythological frameworks depending on the culture and time period in which it happens.'"[10]

Some subject matter, while tangentially related, has been omitted from this book for brevity. Historical accusations of theft by gypsies, real life cults, the Montauk Project, and the infamous "Satanic Panic" of the late 20th century are not addressed (though all bear clear fingerprints of the themes at hand)—nor will we be tackling supernatural attacks upon or spiritual possession of children. Rather, this book primarily focuses upon the entities accused of stealing those most precious to us.

The thieves in the night.

LILITH, MOLOCH, MYTH, AND MODERNITY

Pinpointing which entity was first blamed for missing children is difficult. Thousands of spirits have been accused throughout human history, a majority of their names lost to time. Certainly the *pmere kwetethe* of Australian aboriginal lore are candidates, given their association with the oldest civilization on earth,[11] but there is no shortage of guilty contenders worldwide. Many of these, from the *pmere kwetethe* to beings found in European pagan traditions, are covered later.

Abrahamic religions, on the other hand, can clearly trace their beliefs in paranormal child abduction to Lilith. First appearing in a Hebrew inscription circa 800 BC, Lilith likely has earlier antecedents in Mesopotamian mythology: ancient Sumerians spoke of the bird-footed, lion-headed Lamashtu, a spirit fond of stealing children, even from the womb, only to kill them by nursing (one sees these same motifs in the Indian subcontinent's Hindu mythology, where the demoness Putana nursed the goddess Krishna in an attempt to kill her with poisoned breasts).[12] Other scholars contend that Lilith may have grown out of belief in Obyzouth, a demoness from the first century *Testament of Solomon*.[13]

Whatever her origins, Lilith appears in numerous ancient texts, listed alongside monsters and other unclean beasts. Particularly horrifying is her confrontation with Elijah in the Jewish *Zohar*, to whom she hisses: "I am off to the house of Mistress X who is expecting a child. I am going to plunge her into the sleep of death, take away her babe, suck its blood, drain its marrow and seal up its flesh."[14]

The prophet rebuked the demon, declaring the Lord would turn her to stone; in response, Lilith vowed to depart whenever her name was seen or spoken. Thus was born an early repellant of supernatural harm: the offending entity's name.[15] Inscribed amulets became a common childbirth precaution not only against Lilith but other witches called the *Benemmerinnen*, said to lurk about mothers in labor intent on stealing newborns.[16] Such precautions were utilized for weeks after delivery (males were vulnerable up to one week after birth, females three).[17]

Judeo-Christian superstition gave Lilith the attributes of a succubus, raping lonely men in their sleep, causing miscarriages, and stealing children by slipping through cracked windows.[18] Sometime around the ninth century she was retroactively named Adam's first, inferior wife, made from the same dust as her husband. After demanding equality alongside Adam, God's angels punished Lilith, turning her children into demons and thus igniting her hatred for infants and mothers.[19]

When the same angels threatened to slaughter one hundred of her demon spawn each day, Lilith refused to repent. "Go ahead," she is said to have hissed. "But don't you know that I was created to strangle newborn infants, boys before the eighth day and girls before the twentieth?" In this retelling, she made a pact to flee at the sight of the angels' names, rather than her name, on an amulet.[20]

Multiple variations on this myth exist. In one, Lilith was created from filth, rather than dust. In another, her offense was refusing to lie underneath Adam during intercourse, while other stories claim her evil progeny were birthed via demonic promiscuity.[21] According to some Judaic traditions, Adam and Eve, during an extended separation, were violated by demonic forces and spawned their own evil progeny: the *mazikeen* or *mazakim*, born out of lustful isolation.[22]

In Judaism, the act of circumcision represents an important covenant with the Lord, and boys are vulnerable during the period leading up to their *brit milah*. In one tale, a Rabbi holding *wachnacht*—the night preceding circumcision, when boys were especially susceptible to evil spirits—spotted a black cat leaping toward the child's crib. The Rabbi jabbed his iron-tipped cane in the feline's eye, and the next day he found the midwife with her eye bandaged. She was revealed as a servant of Lilith, seeking babies for her mistress.[23]

Less surreptitious than Lilith—but equally unsettling—

was Moloch. According to Hebrew tradition, the ram-headed Canaanite god demanded child sacrifices of his followers, who placed their offspring in his idol's arms, outstretched over a roaring furnace.[24] Though some scholars argue this act was a symbolic ritual purification by fire rather than a literal sacrifice, the mandate nonetheless informed Jewish tradition for millennia.[25]

These Biblical anxieties naturally found their way into the folklore of Europe, placing children under perennial threat from supernatural sources. Fairytales like "Rumpelstiltskin," wherein an imp imprisons a miller's daughter, took root shortly after Eastern and Western Indo-European languages split—4,000 to 5,000 years ago.[26] Sometime before 1592 a stained glass window was installed in a German church depicting a mysterious musician leading children from their homes; whether the 14th century Pied Piper of Hamelin incident was real or a metaphor for disease, starvation, or the Children's Crusade of 1212 remains uncertain.[27]

These anxieties returned centuries later, when a wave of "phantom social workers" swept the United States and particularly the United Kingdom in the early 1990s, showing up at homes out of nowhere with false credentials and a preternatural knowledge of the family's activities. After expressing their intent to examine or take the children of the household into their custody, these odd visitors fled at the slightest sign of parental suspicion.

"The visitors were mostly one or two women, but sometimes a woman and a man," wrote the English author Patrick Harpur. "The women were typically in their late twenties or early thirties, heavily made up, smartly dressed and of medium height. They carried clipboards and, often, identification cards."[28] None were ever caught, and evidence of their existence remains elusive, outside of eyewitness testimony.[29]

Modern fictions still concern themselves with the lure of children to the supernatural. J.M. Barrie's famous 1904 *Peter Pan* wrapped paranormal child abduction motifs in a relatively inoffensive stage play. More contemporary fare such as Jim Henson's 1986 creation *Labyrinth* embraced these themes, yet unlike *Peter Pan*, refused to shy away from their more menacing overtones.

The 21st century has birthed at least one such legend, the fictional internet sensation "Slender Man." This lanky, besuited wraith, created in an online contest, is said to target children. Despite its fictitious origins, anyone doubting the archetype's power need only refer to the 2014 case in Waukesha, Wisconsin, where a 12-year-old girl was nearly fatally stabbed to death by two of her peers in hopes of appeasing the entity.[30]

Perhaps no region's folklore has contributed more to these modern expressions of paranormal child abduction than the British Isles. Here, we see a rich repetition of foundational motifs to which today's interpretations owe a direct debt of inspiration. Amidst verdant hills, weathered heaths, and imposing cliffs, children of England, Scotland, and Ireland were under near-constant threat of being spirited away by the land's first inhabitants.

By the faeries.

Chapter 2
"Too Bad for Heaven & Too Good for Hell"
A Primer on the Fae Folk and Faerie Abduction

Rest thee, babe! I love thee dearly,
And as thy mortal mother nearly;
Ours is the swiftest steed and proudest,
That moves where the tramp of the host is loudest.
Shuheen sho, lulo lo!

        — Edward Walsh, "The Fairy Nurse"

Everyone agreed that, even though Shuï Rhys came from a poor farming family, few girls in Wales were as beautiful as she was. Her delicate white skin, black hair, and dark eyes made the 17-year-old ill fitted to her daily chores and cattle droving. Indeed, she had little interest in helping around the farm, choosing to dally through the countryside before returning home late.

Shuï was regularly scolded by her mother for procrastination until one day she told her, "I couldn't help it; it was the *Tylwyth Teg.*"

Her mother, shocked, listened as her daughter confessed to consorting with the Welsh forest faeries, whose harps, tiny green coats, and beautiful language kept her spellbound. Following this revelation, Shuï was no longer scolded for tardiness—for fear of offending her newfound friends—until one day she failed to return at all. Neither field nor forest yielded sign of the girl.[31]

Though Shuï was older than most children abducted by the faeries, the story related in Wirt Sikes's 1880 *British Goblins* illustrates the typical beguiling influence they exerted upon young people. The Good Folk, Wee Folk, Gentry, People of Peace—believers used countless euphemisms to avoid their wrath and spare their children. Faeries were a very real part of their world, and so was the risk of offending them.[32]

The notion of faeries possessing emotions other than kindness runs counter to modern expectations. Genteel post-Victorian depictions of faeries belie a dark tradition where powerful beings were historically feared and respected in equal measure. In reality, faeries could be benevolent helpers or mischievous tricksters. Appeasing them with food and respect brought good fortune, a clean house, or a bountiful harvest; on balance, any offense incited ill luck, blighted crops, physical torment, illness, or, of course, abduction.[33]

The phenomenon's complexity is exemplified by its diversity. Though generally attributed short stature and underground dwellings, faeries came in varying shapes and sizes, including what we would recognize today as mermaids, giants, gnomes, sprites, ogres, trolls, etc. They possessed varying degrees of corporeality, from physical beings to purely ethereal spirits, and inhabited every nook of the world: forests, lakes, streams, mountains, caves, and woodlands, even people's homes.[34]

They also inhabited every *continent*. Though this portion of the book largely discusses European faerie folklore, there is no shortage of uncannily similar traditions from around the globe, many of which feature in later discussion. Unless deliberately specified, however, most of the faerie lore herein should be assumed to come from the British Isles.

ORIGINS

Whatever the faeries truly were is lost to time, because anecdotes, true tales, and folklore blend together so effortlessly.

Numerous proposals have been made over the years regarding the origins of faerie belief, or the "Fairy Faith," as it came to be known.

Once it was vogue to interpret faeries as ancestral memories of conquered indigenous peoples. W.Y. Evans Wentz, whose 1911 *The Fairy Faith in Celtic Countries* remains foundational in its field, admitted "it is very highly probable that a folk-memory of Lappish, Pictish, or other small but not true pygmy races, has superficially coloured the modern fairy traditions"; however, by-and-large, "the testimony of Celtic literature goes to show that leprechauns and similar dwarfish beings are not due to a folk-memory of a real pygmy race, that they are spirits like elves."[35]

Ample evidence suggests faeries were demoted pagan gods, clinging to memory long after Catholicism asserted itself in the British Isles.[36] Minor pre-Christian deities of the landscape—*genii loci*—inhabiting features like trees and rocks naturally overlapped with late 19th century interpretations of fae folk as elementals or "nature spirits."[37] Traditions of protective household spirits and family ancestors were also folded into the concept of the faeries.[38]

Rural populations exerted themselves attempting to reconcile the Fairy Faith and Christianity. Some flatly relegated faeries to demons, while others adopted more inventive explanations. One popular explanation held faeries were fallen angels from Lucifer's rebellion—those too bad for Heaven and too good for Hell,[39] or those caught outside both realms at the war's conclusion. Cast aside, they fell to Earth and, to quote Irish storyteller Eddie Lenihan, "the ones that had fallen to ground, they're the ones that live in the earth; the ones that had fallen into the sea, they're the sea faeries; and the ones who were still in the air, they're the air faeries today."[40]

Icelandic legend contends the *Huldufólk* ("hidden folk") were holdovers from Eden. According to folklorist Jón Árnason, the Lord paid a surprise visit to Adam and Eve to see their children. Eve, in the process of washing her progeny (more than just Cain and Abel, it seems), presented her clean children, as she was ashamed to let the Lord see the dirty ones. Knowing this, He proclaimed, "What man hides from God, God will hide from man." Immediately "these unwashed children became forthwith invisible, and took up their abode in mounds, and hills, and rocks."[41] In other parts of Scandinavia, it was believed the *vættir*, nature spirits, began human-sized, then shrank as Christianity spread throughout the region.[42]

Variations on the Eden legend can be found throughout Europe. At least one holds that the hidden children were not those of Adam and Eve, but Adam and Lilith;[43] another, from the Welsh island of Anglesey, replaces Adam and Eve with a common woman embarrassed by her fecundity.[44] Each variation ends with the Lord banishing the children and creating the faeries.

A strong connection existed between faeries and the dead, especially in the British Isles. "When the soul has left the body, it is drawn away, sometimes, by the fairies," wrote poet and folklorist W.B. Yeats. "I have a story of a peasant who once saw, sitting in a fairy rath, all who had died for years in his village."[45]

Folklore tells of mourners seeing or visiting deceased loved ones among the fae folk. In one tale collected by Lady Wilde (Irish folklorist and mother to Oscar Wilde), a young lady of Inishark was weeping for her dead lover when a beautiful lady, clad in white, offered her a wreath of herbs. Whenever she plucked its leaves a magical trance-inducing smoke would appear and the fae would whisk her to Fairyland to her waiting lover—provided she gave no Christian prayer or sign. This enchantment was quite efficacious until her devout mother made the sign of the cross over the sleeping girl, who, terrified, shouted "Mother! mother! the dead are coming for me!" Soon thereafter, the girl died.[46]

The strength of this connection makes it difficult to discern whether the departed and faeries were one and the same. Scandinavia's *döckalfar*, for example, dwelt in burial mounds and possessed an unhealthy pallor, making them sound strikingly similar to the restless dead.[47]

"In Irish mythology, and in other Celtic mythologies, such as Breton and Welsh, the realm of the dead and the realm of supernatural beings are sometimes described in a way that hints they are the same location," wrote Jenny Butler, Lecturer in the Department of Study of Religions at University College Cork. "It has been suggested, indeed that the *sídhe* and the human dead are one and the same and that veneration of the ancestors carried on as customs of leaving offerings for the fairies."[48]

This attitude is echoed by former Sorbonne historian Claude Lecouteux:

> When a man was remembered well after his death, when his life was beneficial to the community, he enjoyed for a short time after his departure a particular status: the pagans made him a god or spirit, the Christians a saint, but the reaction is the same...
>
> In fact the good dead and the spirits were distinct from one another originally...
>
> This amalgam came about on two levels, in my opinion: 1) the local spirits and the dead worthy of offerings were merged with elves by virtue of the latter's beneficial nature and their habitat; 2) all were the object of agrarian and/or domestic worship, and they were demonized by the Church and merged with the dwarves, creatures reputedly malevolent and dreadful.[49]

Further complicating matters is the identical language used to describe the dead, the mentally ill, and faerie abductees as "taken" or "away." Death, affliction, and faerie abduction—of the non-physical variety—often appeared the same or, seen another way, death and illness *were* faerie abduction.

"To be 'away' while physically present in this world meant that while pursuing ordinary tasks one was also in the power—and world—of the fairies," said professor Carole Silver. "Among the symptoms of this condition were the dazed look and the vacant mind; fainting fits, trances, fatigue or languidity, even long and heavy sleeping."[50] This was sometimes referred to as the *fairy stroke*, a term modern medicine borrowed to describe a lack of blood flow to the brain.[51] In Scottish lore, this was referred to as "in the hill," meaning one was under the influence of the *trow*.[52]

It is unclear what exactly the Fairy Faith described, but its features are consistent with a variety of phenomena recorded through the present. Certainly they should not be viewed through the reductive Judeo-Christian dichotomy of good versus evil. Perhaps it is best not to think of the Fae Folk literally as spirits, little people, or the dead, but rather as a concept, an idea—a stand-in for a nonhuman *other*.

FAELIENS?

Two boys lying on a hill were enjoying a Surrey summer day when a sensation of peace settled over them. Hearing a strange voice, the boys sat up and saw a pair of odd men in shimmering clothing, conversing in a strange language and accompanied by a bright light. They neared, switching to English to tell the boys they came from far away and knew the future. They urged the lads to sleep. After awaking and walking home, the boys realized they had been missing a full 24 hours.[53]

Anyone would be forgiven for assuming this is a tale of the faeries. In reality, the story comes from the 1940s, and is cited as evidence of UFO, rather than fae folk, contact. It all depends on the prism through which we observe the phenomena.

Wrote folklorist Thomas E. Bullard:

> Comparativists struck perhaps the richest vein of parallels in the traditions of fairy lore. Belief in diminutive supernatural beings is worldwide and age-old, but the typical short UFO humanoid

fits the functional role of these beings with little obvious difference than a change of address and mode of transportation. The entrance to Fairyland is often a hill or an ancient burial mound that rises on luminous pillars during nights of fairy revelry to resemble a landed UFO. Fairyland itself has a luminous but sunless sky similar to the alien Otherworld or UFO interior described by abductees...

A close encounter with fairies is perilous business. Any human who spends an hour or so in their company may return home to find that fifty or one hundred years have passed—a motif called the 'supernatural lapse of time in Fairyland,' with hints of the time-lapse phenomenon in abductions.[54]

Additional comparisons are worth drawing, observed not only by Bullard himself but also preeminent UFOlogist Jacques Vallee in his landmark book *Passport to Magonia*. The reproductive obsession has already been noted, but consider how both faeries and modern "aliens" are seen carrying wands, seemingly with the power to levitate or paralyze witnesses. Modern UFO experiencers find themselves drawn to lonely locales before abductions, just as faerie victims might be *pixie led* to a field full of *faerie lights*. Yesterday we had faerie rings and subterranean passages leading to earthen faerie forts; today we have crop circles and alleged underground bases. Faeries pinched and poked their victims; aliens perform surgery on theirs. Modern farmers might blame unexplained livestock mutilation on aliens, while their ancestors would have accused the fae folk. In folklore, a taller Faerie Queen sometimes led shorter faeries; in abduction accounts, short Grey aliens are often led by a taller supervisory figure.

Much of this book's purpose is to highlight the internal consistencies between the mythic and the modern. Some comparisons are made as they arise, while others must wait until UFOs are discussed in greater detail; regardless, striking parallels exist between these phenomena, even when examining a tiny, niche aspect such as child abduction.

FAERIE ABDUCTION

After their diminutive height and proclivity for subterranean dwellings, the most commonly shared trait of all faeries was a love of theft. Their kleptomania was so renowned the English language incorporated the word *bogart*, meaning "to selfishly appropriate or keep" a substance. Though attributed to actor Humphrey Bogart,[55] it is suggested to have earlier roots in the *boggart*, a particularly thieving faerie.[56]

Abduction was common among all fae folk, regardless of their disposition, and it was not only youths at risk. *Drows* were said to stalk churches in the Orkney Islands for the purpose of stealing "pious deacons and deaconesses."[57] "Even the milder, more generally benign *Tylwyth Teg* of Wales were inveterate kidnappers," according to Silver.[58]

Women and children were favored targets, however. "All bugbears [faeries] worthy of the name take away children," wrote Scottish folklorist J. Gregorson Campbell.[59] After all, *bugbears, bogies, boggarts, bogles*—all these faerie names are the origins of the modern *boogeyman*.[60]

It was common for parents to keep unruly brats in line with warnings of faerie abduction. "You mind, or the *Tylwyth Teg* will take you away," Welsh mothers would threaten.[61] "The goblin will gobble you!" they warned in France.[62] German children on the Isle of Rügen were warned the Brown Dwarfs would take them away to work for 50 years.[63]

Despite these warnings, examples exist where well-behaved children disappeared. Evans Wentz was told of a woman whose sister had been taken for her *good* behavior.[64] In Greece, faeries abducted "clever" children, but usually returned them "laden with gifts, lovelier in person than when they were taken from home."[65]

Accounts of faeries taking children were also used to write off children who disappeared in an unexplained—or unpleasant—fashion. A Devon gamekeeper's eldest daughter disappeared and was found after several days, naked. "It was assumed that she had been abducted by the pixies but subsequently returned," wrote folklore researchers Mark Norman and Jo Hickey-Hall. "The child presumably got lost and the pixy stories were wheeled out to explain the event."[66] In early 20th century America, the term "faerie" was sometimes employed as a euphemism for "prostitute"; thus, when families told others their daughter was "away with the faeries," they were saved the awkwardness of admitting her true whereabouts.[67] Indeed, narratives of faerie interference were used to conceal a host of deviant behavior "such as extreme tardiness, premarital sexual relations, infidelity, incest, child molestation, wife battering, and sexual assault," wrote Peter Narváez, folklore professor at Memorial University of Newfoundland.[68]

Did adults of the Old World believe faerie stories, or were they purely a means of behavioral control? Influential Swedish folklorist Carl Wilhelm von Sydow wrote:

> All these bogy figures that the folk scare children
> with: the old man of the well who catches them if
> they go too near the well; and the wolf, witch, etc.,
> who catches them if they trample down the corn,
> etc., are *purely fictitious* beings that the adults only
> pretend exist, but do not believe in themselves...
> The elders talked about the dangerous beings in the
> corn before it was cut, but when it is, the beings
> do not appear. And then they may jokingly say, as
> in Russia, that the beings were previously as high
> as the corn, but after harvest no higher than the
> stubble; or they may also say, jokingly, that the wolf
> or witch is caught in the last sheaf; and may also try
> perhaps to make an animal or human figure out of

the last sheaf, this too being pure joking. Or those who fell ill or hurt themselves during harvesting were said to have been bitten by the wolf, etc.; yet no one believes it, knowing quite well that it is *only a joke.*[69]

The sheer number of stories related to ethnographers and cultural anthropologists by earnest, sober informants undermines von Sydow's contention. Two such tales exhibit common faerie (and UFO) abduction motifs, ones that will become familiar by the end of the book. The first comes from Norway:

> The farm Snöva, which lies above the river, was haunted a great deal by *huldre*-folk. Once a three-year-old boy, named John, was taken by the underground folk. One day he was playing with some other children in the farmyard, when all of a sudden he was gone. Folk understood that the child must have been taken away to the mountains, and they tried to exorcise it forth by reading from the Gospels, singing psalms, and ringing the church bells—but all in vain. When all this proved of no avail, they tried to call upon the "Evil One" to help them, by oaths and evil speaking. This way was the most effectual, for straightaway the child appeared, in the same place and position as when it vanished. Rain had now come, and it was muddy in the farmyard, but the child was absolutely clean and dry. He told how he had been to the abode of the underground folk, and that there he was treated with herring bones and eyes. John grew up afterwards, and he became an influential man.[70]

The second comes from Welsh storyteller Shone Tomos Shone Rhytherch. "I tell you that fairies were to be seen in the days of my youth by the thousand, and I have seen them myself a hundred times," he said. "Indeed, when I was a boy, it was dangerous to leave children in their cradles, without some one to watch them; so common was it for the fairies to steal them away." Rhytherch told the story of Gitto Bach, a young boy fond of playing with faeries. As proof of his mountaintop rambles, Gitto produced lettered scraps of peculiar, white "faerie paper."[71] (It is tempting, if recklessly speculative, to compare the boy's lettered paper to the "mystery metal" allegedly found at the 1947 Roswell UFO crash, a thin, pliable material embossed with hieroglyphic-style writing.[72]) One day Gitto disappeared, and the community searched to no avail; two years later, the boy reappeared on his mother's doorstep, dressed as he had the day he disappeared, claiming to have only left yesterday.[73] In his hands, he carried a white paper garment he had worn among the faeries—similar to what famed UFO experiencer Whitley Strieber was asked to wear during one of his encounters.[74]

In addition to straightforward abductions like these, faeries also had a keen interest in retrieving what rightfully belonged to them, including hybrid children. According to Icelandic legend, a young girl named Olōf showed consistent kindness to an elf boy, giving him milk when her sister did not; after years of this interaction, Olōf found herself with child, presumably from her visitor. Following the baby's birth, its father and an elderly couple returned to Olōf and took the child.[75]

Faeries were not indiscriminate thieves, however. There were circumstances rendering some children more susceptible to their grasp.

Chapter 3
"Chief Victims of the Fairy Stroke"
Risks, Methods of Abduction, & Destinations

Who are the norns
who are helpful in need
And the babe from the mother bring?

— "Fáfnismál"

Among the oldest recorded, rather than folkloric, child faerie abductions is an account by early church chronicler Ralph of Coggeshall, compiler of the *Chronicon Anglicanum*. In the 13th century, he wrote, the voice of a girl named "Malekin" could be heard in Dagworthy Castle, Suffolk. The disembodied spirit said she was taken by the fae folk while her mother went to work in the field but would rejoin the mortal plane in seven years' time. The story, which could also be interpreted as a poltergeist incident, is perhaps the only known account from the taken child's perspective.[76]

It is also one of a handful to feature a female abductee—male infants were significantly more likely to disappear.

RISKS: CIRCUMSTANCES OF BIRTH, DAYS OF THE WEEK, AND CLOTHING

"They took only boys, never girls," Welshman John Jones informed Evans Wentz.[77] This gender bias, according to retired

University of Pittsburgh professor D.L. Ashliman, illustrates the folk belief that "fairies… have but little use for a female human child."

Besides gender, other circumstances of birth played a significant role in determining a child's likelihood of abduction. Certain birthdays, such as Fridays[78] or Whitsuntide (around Pentecost),[79] brought bad luck, while Sundays granted good fortune.[80] In the British Isles, babies were most vulnerable three to nine days after birth.[81] In Germany this period was extended to six weeks,[82] and in Slavic countries 40 days.[83] There are, however, a great number of reports of children taken at seven—a regularly recurring age amongst all child abductees—and disappearances of children as old as nine were recorded (to say nothing of adult abductees).[84] Even the act of preparing for childbirth could alert faeries, making both babies and new mothers targets for kidnapping.[85]

Once this culturally mandated period of greatest danger passed, a child's first sneeze decreased the kidnapping risk,[86] simply because it represented a failed faerie abduction[87]— in rare cases, sneezes were said to break spells like the "evil eye,"[88] or return those trapped in Fairyland.[89] Children remained in jeopardy throughout infancy, however, especially if they were beautiful or possessed fair hair.[90]

"Young women, remarkable for beauty, young men, and handsome children, are the chief victims of the fairy stroke," Lady Wilde wrote of the faeries' affinity for attractive individuals.[91] Homes with lovely babies (and wine) attracted French goblins,[92] as well as the Welsh *Tylwyth Teg*.[93] Saying "Bless you"[94] or "God bless you"[95] to a comely child warded off calamity; otherwise, it could be "over-looked," drawing attention from the fae folk.[96]

There appeared to be an inheritable component to these abductions—some families were kidnap-prone, especially if the parents had offended the faeries.[97] Evans Wentz heard of a woman who had three children exchanged for faerie babies (the changeling phenomenon, addressed in the next chapter).[98] It was also common for individuals to become recurring abductees, visiting the Otherworld throughout their lives just as modern UFO witnesses claim. In another tale collected by Evans Wentz, a Cornish boy was "carried away in his cloak" by *piskies*, "but the boy got home. Then the *pisky* took him a second time, and again the boy got home. Each time the boy was away for only an hour."[99]

Certain days of the week were more perilous than others. Faeries were most active on late November days,[100] Wednesdays,[101] Fridays,[102] May Day,[103] Whitsuntide,[104] St. John's Eve,[105] and, of course, Halloween,[106] after harvest when the wilds were surrendered to them once more.[107] (Regarding these correlations with days of the week, consider how John Keel noticed UFO sightings disproportionately occur on Wednesdays, a data point he deemed the "Wednesday Phenomenon."[108]) Inclement weather could render these dates even unluckier, a detail important to later discussion: abductions were more likely on misty days,[109] during storms,[110] or on days of *gwlithlaw*, the Welsh term for "dew-rain."[111] In Norse folklore, the god Höðr loses his way while hunting after a mysterious fog descends upon the forest; shortly thereafter, he finds himself in the company of *virgines silvestres*, beguiling faerie forest maidens similar to the Germanic *norns*.[112]

Since the color was so closely associated with faeries, it was ill advised to clad children in green, especially in parts of Scotland.[113] Doing so brought them to the attention of the "little green men," increasing the likelihood of kidnapping.

"Fairies were believed to take umbrage when humans wore [green], and could cause trouble for such miscreants," wrote Patricia Monaghan in *The Encyclopedia of Celtic Mythology and Folklore*. "A century ago, many women in the Scottish Highlands refused to wear green on the grounds that it was unlucky."[114] This superstition carried over into the New World where, in Newfoundland, it was said the 1892 St. John's fire and Bank Crash of 1894 were caused by the issuing of green postage stamps, which invoked the faeries' wrath.[115]

RISKS: UNBAPTISED CHILDREN

Patrick Kennedy's *Legendary Fictions of the Irish Celts* tells of a woman from Grange who birthed a baby boy while her husband was at sea. The christening was delayed to accommodate the father's attendance, a dangerous proposition in the eyes of the villagers. "She and her husband were not natives of the country, and they were not as much afraid of leaving the child unchristened as our people would be," Kennedy wrote.

Neighbors watched anxiously as the child, untouched by Holy Water, grew into a healthy boy. Eighteen months after birth, the mother heard "a great rush like as if a whole number of fowls were flying down the chimley... then another sound like as if the fowls were flying out again." The boy grew deathly ill and irritable, but the neighbors knew the truth: *Duiné Sighe*, the faeries, had taken her child.[116]

"Fairy-Folk were believed, in general, to have power over none but unbaptized children," American poet and essayist Louise Guiney wrote in 1888.[117] Without question, the greatest indicator of risk came from a child's status within the church. Mothers refused to travel between childbirth and baptism,[118] and failure to christen children during the calendar year of their birth was unlucky.[119] Baptism held a profound power in every Christian country, where folk beliefs contended children never thrived until christened, or that the rite could heal afflictions.[120] Baptism was even claimed to grant Christian souls to illegitimate human-faerie hybrids, should they ever get the chance.[121]

"Even in Pagan times the nameless state of the baby may have been thought to expose him to danger," wrote folklorist Katharine Briggs.[122] Entry into the church via baptism mirrors pre-Christian beliefs, where naming a child or undergoing a rite of passage marked recognition of personhood in the community, safeguarding against supernatural forces.[123]

"Christening meant incorporation and a termination of the liminal period," said University of Tromsø professor

Ann Skjelbred.[124] *Liminal periods*—times of transition, of the threshold—are favored by faeries; it is why they are active at dawn and dusk, and why they linger under bridges and at crossroads or at the forest's edge. For Christians, the time between birth and baptism is liminal, born into the world but not into the church. Unchristened babies were essentially unclean heathens and, in some traditions, considered untouchable.[125]

To late medieval European Catholics, death within this liminal period sent infants to Limbo; for some contemporary practitioners of the Fairy Faith, it meant they joined the ranks of the fae folk, becoming *pixies* or *Will-O-the-Wisps*.[126] Such spirits appeared as lights leading unwary travelers off course.[127]

The unchristened even attracted supernatural phenomena in death. "Unbaptized children and abortions are generally buried under 'monument bushes,'" wrote John O'Hanlon of 1870s Ireland. "Ghosts or monsters were occasionally conjured up, before the excited imaginations of credulous or timid persons, when passing these objects at night."[128]

Again, we see faeries asserting their relationship with the dead.

RISKS: ENVIRONMENT

Regardless of the origins ascribed to faeries, all traditions closely associated them with the landscape. Many European cultures regarded boulders as faerie homes; ergo, wandering among them was treacherous, lest one disappear.[129]

"A heap of stones in a field should not be disturbed, though needed for building—especially if they are part of an ancient tumulus," Evans Wentz wrote of Irish practice around the Knockma Woods north of Galway. "The fairies are said to live inside the pile, and to move the stones would be most unfortunate."[130] In parts of Scandinavia, construction projects are still diverted around large boulders traditionally held as elven dwellings.[131]

Vertical boulders were used throughout Europe to delineate boundaries and provide intertribal meeting areas—liminal zones, in this case the threshold between territories and neutral gathering places, respectively.[132] This may be one reason megaliths, boulder fields, etc. were so closely associated with the fae folk.

Other features of the land were not to be trifled with. Circular earthworks and stone structures known collectively as faerie forts, ringforts, mounds, knowes, hills, ráths, lios, dúns, etc. were deemed traditional faerie dwelling places and were avoided at all costs, for to wander among them increased the likelihood of being taken.[133] Various sources cite between 40,000 and 60,000 such sites in Ireland alone. Though some correctly understood these structures as Neolithic or Early Christian in origin, it was nonetheless held the fae folk moved into these areas after their human occupants vacated.[134] This association between ancient sites and the Good Folk was drawn on the European continent as well, where, according to Guiney, French faeries "guarded cromlechs [megaliths] with care."[135]

Any wild areas, particularly forests, were considered the faeries' domain. The etymology of the word "panic" clearly demonstrates this association. The term originates from the Greek *panikon*, "literally 'pertaining to Pan,' the god of the woods and fields who was the source of mysterious sounds that caused contagious, groundless fear in herds and crowds, or in people in lonely spots." Greek mythology represents Pan as a satyr or faun, a depiction often used for various fae folk (and, of course, adapted into Christian depictions of Satan).[136]

Other notable sites of danger included "faerie rings," naturally occurring circles of mushrooms; any child who dared circle a faerie ring nine times in England's Northumberland County tempted fate.[137] As with so much faerie lore, this darker belief eroded over time into childish fancy: "If you can run nine times round a ring without drawing breath, a fairy will appear and bring you something good," late Dorset lore held.[138]

In other regions, like Germany, the taboo against certain areas remained. Grain fields were the domain of the *Roggenmutter*, or Rye-Mother, and her fondness for stealing children was well known: "Hold your mouth or the *Roggenmutter*, with her long black tits, will come and take you away!"[139]

In England, specters of Bloody Bones, Rawhead, Grindylow, or Jenny Greenteeth, ostensibly water demons, lurked beneath ponds, waiting to snatch youth wandering by the banks: "Keep away from the Marl-Pit or Rawhead and Bloody Bones will have you!"[140] Any body of water was often considered the dwelling of spirits and faeries, particularly of the feminine variety (not coincidentally, apparitions of the Blessed Virgin Mary in the Christian era are almost always associated with underground springs, creeks, or other water sources).

"We most often meet fairies by the shores of lakes, fountains, or springs," Lecouteux wrote. "The co-occurrence of these sites and a lady—regardless of what name she bears—has commanded the attention of researchers who have long realized that fairies could very often be considered as aquatic spirits: an anthropomorphic expression of the *numen* reputed to dwell in such places. Fairies rarely wander far from what clearly seems to be their natural element...."[141]

Children might be pulled to these dangerous areas despite warnings; such wandering was known as being *pixie led* or *pouk-ledden*. Victims found themselves inexplicably drawn to unfamiliar areas, or familiar areas rendered unrecognizable, where they typically *panicked* and returned only with great difficulty. If pixie led children encountered faeries, it was advised they accept nothing from them—especially food—else they would be abducted.

Youth's aimless rambles indicated parental negligence, another risk factor. Innumerable tales exist where the failure to watch children created an opportunity for their disappearance, and it was particularly dangerous to leave an infant unattended while performing daily duties like harvesting or shearing.[142] One Welsh mother, well aware of the risk, was pressed to make a short trip to her neighbors. She hastened home after spying "old elves of the blue petticoat," but the damage was already done, her twins taken.[143]

A dreadfully perilous act to engage in without adult supervision was berry picking. A County Donegal seer told Evans Wentz:

> One day, just before sunset in midsummer, and I a boy then, my brother and cousin and myself were gathering bilberries (whortleberries) up by the rocks at the back of here, when all at once we heard music. We hurried round the rocks, and there we were within a few hundred feet of six or eight of the gentle folk, and they dancing. When they saw us, a little woman dressed all in red came running out from them towards us, and she struck my cousin across the face with what seemed to be a green rush. We ran for home as hard as we could, and when my cousin reached the house she fell dead. Father saddled a horse and went for Father Ryan. When Father Ryan arrived, he put a stole about his neck and began praying over my cousin and reading psalms and striking her with the stole; and in that way brought her back. He said if she had not caught hold of my brother, she would have been taken forever.[144]

In Ireland's County Tipperary, the presence of the *pooka* put a specific deadline on when berries could be picked:

> Young and old would not pick berries off bushes after Nov. 1st. On that night it was believed that the 'pooka' destroyed all the berries and particular attention was given to the sloe bushes and plum trees. The black sloes… would not be picked after [the first November] night. Neither would haws or plums…[145]

These beliefs traveled with immigrants to the New World. Peter

Narváez collected dozens of such stories from Newfoundland. Local lore claimed bread, taken while berry picking, could be fed to the faeries to avoid their wrath.

In one case collected by Narváez, a young boy forgot this precaution. "The next night he went and never came back for three days and three nights. After he returned he could only say a few words and appeared to have gone 'silly.'"

In another Newfoundland account a group of berry-picking children was approached by "a little boy without hair" who offered them something in a mug—they refused, aware of the consequences of taking anything from the faeries. Narváez interpreted berry picking areas as another liminal zone, in this case representing boundaries between communities.[146]

Despite the dangers of the wilderness, children were not necessarily safe indoors either. Orientation, even a child's placement in the home, could attract faeries. In Scotland it was unadvisable to leave a baby—even baptized—near a west-facing window, lest the *sluag* take them.[147] One Irish folktale mentioned a child who was left near a window hit with "a sheaf of straw," and turned into a changeling.[148] In Germany, alternating infants from arm to arm was considered risky, as this "changing" could also produce a changeling.[149]

METHODS OF ABDUCTION: LEVITATION, WHIRLWINDS, & MISCARRIAGES

Faeries were opportunists; as noted, unattended babies were at greatest risk.[150] Any accident could be utilized to their advantage—famed Irish folklorist Isabella Augusta, aka "Lady Gregory," told of a boy taken by sea faeries after a conger eel upset his boat (given conflation between faerie theft and death, this claim is unsurprising).[151]

Faeries were not above making their own opportunities. Shouts of "Fire!" drew a family out of their cottage in one Manx tale, and as they returned an invisible force was lifting the newborn from its cradle. The child was dropped, but two subsequent diversions (including a clatter in the cattle barn) finished the job.[152]

Settlers to the British Isles, likely fueled by discoveries of Pict arrowheads in newly plowed earth, claimed illness—which, as noted, was viewed in some contexts as faerie abduction—was the result of *elf-shot*. The notion held fae folk literally targeted victims with tiny arrows.[153]

Faeries frequently employed subtler methods when abducting infants. Simple touch, for example, even the act of handing a child to a faerie crone for a moment, could produce a changeling.[154] They also employed the "evil eye," as when a Galway mother let an old crone into her home—the guest looked upon the baby without blessing it, a scenario already noted for its risk.[155] A case could be made that such legends speak of witches, not faeries, but the lines between them blur too often to be certain; in 1566, English legal records officially named faeries "familiar spirits in the crime of witchcraft."[156] As British historian Simon Young said, "What witches are blamed for, fairies are often blamed for."[157]

Witnesses to thwarted abductions described infants lifted as if by unseen hands. Sometimes this evidence was circumstantial; the Brothers Grimm told of a Leipzig child found "lying crossways and uncovered in its cradle" on three different nights, presumably the work of faeries.[158] The best-known eyewitness to attempted baby abduction was Jennet Francis, a Welsh mother whose ordeal was described by Wirt Sikes. After feeling her baby being wrestled from her embrace one evening, Francis fought back, persevering only through physical exertion, screams, and prayers.[159]

In another Welsh story from Richard Suggett, faeries tried spiriting away the daughter of Dacey and Abel Walter of Glynebwy. After discovering her infant missing in the middle of the night, Dacey found the babe perched atop the cupboard-bed, "and it was concluded that the fairies had left it there after failing to convey it any further."[160]

Modern accounts still mention levitating babies, though faeries usually escape the blame. In 1930—centuries after the Fairy Faith diminished and thousands of miles away from Europe—owners of Virginia's Woodlawn Plantation placed a babe in its crib, only to hear it crying moments later. It was found atop the dresser.[161]

Levitation was an extension of the fae folk's innate abilities, since many possessed powers of flight.[162] This locomotion was sometimes achieved by traveling on storms or whirlwinds.[163] Bampton Hunt, in *Folk Tales of Breffny*, described a faerie tempest as "a powerful great storm... There were strange noises in it, too, music and shouting...."[164] These powerful winds were another method of abducting children.

"The Irish believe that the fairies are rushing by in the whirlwind intent on carrying off some mortal victim to the fairy mansions," wrote Lady Wilde.[165] An account from the National Folklore Collection of Ireland described "a rustling, whistling sound" just prior to a faerie abduction, causing "the hay to rise in swirls all over the field."[166]

The UFO parallels are obvious, made more compelling in a story retold by Yeats. As a man's seven-year-old daughter was dying, she requested a candle to hold, which he obliged. Returning home one night a year later, he was caught in a storm and beheld "a great black ragged cloud, whirling round and round with furious gusts of wind" bursting from a location known as Demons' Rock.

"The whirlwind swept nearer, till at last, in a sort of dim, shadowy light, he saw the black cloud full of frightful faces, all glaring straight at him... At this moment a bright light dropped down from the sky and rested in front of the cloud; and when he looked up, he saw his little [deceased] child floating in the air between him and the demons, holding a lighted candle in her hand." The light beam repelled the demonic cloud, allowing his safe return.[167]

This association of faeries with wind and storms carried over into the New World. In Newfoundland, the phrase "fairy squall" is still employed to describe a sudden gust of wind.[168]

Whirlwinds, according to a variety of world superstitions, also caused miscarriages—the motivic resonance with child abduction, albeit *in vitro,* can be compellingly argued.[169] In the west, fear of whirlwinds is likely tied to one of Lilith's alternative origins, that of the Mesopotamian wind and storm demon *Lilitu;*[170] however, there are similar New World superstitions, exemplified in Pueblo fears that entering a whirlwind could lead to miscarriage and that winds were sent by witches to steal children.[171] Today, such whirlwinds are referred to as "dust devils," implying these underlying superstitions.

As among the Pueblo, miscarriages, stillbirths, and barrenness in Europe were more commonly attributed to witches than faeries (though both were common scapegoats).[172] For example, Danish noble Lady Christence Kruckow was found guilty of causing at least 15 stillbirths and infant deaths before being burned as a witch in 1597.[173] In the British Isles, any household with recurring birth complications was deemed haunted or cursed. Lady Gregory told of a cursed home beset by miscarriages and stillbirths where only two children survived: one, living just nine months, "had less flesh on it" than "the day it was born," while the other was "crabbed" and sickly after her first year.[174]

One of the few extant stories where faeries caused birth complications featured stillbirths, not miscarriages. The legend of Clan MacLeod claims its patriarch once forsook his Scottish faerie bride and married a mortal. Incensed, his spirit wife cursed his people, causing stillbirths—both human and bovine—across the Isle of Skye.[175]

METHODS OF ABDUCTION: LURES

Infants were easy prey for faeries, but cautious, older children called for more creative plans; once a child could walk, it was more effective to *lure* them into the faeries' grasp, rather than *seize* them outright. While an infant could never be pixie led for purely ambulatory reasons, toddlers were prime targets.

Music made common bait.[176] In the apocryphal story "The Fairy Wife" from *Lore of Prosperine,* a captured faerie named

Thumbeline escapes and "bewitches" the narrator's daughter with the "curious performance" of a "winding, wandering air she had been singing."[177] In a Cornish tale collected by antiquarian Robert Hunt, a child pulled by "exquisite, ravishing" music into the woods followed "a beautiful lady through palaces of the most gorgeous description. Pillars of glass supported arches which glistened with every color, and these were hung with crystals... Many days passed away before the child was found by his friends, and that at length he was discovered one lovely morning sleeping on the bed of ferns, on which he was supposed to have fallen asleep on the first adventurous evening."[178]

Anyone spotting faeries likely caught them singing and dancing, and if their gaze was returned found themselves compelled to join. (The belief fungal faerie rings were caused by the fae folk's circular dancing is why they were avoided in Western European superstition.[179]) Dancers disappeared, returning months or years later with little recollection of where they had been.[180] Returned abductees often appeared sickly, skeletal,[181] or pale.[182] Yeats told of a woman taken in her youth for seven years, only to return with all of her toes missing—"she had danced them off."[183]

Evidence suggests this supernatural lapse of time was deliberately controlled by the fae as a means of abduction, rather than an innocent byproduct of sharing their revels. One Welsh girl claimed she regularly cavorted with faeries dressed in blue and green aprons under a crabapple tree, stopping to dance while traveling to and from school, to no ill temporal affect. When she abruptly ended these rendezvous three or four years later, her dancing partners dislocated her leg for the offense.[184]

In another example, Annie McIntire swore faeries took her on Halloween night 1839 in Donegal. She was trapped in their dancing ring when, to her good fortune, her brother caught sight of them and tossed a book into their midst, breaking the fae folk's hold upon her.[185] Again, no missing time was noted.

Faeries also played with children, luring them with simple childish amusements—the aforementioned tale of Gitto Bach is a good example—as well as more structured activities, like hurling[186] or ball sports.[187] In one tale, the prospect of playing with a strange faerie dog was too much for a young Irish lad to resist; he disappeared into the hills, only to return "changed."[188]

An earlier newspaper article from Dublin reported that a John Keely (no relation to John Keel) and his friends watched several little men skipping rope in the forest one day in 1938. Keely revealed himself after a time and the faeries, apparently wishing to depart, took him by the hand. When Keely's comrades stepped forward, the little men fled into the brush.[189] Tales of faeries using play to attract children continue through the modern era. In 2002, a rural Minnesota witness told investigators in no uncertain terms that she remembered, "playing with elves in the woods near her house" in the early 20th century.[190]

The most unsettling tales involve faeries imitating a child's parents. A 1596 letter by Icelandic scholar Arngrímur Jónsson claimed "elves take on the parents' likenesses and imitate their speech, and so find it easier to lure them away."[191] These imposters caught a child's attention then fled into the wild, enticing them to follow.[192] Variations on this technique existed in the British Isles. In Scotland, names called by faeries lured children away from home;[193] these voices often sounded like other children, making them more palatable to youngsters.[194]

In one tale from Dartmoor, a young farmhand was drawn from home after hearing his name called across the moors. His friends were certain the strange calls were from the *piskies*, and they would return him in 366 days—but he disappeared forever.[195]

It is worth noting that anomalous childlike voices in the woods, once a common faerie lure, are still heard today. In 1976, a birdwatcher in southern New York heard the sound of children quarrelling and observed two short, bearded figures in dark green clothing and red caps. They bickered for several moments before walking away.[196]

More recently, Daniel Klemsrud and his girlfriend become lost while hiking near Boscobel, Wisconsin, in 1995. A thick mist had settled over the trail when Klemsrud heard "the sounds of giggling, like small children laughing at play." Peering through the foliage, he caught the impression of two small figures diving into a warren at the base of a hill. Klemsrud intuitively tossed two coins at the mouth of the tunnel, dissipating the mists and revealing the trail leading out of the forest.[197]

Though not children, the couple's account is striking: on a misty day in modern America they were pixie led, only escaping after respecting tenets of the Fairy Faith.

DESTINATIONS

It was commonly held that faerie abductees were taken to Fairyland. But where was this magical place? Most who returned had extreme difficulty recalling the specifics of this marvelous land.

If Fairyland had a physical location—more on this in a moment—it was most certainly underground. Germanic and Scandinavian texts were explicit about their subterranean realm, calling the faeries "underground people," resonating nicely with connections between faeries and the dead.[198] Sixteenth century Swiss polymath Paracelsus coined the term *gnome* to describe those dwarfen earth-spirits "who lived in their own element, the earth."[199]

This subterranean association coincided with English, Irish, and Scottish superstitions surrounding faerie mounds and forts, which often had entrances to underground tombs and passageways known as *souterrain* systems.[200] A folktale collected by Evans Wentz detailed a lost shepherd boy who, after following an old faerie man to a *menhir* (a standing stone), descended a set of stairs awash in bluish white light. Underneath the stone was a beautiful subterranean countryside: Fairyland.[201] In another story related by Irish antiquarian T.C. Croker, a young hero descended the Giant's Stairs, emerging in an underworld cavern "of vast extent, and filled with lights; along either side of which were rows of children, all apparently seven years old, and none beyond that age, dressed in green, and every one exactly dressed alike."[202]

The presence of children in one modern eyewitness account echoes Croker's tale. Around 1950 an Icelandic boy named Roskinkrans noticed seven children, each between four and ten years old, emerge from a small cave above his home. Roskinkrans joined them regularly, playing with insects and flowers before eventually moving to Reykjavik. He claimed to have seen them nearly every month before realizing he had actually met the *Huldufólk*—or perhaps their captives.[203]

Much can be discussed regarding the psychological trappings of Fairyland, none of it better said than by Patrick Harpur. His view on the realm of lake monsters like Nessie and Champ equally applies to the subterranean locale of Fairyland: "Regardless of the actual characteristics of the lake, it is transformed by the Imagination into a reflection of the unconscious self, becoming a dark, impenetrable kingdom which does not yield up its dead."[204]

As the unknown of mankind's shadow-self resides in our subconscious, the unknown of the Otherworld exists just below the surface of our reality. Earthen faeries took captives below ground, while water faeries such as *sirens* and *nixen* dragged their victims under the waves.[205] These themes retain remarkable consistency across all paranormal phenomena to the modern day—a small contingent of contemporary anomalists claim underground spaces are filled with Sasquatch, alien bases, and reptilian beasts.

For these psychological reasons, it is equally valid to posit Fairyland was an incorporeal destination. As mentioned, the ill were often understood as cavorting with faeries; ergo, Fairyland and trance states were seen as one-and-the-same. Evans Wentz was quite bullish on the notion that faerie abduction and, by extension, Fairyland, were non-physical. He commented on the legend, recorded by Sikes, of a French abductee restored from Fairyland: "the real child... as though all the while it had been in an unconscious state—which has a curious bearing on our Psychological Theory—stretches forth its arms and awakening exclaims, 'Ah! mother, what a long time I have been asleep.'"[206]

While many tales recount the theft of children without substitute, exchanges commonly took place between faeries and humans. In an attempt to conceal their transgression, the fae folk left behind something alien in the mortal's stead, an unsettling imposter of the crib: a changeling.

Chapter 4
"Not Your Child, nor Is He a Child"
Changelings

Come away! O, human child!
To the woods and waters wild,
With a fairy hand in hand,
For the world's more full of weeping than
you can understand.

— W.B. Yeats, "The Stolen Child"

Once upon a time there was a couple blessed with a beautiful baby boy. They were happy as they could be, until one day the mother went sheep shearing and left the child in its crib. Upon returning, she found the infant wailing in an unusual manner. Thinking him hungry, she attempted to feed the babe, but he proved insatiable.

Around the same time, a tailor called to work upon some homespun cloth. "Pay no mind to the boy if he cries," said the mother, returning to her shearing duties. "I'll tend to him when I return."

Several hours later, the tailor was startled to see the baby reach to a nearby shelf for a bagpipe chanter. He took the instrument and played a lively tune, filling the house with a dancing faerie host. The tailor was compelled to join.

Two hours later, the playing ceased and the faeries disappeared. "Tell not my mother what happened today," the infant said, and when she returned the tailor had no defense for why his task was left undone.

When the tailor arrived the next day to finish, the entire series of events unfolded as it had the day prior. This time, when the mother demanded an explanation, he said: "I urge upon you after going to bed to-night not to fondle that child, because he is not your child, nor is he a child: he is an old fairy man. And to-morrow, at dead tide, go down to the shore and wrap him in your plaid and put him upon a rock and begin to pick that shell-fish which is called limpet, and for your life do not leave the shore until such a time as the tide will flow so high that you will scarcely be able to wade in to the main shore."

The mother did as told, and while wading, the infant spoke. "You had a great need to do what you have done," he said. "Otherwise you'd have seen another ending of your turn but blessing be to you and curses on your adviser." Upon returning home, she found her own boy, not the changeling, in his cradle.[207]

"The Tailor & the Changeling" is one of the most popular and geographically widespread faerie stories, even imported to America by Scottish immigrants.[208] Innumerable variations exist: sometimes the tailor takes action into his own hands, sometimes the dancers are absent, sometimes the method of resolution differs.[209] But the motifs of the tailor, the changeling, and the music remain the same.

"The smallness of fairies… and the belief in changelings are the two most prominent characteristics of the Fairy-Faith," wrote Evans Wentz.[210] The scenario plays out in a nearly identical manner every time: an oft-unhappy mother leaves her child, usually a boy, unattended; the babe exhibits undesirable traits and/or appearance; advice is sought of a wise man or woman; a ritual is carried out, usually a Christian rite, abuse, abandonment, or an effort to bewilder the changeling; and the original, mortal child is returned to the parents.[211]

Abundant, vaguely cited tales can be found at the murky intersection of fact, folklore, and fiction.

- A story from John Rhŷs' *Celtic Folklore, Welsh and*

Manx tells how the *Tylwyth Teg* stole a baby from its dozing grandmother, leaving behind "a slender, wizened old man moving restlessly and peevishly about"—a *crimbil*, or changeling. Its mother found the child inconsolable and hideous, and a man "skilled in the secrets of the spirits" was fetched from Trawsfynydd. He advised they trace the shape of a cross in salt on a shovel, heated in a fire. The sight of this made the changeling flee through a window, and the actual child appeared on the doorstep unharmed.[212]

- One novel story from Croker tells of two Scottish whisky distributors who, while measuring their load in a friend's cottage, heard her infant shriek in its crib. The mother comforted the child, making the sign of the cross over it as the distributors left. When they drove off, a child—recognized as their friend's—was found in the road. The distributors surmised the faeries had attempted to take the babe but were unable to complete the theft after its mother intervened. Pressed for time, they cared for the child and returned a fortnight later, finding the mother at wit's end: the child at home was sickly and crying constantly. The distributors presented her real child and "lighted a bundle of straw to throw the changeling in, but at the sight of it the Elf made its escape through the chimney."[213]

- A North German mother was convinced her baby was a dwarfen changeling. Following the advice of a friend, she brewed oil and placed empty walnut shells about the fire. The child asked what she was doing, and she replied, "Brewing beer." The child said, "Now I am old as the Harz Wood, and I've never seen anything like this, my entire life long. Brewing beer in walnut shells!" His identity revealed, the mother threatened to kill the changeling if he did not bring her child back. The dwarf asked her to leave the cottage, and when she returned, her baby had also.[214]

- James MacDougall's *Folk Tales and Fairy Lore in Gaelic and English* records the tale of a Glengarry widow with a young son who went to the well to fetch water. When she returned, the boy was screaming, and nothing could silence him. As she took him to her breast, she spied teeth and a withered face, and knew he was a changeling. The next day she took him to the river. "A bug burn ran across her path, and when she was going over the ford, the creature put his head out of the shawl and said: 'Many a big fold have I seen on the banks of this stream!'" She tossed the child into the river below the ford, "then heard a sound like that of a flock of birds flying about her." At her feet was her true child.[215]

- Jacob and Wilhelm Grimm adapted several German changeling tales for their famous collections. "A mother had her child taken from the cradle by elves. In its place they laid a changeling with a thick head and staring eyes who would do nothing but eat and drink. In distress she went to a neighbor and asked for advice. The neighbor told her to carry the changeling into the kitchen, set it on the hearth, make a fire, and boil water in two eggshells. That should make the changeling laugh, and if he laughs it will be all over with him. The woman did everything just as her neighbor said. When she placed the eggshells filled with water over the fire, the blockhead said: 'Now I am as old as the Wester Wood, but have never seen anyone cooking in shells.' And he began laughing about it. When he laughed, a band of little elves suddenly appeared. They brought the rightful child, set it on the hearth, and took the changeling away."[216]

As noted earlier, any unbaptized baby presented an opportunity for a faerie exchange, and some families were unfortunately changeling-prone. Lady Wilde told of a family who had slighted the fae folk and had no less than *six* changelings, each of whom pined away and died.[217] A family could also suffer multiple changelings at the same time: Wirt Sikes recorded a story of changelings who were twins.[218]

A HISTORY OF BELIEF

The word "changeling" originally meant "turncoat."[219] Later it evoked royal children substituted to some nefarious end[220] before becoming closely associated, alongside the word "exchangeling," with faeries.[221] While changeling belief was most robust in the British Isles, identical tales were told throughout Europe. Scandinavians called them by a host of names: *killkrack,*[222] *skiptingr, vixlingr,* and *bytingr*[223] (the last term was once an insult in Iceland).[224] Germanic peoples had multiple terms as well: in Holland they were called *wisselkind,*[225] likely derived from the German *wechselkind; wechselbalg* was popular, but it was also common to hear *dickkopf* or *kielkropf*[226] (anglicanized as *killcrop*[227] and used to denote not only a changeling, but a spontaneously aborted fetus as well).[228] Polish mothers feared the *Dziwozony,* tall women of the woods fond of taking a human baby and leaving their own kind in its place.[229] Other Slavic countries called changelings *divious, premien,*[230] *podmenek,*[231] or *odmieńce,*[232] depending on one's geography and ethnic group.

Like the origins of faeries themselves, the changeling legend's genesis is up for debate. Though adults are lured to Fairyland in pagan stories, belief in the substitution of children does not pre-date Christianity in Ireland, suggesting roots in Abrahamic tradition (at least in Europe—global traditions, addressed later, undermine this assumption).[233]

The Babylonian Talmud described the concept of *b'nei temurah*, a "child of substitution," created when parents thought of someone other than their spouse during conception.[234] The *Zohar* clarified the concept, declaring, "The body of the child that [a father] begets is called 'a changeling' [because the body was created while the father 'changed' his thoughts during procreation]."[235]

Some scholars cite fifth century church father Saint Augustine's exegesis of Psalm 17, which spoke of estranged children (*filii alieni*), "not worthy of being called mine, aliens who were rightly told 'You are of your father the devil,'" as another step in the evolution of the belief. Though more likely anti-Semitic rhetoric than an account of changelings, it illustrates the early church's language as a guiding factor.[236]

In the 13th century, William of Auvergne, philosophical theologian and Bishop of Paris, authored "the earliest extant texts to mention the actual substitution story."[237] Using the Latin term *cambio* (from *cambiti*, "exchanged"), William described "the sons of *incubi demons*," thin and insatiable, left with mortal mothers. He maintained these were not literal substitutions but instead demonic illusions, explaining their sudden disappearance when banished.[238]

Suffice to say the belief was ensconced in Europe by at least the 1200s, if not earlier. Christianity and the Fairy Faith syncretized around a shared belief in changelings to the extent that Martin Luther—father of the Protestant Reformation—"saw and touched" one in Dessau in 1532:

> It was twelve years old, and from its eyes and the
> fact that it had all of its senses, one could have

thought that it was a real child. It did nothing but eat; in fact, it ate enough for any four peasants or threshers. It ate, shit, and pissed, and whenever someone touched it, it cried. When bad things happened in the house, it laughed and was happy; but when things went well, it cried.... Therefore, I said: "Then you should have all Christians repeat the Lord's Prayer in church that God may exorcise the devil." They did this daily at Dessau, and the changeling child died in the following year....[239]

The church also exhibited a general distrust of midwives and assumed their complicity in swapping children.[240] A 1554 treatise on the practice by Jacob Rueff blamed changelings on Satan,[241] and by 1567 English midwives were forced to swear they would aid neither the devil or mortals in exchanging mortal infants.[242]

The notion changelings might be explained by spirit possession is one Forteans should carefully consider. The idea, popular among Victorian occultists, was considered by Evans Wentz,[243] and folkloric evidence suggests the idea of faerie "walk-ins," or possessions, were possible, particularly near death.[244] This talking point is regularly touched upon throughout this book.

On balance, UFOlogical connections should not be dismissed either. As early as 1638 authors were playing with the idea of changelings and extraterrestrials: *The Man in the Moon: or a Discourse of a Voyage Thither*, a work of fiction by Francis Godwin, told of superior Lunar inhabitants who exchanged problem infants with healthy earthlings.[245] While there are further specific UFOlogical analogues to changelings—some commonly noted, others less so— they are largely withheld until much later in the book. This and subsequent chapters seek to establish the richness of changeling lore to inform our future speculation and comparison.

For at least 500 years changelings have influenced our popular culture. The trope and its variants inspired Shakespeare, Brontë, Dickens, and Yeats, to name but a few. Lest changeling tales seem too distant and mythic, consider how Evans Wentz spoke with numerous individuals—circa 1911—who still believed faeries stole mortal infants.

ATTRIBUTES

"A remarkable feature of the changeling narrative... is its stability," wrote English professor Joyce Underwood Munro.[246] It is not only consistent in its narrative beats but also in its description of changelings.

They were, put bluntly, hideous. Perhaps Peter Christen Asbjørnsen, reteller of Norwegian folktales, dramatized their appearance best: "The child looked like an old man with a weather-beaten face, his eyes were as red as fire, and glowed like an owl's eyes in the dark. He had a head as long as a horse's head and as round as a cabbage; the legs were as thin as a sheep's, and his body looked like last year's dried mutton."[247] These were the general attributes, moderately embellished, expected from faerie imposters.

- **Stature and body shape.** Changelings, nearly always boys,[248] were commonly deformed or hunchbacked.[249] They were consistently tiny, sometimes hyperbolically so ("not as big as a mushroom," Lady Wilde claimed), remaining small their entire lives, no matter how long.[250] One German tale described a two-year-old "no longer than a shoe,"[251] one Irish changeling was the size of a three-year-old at age six,[252] and Evans Wentz was told of a 20-year-old no bigger than an infant.[253] They had "pale, wrinkled skin as that of an old person."[254]

- **Build and weight.** Alexander MacGregor described the changeling in *Highland Superstitions* as "a withered, little, living skeleton of a child."[255] It always seemed they were "dying, yet would not die."[256] This weakness was a hallmark of change-lings. "They are always ailing and do not grow…" it is written in the *Malleus Maleficarum*, "though they are very heavy."[257] This description matches super-stitions surrounding demonic succubi and incubi, whose offspring were believed frail-yet-heavy.[258]

- **Head, neck, and eyes.** The German names *kielkropf* and *dickkopf* directly reference the large head and neck of changelings (meaning "crop in the throat"[259] and "thick head," respectively). North German peasants believed small, grey *nickerts* replaced their infants with tiny, large-headed changelings.[260] Eyes were occasionally described as burning like coals,[261] "goggly,"[262] "big,"[263] "bulging,"[264] or "large [and] unblinking."[265]

- **Limbs.** "His hands were like kite's claws, and his legs were no thicker than the handle of a whip, and about as straight as a reaping-hook," wrote Yeats in *Irish Fairy Tales*.[266] Limbs were awkward,[267] some-times growing too quickly,[268] and often short.[269]

- **Face.** Changeling faces were shriveled,[270] pinched, and withered.[271] They were sometimes recognized by failure to teethe or grow hair,[272] while other times too many teeth,[273] long teeth,[274] or even fangs[275] gave them away. Beards were a dead give-away, of course.[276] A Scottish child born with a caul over its face was considered a changeling.[277]

- **Voice.** "The ugly, shriveled Elf in the Irish legend speaks in a snarling and piercing tone, which terri-fies men," wrote Croker. "As a changeling, he does not speak at all, but howls and screams in a frightful manner; and, if compelled, his voice sounds like that of a very old man."[278] Their voices were described as "small and squeaky"[279] or "hollow."[280]

Occasionally the exchange went unnoticed, the faerie *glamour*, or illusion, strong enough to make the changeling appear mortal for a time.[281] Welsh faeries took well-behaved and handsome children, leaving behind an identical *plentyn-newid* that slowly turned hideous.[282] Greek faeries took children but usually returned them; if not, the exchanged faerie never revealed its true self until adulthood.[283]

Rarer still—but not unheard of—were beautiful changelings. In a 1726 visit to the Isle of Man, George Waldron described a changeling as beautiful beyond compare, with a delicate complexion and fine hair, but entirely immobile with long, thin limbs. The child seldom smiled, "but if anyone called him Fairy-Elf, he would frown and fix his eyes so earnestly on those who said it, as if he would look them through."[284]

All changelings made unpleasant company. They cried nonstop[285] in an inhuman wail[286] and were generally "cross and ill-tempered."[287] Their reputation was so notorious parents of peevish children might jest their true offspring were taken by the faeries.[288] "When we see a child good for nothing we say, 'Ah, you little faery,'" Lady Gregory learned.[289] Edmund John William claimed his own son was taken and was swapped with "an idiot" who made "very disagreeable screaming sounds."[290]

Changelings were also listless, appearing as dullards around their "parents" and avoiding eye contact.[291] Even when of age, they never walked—unless alone. Irish writer Thomas Keightley described one changeling: "...when there was no one in the place, he was in great spirits, ran up the walls like a cat... but sat dozing at the end of the table when any one was in the room with him."[292] They were believed to engage in all sorts of raucous activity when alone, such as dancing, stealing and breaking valuables, [293] having their hair combed by faeries, and playing music.[294]

Anyone spying upon a changeling might catch a demonstration of its musicianship. Many tales mention them playing bagpipes when alone, usually in variations on "The Tailor & the Changeling"[295]—in Wilde's retelling, the baby played "such sweet music" on four straws "as if they were pipes."[296] Sometimes the instrument is a fiddle, as in one variant told to Evans Wentz,[297] or "The Fairy Child of Close Ny Lheiy," a version contemporaneously published in Sophia Morrison's *Manx Fairy Tales*.[298] These musical abilities magically compelled listeners to dance.[299]

Around others, changelings only showed enthusiasm in their insatiability, existing to "only eat and cry" for more.[300] They were constantly "wawling and crying for food and attention in an apparent state of paralysis," said Briggs.[301] No amount of food satisfied or fattened changelings, who in some accounts ate four times more than mortal infants[302] or as much as a grown man[303] (one notable exception is George Waldron's beautiful changeling who, keeping with its contrarian nature, *never* ate).[304] Evans Wentz recorded one story where the babe's usual diet of porridge and milk could not ease its hunger; perhaps, as believed on the Scottish Isle Benbecula, only meat could satisfy it.[305]

So prodigious was their appetite that faeries sometimes left behind a sort of alimony to help raise the changeling, small sums placed in the same location of the home daily provided the family told no one their secret.[306] In "The Gors Goch Changeling," a *Tylwyth Teg* host was allowed inside an English home to wash their children, leaving money behind in appreciation but exchanging the family's infant for one of their own. The mother died of a broken heart while the father prospered on faerie riches.[307]

While most changelings were infants, adults (particularly young women and mothers) were susceptible as well. Danish legend tells of a smith who rescued a pregnant woman from a troll. After helping her birth twins, the smith escorted the wife to her husband and discovered a changeling in her place, which he hacked to pieces.[308] Changelings were also used to scapegoat adults whose behavior abruptly changed, as in the legend of young Rickard the

Rake, who—following his collapse at a feast—emerged from his convalescence ornery and insatiable.[309]

In many cases these adult changelings simply appeared ill or as a corpse. The Irish commonly held that anyone with consumption or other wasting diseases was in good health in Fairyland, while the physical body represented a changeling.[310] Women who passed away in childbirth were not dead—they were taken by the faeries.[311] Once more, the connection with the dead makes categorization of abduction difficult and raises the question: what *were* changelings, anyway?

TRUE IDENTITIES

Given the faerie/dead connection it should come as no surprise that a handful of grim accounts actually describe changelings as dead children. In one Irish tale, a morning commuter heard two faerie women at an open window say, "There is a beautiful boy in this house, go in and hand it out to me, and we'll leave the dead child in its place." The commuter, signing the cross over the sleeping boy, intercepted the exchange and restored the baby to its mother.[312]

Such tales are rare, however. As one might surmise from their wizened visages, changelings were more often thought to be old faeries, hence their advanced abilities of musical performance and speech.

"I have heard my father say it was the case that fairy women used to take away children from their cradles and leave different children in their places," said 94-year-old John Campbell, who spoke to Evans Wentz. "And that these children who were left would turn out to be old men."[313]

Attempts to explain the incongruity of infantile bodies and aged faces led many 19th century occultists to declare changelings had less to do with fae folk and more with "the souls of the dead returned to inhabit the bodies of mortal children," i.e., reincarnation.[314] Lady Gregory anecdotally provided support for this notion via the tale of an old Aran man who, three days after his death, "appeared in the cradle as a baby" with "an old look on his face."

"He won't be with you long," a wise woman told the mother. "He had three deaths to die, and this is the second." The child passed away six years later.[315]

Icelandic folklore held faerie women "go to the cradles of young babies, and take with them their husbands, eighty years old, whom they knock, and kick, and squeeze until they are small enough to get into the cradle."[316] In one story, a startled mother saw her changed "child" yawn and stretch all the way up to the rafters of the house;[317] perhaps the heavy weight of changelings was due to this compression.

Alongside these beliefs others contended changelings were faerie babies who just so happened to *look* elderly,[318] possibly due to illness.[319] Elias Owen wrote, "the Fairies exchanged their own weakly or deformed offspring" with mortal babies,[320] while Yeats also contended it was "some sickly fairy child," not an elder, left behind.[321]

Abandonment of faerie children to mortals was not always consensual on the behalf of their Otherworldly parents. The story of "Coleman Gray" tells of an abandoned *piskie* child adopted into a Welsh family, raised to good health; after some time, its parents came and retrieved the child, never to be seen again.[322]

In another unique tale, the faeries left behind a hairy changeling quickly rescued by its mother. "This is my own child that was stolen from me tonight because my people wanted to take your beautiful baby," she told the parents. "But I'd rather have ours; if you let me take him I will tell you how to get your child back." They were instructed to burn "three sheaves" at the nearby faerie mound, threatening to burn the faerie's home if their child was not returned.[323] By now readers have doubtlessly noticed the peculiar methods by which changelings could be banished and mortal infants returned; these are discussed at length later.

Arguably the most intriguing changeling tradition held they

were not living beings at all, but instead *fetches* or *stocks*, logs cloaked in glamour to appear as living children.[324] Faeries had a knack for masking rubbish as something different, including food, so stocks were a natural extension of this ability.[325] Belief that changelings were inanimate hunks of wood was a reference to their immobility, described by one father as "stiff as an aik tree, unable to move."[326]

In Yeats' retelling of "Jamie Freel & the Young Lady," the protagonist saw "the young lady lifted and carried away" by the faeries, "while the stick which was dropped in her place on the bed took her exact form."[327] Another female changeling, the grown protagonist of the Finnish folktale "The Kantele Player," throws her imposter into a roaring fire, revealing it as an alder stump.[328]

Stocks were commonly employed when abducting new mothers, or mothers and children. In one famous tale, a husband heard the faeries working on his wife's stock, shouting, "Mind da crooked finger!" The man lit a candle, opened a Bible, and grabbed a knife; the faeries were frightened by this, and fled when he tossed the Bible into the cowshed. Inside he found a carved effigy of his wife, accurate down to her deformed finger, which he used for a chopping board thenceforth.[329]

This deception was not limited to changelings—sometimes stocks were used for simple pranks. Dinah Moore of the Isle of Man told Evans Wentz:

> One night the man was out on horseback and heard a little baby crying beside the road. He got off his horse to get the baby, and, taking it home, went to give it to his wife, and it was only a block of wood. And then the old fairies were outside yelling at the man: "*Eash un oie, s'cheap t'ou mollit!* (Age one night, how easily thou art deceived!)"[330]

Stocks could also replace limbs and digits, usually as a result of a wrathful whirlwind, or "faerie blast."[331] Anyone unfortunate or foolish enough to cross a faerie might suffer this affliction, resulting in a pustule or tumor-like protrusion on an arm or leg, filled with detritus: grass, moss, splinters, etc.[332]

Variations on stock/fetch changelings included bits of sod,[333] turf,[334] a broom wrapped in cloth,[335] or a waxen effigy stuck with pins, all left as placeholders for mortal children.[336] The last example comes from the Celtic black magic practice of a "corp criadh"—essentially a Gaelic voodoo doll used to inflict consumptive illness.[337]

In spite of various "faerie artifacts" collected over the years—miniscule chalices, pipes, shoes, jackets, flags, etc.—no faerie stock, or any of the above substitutes, has ever been found.[338] Dr. Hugh Cheape, Curator of Scottish Modern Collections, said that although the National Museums of Scotland are "comprehensive... I must say I do not have an example of this. I have looked at similar collections in other museums in Scotland and England and have never seen such a thing."[339]

The nomenclature surrounding these glamoured logs is worth discussion. Consider how the Welsh term for changeling, *plentyn-newid*, derives from the word *plentyn*, or "child." *Plentyn* shares an Old English root with *plante*, or seedling.[340] *Fetch*—in addition to its modern meaning, "to take," appropriate for faerie abduction—is an antiquated term for "trick" or "deception."[341] In the folklore of the British Isles, a fetch was also a doppelgänger or eidolon,[342] a living person's double which, seen at night, was a death omen.[343] In one story recorded by folklorist Christina Hole, a Sir William Napier was shown his room at an inn one evening and perceived his corpse upon the bed. After finishing his journey, he promptly died.[344]

The *Oxford English Dictionary* defines a *stock* as "the trunk or woody stem of a living tree or shrub, especially one into which a graft (scion) is inserted."[345] In modern horticulture, stocks join separate plants so they grow together and asexually propagate.[346] This definition has significant metaphoric resonance with later themes in this discussion, specifically the motivations behind alien and faerie abduction.

Chapter 5
"Fresh Blood and Human Vigor"
Motivations Behind Faerie Abduction

Besides, by partial fondness show,
Like you, we dote upon our own.
Where yet was ever found a mother
Who'd give her booby for another?
And should we change with human breed,
Well might we pass for fools indeed.

— John Gay, "The Mother, the Nurse, and the Fairy"

The prevalence of kidnapping in faerie lore suggests compelling reasons to engage in such compulsive behavior. Unsurprisingly, a myriad of reasons have been proposed to explain the fae folk's kleptomania.

Reasons behind adult abductions frequently differed from those involving children. "It will be seen that various motives were ascribed for captures of mortals," Briggs wrote in *An Encyclopedia of Fairies*, among them "the acquisition of bond-slaves, amorousness," and "the enrichment brought by musical talent."[347]

Interpretations colored the phenomenon's exact explanation. For example, those contending changelings were elderly faeries argued that the substitution provided them with a sort of retirement or hospice arrangement; if changelings were faerie babies, on the other hand, the exchange might be motivated by a desire to have humans raise the child.[348] More metaphysical approaches—as favored by Evans Wentz—suggest the child's *soul* was kidnapped for other reasons entirely (addressed later).[349]

The driving forces behind child abduction were not exclusively negative. German mythologist Karl Simrock speculated faerie abduction stories originated in benevolence, that "even the theft of children was dictated by their care for the best interests of mankind," before being twisted into narratives of evil kidnappings.[350] Indeed, young captives in Fairyland were rarely mistreated, an interpretation supported in the record.[351] An 1188 Latin text recorded by Giraldus Cambrensis spoke of "Elidurus," a child who skipped his studies "to avoid the severity of his preceptor"; after watching him fast two days under a riverbank, the fae folk took pity on the boy, spiriting him to Fairyland where they feasted upon a peculiar milk-diet.[352]

Some faeries simply sought the love of a beautiful human baby.[353] Others, like the *korrigans*, stole children to protect them from harm.[354] An old Scottish folk tale from John Gregorson Campbell follows:

> The Elves sometimes took care of neglected children. The herd who tendered the Baile-phuill cattle on Heynist Hill sat down one day on a green eminence (*cnoc*) in the hill, which had the reputation of being tenanted by the Fairies. His son, a young child, was along with him. He fell asleep, and when he awoke the child was away. He roused himself, and vowed aloud, that unless his boy was restored he would not leave a stone or clod of the hillock together. A voice from underground answered that the child was safe at home with its mother, and they (the 'people') had taken it lest it should come to harm with the cold.[355]

Regardless, folklore eventually (justifiably?) embraced negative interpretations of child faerie abduction. It incentivized good behavior, saying prayers, etc., reflecting Christianity's influence on the Fairy Faith. Even when not outright labeling them demonic, religious figures claimed faeries owed a *teind* (tithe) to the devil, paid in unbaptized souls to spare their own offspring.[356] Scots believed Satan annually took a tenth of the *daoine sith*, increasing the demand for child substitutes.[357] This debt was supposedly owed every seven years (a number derived from Ralph of Coggeshall; this, however, is a misreading, as Malekin was taken seven years prior, then released in seven *more* years' time, rendering a 14 year timeframe).[358]

Other Christian dogma asserted faeries exchanged their babies with humans to have them baptized. In northern Spanish mythology, the *xana* swapped her children with mortal babies to this end,[359] a sentiment shared by an Icelandic priest who said any faerie women bearing human children "were very anxious to have their offspring dipped in the sacred font."[360] Christian propaganda—in the guise of folklore—featured numerous tales of faeries lamenting their inability to attain Christ's salvation.[361]

NEW BLOOD & HYBRIDS

Pagan explanations suggested faeries needed something else from humans, something they lacked. According to German folklorist Karl Bartsch, it was "earthly beauty," which could be obtained by a sojourn among mortals.[362] In rare cases this meant procuring blood; Isle of Man folklore claimed any faeries denied water offerings extracted blood to make into cakes,[363] while other tales spoke of a green-clad faerie mistress who fed her offspring with—or washed them in—the blood of children, explicitly rendering faerie fecundity "dependent upon human death."[364]

By and large, examples of vampiric exsanguination by faeries are poorly supported; while both faeries and vampires were blamed for diseases like consumption, few faeries in folklore consumed blood.[365] Thematically speaking, the closest reliable narratives come from Iceland, where trolls took children because they made easy snacks.[366]

Claims of faerie interest in blood are more likely a reference to their interest in *bloodlines*. Most often, faeries simply sought to diversify their gene pool. The fae folk's "chief motive was to inject the dwindling stock with fresh blood and human vigor," Briggs wrote.[367] It was the primary reason why faeries, hairy and swarthy, preferred fair-featured babies,[368] and why the fae folk quickly assimilated deceased children—Germanic *nixies,* for example, with their "large, dreadful eyes," were said to be drowned babies.[369]

Naturally, this implied that mortal youths disappeared to live among faeries and swell their ranks. Historians attributed this superstition to ancestral memories of suppressed aboriginal peoples—Picts in the British Isles, Sami in Scandinavia, Gauls in Western Europe—replacing their own malnourished infants with invaders' healthy babies.[370] From a folkloric perspective (since faeries like the *Tylwyth Teg* and *korrigans* feared their races' death),[371] it was speculated generations of inbreeding caused faeries to seek out genetic diversity.[372]

It is unknown why the fae were so preoccupied with mortality. After all, they were by all appearances dead or immortal, and in some cases, could even transmit this longevity to their child captives;[373] in Ireland, children were taken to Lough Gur, one of the entrances to *Tír na nÓg* (Fairyland), to undergo an "unearthly transmutation from the human to the fairy state."[374]

Incorporation of human children into the faerie bloodline raises the question of faerie-human hybrids, for which folklore provides countless precedents. Irish stories, for example, explicitly asserted faeries took children for breeding stock.[375] The Irish tale of Tam Lin combined many themes: a maiden, wandering in a forest, happened upon a mysterious stranger and soon found herself pregnant; when she asked if he be fae or human, he told her he *was once* a mortal, but fell in with the fae and, every seven years, was forced to deliver a soul to Hell.[376] Historical accounts of alleged human-faerie hybrids living among those in the British

Isles described them as artistic, handsome, strong, passionate, vengeful,[377] tall, and matured beyond their years.[378]

The human-other hybrid motif persists even into modern UFOlogy, where human-alien hybrids are commonly alleged, and is widespread in world folklore. In India, a dapper man visiting a lady at night might generate such a union; in one example, a spirit pulled his bride into a whirlwind which deposited them atop a tall tree, where he fathered two supernatural children.[379] In New Zealand's Maori culture, any albino is considered the result of a relationship between mortal women and forest spirits.[380] South American tribes still fear Otherworldly spirits masquerading as river dolphins, procreating in the guise of handsome partners,[381] while Eastern royalty, centuries past, proudly championed genealogies imbued with "dragon-blood."[382] Despite the power these offspring represented, they were often physically deficient, pale, and weak—Amazonian superstition says copulations between female humans and male nutria (large aquatic rodents) produce sickly children with "white skin and white hair."[383]

Biblical mention of the Nephilim preceded later Christian descriptions of human-incubi/succubi progeny with "two mouths, two heads, six fingers, two sets of teeth, beards, four eyes, three hands, and three feet." Some were amorphous blobs, while other possessed beaks or tails.[384]

Human-other hybridity in the Fairy Faith is represented by the symbolism of the stock, the log faeries sometimes used to replace abducted children. Recall how the stock, horticulturally speaking, intertwines two separate plants—itself an elegant metaphor for hybrid unions.

In light of the stock metaphor, it is interesting to note the Book of Enoch, an ancient Jewish text, opens with the following on the Nephilim: "And they took wives for themselves, and everyone chose for himself one each. And they began to go into them and were promiscuous with them. And they taught them charms and spells, and showed to them the cutting of roots and trees."[385]

MOTHERS' MILK

The faeries' need for mortal genetic material was echoed in the most commonly cited reason behind child exchange: the acquisition of human milk. Faerie milk, like their stocks and food, was a sham, meaning changelings served a dual purpose: while fae folk assimilated human babies, their own offspring were nourished by[386] (or, in the case of some elderly faeries, imbued with mortal souls through) human milk.[387]

A Scottish variant of "The Tailor & the Changeling" ends:

> When he returned he found the wife before him, and the changeling in the cradle, ready to burst with crying. The wife took him up, and gave him a drink, and then put him back in the cradle again.
>
> He was not long there till he began to scream and cry once more. She took him up, and gave him another drink. But to all appearance nothing would please him but to be left always on the breast.
>
> This game went on for a few days more. But when the patience of the tailor ran out, he sprang at last from the work-table, took in a creelful of peats, and put a big fire on the hearth. When the fire was in the heat of its burning, he sprang over to the cradle, took with him the changeling, and before any one in the house could interpose, he threw him in the very middle of the flames. But the little knave leaped out through the chimney, and from the house-top cried in triumph to the wife: "I have got so much of the sap of thy breast in spite of thee," and he departed.[388]

Changelings were not always employed in the acquisition

of milk. Sometimes adult faeries directly appealed to nursing mothers, as in an Icelandic tale where a faerie appeared to a woman in a dream and begged to feed her child on mortal milk.[389] This story bears similarities to a Galloway legend, wherein a human voluntarily revived a faerie babe by bringing it to her breast;[390] a Nithsdale variant sees this act rewarded with fine clothing and food.[391] Grimm also chronicled a German story wherein a faerie caught in the act of stealing a child refused to hand it over until it was given "the generous milk of human kind."[392]

A vast array of European belief surrounded milk, both human and bovine. Practitioners of the Fairy Faith often left out a saucerful to appease the fae folk, while some in Lower Brittany poured milk over the tombs of the dead on All Saints Night for similar reasons.[393] Gypsies claimed the suckling of earth spirits, or *Pçuvus-wives*, caused a host of nursing problems, including difficulty lactating.[394] Elsewhere, changelings were accused of suckling their mothers to death.[395]

Some faeries were breast-obsessed. The *barabao*, an Italian spirit, was known for changing into a thread and sneaking between a woman's breasts, all the while yelling "I'm a titty-toucher!"[396] A curious Danish anecdote from Keightley spoke of three children who awoke in the night, crying something "had been sucking them. Their breasts were found to be swelled." The father attributed these injuries to spirits attached to their room, which was floored with elder, a sacred faerie tree.[397]

WET NURSES, NURSEMAIDS, & MIDWIVES

This desire for milk was why faeries targeted women following birth: new mothers made perfect Otherworld wet nurses.[398] The partial ballad "The Queen of Elfan's Nourice" detailed a woman taken from her four-day-old infant to nurse the faerie queen's progeny (the story also contains the profound, poignant detail of two roads leading from Fairyland: one to Heaven, one to Hell).[399]

Stories of faeries taking women for childcare are nearly as

common as changeling stories. The oldest extant example comes from Gervase of Tilbury, a contemporary of Ralph of Coggeshall who claimed to have met a French woman taken by river *dracs* into the Rhône and "made nurse to her captor's son."[400]

Four centuries after Gervase, Robert Kirk wrote of this trend:

> Women are yet alive who tell they were taken away when in Child-bed to nurse Fairie Children, a lingering voracious Image... left in their place, (like their Reflexion in a Mirrour)... The Child, and Fire, with Food and other Necessaries, are set before the Nurse how soon she enters; but she nather perceaves any Passage out, nor sees what those People doe in other Rooms of the Lodging. When the Child is wained, the Nurse dies, or is conveyed back, or gets it to her choice to stay there.[401]

More recent first-person accounts of faerie nurses abound. One Grange woman described by Yeats was "compelled to nurse the child of the queen of the fairies."[402] In another—sure to make UFOlogists salivate—an Irish mother told Lady Gregory she was taken to a large, circular "house," where a robed "woman," taller than the other faeries, touched a "stick" to her breast and demanded she nurse faerie babies.[403]

These mothers suckled both faerie babies and human infants held captive in Fairyland.[404] Depending upon circumstances, they died, were released unharmed, opted to stay with the fae, or—rarely—escaped.[405] One shrewd wet nurse negotiated her departure from Fairyland by offering up her husband's lactating mare in her stead, which was drained to the brink of death.[406] Others were released nightly to suckle their mortal children, though they often appeared as an ominous specter or *fetch*. This presented an opportunity for her salvation through a hodgepodge of folk remedies: any husband could restore his returning wife provided he asked no questions, fed her, tied a red thread at the threshold, and splashed her with Holy Water to restore her appearance.[407]

Many never returned because they were already deceased. Lady Gregory recorded numerous stories of wet nurses who were taken in death or died after accepting their duty (these narratives were related, if not identical, to her collection's tales of deceased mothers returning to nurse bereaved children).[408]

> Cloran the plumber's mother was taken away, it's always said. The way it's known is, it was not long after her baby was born but she was doing well. And one morning very early a man and his wife were going in a cart to Loughrea one Thursday for the market, and they met some of those people and they asked the woman that had her own child with her, would she give a drink to their child that was with them, and while she was doing it they said, "We won't be in want of a nurse tonight, we'll have Mrs. Cloran of Cloon." And when they got back in the evening, Mrs. Cloran was dead before them.[409]

In addition to wet nurses, faeries also desired nursemaids and midwives. Generally speaking these services were acquired voluntarily, rather than by abduction or force (making them more of a kind with 1950s UFOlogical contactee lore, compared to the involuntary alien abductions seen from the late 1970s onward). Most narratives feature a stranger begging a woman for help; after a short period of transit, they arrive in Fairyland to find a faerie in labor, a mortal woman living among the faeries in labor, or faerie children to care after. Once she performs her duties, the woman is offered a reward—or punished for some transgression.[410]

- According to Sikes, a Welsh lady "was addressed by a very noble-looking gentleman all in black, who asked her if she would be a nursemaid, and undertake the management of his children for a time."

Eagerly agreeing to his hefty wages, she mounted his "coal-black steed" and arrived presently in "a beautiful palace lighted up by more lights than she could count," full of handsome children. The mysterious stranger "gave her a box containing ointment, which she was to put on their eyes," after which she *must* wash her hands. One day she itched her own eye after the task and saw the faerie realm for what it truly was: the children were impish, the palace dark, the surroundings bleak. Years after her release she greeted her old faerie master at a fair, revealing she could see him and had disobeyed his orders. She was blinded for the transgression.[411]

- A Swedish variant featured a clergyman's wife summoned by a troll. Again, the woman arrived at a sumptuous home. Aided by her mortal midwife, the mother easily gave birth and recovered within minutes, then fetched refreshments for her guest. Aware of the taboo on consuming faerie food, the midwife politely declined both the refreshments and the gold offered. She was later blessed with reward in the form of "half a dozen large spoons of pure silver" which became family heirlooms (a similar event, or perhaps the same, was sworn to in an April 12, 1671, affidavit from Sweden).[412]

- In the mid-20th century, a Yorkshire nurse claimed to have been lured by a stranger aboard a bus, where she was allegedly taken to a Greenhow Hill cave inhabited by a family of *pixies*. "The interesting point here, since the *pixies* are not native to Yorkshire…" Briggs wrote, "is that Greenhow Hill was said to have been mined by Cornishmen"—as though they brought their native faeries with them.[413]

Faeries in similar narratives seemed less concerned with midwifery skill and more with simple mortal touch. According to Icelandic lore, elf-women in labor needed human hands to touch them before giving birth.[414] In the Swedish legend of Güngu Hrólf, the protagonist encounters a mysterious woman who leads him to her daughter, who is in labor. They enter a mound of earth and—through mere touch—Hrólf successfully delivers the child. As reward, he is granted a magic ring that will guide him further on his quest.[415]

"The midwife's passage to and from the Otherworld is comparatively easy because she is already a borderline, liminal figure," Harpur wrote. "Her special status stemmed above all from the fact that she presided over the rite of birth, when the ante-natal Otherworld draws very close to this world and the midwife... has to straddle the same threshold." Harpur adds that "young children are especially vulnerable to abduction for the same reason: they have not yet been officially received, or received back, into this world—they still have one foot in the other."[416]

In his *The Science of Fairy Tales*, E. Sidney Hartland astutely noted commonalities between the "midwife to the faeries" narrative and one late rabbinical story: a man summoned by a stranger to perform a circumcision was brought "to a lofty mountain, into the bowels of which they passed, and after descending many flights of steps found themselves in a great city." Upon reaching the child's mother—a human Jew—the visitor was warned to consume no food or drink during the procedure, for they were in the land of the *mazikin* (demons, also spelled *mazikeen* or *mazakim*). The woman "had been carried away when little from home and brought thither."[417]

FAERIE OINTMENT

One crucial detail in these accounts is the glamour-dispelling faerie ointment, an exceedingly common plot point in such narratives.[418] The substance resolves stories with striking uniformity: a midwife touches her eye with faerie ointment, revealing their true nature and violating a taboo for which she is blinded. Even the earliest tale from Gervase of Tilbury features an eel pasty given to the nurse by the *drac*—after some of its grease touched her eye "she acquired a clear and distinct vision under the water" but was blinded years later after greeting her captor at market.[419] A Scottish folktale described a mother and child taken by the faeries; she witnessed them mixing "various ingredients" in a "boiling kettle" before rubbing their eyes with the product and, following suit, beheld Fairyland as a drab cave. Once more the woman's former captor blinded her in public, this time after she asked him about her child's well-being.[420]

The narrative's consistency leaves little need to discuss its innumerable iterations, though a few variations are of note. Stories attributed assorted motivations to the midwife—sometimes the application of the ointment was deliberate, sometimes because of an itch[421]—while a handful like "Cherry of Zennor" (one of the more detailed retellings) features context clues suggesting only human-faerie hybrids received this ointment, so they might see their half-siblings.[422] Other tales described midwives touching their eyes not with ointment but with the water used to wash faerie babies.[423]

A novel Welsh version described a kind woman who took in what she believed to be a human infant, only to find its needs mysteriously provided for each morning: milk and clothing, as well as gloves and a box of ointment, complete with instructions to anoint the child's eyes. In this variation, she itched her eye and discovered the foundling was a faerie. It disappeared the next day.[424]

What was this strange substance, and how did it appear? According to some it was green,[425] keeping with the fae folk's love of the color and perhaps resulting from four-leaf clover, a purported essential ingredient.[426] One 17th-century text provided a recipe, though its authenticity is obviously up for debate:

> Put a pint of clear oil with rose-water and marigold water into a glass, and add hollyhock buds, marigold flowers, hazel buds and the flowers of wild thyme— and the thyme must be gathered near the side of a hill where the fairies habitually go. Take grass from a fairy throne and add it to the glass, then leave the glass in the sun for three days. It can then be used.[427]

A similar version of the recipe called for the addition of sallet oil—used to lubricate and polish armor—and required application to the eyes morning and evening.[428]

A rare example of this ointment's appearance in a non-"midwife to the faeries" tale comes from T.J. Westropp. One Mary Callan of Shark claimed she was taken to Fairyland where, upon procuring and applying faerie ointment, she saw dozens of dead children awaiting Doomsday; one gave her a magical leaf and helped her escape the faerie fort. Running home, she found her own babe dying—he would have disappeared had the bedside candle extinguished—and, crushing the leaf, restored him to health.[429]

Tales of faerie wet nurses, nursemaids, and midwives "reflect the dangers and anxieties of childbirth and the fact that women do sometimes die or almost die," wrote Irish historian Angela Bourke. "They also reflect the anxiety surrounding the whole question of human fertility."[430] We might add that such stories are consistent with the motifs presented thus far: they underscore the essentiality of human beings to the existence of those in the Otherworld.

Chapter 6
"Mastery Beyond the Light of the Campfire"
Preventing and Thwarting Child Faerie Abduction

"Ah—Cold Iron," he said at last to the impatient children. "Folk in housen, as the People of the Hills say, grow so careless about Cold Iron. They'll nail the Horseshoe over the front door, and forget to put it over the back. Then, some time or other, the People of the Hills slip in, find the cradle-babe in the corner, and—"
"Oh, I know. Steal it and leave a changeling," Una cried.
— Rudyard Kipling, "Cold Iron"

"Anything more trivial than this, as a matter for the consideration of grave and scholarly men, one could hardly imagine," wrote American journalist and Welsh folklorist Wirt Sikes of the practices designed to protect children against faerie abduction. "But it is in precisely these trivial or seemingly trivial details that the student of comparative folk-lore finds his most extraordinary indices."[431]

Human belief is an odd thing. It is mutable. It makes erroneous connections where none exist. It feeds upon illogic and breeds superstition.

The core forces driving such superstitions, however, never change. They are steadfast. How we interpret, react to, and safeguard against the supernatural adapts over time and reflects contemporary belief, but the phenomena collectively—be it an objective other, an exteriorization of psychological anxiety, or something else entirely—remains a fixed point.

Much of what follows in the next two chapters seems contradictory, foolish, primitive, and, in some cases, barbaric to modern readers. Regardless of the logic behind such practices, efforts to prevent, intervene, confirm, and resolve changelings and child abduction were fundamental to the Fairy Faith.

GENERAL SUPERSTITIONS & FIRE

While avoiding risk factors, supervising children, having infants christened, etc., were most potent in discouraging child abduction by the fae folk, more obscure methods were implemented as well, varying widely from region to region. These protective measures were used in varying combinations, often syncretizing Pagan and Christian belief.

Region-specific practices were often so cryptic their true meaning is lost to time. In one enigmatic example learned by Evans Wentz, a mother in the Hebrides was nursing her child when a faerie woman arrived and intoned, "Heavy is your child."

"Light is everybody who lives the longest," the mother responded in kind.

"Were it not that you have answered my question and understood my meaning, you should have been less your child," the faerie replied before disappearing. Perhaps this exchange referred to the excessive weight exhibited by changelings? The true meaning and intent behind these statements—which sound more like modern espionage code phrases than snippets of 19th century Scottish conversation—remains more or less a mystery.[432]

Such arcane knowledge could prove quite useful. As with Lilith and her demonic brood, if one knew the name of a faerie, one possessed power over it.[433] A Welsh tale featured a mother who learned the name of her child's kidnapper via eavesdropping; when the faerie visited her and wagered her babe against a pile of gold that its name would go unspoken, the mother prevailed, both saving her baby and becoming rich in the process.[434]

The power of names played into another protective measure. "Elaby Gathan" was invoked in magical spells among the 17th century English when tucking babies in for the night, in the belief this benign faerie would watch over the child and prevent an exchange. Some speculate the word *lullaby* was derived from this name,[435] though there is evidence to suggest it may also be a portmanteau of the Hebrew "*Lilla, abi,*" or "*Begone, Lilith!*"[436]

Other protocols made varying degrees of sense. Some households kept black cockerels in the practical hope they might raise an alarm during faerie home invasions.[437] Less logically, Scandinavian grandmothers held it was bad luck to toss out a newborn's bathwater.[438] Best practice in Ireland's County Leitrim saw a newborn's bathwater "burnt,"[439] while other residents of that locale believed "if children in arms [were] met, they should be spat on or around, to keep off the fairies."[440] Inhabitants of the Isle of Man, according to a 1902 newspaper article, used "fanciful patterns drawn in white chalk on the doorsteps" to "keep the fairies away."[441] In other areas, "stones with natural holes in them placed in a pocket"[442]—also called *hag stones*—were useful deterrents.[443] Hungarian mothers plugged keyholes and tied doors shut with string from their undergarments during childbirth to discourage any abduction.[444]

Many cultures across the world thwart evil spirits by engaging their compulsive desire to count or catalogue—African American cultures, for example, warded off Old Hag (*Boo-Hag*) attacks by leaving out a colander or broom, the holes or straws of which the entity obsessively counted until sun-up.[445] Similarly, the devil might be distracted if tasked with enumerating grains of sand, stars, or waves.[446] In the Fairy Faith, this belief manifested itself in lore regarding French *lutins*, who, when confronted with a collection of peas, grain, or ashes during intended abductions, would knock over the vessel and become lost in counting.[447]

Keeping with prejudices of the past, faeries feared men more than women. A father remaining at home following birth was an effective safeguard, for "as long as the husband's breath is in the house [faeries] can do no harm."[448] Fathers would also pantomime childbirth to distract thieving fae folk—absurdity and inversion commonly crop up in preventative faerie lore.[449]

Any premises in the Scottish Highlands housing a newborn was to be guarded by torchbearers "carrying fire in the right-hand, and therewith running around the premises from right to left." To reverse direction would negate this protective measure.[450] (Circumambulation of a settlement or home is a widespread defensive practice—one can read Joshua's Biblical six-day march around Jericho as an inversion of this theme, the defensive made the offensive, culminating in the God of the Israelites asserting His dominance over the city's guarding deities.[451])

In the British Isles, babies were passed through fire to ward off evil spirits or the "evil eye,"[452] and in parts of Germany, Denmark, England, Ireland, and the Baltic, it was customary to keep a fire continuously burning beside an unbaptized child, a holdover of ancient Roman and Zoroastrian practices employed to keep demons at bay.[453] On the island of Lewis, this fire encircled mother and child 24 hours daily,[454] and some even incinerated the after-birth.[455] Fire and heat also played an integral role in confirming and resolving changelings (addressed later).

A Mecklenburg mother who prematurely extinguished her lamp one moonlit night inadvertently discovered the protective power of even the smallest flame. As soon as the lamp went out, a small figure appeared in her doorway: a faerie woman. The intruder rushed to the bedside and seized the woman's baby, to which she held fast. The struggle ended when the mother called for her husband, frightening the kidnapper away.[456]

FOOD

Given the taboo on consuming their food, it should come as no surprise that certain comestibles held power over faeries. Particularly potent were bread and salt, given their sacred association with life and eternity.[457]

We have already noted the protective role of bread in berry picking, and it had other applications as well. In Wiesbaden, amulets and breadcrumbs left in a baby's swaddling clothes fended off any witches or faeries encountered on the road to baptism.[458] Robert Kirk described the Gaelic practice of placing bread in a woman's bed during labor for protection,[459] to which some added a Bible and cheese.[460]

Salt—whose preservative powers seemed magical—was a powerful repellant against all supernatural forces.[461] Its power straddled the line between Paganism and Christianity. For centuries, salt was given to candidates just prior to baptism,[462] perhaps borrowed from the Fairy Faith belief that consuming salt after a faerie stroke could prevent a full-fledged abduction.[463]

It was not uncommon for the superstitious to put salt in the cradle of an unchristened infant.[464] Beatrix Lesley, a Scottish midwife, admitted in 1661 she regularly "stuck a bair knyfe betwixt the bed and the straw" and sprinkled salt about the childbirth bed before reciting, "Lord let never a worse wight waken thee nor hes laid thee downe."[465] Salt not only protected mothers and children, but also livestock; a cow encircled with it was protected from any *pixies* who wished to steal its milk.[466]

Rarely was food actually consumed to ward off faeries, though a few examples exist. "To guard against [changelings] even in the Scottish Highlands, midwives were accustomed to give a small spoonful of whisky, mixed with earth, to newly-born children, as their first food," wrote O'Hanlon.[467]

This curious intersection of food, earth, and protection is further borne out in the Irish belief that "giving mother and child the milk of a cow which had eaten of the *mothan*" would thwart faerie abduction.[468]

PLANT ALLIES

Plants guarded children against the fae folk throughout the British Isles. According to Celtic folklore, *mothan*, or pearlwort, derived its sanctity from being the first plant stepped upon by the resurrected Christ; faeries could not attack anyone carrying the weed, including cows, which were traditionally fed pearlwort on Beltane Eve (April 30) and Samhain (October 31).[469] In Wales, hedges of eithin, or prickly furze, were considered impenetrable by the *Tylwyth Teg*,[470] while far to the north on Rathlin Island, a blackberry jag under the fingernail meant any faerie captive must be returned.[471] Those in France's Aude Valley would spread barley and wheat in front of their homes whenever a strong wind arose, just in case the gust was an invisible *follet* hoping to assault a young girl.[472]

Other parts of Europe utilized herbs and spices placed strategically throughout the home. Germans employed orant (horehound), blue marjoram, and black cumin, while the Danes preferred garlic to ward off faeries .[473] (Garlic's reputation as a supernatural prophylactic not only extended to vampires, but also to New World creatures like the Jamaican *duppy*, covered later.[474]) On the other hand, herbs like thyme, closely associated with fae folk, were avoided at all costs.[475]

Another plant beloved by faeries was bundweed, otherwise known as ragwort. Yet in Scotland, "if a mother takes some bindweed [sic] and places it burnt at the ends over her babe's cradle, the fairies have no power over the child," Evans Wentz was told.[476] The spelling discrepancy is notable, according to plant folklorist D.C. Watts, who was adamant Evans Wentz meant bundweed.[477]

Perhaps the act of burning turned faeries' affinity for bundweed to revulsion. The act of igniting plants has long been used to repel evil forces—sage smudges in Native American culture, incense in magical traditions, etc. In faerie lore, burnt plants in Ireland included "a lighted wisp of straw... turned round the baby's head" which, in conjunction with "a quenched coal... under the cradle" could keep the fae at bay.[478]

Indeed, the faeries around Ireland's Lough Gur were off-put by burning tobacco. In one folktale from the region, an older boy entered a crack in the hollow hill of Knockfennel, only to have faeries toss fern seed in his eyes, blinding him, and shove elder wood in his ears, deafening him. It was only by his wit he remembered his pipe, which, when lit, caused the faeries to expel him from their mountain.[479]

Draping children in flowers like daisy chains and coronals, symbolic of the sun, was deemed protective.[480] Daisies ("day's eyes") were commonly decocted into protective eyewash in the British Isles, drawing intriguing parallels to faerie ointment.[481] As an alleged ingredient in faerie ointment, clover—specifically shamrocks—dispelled glamour[482] and even restored infants exchanged by faeries.[483]

One antiquated recipe lists the plants of an anti-faerie salve:

> …take the ewe hop plant…wormwood, bishopwort, lupin, ashthroat, henbane, harwort, vipers bugloss, heathberry plants, cropleek, garlic, grains of hedgerife, githrife, fennel; put these worts into a vessel, set *them* under the altar, sing over them nine masses, boil *them* in butter and sheep's grease, add much holy water, strain through a cloth, throw the worts into running water. If any ill tempting occur to a man, or an elf or *goblin* night visitors *come*, smear his forehead with this salve, and put it on his eyes, and where his body is sore, and cense him with incense, and sign him frequently with the sign of the cross; his condition will soon be better.[484]

A much less labor-intensive method of protection advised keeping certain pieces of wood at hand. A sprig of box-wood, blessed on Palm Sunday and placed in the crib, was believed to prevent changelings in France.[485] Being an evergreen, box-wood has connections to eternal life and, in some traditions, was one of the timbers used to construct Christ's cross.[486]

Oak was useful when combined into a wreath with ivy "in the increase of the March moon." These wreathes were kept till the following year, after which any child suspected of faerie influence was "pass[ed] thrice through."[487]

Ash, sometimes used in divination, was effective against both faeries and witchcraft;[488] "therefore branches of it were wreathed round the horns of the cattle, and round the children's cradle to keep off evil influence," Wilde wrote.[489] Children clutching a bit of this wood could escape faerie circles in Ireland,[490] while Highlands tradition fed newborns a drop of protective ash sap.[491] The tree was hallowed in many European mythologies: Scandinavian belief held Yggdrasil, the world tree, was a gigantic ash, Teutonic mythology claimed it was an ash which spawned mankind, and ancient Greeks believed the wood repelled serpents.[492]

According to Briggs, rowan offered the best protection from faeries, hence its common presence outside Scottish homes.[493] Some Irish believed witches used the smoke from morning fires in May to curse households, unless it was rowan smoke.[494] Rowan was said to derive power from its red berries,[495] a repellant effect magnified by red thread: "Rowan-tree and red thread / Haud the witches a' in dread," went a Northumbrian rhyme.[496]

CLOTH, CLOTHING, & THE COLOR RED

Sikes' "trivial details" are no more apparent than in superstitions regarding clothing. Expectant mothers were layered with blankets, old shoes were burned,[497] and left stockings and right shirtsleeves were arbitrarily ascribed special potency—all in the name of preventing faerie abduction.[498]

Unsurprisingly, articles associated with men were deemed most powerful. Husbands' breeches[499] or waistcoats[500] were draped in or around the crib,[501] providing the illusion of a watchful father guarding his child.[502] This belief was particularly widespread;

a maternal superstition practiced in China frightened away evil spirits by placing the fishing nets of men near newborns.[503]

Motifs of inversion and absurdity abound in clothing beliefs. Inverting an article, especially a coat or stocking, was a common means of neutering enchantments[504] from child abduction to being pixie led.[505] In Ireland, boys were dressed as girls to fool faeries[506]—recall they desired females least—and Croker claimed, "If a mother wishes to protect her child… she must let its head hang down when she is dressing it in the morning."[507]

For Christian practitioners of the Fairy Faith, a thrice-knotted thread—symbolic of the Trinity—blessed by a priest and placed across the cradle kept away both faeries and the devil.[508] While its color did not matter to the priest, red thread occurred frequently in good luck folk charms: strung across doorways, it kept faeries from entering homes,[509] while red thread tied about their necks rendered children untouchable[510] (a practice seen both in Jamaica[511] and in China, where red thread was tied into a babe's hair).[512]

The color red also empowered cloth. Some Irish mothers refused to let their children out of the house without a bit of scarlet flannel pinned to their chests, and anyone finding fae loot could secure it by affixing a red handkerchief.[513]

Similar belief can be found in Germanic countries. The *Zimmern Chronicle* of 1566 told of a weaver who "rewarded the gnome in his service by offering him a pair of shoes and a black blouse, which the other gratefully accepted. He later gave the gift of a red cap, which the other received reluctantly before leaving, never to return."[514]

Why red? Opinions differ. Some cite Genesis 38, where a midwife places a red string around the wrist of a firstborn twin as a means of child identification, but evidence of belief in red thread's protective qualities is found in Hindu and Buddhist practice as well.[515] Hartland proposed pagan roots: "In Sweden the babe is wrapped in red cloth, which we may be allowed to conjecture is intended to cozen the fairies by simulating fire."[516]

An informant from the Irish midlands suggested to Patricia

Lysaght:

> ... that the fairies' hatred of the color and their
> desire to avoid it is because it reminds them of
> their own bloodless state and their hopeless quest
> for reinstatement in Heaven. Not only will the
> fairies avoid anything which is red in color, such
> as red cloth, red fire, meat, even the red comb of
> the farmyard cock, but they will also avoid sharp,
> pointed objects... which might prick them, remind
> them of their lack of blood, and 'make them
> hysterical.'[517]

This bloodless quality should give Forteans pause—after
all, the ubiquitous "Greys" described in so many modern alien
abductions possess a pallor suggesting a lack of blood. At the
same time—while it is true certain types like the Orkney *trows*
were famed for dressing in grey—not all fae folk avoided the
color red.[518] In fact, some malicious English faeries were known
alternately as Redcaps, Redcombs, or Bloody Caps, named for
their crimson garments.[519] According to some traditions, it was
as closely associated with faeries as the color green, and wearing it
could invite similar consequences.[520] To see any fairy clad entirely
in red was considered an ill omen... often portending war[521] or a
child's death.[522]

BELLS & CHRISTIANITY

"There was anciently a belief that the sound of brass would
break enchantment," wrote Sikes. "It is presumed that the original
purpose of the common custom of tolling the bell for the dead was
to drive away evil spirits," entities ready to seize upon the newly
vacated body of the dying. The Welsh even contended bells could
"perform miracles, detect thieves, heal the sick, and the like."[523] It
was for this reason bells were believed to drive away faeries[524] and

were sometimes worn around the neck as an amulet with a bit of coral.[525]

This belief has deep Pagan roots, stemming in part from the same source as the English Morris dance, in which bells on dancers' legs drive anti-fertility spirits away from communities.[526] Christian teachings—where church chimes repelled witches and the devil—evolved from these earlier superstitions.[527] In one fascinating Devon tradition, *pixies* actually went out of their way to abduct bell-ringers, for they feared their presence would undermine faerie power over the region.[528]

Europeans used anything and everything Christian to protect children from faeries. Iconography and sacred items were most popular, including church books: Bibles,[529] prayer books,[530] and hymnals[531] were regularly placed underneath the heads of both infants[532] and mothers in labor.[533] Wary parents hoping to ward off faerie intrusion might also mount crosses or crucifixes in nurseries or make the sign of the cross over the cradle.[534]

In Iceland, crosses were placed both above and below the crib.[535] From J. Simpson's *Icelandic Folktales and Legends:*

> Two elfin women once went to a farm to leave a changeling there. They came to where the baby they wished to take was; it was lying in a cradle, and there was nobody nearby except for another child, which was two years old.
>
> The younger and less cautious of the elf-women goes straight up to the cradle and says:
>
> Let us take him, take him, do!
>
> Then the elder says:
>
> We can't for that would harm us too:
> A Cross above, beneath, they drew;

And by him sits a child of two,
And he will speak of what we do.

At that they went off without doing anything, partly
because of the Cross marks which had been made
over the cradle and also beneath the baby before it
was laid there, and partly also because of the two-
year-old child who was sitting by the cradle, and
who later told everyone what had happened.[536]

Some Irish preferred wearing a cross at the neck[537] or making
"a fiery sign of the cross over a cradle" with a lit straw before placing
the infant inside.[538] If a cross was unavailable, blades and scissors
in the shape of a cross sufficed.[539] Missionaries spread similar
traditions far and wide—to prevent nursing a demon, Chinese
Christians made the sign of a cross on their child's forehead using
the ashes of a burned banana skin.[540]

Christian anti-faerie practice regularly syncretized indigenous
folk belief. An excellent example comes from Italy: to fend off both
faeries and witches—who terrifyingly "tore faces off infants"—
Italian mothers kept a light burning; pinned to the door the portrait
of a saint, an unfurled napkin, and a rosary; and left a brush and a
jar of salt behind the door (thresholds and doorways being liminal
spaces).[541] The potency of salt has been addressed—elsewhere in
Europe other substances were deemed equally effective, such as
mold from a church graveyard[542] or, in warding off French *lutins*,
holy water.[543]

The most devout eschewed these Pagan remnants, claiming
Christian piety alone reduced the risk of abduction.[544] Special
emphasis was placed upon prayers,[545] in particular the Lord's
Prayer, recited either by children or their guardians.[546]

We have already noted the importance of blessing beautiful
children, as well as christening. There were certain rituals
surrounding baptism, however, which reeked of Pagan holdovers.
Wrote MacGregor of the Highlands:

Another fret was observed, that immediately after a child was baptised, he behoved to be secured from the power of the fairies, and of all evil spirits. For this purpose a basket was taken, which was half filled with bread and cheese, wrapped up in a clean linen cloth. Over this parcel the child was laid as if in a cradle. The basket was then taken up by the oldest female in the family circle at the time, carried three times round the fire, and then suspended for a few seconds from the crook that hung over the fire. The child was then removed from its temporary berth, while the bread and cheese were divided among the company present, as nourishment to guarantee their health for another year. [547]

Other Scottish post-baptismal practices included refraining from washing the infant after christening, for fear the evil-repelling holy water might be removed before the child's first post-Baptismal sleep.[548]

IRON

A tale from Ireland's Boyne Valley described a family beset with changelings. When the Faerie Queen ordered a trio of her people to take the couple's third child, they were astounded by the presence of a heavy iron beam laid across the infant's breast. None of the three could move beam nor child, nor could the Queen when she intervened. What the faeries perceived as an immoveable iron beam was, in fact, merely a simple needle fastening the child's clothes.[549]

The most potent means of avoiding faerie abduction was the use of iron, second only to baptism. It was placed in households and cribs, hung over doorways,[550] fashioned into amulets,[551] and even carried in pockets while traveling[552] in any form, including needles and pins.[553] It could be used as an outright repellant, or as a sort of insurance against unsavory interactions. The Welsh *gwyllion*, said to visit homes during storms, were to be greeted with hospitality—should the meeting turn sour, however, they could be banished with cold iron.[554]

Iron not only frightened faeries, but also drove changelings from homes and restored taken infants (discussed later).[555] Celtic superstition held a combination of rowan, juniper, and iron dispelled any witch's "evil eye," a curse already demonstrated as one means of producing a changeling.[556]

Spades[557] or iron tongs were popularly mounted over[558] or placed across cradles.[559] While the latter method may have simply served the practical purpose of keeping rowdy children confined, potential faerie abductors in one Irish story spied a pair of tongs and were so stumped they could only laugh and begin playing cards.[560] By contrast, "The Llanfabon Changeling" tells of a mother who, running outside to check on the livestock, forgot in her haste to lay protective tongs across her child's cradle; though nothing seemed amiss with the cattle, the babe was exchanged upon return.[561]

"A bunch of keys, or a rusty nail, was as effective as the most lethal weapon," J.G. Campbell wrote.[562] While any old bit of iron seemed to suffice, weapons were favored, inducing the faerie's aforementioned fear of sharp objects. "It is no matter of surprise, that a sword, or dirk, or knife, should have miraculous powers ascribed to it."[563] Blades and nails were driven into children's headboards—swords drew additional power from their hilt, which formed a sort of crude cross.[564]

Needles were placed alongside babies, safety concerns notwithstanding.[565] To modern eyes, these children were more at risk from heavy and sharp objects than faeries, but even more extreme methods were practiced. Sometimes knives or scissors would be placed *in the crib*, rather than the headboard,[566] and in one striking example of poor judgment, a sleeping Yorkshire babe was protected by suspending a carving knife from the head of its cradle, the point dangling just above its face.[567]

While iron was most common, a handful of accounts indicate other metals were employed. The aforementioned Thumbeline story claimed she could neither pass over nor touch zinc, though this may indicate the tale's dubious origin.[568] It was most common to replace iron with steel, especially in Scandinavia.[569] This substitution was logical, given steel is an iron alloy, purified by human hands.[570] The protagonist of one Shetland legend encountered a troop of faeries absconding with an infant—thinking quickly, he drew his steel knife and pressed it to the child's head, forcing the kidnappers to drop it.[571]

Contradictory lore suggests not all faeries feared iron and steel. Some, like *gnomes* and *dwarfs*, were renowned metallurgists.[572] Such was the case in one Scottish story, where a father wishing to rid himself of a *sibhreach* (changeling) eventually found his son working a faerie forge.[573] Another changeling tale from Ireland told of a father who criticized a blacksmith's handiwork. "Well, whoever told you that is as good a blacksmith as I am," the craftsman retorted. The father said it was his own sickly child, which the smith surmised must be a changeling, to be so knowledgeable. He advised the father to casually mention that the nearby faerie fort was ablaze upon arriving home. The father followed this suggestion and the child exclaimed, "My word! My bellows and tools are all burnt." The changeling fled, never to return.[574]

Before speculating on the reasons behind iron's efficacy, its accompanying folklore must be contextualized. Faeries were not the only beings said to possess the aversion—iron also impeded witches and evil spirits.[575] In France, it was once held that any curse could be repelled by obtaining a cow heart and driving a handful of iron nails into it, then affixing it to the main beam of a home between 11:00 p.m. and midnight.[576]

Belief in iron's potency was not exclusive to the West; ancient Chinese custom saw iron nails hammered into trees to exorcise demons.[577] "In India, iron is believed to repel the *djinn*, the demonic children of Lilith and the Devil," wrote Rosemary Ellen Guiley. "In classical times, iron was used to ward off illness and bad luck, which were believed to be caused by evil spirits." (It is worth noting this ability did not affect vampires or ghosts.)[578]

Indeed, an entire book could be written on the global intersection of iron and the paranormal. But *why* was iron deemed so useful?

An anecdote described by Evans Wentz is worth retelling:

> By experiments on his own perfectly healthy children, [a mister] Wienholt proved that there are natural forces existing whose stimulations are never perceived in waking life: he made passes over the face and neck of his son with an iron key at the distance of half an inch without touching him, whereupon the boy began to rub those parts and manifested uneasiness. Wienholt likewise experimented on his other children with lead, zinc, gold, and other metals, and in most cases the children "averted the parts so treated, rubbed them, or drew the clothes over them." Therefore, in sleep the consciousness perceives objects without physical contact and this not inconceivably might suggest, inversely, that in sleep the human consciousness can affect objects without physical contact, as it is said fairies and the dead can, and in the way psychical researchers know that objects can be affected.

We might wonder if this stimulation of sleeping consciousness might be the actual reason objects were left in cribs. Perhaps this stimulation prevented sleepers from falling too deeply into the astral realm, a metaphysical state parapsychologists claim is accessed during slumber and, it should be noted, where a variety of cultures claim spirit predation takes place.[579] Metaphysicists have posited other reasons for iron's use; popular theories hold that spirits absorb ambient energy to manifest, and iron may somehow interfere with this effort.[580]

Why iron specifically? Iron is synonymous with strength,[581] and its ferromagnetic properties no doubt appeared supernatural to primitive peoples,[582] as did its common arrival from the heavens in the form of meteors (meteoric iron, imbued with nickel, yields exceptionally strong blades).[583] Iron also gave mankind the ability to bend nature to its will—Pliny the Elder said in the first century, "It is by the aid of iron that we construct houses, cleave rocks, and perform so many other useful offices in life."[584]

"It is a trickster or devil-delivered technology that sets us apart," said author, alternative historian, and chaos magician Gordon White. "If you look at the archaic Greek versions of the origins of metallurgy, they sort of match similar things you'll find in other cultures—this is a god-given or god-stolen skill… As a result, it's associated with power over and mastery over the things that are beyond the light of the campfire."[585]

This assertion of technology over nature is why cold iron—i.e., iron worked by a human blacksmith—was more feared by faeries than the raw element itself, according to some folklorists and authors.[586] It has also been suggested that faeries resented mortals' mastery of this craft,[587] or, as "representatives of the stone age," they feared the technological progress iron represented.[588] Many historians favor this interpretation, contending aboriginal peoples of the British Isles, being unfamiliar with the strength of invaders' iron implements, feared its power and gave rise to faerie legends.[589]

INTERVENTION

"Welsh fairies have been caught in the very act of theft, and a pretty fight they made, every time, to keep their booty," wrote Guiney. "But the strength of a man or a woman, was, of course, too much for them to resist long."[590]

Any parent foolish enough to ignore these precautions was left with few options should faeries decide to take their children. As in the tale of Jennet Francis, a physical struggle just might succeed. Lady Gregory wrote:

There was a woman woke one night and she saw
two women by the fire, and they came over and
tried to take away her baby. But she held him and
she nudged her husband with her arm, but he was
fast asleep. And they tried him again, and all she
could do wouldn't waken the husband, but still she
had the baby tight, and she called out a curse in the
devil's name. So then they went away, for they don't
like cursing.[591]

Note the unwakeable spouse, a detail common in modern alien abductions.

Given the faerie association with weather, it was advisable to toss clods of dirt,[592] nails,[593] or knives[594] at suspicious whirlwinds, whereupon any stolen children would be dropped. "In Irish lore, if you passed by fairies on All Hallow's Eve, you should throw the dirt from your footprint after them, which will force them to surrender any humans they have taken captive," wrote Rosemary Ellen Guiley.[595] Prayer could be used for additional effect.[596]

The simple act of noticing abduction could force faeries to abort. In a German account, a mother returning from cherry picking saw a strange being by the cradle; upon crying out, it disappeared, leaving behind only a handprint on the canopied bed.[597] Another story collected by Evans Wentz ended similarly after a Scottish mother awoke abruptly—caught in the act, the faeries grumbled, "Oh, let us leave this one with her as we have already taken so many!"[598]

The kindness of strangers could prove helpful, as in the case of an Irish tailor who spied a faerie holding a child out the window of a roadside cottage. Its confederate was nowhere to be seen, so when the faerie shouted, "Who'll take the child?" the tailor snatched the babe and delivered it to a neighbor. The next day, the changeling left in the first house appeared to have died in the night, but the neighbor shortly delivered the true baby.[599]

Another stranger came to the rescue in a Swedish folktale, employing a "shell game" strategy to rescue an infant.

A resident of Vingåkir, who made frequent trips to Nyköping with loads of flour, was in the habit of halting for the night at the house of a farmer in Verna. One summer night he arrived later than usual, and, as the people were already in bed and asleep, the weather being pleasant, he did not wish to wake anyone, so unhitched his horse from the wagon, hitched him to a haystack, and laid himself under the wagon to sleep.

He had been some time under the wagon, yet awake, when, from under a stone nearby, an ugly, deformed woman, carrying a babe, made her appearance. Looking about her carefully, she laid the child on the stone and went into the house. In a short time she returned, bearing another child; laid it upon the stone, and taking up the first one, returned to the house.

The man observed her actions, and divining their purpose, crept cautiously from his resting place as soon as the woman had disappeared into the house, took the sleeping child and hid it in his coat under the wagon. When the troll returned and found the child gone, she went a third time to the house, for which she returned with the child she had just carried in, whereupon she disappeared under the stone.[600]

Chapter 7
"The Acorn Before the Oak"
Changeling Confirmation & Resolution

A bar of metal I heated red
To frighten the fairy from its bed,
To put in the place of this fretting wean
My own bright beautiful boy again.
— Dora Sigerson, "The Fairy Changeling"

Sometimes the mere suspicion of a changeling was enough to set in motion the barbarous process of expelling it from the crib. The more cautious, however, first sought confirmation of their true child's absence; many of these methods have already been alluded to or mentioned briefly.

The faerie fear of iron, for example, could be utilized to both assure parents they had a changeling and restore the abducted infant. A child who screamed when placed upon an iron-bladed shovel was almost certainly one of the faeries and could be tossed aside with little guilt.[601] Another technique suggested tossing a piece of iron at the child, at which changelings would wail and flee.[602]

While offensive to modern sensibilities, this process pales in comparison to other tactics. What follows is not for the faint of heart.

CONFIRMATION OF CHANGELINGS

A variety of methods existed to determine if one's baby was a changeling. In some regions, animals ferreted out the imposter: in Sicily, snakes ignored mortal babies but bit changelings, while elsewhere a wild stallion colt, smelling two infants, would lick a human child and attempt to kick a faerie.[603]

Typically, a changeling's identity was confirmed when it betrayed its age via the exhibition of advanced abilities, sometimes of its own volition—they commonly raised suspicions by displaying musical talents as in "The Tailor & the Changeling."[604] Similarly, the Nordic *näkk*, excited by the prospect of baptism, revealed itself as a changeling by speaking en route to the christening.[605] Other tales described changelings whose laughter,[606] psychic abilities,[607] or—in cases of slightly older children—feats of strength or labor give them away.[608] The servant girl of one Nithsdale folktale bemoaned her duties in front of the family's exchanged child, only to find all of her work finished by a great gust of faerie wind that revealed the imposter in their midst.[609]

Most changeling stories, however, involved tricking them into revealing their age. This usually involved betraying an adult intellect, i.e. speaking. Some deceptions were relatively straightforward, as in the story "The Fairy Hill's Afire," where, as the name suggests, all one needed to do was announce the nearby faerie mound was burning; alarmed, the changeling would exclaim, "Waes me! what'll come o' my wife and bairns?" and disappear up the chimney.[610]

Other tricks were more convoluted. With few exceptions, these techniques baffled the creature with some nonsensical activity, prompting questions or exclamations no mortal child would make.

CONFIRMATION OF CHANGELINGS: A BREWERY OF EGGSHELLS

The most common method of confirming a changeling's presence was the preparation of foodstuffs in broken eggshells,[611] a motif consistently seen in tales from every corner of Europe.[612] In these narratives, a parent, noticing their baby's odd behavior, solicits assistance from a cunning man or woman who prescribes the eggshell method. In some tales only one eggshell is used, in others a dozen;[613] the food might be ale, beer, porridge,[614] dough,[615] potage,[616] or simply water,[617] but it is almost always heated or boiled by a fire[618] (in rare examples the eggshells themselves are "brewed," omitting food entirely).[619]

The astonished changeling watches this absurdity unfold with great interest, asking the parent what they are doing. Invariably the tale ends with the faerie laughing like an adult[620] or declaring, despite its advanced age, it has never seen the like. Most changeling exclamations riff on a rhyme collected by folklorist Joseph Jacobs: "Acorn before oak I knew / An egg before a hen / But I never heard of an eggshell brew / A dinner for harvest men."[621]

A variant from Wales and Brittany concluded thusly:

> A mother whose infant had been spirited away, and who was much perplexed over what she took to be a changeling, was advised to cook a meal for ten farm-servants in one egg-shell. When the queer little creature, burning with curiosity, asked her from his high-chair what she was about, she could hardly answer, so excited was she to hear him speak. At that he cried louder: "A meal for ten, dear mother, in one egg-shell? The acorn before the oak have I seen, and the wilderness before the lawn, but never did I behold anything like that!" and so gave damaging evidence of his age and his unlucky wisdom. [622]

In an Irish version, a beggar woman calling upon a housewife learned of her child's incessant wailing and advised her to place a circle of eggs in the center of the room. Doing so, the babe asked, "What are you doing in that manner?"

"I am making a brewing cauldron," the mother replied.

The changeling gasped, "I am more than 300 years old and I never saw a brewing cauldron like that!" Identity confirmed, the housewife gazed out the window and claimed the faerie mound was ablaze, prompting the changeling to flee.[623] This faerie was a whippersnapper—another Irish changeling shouted, "I'm 1,500 years in the world, and I never saw a brewery of egg-shells before!"[624]

Responses varied region-to-region. A Breton variant ended with the changeling exclaiming, "I remember when they were building Babel, and never heard before of a brewery of egg-shells."[625] In Germany, the babe scoffed, "Well, I am as old as the Westerwald, but I never before saw anybody cooking in egg-shells!"[626] In Lithuania, the imposter cried, "I am so old, I was already in the world before the Kamschtschen Wood was planted, wherein great trees grew, and *that* is now laid waste again; but anything so wonderful I have never seen."[627] In Normandy, changelings remarked they had "seen the Forest of Ardennes burnt seven times"; in Scandinavia, "the wood fall in Lessö Forest"; in Denmark, "a young wood thrice upon Tiis Lake." But in each case, never was such absurdism beheld.[628]

A handful of notable variations substituted eggshells with the husks of acorns,[629] walnuts,[630] or shellfish.[631] Other accounts described boiling oil, rather than food;[632] a curious version from Ireland's County Longford dispensed with eggshells entirely, choosing to bewilder the changeling with the food itself (meal and two egg whites combined in a type of "porridge" the creature had never seen).[633] French lore suggests the brewery of eggshells could be employed preventatively to discourage faeries slipping through the chimney.[634]

No academic consensus accounts for the eggshell method's popularity and distribution. Possibly, like superstitions surrounding clothes, it represented an inversion of norms. More likely, however, the eggshell method expressed fertility themes—changeling stories, after all, have an undercurrent of anxiety regarding reproduction.

Eggs appear prominently in faerie tales. In 1883 P.C. Asbjørnsen retold a changeling story in which a giant egg was discovered, later hatching a faerie baby.[635] A casual aside from Waldron's *Description of the Isle of Man* claimed humans, in the opinion of mermaids, were ignorant because they "throw away the water they have boiled eggs in."[636] In another tale, a girl was advised to take the "sweat" of an egg roasted on three Sundays and apply it to her eyes to "see and know any thing she desired"—essentially faerie ointment.[637]

"The significance of the eggs has been debated by others," wrote "Dr. Beachcombing," *nom de plume* for the academic-professor-cum-curator of *Beachcombing's Bizarre History Blog*. "Are they a memory of a time when the changeling was boiled? Are they a psychological symbol of individuation? Or are they just a chance motif thrown up by the European folklore tradition—such tales stretch all the way through northern Europe?"[638]

While eggshells are common, they are not present in every changeling confirmation. The main goal—to kindle changelings' curiosity—remains intact in each of these examples, even if eggshells are absent.

- A commonly cited Icelandic technique involved the construction of an enormous "spoon," using rods fastened to the end of an ordinary porridge spoon. In these tales, the handle stretches all the way up the chimney, prompting the changeling to mutter, "Well! I am old enough, as anybody may guess from my beard, and the father of eighteen elves, but never, in all my life, have I seen so long a spoon to so small a pot."[639] Occasionally, the spoon was placed in an eggshell half, creating "a little porridge pot" to marvel at as well.[640]

- A shrewd woman slaughtered a pig in another Scandinavian tale and placed it, hide and all, into a black pudding. Upon presenting the dish to her ravenous child, he exclaimed, "A pudding with hide!—and a pudding with hair!—a pudding with eyes!—and a pudding with legs in it!" Never had he seen such in all of his years, and he promptly fled.[641]

• The Saami of the Arctic Circle told of Little People who exchanged "old men" for human children. Making "stone soup"—boiling rocks in a pot—revealed any suspected changeling, who exclaimed they had never beheld such a sight.[642]

• A unique French variant featured a well-dwelling *poulpican* who exchanged her hairy child. One night the changeling saw a butcher ride past with "a calf, tied by the legs, before him on his horse, so that man, horse, and calf looked like one strange beast in the half-darkness." "I saw the acorn before the oak, but this is neither sense nor joke," it exclaimed. The mother then lined up one hundred broken eggshells "like a procession of priests"; after hearing the same response, the father threatened to kill the boy, at which point the *poulpican* returned their true child.[643]

Since many changelings were simply afraid of being caught, some fled once exposed. In most cases, however, the process of retrieving a mortal child was just beginning.

RESOLUTION: RETRIEVAL

Some Germanic communities held that any changeling not restored within nine days would waste away and die.[644] Celtic folklore traditionally held those kidnapped to Fairyland could be retrieved after 366 days, though changelings were regularly expelled much sooner in Ireland, Scotland, and England.[645] The timeframe of a year and a day has possible origins in the Irish custom of "Telltown marriages," a matchmaking tradition wherein couples were blindly married at a faerie rath, with the provision their union could be dissolved after exactly 366 days—apparently the fae folk, given their affinity for breeding with humans, adopted a similar custom.[646]

Salvation often rested in the hands of the abducted.[647] Accounts tell of children relinquished from Fairyland after refusing to eat faerie food, touching iron,[648] sneezing,[649] or, in one tale, drinking from a forbidden fountain.[650] Sometimes the best course of action was to ignore abductions and hope the faeries would return captives of their own accord—folklore on Rathlin Island, for example, held if children were released at all, they would be relinquished by the third day without warning, ceremony, or reason.[651] Examples persist where treating a changeling as one's own,[652] or showing little reaction to the discovery of an exchange, hastened the real infant's return.[653] In "The Queen of Elfan's Nourice," it was insinuated mother and child would be reunited if she nursed a faerie child for a time, letting it drink its fill of human milk.[654]

On the other end of the spectrum, the direct confrontation of some entities literally shamed them into releasing captives. In Hungary, knock-kneed children were labeled changelings, only remedied when their mothers sat in doorways on days when witches roamed—Tuesdays or Fridays—shouting, "Pfui! Pfui! you scoundrels! Give it back!"[655]

Mounting a physical rescue was nigh impossible, though tenacious parents sometimes took their fight to the faeries through great effort.[656] The proactive blacksmith of one Scottish legend, after employing the eggshell method and ridding himself of a changeling, infiltrated the nearby faerie mound armed with a dirk, the Bible, and a rooster. The Bible warded off enchantments; the dirk, thrust into the mound's threshold, kept it from sealing and trapping him underground; and the cock irritated the faeries until they discharged his son.[657]

The Orkney mother of "The Rousay Changeling" was instructed

to visit a rock cleft above a certain loch and drive into it a wedge of steel. The fissure widened, revealing a faerie bouncing the missing child upon her knee; the mother smacked the abductor in the face three times with a Bible and returned home, where she found her child returned.[658]

In another tale from Scotland, a *gruagach*—faerie wizard— visited a fisherman, convincing him to part with his son for a year and a day, so he could learn the arcane arts. The father agreed but made the *gruagach* give his word to bring the boy back. Upon his homecoming, the *gruagach* again asked to take the boy for an additional 366 days; the father once more agreed but failed to secure any promise of return. The *gruagach* kept the boy permanently, and the father set off to rescue his child. After months of searching, he came upon the home of an old beggar woman with second sight who set him off in the direction of the *gruagach*'s cottage. The father finally found the thief, who told him he had transformed all his victims into birds. The father could have his boy back the following morning—but only if he could select him from all the birds within a league. That night, the boy whispered in his father's ear that he would be the only bird lagging behind, pecking at the others; armed with this knowledge, the child was identified and returned home with his father. The boy thenceforth had the ability to shapeshift and possessed a "strange wisdom" in his eyes.[659]

A recurring Irish motif featured abductees roving the countryside with the faerie host astride a great white horse. From the National Folklore Collection of Ireland:

> After a few weeks the father was visited by his own child and he told him to be at the edge of the river nearby on a certain day and he would be riding a white horse and if he could catch the white horse they could have him back. This father went to the edge of the river and with great difficulty he caught the white horse on which the boy was riding. When they went home the queer child was gone and they

had their own child again.[660]

RESOLUTION: MAGIC

A compelling argument could be made that all child retrievals involved ceremony, ritual, or magic. There are, however, more explicit examples, like the lore surrounding "Saint" Guinefort.

Unlike canonized saints, Guinefort was not human—rather, he was a greyhound. The story holds that a French knight, returning home, found the nursery in shambles, his child missing, and Guinefort's muzzle bloodied. After slaying his dog, the knight was heartbroken to discover the infant unharmed and a dead snake alongside the crib, killed by the loyal hound. The knight erected a shrine in Guinefort's memory, and since the 13th century the dog has been regarded as a folk saint.[661]

The shrine was revered as a place of child healing and, naturally, changeling resolution. According to local tradition, the exhaustive process for restoring an exchanged child involved offering Guinefort salt; hanging the child's clothing on nearby bushes; driving a needle into an adjacent tree; passing the nude changeling between two trunks; tossing the child nine times between mother and wise woman, while beseeching the *fauns* to take their child back; laying the changeling at the foot of a tree atop bedding straw; waiting for two lit candles in the branches above to burn out; and, providing it was still alive after such an ordeal, dunking the child nine times in the Chalaronne River.[662]

Elsewhere in Europe, methods were less convoluted. Changeling stories typically featured the guiding wisdom of wiser community members, varyingly called *dynion hysbys,*[663] *dyn hysvys,*[664] magicians, sorcerers, faerie doctors,[665] or faerie men/women.[666] Such individuals required their advice be followed "faithfully and minutely," no matter how cruel or absurd.[667]

- In Wales, a changeling was once restored after its mother swore to dunk it in cold water each morning for three months, on the advice of a wise woman. By the end of this period, wrote Rhŷs, "there was no finer infant in the Cwm."[668]

- Another Welsh faerie doctor advised cooking a black hen (feathers and all) above burning peat. After its feathers fell off, any exchanged child would be restored.[669]

- In Cornwall, magicians once instructed parents to pass changelings through the Mên-an-Tol, a series of standing stones near the western shore. It was believed benevolent *pixies* at the Mên-an-Tol would undo any faerie exchanges.[670]

Methods were commonly mixed and matched. Prayers and chants accompanied other tactics. In one Irish account described by Patrick Kennedy, a changeling was dumped "on a wisp of straw which crowned the manure heap," around which observers joined hands while a faerie doctor intoned:

> Come at our call, O Sighe mother!
> Come and remove your offspring.
> Food and drink he has received,
> And kindness from the Ban-a-teagh.
> Here he no longer shall stay,
> But depart to the Duine Matha.
> Restore the lost child, O Bean-Sighe!
> And food shall be left for thy people
> When the cloth is spread on the harvest field,
> On the short grass newly mown.
> Food shall be left on the dresser-shelf
> And the hearthstone shall be clean,
> When the Clann Sighe come in crowds,
> And sweep in rings round the floor,

And hold their feast at the fire.
Restore the mortal child, O Bean-Sighe!
And receive thine own at our hands.[671]

Chants were essential to rituals in other parts of the British Isles. Shetland faerie doctors advised a family gather inside a doorway—again, a liminal zone—before breakfast, drawing a circle around themselves while repeating, "Outside this ring ye your power may tine / Inside this ring, Lord, keep me and mine." Once complete, the circle and everything within it was vigorously swept out the open door, after which their child would appear inside the ring.[672]

Being magical creatures, faeries were obsessed with fairness and pacts. Offering something of one's own in exchange compelled them to release their captives. Irishman John Roy rescued a young lady by tossing his cap on the ground and proclaiming, "Mine is yours, and yours is mine!" The faeries were obligated to accept the bargain.[673]

Other trades involved comestibles. Northern Scots left changelings in faerie-frequented areas accompanied by "bread, butter, cheese, eggs and flesh or fowl." If these offerings were missing upon their return, children were deemed restored.[674]

RESOLUTION: EXPOSURE & ABANDONMENT

Sickeningly, the abandonment of disabled infants is a longstanding tradition in cultures worldwide.[675] The practice conveniently mirrored belief that faeries came to the aid of their abused or neglected babies, reinforcing a culture of unintentional and deliberate infanticide.

While some advised abandoning changelings anywhere outside the home, [676] specific locales worked best: aside ancient cairns,[677] beneath sacred oak trees,[678] at church entrances,[679] or, in the case of Greek islanders, on altar steps.[680] These were frequently liminal locations, as in southern Ireland, where changelings were left before nightfall at the intersection of three rivers or borders.[681]

Other practices took the child to a crossroads—a classic liminal zone—where a corpse was passed over it.[682] Coastal cultures employed liminal areas like the seashore[683] or a rock at high tide,[684] accompanied by a food offering.[685] Ironically, it was regular for such barbaric abandonment to include Christian trappings, such as dunking the child thrice in the name of the Trinity.[686] Parents also visited these liminal locales hoping to spy their mortal child among its faerie captors.[687]

The faerie-dead association manifested in examples where changelings were left overnight in open graves,[688] a technique rendered more effective on quarter days (religious festivals approximately three months apart near solstices and equinoxes).[689] This method also supposedly mitigated the bad luck of Whitsuntide births.[690]

Wells featured prominently in changeling tales. In Germany, suspected faerie imposters were forced to drink from a special well and abandoned for nine days,[691] directly paralleled in parts of Ireland.[692] Other techniques included dipping changelings thrice in County Wicklow's Tubber Rowan (or the "Well of the Ash Tree")[693] or, in County Kilkenny, tossing them into a well outright.[694] These methods bear a passing resemblance to baptism, explaining their efficacy within a Christian context.

This water theme continues with rivers, into which changelings were thrown,[695] particularly in Denmark and Sweden.[696] Water revealed changelings' true nature—parents tossing babies into rivers might only see old men floating downstream,[697] or watch their children wither in mid-air, intercepted by their faerie brethren before hitting the water.[698]

Vestiges of this belief still exist in the form of a macabre joke told among medical students: a foreign student tells his attending physician about cantankerous "reever babies." When asked to elaborate, he explains, "In my country, you throw such babies in the reever."[699]

Like vampires, faeries could not cross running water.[700] The contradictory nature of folklore rears its head again, however, when one examines the many tales where changelings willingly jumped into streams,[701] or—in the case of German *nickerts*—crossing a river actually *allowed* faeries to steal infants.[702] (This association between water and the supernatural is echoed in modern UFO, Sasquatch, and [obviously] lake monster stories, where a disproportionate amount of sightings take place near bodies of water.[703])

One of the more popular places to abandon changelings was atop dunghills or rubbish heaps, compost stockpiled just outside the home for fertilization of the spring crop.[704] According to Kennedy, following the eggshell method "the Breton or Irish housewife... summons her relations, and they get rid of [the changeling] by taking him on a shovel, and *landing* him comfortably in the middle of the dung-lough at the bottom of the bawn, and letting him cry his fill. His fairy relations come to his rescue with little loss of time..."[705] Any Cornish mother fearing *spriggans* had exchanged her child might take a broom and deposit the infant on a trash heap,[706] while German women literally swept changelings out of houses like so much rubbish.[707] Similar practices among gypsies advised taking a convulsive infant to a dried dung mound in "which the hair of the father and mother have been mingled... [the mother] chants, 'Hair, hair, burn! / Dirt and hair burn / Dirt and hair burn / Illness be burned!'"[708]

The logic guiding this practice, according to some, was that faeries were "pure" spirits who could not abide defilement.[709] They did seem averse to filth—not only could tossing dirt clods at whirlwinds foil abductions,[710] but there are also tales where the fae folk so obsessively cleaned a dirty baby they failed to notice the sunrise, forcing them to release their captive.[711]

Anyone happening upon an abandoned changeling was warned against interfering. In the best-known tale, "Yallery Brown," a faerie baby was discovered by a kind-hearted man named Tom Tiver. Taking Yallery home, Tiver received assistance from the faerie child with household chores until the community began accusing him of witchcraft. Tiver was forced to ask Yallery to leave. He obliged but cursed his benefactor with bad luck from that day forward.[712]

RESOLUTION: ABUSE

By far the most prevalent means of expelling a changeling was abuse, the simple threat of which could frighten them into leaving[713]—a Russian changeling, fearful of axes, was once exorcised after its hosts began chopping firewood.[714] As in cases of abandonment, prevailing wisdom held faeries disliked seeing their kind mistreated, but this logic could backfire.[715] In one Scandinavian tale, a mother's baby was only restored because she *didn't* mistreat the substituted child.[716]

Abuse took many forms. Children were pinched, underfed,[717] splashed in the face with urine[718]—even stabbed.[719] Most commonly, however, they were simply beaten, a practice common across Europe.[720] For example, after dumping them on an ash pile, changelings in Cornwall were "belabor[ed] with brooms" by all the women of the village.[721] This worked best on Thursdays, typically held as Christ's day, when faerie powers were at their weakest.[722] A Norwegian babe, supplanted by a witch in one tale, was restored by beatings every Thursday for three weeks.[723]

Certain plants were prescribed as whipping switches. "Weeping birch" branches did the trick in some parts of Germany,[724] while in Bohemia the child was bound with "a weed growing at the bottom of the lake" and "beat[en] with a rod of the same."[725] In a tale from Lady Gregory, a father was advised to gather "a bundle of sally rods that will be thin as rushes, and divide them into six small parts and twist every one of the six parts together," with which "he beat the child on the head with them one after another." The child was restored the moment it "fell asleep" (or passed out from pain).[726] These themes are echoed in gentler practices, such as one technique described by Silver of placing a child on a bed, "his feet on a bolster and his head at the foot, while a dish of salt with two rushes across it was laid on [the] chest."[727]

One plant of note was foxglove, employed in abuse of a different sort. Also known as *digitalis* or *lus-mor*, this species compelled faeries to take their changelings back through its renowned toxicity.[728] In this sense, parents used foxglove as a catalyst to resolve the faerie stroke: it either hastened death or initiated a return from Fairyland (unsurprisingly, there are records of mortal children, mistaken for changelings, dying from this technique).[729] In its powdered or liquid form it could be made into a bath,[730] placed on the tongue or in ears,[731] mixed with milk and drunk,[732] or, more benignly, placed under a pillow.[733]

RESOLUTION: BURNING

The primary goal was to make changelings—or their faerie families—fear for their lives. For this reason, the importance of heat and fire as means of expulsion cannot be overstated. As with other forms of abuse, the mere threat served enough to drive changelings out: threats of burning not only them, but also their mounds and the faerie thorns (typically hawthorn) found there.[734]

In these examples, confirmation and resolution could be one-and-the-same, as a changeling's reaction to fire was so extreme it would abscond at its very sight or suggestion. In one retelling of "The Tailor & the Changeling," the faerie child watched a fire being prepared and conveniently let a ball slip from his pocket, providing an excuse to wander away. As it rolled off he followed, never seen again.[735]

An adult changeling tale from Hartland:

> A tale from Badenoch represents the man as discovering the fraud from finding his wife, a woman of unruffled temper, suddenly turned a shrew. So he piles up a great fire and threatens to throw the occupant of the bed upon it unless she tells him what has become of his own wife. She then confesses that the latter has been carried off, and she has been appointed successor. But by his determination he happily succeeds in recapturing his own at a certain fairy knoll near Inverness.[736]

Empty threats were one of several relatively harmless methods by which changelings could be disposed of using fire.

- One Irish wise woman advised a mother obtain a strip of the faerie abductor's cloak and burn it by the child's face, prompting an enchantment-breaking sneeze.[737]

- Macabre though equally benign was tossing a dead child, suspected of being a stock, upon burning turf and declaring, "Burn, burn, burn—if of the devil burn; but if of God and the Saints, be safe from harm." If a changeling, it would fly up the chimney. Otherwise, parents cremated their dead child.[738]

- Some Irish practitioners placed a changeling in a ring of fire, "not intending to do bodily harm to it independently," should it not transform into "a sod of turf."[739] Passing a child through fire not only prevented faerie theft but also restored taken infants, as early Christian belief held passing them between two fires protected from evil.[740]

In one Irish oral account collected by Richard Breen, a young girl returned from playing by a faerie fort "sick... loss of memory and crying and fooling." A fortnight passed and her mother needed to go milking, so she enlisted a drunken neighbor for a babysitter.

> He was sitting by the fire... and he made a roar at the child. He said "Shut up" says he. "Or if you don't shut up, I'll stick the tongs into the fire and I'll scald you. I'll burn you... You're only blackguarding and petting and all this... Get out anyway, out to play with your kids outside... There's nothing wrong with you..." He just got that kind of a brainwave.

The child got up, walked out of the door, got up
and walked out—she got in dread of him you know.
The right child walked in after about ten minutes.
They'd kept her (i.e. the fairies) and they'd sent the
bad one. She was going to be the cause of the death
you see.[741]

Iron tongs, known for warding away faeries, were heated and
clasped to the changeling's body, typically the nose.[742] In other
instances, they were used to press burning turf on the imposter.[743]
Another favorite heated tool was the shovel, particularly in Ireland,
Denmark, and Sweden:[744] any changeling placed on a shovel and
held over a fire would surely flee.[745] Other efforts to exorcise
included holding red-hot shovel blades close to changelings'
faces[746] or branding them with the symbol of the cross using a
heated poker.[747]

Shockingly enough, faerie doctors prescribed even more
violent instructions. In Scotland, changelings had their toes burnt
with hot coals,[748] were placed on gridirons[749] and in pots above
fires,[750] or laid atop burning straw.[751] Fearful German mothers
might literally bake changelings in their ovens.[752]

More often than not these burnt changelings fled through the
chimney,[753] a common point of faerie/spirit ingress.[754] (You can
draw your own conclusions about the origins of Santa Claus, or the
nature of modern alien Greys appearing in homes without using
windows or doors.) For example, one legend holds that Ghengis
Khan's divine ancestor was conceived by a spirit who entered his
mother's belly through the yurt's smoke hole. It was for this reason
that most Europeans sealed every other entrance to the home
prior to burning a changeling, to encourage this point of exit.[755] In
one tale from Wilde, a changeling tossed upon the fire turned into
a "black kitten, and flew up the chimney and was seen no more."[756]

Chimneys are notably a liminal threshold. "The chimney is
thus a link between heaven and earth," wrote Lecouteux. "At its
base, it is anchored in the hearth, and its smoke rises up to heaven.

This confers upon it the quality of an *axis mundi*, which explains its ties with the other world, either higher or lower, that it connects to our own."[757]

Sometimes a single window was left open instead. Like chimneys, windows were seen as common access points for a variety of spirits, including the devil and Death itself. During childbirth throughout Europe, windows were closed and covered to avoid drawing demonic forces attracted by blood, which might harm mothers or infants.[758] In County Limerick it remains common practice to this day to open a window when someone passes away so his or her soul might exit the home.[759] Similar practices can be found in the traditions of Germany, England, Armenia, and Slavic countries.

Changeling lore reflects this practice. In one Welsh tale, a father was advised to cover a shovel in salt, into which the sign of the cross was made; then go to the changeling's room and open the window; and finally place the shovel on the fire until the salt was burned. When the salt grew white-hot, the changeling disappeared, and the original child was found in perfect condition on the doorstep.[760]

Fire, like iron, is an example of Gordon White's god-stolen technology (indeed, Promethean by definition), asserting mankind's dominance over the natural world. Fire has long been portrayed as a purifying substance with the ability to transform[761]—just as wood reduces to ash, the changeling is exposed as an imposter.[762] Indeed, the practice of rooting out the supernatural with flame is one origin of the contemporary phrase "trial by fire."[763]

INFANTICIDE: A TRAGIC LEGACY

Unsurprisingly, there are dozens of historical examples where innocent children were killed as suspected changelings. It would be disingenuous to downplay this ugly side of faerie lore and suggest every changeling case, or even a majority, involved the supernatural. One can only guess how many times the Fairy Faith was used to justify child abuse and murder.

"Incidences of suspected infanticide were reported on a weekly basis in the latter half of nineteenth-century Ireland," wrote Elaine Farrell in her excellent book, *'A Most Diabolical Deed': Infanticide and Irish Society, 1850-1900.* It is recommended reading— alongside Angela Bourke's *The Burning of Bridget Cleary*, detailing the most famous adult "changeling" tortured to death—for anyone interested in this grim corner of history. To give some sense of the scope of the problem in Ireland, Farrell examined 4,645 cases of child murder from a 50-year period—*only including children less than three years old.*[764]

In point of fact, there are far too many tragic "changeling" murders to exhaustively recount here. No doubt some parents had the best intentions, but in many cases it was, to quote one scholar, "little more than socially-countenanced forms of infanticide,"[765] for irresponsible adults to reject their parental duties.[766] Given the moral and practical complications of abortion in 19th century Ireland, sometimes the murder of a child—or, to absolve one's guilt, a "changeling"—was a preferable option to placing further strains on finances and meals.

In 1884, two women from Clonmel were charged with cruelty to a three-year-old boy they placed naked on a red-hot shovel.[767] Earlier that century in the same county, a six-year-old Tipperary girl was fatally dosed with foxglove.[768] In 1826, young Michael Leahy's grandmother drowned him in the Flesk River; she was acquitted for only trying "to put the fairy out of it."[769] In 1862, police found a newborn boy abandoned "at a place called the Fairy Bush" between Waterford and Dunmore—shortly thereafter he died, leading to his mother's arrest.[770]

These are but a fraction of 19th century Irish cases. Reality saw this happening across Europe—a contemporary Scottish case detailed the death of a sickly child left atop a faerie mound,[771] while a Scandinavian mother was taken to court for placing her own child in an oven.[772] The practice even made its way to the New World, where a New York couple in 1877 allegedly "burned their child to death under the delusion that they were ridding themselves of a changeling."[773]

Such barbarism is not confined to the distant past. On Christmas Day 2010, authorities discovered 15-year-old Kristy Bamu mutilated in a London flat. Investigators revealed his sister, Magalie, and boyfriend Eric Bikubi "were convinced the boy was a witch, possessed by spirits who wanted to bring evil into their home."[774]

Not every case ended in tragedy, however. If superstition has any truth, some children were restored to their former selves— even in cases where they weren't, parents were able to make peace with their new family members.

Chapter 8
"Marvelous or Dire"
Restoration or Resignation

She knew what she was going to find. But she did not guess till she lifted the little frail child she had left upon the shore seven years back, that the secret people of the sea or those who call across running water could have the hardness and coldness to give her again the unsmiling dumb thing she had mothered with so much bitterness of heart.
— Fiona Macleod, "Fara-Ghaol"

For all the talk of motivic consistency within changeling narratives, few point out that the return of mortal children—like the initial abduction itself—is rarely witnessed. They appeared on doorsteps and in cradles when no one looked; Evans Wentz even recorded a story where the mother of a changeling stepped outside, only to find her mortal child fully restored moments later.[775] In the rare event the return was seen (as in the aforementioned case where burning faerie cloth prompted a sneeze), they appeared the same as they had moments before, albeit with a rosier disposition.

This naturally raises the question whether or not physical abductions actually took place in faerie lore. Some belief explicitly argues otherwise. In Germany, *Frau Holle* enjoyed dragging children into ponds, where they were not exchanged, but rather *turned into* changelings.[776] Even in the New World, indigenous lore held *duendes* (a name imported from Iberia) stole baby souls, not physical bodies.[777]

As noted, Evans Wentz entertained the notion that a sort of possession or spiritual abduction took place, at least as one explanation among many modalities. His "Soul-Wandering Theory" cited pernicious beliefs among disparate global cultures where "the human soul can be abstracted from the body by disembodied spirits and by magicians." A variation was his "Demon-Possession Theory," conceptually more familiar to modern Westerners: "demons, who sometimes may be the souls of the dead, can possess a human body while the soul is out of it during sleep, or else can expel the soul and occupy its place."

Parapsychological theories help explain the abusive methods of child retrieval; perhaps they meant to shock evil spirits out of (or mortal spirits back into) the body.[778] At the same time, entertaining such notions does not address worldwide folk traditions wherein abductions were allegedly physical.

RESTORATION

When mortal children were restored, the prognosis was either marvelous or dire. After the faeries took a child, nothing stayed the same: they either never came back, returned changed, or wasted away and died.[779] Those returning from Fairyland might crumble into dust, appear wraithlike, or pine away for the majesty of the Otherworld until they passed.[780]

Vengeance for the rescue of mortals usually came in the form of curses. In Yeats' retelling of "Jamie Freel and the Young Lady," the fae folk cursed the titular rescuee: "Jamie Freel has her awa' frae us, but he sall hae nae gude o' her, for I'll mak' her deaf and dumb!"[781] A British newspaper article from the 1880s claimed two infants, taken by the faeries, were quickly returned following their mother's lamentations; though healthy, the children remained short and stunted the rest of their lives on account of their abduction.[782]

One unsettling account of faerie vengeance is noteworthy for its physicality—following the successful removal of a changeling, the child's godfather returned home.

> He said he would be back in the morning to see if
> the child was still in the bed. He had a dog with
> him, a fierce fighter. It was dark when he left the
> house. When he had crossed two fields he came
> to a ditch; a thorn bush stood near it. He heard
> a noise in the ditch, and something jumped out
> of it at him. What shape it had he could not tell,
> but his dog rushed towards it and drove it off. It
> came again at him from the bush. It had no shape
> that he knew, but was like a big lump. It followed
> him all the way, jumping at him till he reached the
> river. Only for the dog it would have killed him. He
> crossed the river, and was safe. The thing could not
> come across the water.[783]

Even in the best of scenarios, children returned... different. Some were spiritually awakened by their time among faeries. Jennet Francis' child, for example, was merely touched by faeries and became a preacher.[784] In another example, a boy taken by the *Tylwyth Teg* left of his own volition after what felt like two years— in actuality it had been a fortnight. An informant told Evans Wentz "he went back to school, and became a most wonderful scholar and parson."[785]

Early Christian legends claim multiple saints, among them Stephen, Bartholomew, and Lawrence, were taken by the devil in infancy, laying the foundation for their supernatural abilities in adulthood.[786] According to some traditions, the devil took Saint Innocent I from the cradle to a magpie's nest in an archbishop's garden.[787] Satan allegedly stole St. Stephen just after birth; nursed for years by a white bitch, he eventually beheld an Angel who revealed his true lineage. Stephen returned home and supplanted the demonic changeling left in his place, threatening it with fire— years after, he began performing Christ-like miracles.[788]

"Some people receive extraordinary talents from nonhuman entities," wrote folklorist Peter M. Rojcewicz. "Ancient Druids believed that their interaction with fairies and demons could produce power to master natural phenomena and animal processes, as well as to cast spells and see the future."[789] This trend prominently continues to this day—following their experiences, UFO abductees and Near Death Survivors alike claim newfound healing abilities and clairvoyance.[790]

Among the most celebrated faerie abductees was Anne Jeffries, whose experience bears many hallmarks of modern UFO abduction. In 1645 the servant girl fell profoundly ill, claiming upon recovery she had been taken by faeries. While in their paradise, she took a faerie lover but was returned when one of five spurned suitors covered her eyes with his hands. She immediately heard a noise "as if a thousand flies were buzzing around her" and felt herself endlessly twirled about.[791] Following her return, Jeffries famously exhibited clairvoyance and healing through touch, first demonstrated upon her mistress. Years thereafter people visited her for miraculous cures and prophecies.[792]

Less dramatically, returned abductees experienced improved luck or artistry.[793] A Scottish boy rescued from a faerie forge remained silent until one day he saw his father at the anvil. "That is not the way to do it!" he shouted, taking the tools. He then crafted "the finest sword ever seen on Islay," after which father and son were renowned for their smithing.[794] Such abilities could even be passed to family members. A woman returning from Fairyland "might precipitate the emergence of skills—particularly medical or musical—in the children she had left behind as a compensatory gift from the fairies for taking their mother from them," wrote English professor Regina Buccola.[795]

RESIGNATION

Even when faerie doctors' instructions were closely followed, restoration of children was not guaranteed. In 1878 *Celtic Review* published the tale of a mother in the Hebrides who left a changeling on the shore for the faeries to rescue. When she returned the faerie baby was exactly where she had left it, her mortal child lost forever.[796]

"If the child survives the ordeal [of abandonment or abuse] it is accepted as one of the family, though very grudgingly," wrote Lady Wilde. "And it is generally hated by all the neighbours for its impish ways."[797] Crestfallen parents resigned themselves to raising a sickly faerie child, most likely doomed to waste away and die.[798]

Their lifespans were notoriously short: one faerie-cursed family, saddled with six changelings in a row, watched each die in turn before any restorative action could be taken.[799] In another example from Lady Gregory, famous Irish seer woman Biddy Early derived her powers from a changeling encountered as a servant girl; though her friend only lived a few years, "he was friendly to her and used to play tunes for her and when he went away [died] he gave her the bottle and the power."[800]

Despite this trend of short lifespans, testimonies persist where changelings lived among mortals, though their existence appeared significantly truncated. The aforementioned changeling belonging to Welshman Edmund John William lived until 12, "which was judged longer than such children usually lived."[801] One 1879 German account mentioned a changeling who "remained small and ugly, and died in his twentieth year,"[802] while another Welsh changeling[803] and another from Scandinavia both made it to 30.[804] Changelings enjoyed greater longevity if the faeries left treasure behind as child support—a Welsh saying, "Shoe the elf with gold and he will grow," references a changeling whose mortal father received faerie gold, allowing him to inherit a large farm upon his father's death.[805]

Surviving changelings inhabited the fringes of society as fools or oddities, to the extent anyone exhibiting odd interests or qualities might be suspect.[806] Sure signs included left-handedness,[807] small build,[808] "yellow skin and dark hair,"[809] and the inability to speak, or, contrarily, talking to oneself.[810] Superstition held they caused misfortune, though most seemed inoffensive dullards.[811] A Prussian changeling named Matthias, born in 1565, could not stand, walk, or speak at age 20.[812] Nearly three centuries later an eyewitness described a Monmouthshire changeling as "simply an idiot of a forbidding aspect, a dark, tawny complexion, and much addicted to screaming."[813] In Scandinavia, another "hunched and ugly" changeling received baptism but remained nonverbal, only "lowing like an ox."[814]

Though immobility was common, the opposite—wandering and roving—could indicate faerie heritage. One Welsh changeling "often talked to himself, and many believed that he was then holding converse with some of the fairy tribe, only visible to him, who enticed him to ramble among the earns, hills, and moors— their usual haunts."[815]

A strong association existed between mental disability and faerie interference. "The curious word 'oaf,'" wrote folklorist Jacqueline Simpson, "is a medieval development from 'elf.' Its chief present-day meanings are 'rough, bad-mannered fellow' and 'stupid country bumpkin,' but the *Oxford English Dictionary* gives the following range of older meanings: 'An elf child, a goblin child; a half-wit, fool, dolt.'"[816] Some families who offended the fae folk were cursed to always have a "fool" within their ranks.[817]

It should be noted, however, changelings did not universally display these traits; in spite of their unorthodox behavior, their natural gifts occasionally made them worthy additions to the community. As noted earlier, any offspring from a human-faerie union excelled in the arts and matters of intellect.[818] In the tale of "Coleman Gray," an abandoned changeling was found as in "Yallery Brown"—the similarities end there, however, as Coleman proved himself intelligent, active, strong, and good humored until his *pixie* parents returned to claim him years later.[819]

A few notable examples of changelings from the historical record:

- Elis Bach of Nant Gwrtheyrn, son of a farmer, passed away circa 1860. He was described as "deformed, his legs being so short that his body seemed only a few inches from the ground when he walked." His voice was "small and squeaky," but he possessed a keen intellect and was able to navigate the countryside when seeking his father's livestock.[820]

- Robert Elliot (otherwise known as "Little Hobbie o' The Castleton") of southern Scotland was feisty and quick to brawl, though his short legs precluded giving chase to those who turned tail. Sometime in the early 19th century he challenged a 6'3" neighbor who had slandered him, only to watch the coward flee.[821]

- Perhaps the most famous surviving changeling was the "Little *Corrigan*," discussed at length by Evans Wentz. Hailing from Plounéventer, France, he was "no taller than a normal child ten years old" at 30, and "thick-set, though not deformed," according to one account. Others described him as "greatly deformed, hunchbacked, and crooked, and of a black color." He was prone to vice, wandered about in the night, and could predict the future. He apparently attempted to kill his mother on several occasions. As of 1911 he was 70 years old, a detail perhaps precluding his identification as a changeling. Apparently, photographs were taken of the Little *Corrigan*, but none have surfaced.[822]

By now it should be abundantly clear no small portion of changelings were, in reality, human individuals with a broad spectrum of disabilities. While this does not rule out a supernatural component in some accounts—a great deal of this book contends very real paranormal elements are at play, particularly in cases of physical abduction—it is important to remain healthily skeptical of such explanations, instead exhausting all materialist solutions before advocating the fantastic. Having thoroughly indulged in the superstitions surrounding European changelings and child faerie abduction, we now turn a sober eye to how modern medicine addresses this phenomenon.

Chapter 9:
"Horrifying to Tragic"
Medical & Psychological Perspectives on Changelings

Imagine that aliens were stealing one in every two hundred
children... That is what is happening in America today.
It is called autism.

— Cure Autism Now (CAN)

In the mid-19th century, an Irish ear and eye surgeon contributed to a census of the region's epidemiology. On the subject of consumptive illness, he wrote:

> Marasmus was adopted as a generic term, under which to class all those various affections of infancy and early youth returned on the different forms as consumption (infantile), wasting, decay, decline, emaciation, general debility and loss of strength... It is this affection which has given rise to the popular ideas respecting the "changeling," and in this country to the many superstitious notions entertained by the peasantry respecting their supposed 'fairy-stricken' children;—so that, year by year, up to the present day, we read accounts of deaths produced by cruel endeavors to cure children and young persons of such maladies, generally

attempted by quacks and those termed "fairy men" or "fairy women."[823]

The author was none other than Sir William Wilde, father of Oscar Wilde and—ironically—married to one of the greatest Irish folklorists of her day, someone without whom our knowledge of faerie lore would be much diminished. While unappealing, even offensive to practitioners of the Fairy Faith, it is impossible for modern Westerners to disagree with this assessment. Coupled with the prevalence of infanticide in the changeling tradition, a disquieting reality emerges: parents commonly used faerie lore to scapegoat the murder of unwanted babies, particularly children whose disabilities or infirmities placed too great a strain upon the family.

MEDICAL CONDITIONS

Descriptions of the changeling's appearance and behavior pointed to developmental disability and disease long before modern medicine eclipsed superstition. Viewed through contemporary eyes, most changeling stories transform from horrifying to tragic, unsettling tales of an inhuman *other* reinterpreted as heart-rending stories of abused children in dire need of medical assistance.

Pieces begin to fall into place. For example, the advanced abilities displayed by changelings, from talking to musicianship, can be easily read as embellished depictions of "precocious children in declining health," according to ethnographer James Mooney.[824] Males are statistically more prone to congenital birth defects, a fact reflected in the rarity of changeling stories where girls are taken.[825]

"Whether [medical conditions] gave rise to the [changeling] belief or not, it has probably helped a good deal to perpetuate it," wrote R.U. Sayce.[826] A large body of literature examines medical interpretations of changeling tales, so much that every theory cannot be covered here. The work of Carole Silver and congenital disorder expert Susan Eberly is recommended for anyone seeking to explore this topic further.

Even as Europe moved into the Enlightenment—a period of unprecedented rational, intellectual development—philosophers clung to views of the mentally disabled as sub-human. In his 1690 *An Essay Concerning Human Understanding,* English luminary and key Enlightenment figure John Locke advocated using the word "changeling" to describe those "between man and beast," i.e. the mentally handicapped.[827]

One of the earliest interpretations of changelings as medically afflicted mortals comes from the writing of 18th century biologist Carl Linnaeus. On June 10, 1741, an alleged changeling was brought before him on the Swedish island of Öland. The child, aged 13, had no control of his limbs, could not sit, stand, or walk, and constantly mumbled. His front teeth protruded, his legs thin, his flesh loose, and appeared "more like a girl than a boy." After some time, Linnaeus determined the boy suffered from *Hieranosos,* a form of epilepsy brought about by stress in the womb.[828]

Notably—though some afflictions seem to describe their appearance and behavior more than others—no single condition has been deemed the sole source of changeling stories. Consumption, as noted by Wilde, has a longstanding association with faeries and is thus a likely contender. Some scholars suggest sudden infant death syndrome or infantile paralysis were to blame,[829] especially when changelings were suspected of being lifeless stocks.[830] Author Robert Hunt reported the alleged changelings he had seen were uniformly "sad examples of the influence of mesenteric disease," a gastrointestinal condition.[831]

Researchers have proposed misdiagnoses of cystic fibrosis, Down's syndrome, metabolic disorders,[832] and rickets.[833] Conditions simultaneously manifesting in mental retardation, limited language, and physical deformity remain popular theories, such as Hurler's & Hunter's syndromes (called "gargoylism" in years past), or homocystinuria (which additionally causes thin, spidery limbs).[834] Logically—since changeling stories involve the abduction of a non-disabled child after birth—disorders with a delayed onset are more often cited.[835]

A few noteworthy theories:

- **Spina bifida** is the most common central nervous system disorder, more prevalent in the United Kingdom than America. In 80% of cases sufferers possess hydrocephaly, or "water on the brain," where the presence of excess fluid causes an enlarged skull. Eberly suggests hydrocephaly "is probably the disorder described in the changelings with oversized heads." Spina bifida can also cause paralysis.[836]

- **Cerebral palsy** results in loss of muscle control and, because of unequal muscle development and pressure, can cause serious deformity. The muscular motions may be slow and rhythmic or fast and spasmodic. "It is just possible that the 'wild dance' of the changeling may in fact describe the movements of a person with severe cerebral palsy," Eberly suggests.[837]

- **Progeria** is a progressive genetic disorder characterized by extremely short stature and wrinkled or dry skin. Delayed tooth development, an enlarged head, high-pitched voice, and loss of muscle may be observed.[838] Few sufferers exceed age 13.[839] A nine-year-old Hungarian "changeling" touring with a sideshow through England in 1858 likely suffered from progeria: 18 inches tall, with limbs the size of a man's thumb, toothless and silent, with a wizened complexion.[840] Though its symptoms closely match those of changelings, the condition is exceedingly rare, making it a poor explanation (only 100 patients were alive worldwide circa 2014).[841]

- **Phenylketonuria (PKU)**, an inherited metabolic disease, does not present itself at birth. By six months, however, sufferers experience vomiting, seizures, hyperactivity, tremors, slow growth, and irritability. While no shortened lifespan is present, those with PKU are inclined towards mental retardation and a high-pitched voice. Notably, Eberly writes, "Most children who develop PKU are of English or Irish ancestry; today, diet therapy can prevent the disease from progressing if treatment begins early enough."[842]

- **Williams Syndrome** affects one in 10,000 people and, in addition to causing intellectual disorders, also manifests in shortness, kindness, obsession with spinning objects and circles, and a love of music and dance. Infants are typically restless and have difficulty sleeping.[843] Characteristics of those with Williams Syndrome are described as "elfin," including upturned noses, full lips, and prominent earlobes[844] (perhaps this condition explains more agreeable and long-lived changelings, as sufferers can reach at least age 60).[845]

One of the most popular interpretations suggests changelings were actually sufferers of undiagnosed autism.

"Changelings were described as unresponsive, resistant to affection, did not express emotion, cried a lot or did not speak," said Dr. Julie Leask from Australia's National Centre for Immunisation Research and Surveillance of Vaccine Preventable Disease. "The description of changelings is very similar to those given to autistic children."[846] Leask also said that "the features of these stories, including the initial health and beauty of the human child, the change after some period of 'normalcy,' and the specific behaviours of the changeling... are well matched to symptoms in some presentations of autism."[847]

Eberly suggested stereotypy—the repetitive speech patterns common to autism—might account for the singsong or poetic nature of changelings' speech patterns.[848] Moreover, autistic children can react poorly when touched, and the changeling's incessant cry could be a misinterpretation of a sensitive child avoiding such contact. In Martin Luther's encounter with a changeling, he wrote, "When bad things happened in the house, it laughed and was happy; but when things went well, it cried." This possibly reflects the misreading of social cues in some individuals dealing with autism spectrum disorders.[849] Affected children may also have trouble falling asleep—producing an irritated disposition—or staying asleep, perhaps accounting for reports of nighttime rambles, or raucous activity when no one is looking.[850] Like faerie abduction, autism spectrum disorder disproportionately affects boys (one in 42) over girls (one in 189).[851]

In certain instances known as regressive autism, children may actually lose previously acquired skills, especially speech and socialization.

"Regressive autism... sneaks up on parents," wrote James Ball, member of the Autism Society's Board of Directors and current Chair of the National Board. "Generally this child seems to be developing just fine and hits a great many developmental milestones. These are children who walked on time, said their first words on time, played like typical kids, but at some point began to lose these skills." The net effect is the appearance of a healthy, well-developed child who is seemingly replaced by an imposter.[852]

One novel proposal by Joyce Underwood Munro posits the changeling as a "failure to thrive" (FTT) infant, a condition often brought on by emotional deprivation. Because the parents in some changeling narratives seem unhappy, Munro draws a clear connection to FTT babies. Her argument is bolstered by a 1949 testimony where emotionally deprived, hospitalized infants exhibited "listlessness, emaciation and pallor, relative immobility... failure to gain weight properly despite the ingestion of diets which, in the home, are entirely adequate… poor sleep, and appearance of unhappiness."

Munro also cites a 1967 study of emotionally deprived children, all of whom were short for their age. These children displayed an insatiable thirst and hunger leading to consumption of toilet water, rainwater, entire jars of mustard and mayonnaise, packs of deli meat, loaves of bread, boxes of corn flour, cat food, and seven eggs in one sitting (recall the ravenousness of changelings). As with the last chapter's Welsh changeling, "some got up and roamed the house at night."[853]

In some cases, it is possible parents, rather than children, were the ones suffering from undiagnosed medical conditions. In 1923 French psychiatrist Joseph Capgras and his intern Jean Reboul-Lachaux chronicled the case of a 53-year-old woman who, without provocation, suddenly convinced herself her friends and family had been replaced with identical imposters. Though its root cause remains unknown, Capgras Delusion is associated with schizophrenia, mood disorders, Alzheimer's disease, and neurological trauma. In a case from the 1970s, a man developed Capgras Delusion after suffering a massive right frontal subdural hematoma in his brain, after which he maintained his wife and five children were all duplicates of his real family. In an interesting parallel to the faerie blast—wherein limbs, digits, etc. were believed to be replaced with stocks, or filled with detritus—patients with Capgras Delusion can also experience the sensation of duplicated body parts.[854]

COUNTERARGUMENTS

While it is abundantly clear *many* disabled children were labeled changelings, compelling counterarguments cast doubt on whether *all* changelings were medically afflicted. Evans Wentz contended:

> Our examination of living children said to have
> been changed by fairies shows *(a)* that many
> changelings are so called merely because of some
> bodily deformity or because of some abnormal
> mental or pathological characteristics capable of
> an ordinary rational explanation, *(b)* but that other
> changelings who exhibit a change of personality,
> such as is recognized by psychologists, are in many
> cases best explained on the Demon-Possession
> Theory....[855]

Explaining changelings medically has two primary
shortcomings. The first assumes a degree of abject stupidity on the
behalf of Fairy Faith practitioners. This is not to imply Europeans
were not superstitious in centuries past—far from it—but we must
ask why folklore regularly made distinctions between the physically
disabled and changelings, if all birth defects were ignorantly
attributed to faerie abduction? Consider the Irish hunchback
Lusmore, protagonist of the "Legend of Knockgrafton": in
spite of his deformity, no telling of the story ever labeled him a
changeling.[856]

"Witches were believed to *cause* epilepsy, not that epilepsy
is a disorder that witches themselves *have* (as the popularisation
appears to misread)," wrote historian Irina Metzler. "However,
popular myths surrounding disability in the medieval period still
tend to view the period itself as one of barbaric darkness, and one
where people we now call disabled were invariably demonised."[857]
While folklore and fairytales attributed birth defects to spiritual
interference, the defects themselves were not always indicators of
sub-human status and were recognized as medical conditions (e.g.
while a cleft lip might be *the work* of faeries,[858] it was still recognized
as a treatable physical ailment using Anglo-Saxon medicine of the
Middle Ages).[859] To suggest every infant with congenital defects
was branded a changeling is not only disingenuous, it lacks nuance.

"Most stories about [changeling] substitution dwell on the

child's supernatural abilities," wrote medical humanities scholar C.F. Goodey and social work professor Tim Stainton. "The child has an adult intellect and personality which, being diabolic, it tries to hide (the key moment in such stories is often the parents' successful exposure of this). Only a few stories depict anything even resembling disability, such as physical differences or failure to thrive."[860]

Numerous changelings exhibited behavior inconsistent with mental retardation, which is symptomatic of many proposed conditions. How does the cognitively impaired child suddenly become keenly aware of its mother's peculiar brewery of eggshells? From where does its sudden vocabulary spring? What are we to make of children successfully restored to their families? How do we explain faerie stroke victims well beyond infancy? Or children taken without a changeling left behind?

Scientific explanations for the changeling phenomenon would have us believe that—while the bulk of the stories are built upon carefully observed medical symptoms—these outliers simply embody wishful thinking or pure fantasy.

This is not necessarily an argument *for* the existence of supernatural forces, but rather an argument *against* a purely medical reading of the changeling narrative; here we have our second shortcoming. Put another way, explaining every facet of folklore with medicine makes as much sense as explaining medicine with folklore. To cram changeling narratives into a purely scientific materialist worldview robs these legends of their power to articulate archetypal motifs, psychological anxieties, and—dare we suggest, in rare cases—actual contact with the Otherworld.

"The folklore of the changeling, therefore, cannot be interpreted within the frame of folk medicine and definitely not within the frame of scientific medicine," wrote Ann Skjelbred on Scandinavian changelings. "The latter perspective views folk tradition from the angle of natural science and disregards the cultural context of fairylore."[861]

To reiterate: the theory that most changeling stories

represented undiagnosed developmental disorders is not open for debate—these tales were almost certainly *in part* attempts to understand medical tragedies. But it is important to consider the possibility they might simultaneously represent something much more, especially to the comparative Fortean.

PSYCHOLOGICAL EXPRESSIONS

As compelling as the medical angle may be, it is equally valid to interpret child faerie abductions as cautionary tales expressing latent parental anxieties in a pre-industrialized society. In countless changeling stories the abduction directly results from a failing on the behalf of parents or guardians: they fall asleep, take their attention off the child to work, fail to heed traditions, etc. (this trend continues into the modern era, where tales warn of children interfered with or abducted by paranormal forces under a babysitter's supervision). The crippling weight of these parental concerns are touched upon in a tale from Rhŷs: prior to her child's abduction, a mother "was remarkably careful about her son, so much so, that it made some of the neighbours say that she was too anxious about him and that some misfortune would overtake her child." The boy's subsequent disappearance at the hands of the faeries only took a momentary lapse in judgment.[862]

In addition to fears of parental shortfalls, changeling lore articulated the dangers of living in difficult times. Unsurprisingly, given the reverence toward the Fairy Faith exhibited by peasantry of the British Isles, changelings represented very real fears of lost power, security, and hope among lower-to-middle classes.[863] Mooney argued faerie lore provided meaning in a harsh world "of infants which pine away without apparent cause, strong young men suddenly stricken down, and old persons whose illness is of a fitful and lingering nature."[864] Childhood mortality rates—even without factoring in infanticide's prevalence—were horrendous, and diseases took the youngest first: in the summer of 1636, a smallpox outbreak ravaged Scotland. Out of 92 reported deaths in

Dumfries, 89 were children, 36 out of 41 in Kelso.[865]

The Fairy Faith softened this grief. One's child wasn't dead; it enjoyed immortality among the fae folk.

The Irish, traumatized by famines throughout history, no doubt feared the prospect of an extra mouth to feed, to say nothing of an insatiable changeling.

"A peasant family's very subsistence frequently depended upon the productive labor of each member, and it was enormously difficult to provide for a person who was a permanent drain on the family's scarce resources," wrote folklorist Ashliman.[866] This impact multiplied twofold—not only did another consumer contribute to resource scarcity, but an invalid meant one less set of hands helping around the farm.

"Interestingly, as the [19th] century moved on, the fear of losing a child to alien powers seems to have spread from rural folk and the unlettered working classes to the more affluent," wrote Silver. "As the concern about the stability and security of the family grew… and as children themselves became more important, in part because of a decreased birth rate, the fear increasingly affected the Victorian middle class… the feared abductors might sometimes be nurses or gypsies rather than denizens of the elfin world, but the implications were similar."[867]

Certainly the trope of children as "evil others" is ingrained in mankind's psyche, examined in such works as Loretta Loach's *The Devil's Children: A History of Childhood and Murder* and Karen J. Renner's collection *The 'Evil Child' in Literature, Film and Popular Culture*. This concern—that one might be sharing their home with something demonic—appears in adult changelings as well. An Irish informant claimed "the changeling belief also explained changed behavior in men after marriage, men who were perhaps dissatisfied with their choice of wife."[868]

Plainly, the patriarchy could use this lore to their advantage. Stories of changelings "teach that a mother and newborn child will remain happy only if they remain at home," wrote English professor Carl Lindahl.[869] Changeling lore doubtlessly reinforced existing power structures, both masculine and parental. From Silver:

> Significantly, most of the incidents recorded involved the victimization of either children or women—that is, of those who were perceived as dependent or subordinate... [Tales] suggest a widespread if horrifying pattern of how a society deals with an unacceptable transformation, especially in persons viewed as relatively powerless. The belief in supernatural etiology and intervention permits the more dominant group—here adults— to reject an imperfect infant ("It's the fairies' child, not ours") and allows as well for denial ("We didn't do anything; it was born normal"). In this total inversion of Freud's family romance—that is, the child's belief that her or his true parents are other and superior to the putative parents—the attitudes of the dominant figures, with their components of anger and guilt, can be expressed in a socially sanctioned way by rituals of exorcism or guilt.[870]

Perhaps the most important point to remember when analyzing changeling stories through a modern lens is that no singular explanation provides an ironclad solution. Changeling stories undoubtedly describe undiagnosed medical conditions; it is equally true they are an elegant metaphor to cope with hardships in an exceedingly difficult era.

Bearing this in mind, it seems possible a "third rail," controversial in modern academia, also had some bearing upon these stories. The Fairy Faith may not present an unbiased interpretation of this variable's true nature, but its paranormal fingerprints can be found from Iberia to Russia. If one steps back to objectively view the complete picture, the same incriminating evidence can be seen among the spirits who kidnapped ancient Australians, or in tales of modern UFOnauts stealing children in Texas.

It is not the veracity but rather the *stability* of legends that keeps Fortean studies relevant. The goal is not to prove whether faeries, aliens, or Sasquatch objectively exist, but rather to highlight the astounding consistencies of storytelling as they resonate across centuries. For anyone investing the time, earnest examination of these phenomena implies... *something* objective lurking at the fringes of perception.

Armed with this knowledge, let us examine the startling consistency of paranormal child abduction on every inhabited continent.

Chapter 10:
"Nothing More Familiar"
Paranormal Child Abduction Worldwide

SARAH: It bit me!
HOGGLE: What did you expect fairies to do?
SARAH: I thought they did nice things, like... Like granting wishes.
HOGGLE: Shows what you know, don't it?
— *Labyrinth* (1986)

"There is nothing more familiar in the fairy tales of different nations than the idea that the elves steal pretty babies and leave their own offspring instead," wrote William J. Rolfe, author of *Fairy Tales in Prose and Verse*. Every culture has its own version of the boogeyman. While it is impossible to comprehensively list every example, paranormal child abduction legends from indigenous cultures worldwide feature shared themes of striking motivic consistency.

WITCHES

Even cultures with robust faerie traditions warned of other thieves in the night. Chief among these—and worthy of special mention—were witches, who, as noted, had longstanding associations with faeries. Given the stereotypically feminine virtues of nurturing and protecting, witches represented a truly horrifying corruption of gender norms and maternal roles; a cross-cultural constant was the threat they posed to children.[871]

Though common worldwide, Europe is known for its rich witch traditions, both historical and legendary.

- Scotland's "Yellow Muitearteach," a legendary, tusked, one-eyed hag, famously sired a race of giants. Like Lilith's offspring, these giants shared their mother's fondness for kidnapping babies. Yellow Muitearteach loved nothing more than stealing children to roast in her cave.[872]

- Grecian witches were believed to abduct newborns to drain their blood or "prick them to death with sharp instruments." Though often returned, victims were crippled the rest of their lives.[873]

- A Scottish witch, Lord Soulis of Hermitage Castle, was a 14th century nobleman said to be in league with the long-fanged spirit familiar Redcap Sly. Under Sly's bidding, Soulis allegedly kidnapped the children of farmers for his black magic rituals.[874]

- During the mid-17th century several French individuals, including Abbé Guibourg, Catherine Deshayes, and Lemeignan, vicar of St. Eustache, allegedly held Black Masses in their cellars. During these rites it was said young children were sacrificed to Satan.[875]

Modern tales would have us believe witches never left us. From the 1970s through the 1990s the "Satanic Panic"—rumors of Black Magic practitioners abducting children for ritualistic abuse, inflamed by evangelical Christians—gripped communities in

America and the United Kingdom. While a handful of instances may have been generated by actual criminal activity, scholars generally agree it was a product of mass hysteria.[876]

Earlier eyewitness cases, like the disappearance of Mary Scully, are more compelling. A 16-year-old bedridden girl, Scully mysteriously vanished from her aunts' Birmingham home on October 23, 1943. Neighbors claimed to have witnessed the girl *walking out of the house* accompanied by a veiled woman dressed entirely in black; she was never seen again.[877]

In August 1950, seven-year-old Adolfo Calbuyahue failed to return after a trip to gather firewood in Alao, Chile. For three days the island was searched to no avail, until one day Adolfo simply reappeared on a small mound of dirt near a neighbor's home. The boy remained in a daze for some time before eventually claiming "strange men" had appeared in the forest and taken him away. No one explained how Adolfo braved 72 hours of cold and rain; his parents believed "sorcerers of the Cave" had taken the boy underground.[878] (Note the resonances with faerie lore: abduction of a seven-year-old boy, subterranean dwellings, inclement weather, a trance, and a return after three days, as in Rathlin Island folklore.)

While historical accusations of witchcraft cited various motivations, the witches of legend normally wished to devour victims, a motivation rarely ascribed to the fae folk (trolls and goblins notwithstanding). Both the Russian witch Baba Yaga and Japan's "terrible forest witch" Yamamba ate children they found wandering the woods; the former would imitate their parents, drawing victims in close before tossing them in her sack.[879]

Outside of legend, witches were more commonly accused of stealing and sacrificing, rather than eating, children. Victims were preferably unbaptized.[880] These babies were sometimes sold to the faeries, perhaps for their rumored *teind* to the devil.[881] Grim charges from the historical record also alleged witches stole infants to use their body parts in the manufacture of magical potions and salves.[882] One purported recipe called for mixing "aconite, belladonna, water parsley, cinquefoil and baby's fat."[883] Any witch could enhance her magical prowess by boiling an infant, partially drinking the resultant mixture and rubbing the rest over her body.[884] Such ointments were sometimes deemed the source of witches' flight, employed to fly to their sabbats.[885]

As in changeling lore, real human beings suffered from sensationalist paranoia. Any unnatural lump on an innocent person's body might be considered a "witch's mark," a point which their demonic familiars suckled to gain strength (again, we see the common belief Otherworld inhabitants crave human energy).[886] Accusations beginning with the careless gossip of neighbors could snowball into full-out witch-hunts. In 1669—23 years prior to the infamous Salem witch trials—85 people were burned to death in Mora, Sweden, for allegedly taking 300 children to their witches' sabbats.[887] The accused often faced physical ordeals to determine innocence; even if not deemed guilty by these arbitrary methods, the resulting trauma usually meant death.

OCEANIA

Though practically every society has some tradition of witches, sorcerers, cunning men, etc., certain parts of the world describe unique and culture-specific entities with a keen interest in child abduction. Starting southeast and working our way northwest— from an American's perspective—we look first to Oceania.

The Abelam of Papua New Guinea depend upon *wala*, nature spirits living in bodies of running water, for fertility. *Wala* travel into the vaginas of women in or near streams and leave behind a child's soul, to which father and mother contribute flesh and bone. This is a precarious relationship, as the *wala* can also cause complications, even miscarriages, if they are offended. Therefore, pregnant women should not sing too loudly near *wala* dwelling places or step upon stones sacred to them. In a curious parallel to European faerie lore, they despise sharp knives—any pregnant woman using them might find their newborn blinded by the angry *wala*.[888]

While the *wala* are largely benevolent, they should not be confused with the island's *Kilyakai,* which are thoroughly evil. These demonic nature spirits are known for sneaking into towns and kidnapping pigs and, more importantly, children, "in order to imbue their own demonic nature into them in order to populate their race."[889]

Roughly 1,500 miles to the southwest, the Western Arrernte culture of Australia holds that *pmere kwetethe,* "spirits of the land," constantly observe human beings. Only children and dogs can see them; to adults, they appear as fleeting shadows or silhouettes. Like their European brethren, *pmere kwetethe* can be mischievous or helpful, large or small. Some, called *pangkelangke,* are hairy, gorilla-like beings fond of carrying off women and children (it is unclear if there are connections to the Yowie, Australia's version of Bigfoot). A female *pangkelangke,* named *arrkwetye irrentye,* is very strong and can alter her appearance at will to appear beautiful or hideous. *Arrkwetye irrentye* steals infants because, lacking a womb, she can birth none of her own.[890]

While Hawaii's faerie folk, the *menehune,* do not seem overly keen on abducting children, another entity, the Green Lady, regularly takes children from Wahiawa gulch. Conflated with the deity *Wahine-oma'o,* urban legend holds that this scaly, mossy woman began her nightly vigil after losing her child near the gulch. Since then, she prowls the area in search of any children foolish enough to trespass.[891]

SOUTHEAST ASIA

In addition to its imposing mainland peninsula, Southeast Asia boasts approximately 20,000 islands. Its density of cultural diversity is unprecedented; unsurprisingly, this maritime region boasts a wealth of supernatural belief.

On the Indian subcontinent, Hindu belief holds trees as favored dwelling places of spirits—ergo, shrines are often erected beneath their branches. Not all these entities are benign. The Abor and Padam people of East Bengal believe ghosts dwelling in trees kidnap children.[892]

To protect their children from supernatural influence, the Balinese practice *tingkah dadi janma*, essentially a series of ceremonies conveying adulthood. Among these is the creation of a *tjolong*, an effigy made from the stem of a coconut palm. Three months after the child's birth, the doll is abandoned by the side of the road as a sort of substitute for would-be paranormal kidnappers, akin to a faerie stock in reverse.[893]

Expectant mothers in parts of Indonesia and Malaysia fear the vampiric *pontianak*. Though the blood of any mortal will do, it prefers that of infants and pregnant women, ripping fetuses out of the womb if the opportunity arises. The *pontianak* is said to be the spirit of a woman who died in childbirth, as a virgin, or at the hands of another *pontianak*; this curse can be averted if glass beads are placed in the victim's mouth, needles placed in the palms and soles of the feet, and eggs tucked under each armpit.[894] Its cousin, the *aswang* vampire of the Philippines, has similar tastes, using its long fingernails to cut fetuses from mothers.[895]

Malaysia remains a hotbed of paranormal child abduction. In the years 1982-1983 a wave of disappearances fanned flames of belief in the *Bunian*, a race of supernatural beings inhabiting the forests. Both adults and children fell victim.

Medical sociologist Robert E. Bartholomew and author Ahman Jamaludin provided an excellent overview of this flap in a 2000 article from *Australian Folklore*. A few select cases:

- **June 1982:** Twelve-year-old Maswati Pilus failed to return from washing clothes in the Pahang River. She was recovered two days later not far from home, telling of an odd girl around her age who invited her on a walk. The two went to a "strange place... remarkably beautiful." Maswati thought the short walk had only taken a few minutes.[896]

- **July 1982:** Shuhaimi Mohd, a five-year-old boy from Pendang, was last seen walking near a rubber plantation "with a strange old man." A search party of 40 shamans and 600 locals, failing to locate the boy, blamed the *Bunian*.[897]

- **March 1995:** After a lull in activity, the *Bunian* took 14-year-old Jefri Dan, who disappeared on his way to school. Six days later he appeared under a tree behind his house dazed and weak, claiming he had entered a strange place full of friendly villagers dressed in white. He claimed to have eaten delicious, unfamiliar fruits over the course of what he estimated were two days. Several months later, Jefri disappeared and returned once more.[898]

Like other kidnapping spirits, the *Bunian* were also blamed for miscarriages. In 1978 "a young man with a hat" approached the bed of Fatimah Kutty, lifting up her mosquito net. Kutty, who was seven months pregnant, shrieked and roused her husband, who failed to see the entity. The next morning, she experienced vaginal bleeding; the child had died in her womb.[899] That same year, Anita Adnan claimed to have experienced a strange dream the night prior to her due date: "an elderly bearded man appeared before her while she was in bed. He had pulled her legs." Finding her stomach flat the next morning, she rushed to hospital. In spite of being confirmed pregnant earlier, her uterus was now empty.[900]

According to another set of Malay legends, a woman long ago took a ritual bath of vinegar and honey but was so startled by an intruder she twisted her head off, spilling viscera across the floor. Thus was born *Penanggalan*, a disembodied head dangling entrails as it flies through the jungle. It primarily preys upon pregnant women and new mothers, lurking about homes where women are in childbirth. "Squeezing through the cracks in the floorboards and walls, she laps up the afterbirth and scoops up newborns with her tongue," wrote journalist Sarah Bartlett. "If she touches a mother or older child, they soon contract a fatal wasting disease."[901]

Penanggalan's Thai analogue is the *krasue*. Another disembodied head trailing bowels, *krasue* is the spirit of a woman cursed for aborting her child, performing the same practice on expectant mothers with her "proboscis-like tongue." To protect mothers, family members place thorny branches around windows and bury placentas far from home.[902]

JAPAN

A boy from Japan's Aichi prefecture disappeared for several hours on September 30, 1907. When he returned, he was found atop his home, his mouth covered in bits of rice cake. He claimed a stranger had appeared near a large cedar tree and taken him to "many people's houses, where always there was a delicious feast of white rice cakes to eat... The child afterwards became an idiot."[903]

This report comes from Japanese language scholar Carmen Blacker, who compiled quite a few supernatural abductions from the island throughout her career. Numerous parallels to European faerie lore emerge when studying Blacker's work: for example, Japanese boys were disproportionately abducted, while one prescription for returning kidnapped children is the continuous beating of drums, akin to noisy bells in the Fairy Faith. The kidnapped children catalogued by Blacker "were halfwits when they recovered consciousness and were able to relate nothing of their adventures," just as faerie abductees returned in trances.[904]

Japanese families traditionally fear child abduction from several entities. First are the *yamaotoko*, extremely tall, hairy "mountain men," calling to mind Australia's *pangkelangke* or North America's Sasquatch. Given their phonetic similarities, there may be an association between these entities and the witch Yamamba (*yama-uba* is the female equivalent of *yamaotoko*, meaning "mountain old women").[905] They are known for taking children as slaves and abducting women for procreation.[906]

Kappas inhabit deep pools in Japan, waiting to drag under hapless swimmers so they may pull their livers through their anuses. *Kappas* are commonly depicted as humanoids covered in amphibious skin with a shell, beak, and, curiously enough, a water-filled depression atop their heads. If this water spills or evaporates, the *kappa* dies. Like European faeries, *kappas* not only steal children, but also interbreed with women and fear iron.[907]

The being most commonly blamed for child abduction in Japan is the *tengu*. These spirits appear in a variety of shapes but are commonly birdlike and red-faced. Although they possess the ability to take on a humanoid appearance, they retain some avian aspect, e.g. wings, beak, etc. An eagle or mountain hermit might be a *tengu* in disguise. They are fond of luring children with beautiful music, for they love drink, dance, and song.[908]

In the early 13th century, a seven-year old boy disappeared for three days, only to be unceremoniously tossed back into his home through the window by *tengu*. He remained in a daze until his mother enlisted the aid of exorcists, who helped him vomit horse dung the *tengu* had fed him. The boy's age, length of disappearance, and mental state echo the case of Adolfo Calbuyahue; the revelation that *tengu* abductees are given "dirty things which seem to be food" directly correlates with European faerie folklore.[909]

One hundred years later a boy claimed several *tengu*, disguised as hermits, lured him to a mountaintop temple. "The child watched as they danced, when something like a net descended from the sky and seemed to draw itself round the dancers... from the meshes of the net shot forth flames," recorded Blacker. After more dancing the *tengu* sent the child home, unceremoniously dropping him on the roof. He was "in a state of stupefaction" until the priests recited a *dharani* [mantra or prayer] over him.[910]

THE MIDDLE EAST

The Qur'an says that the *djinn* were created alongside angels from "the smokeless flame of fire," but unlike their heavenly brethren possessed free will. After receiving dominion over Earth from Allah, they disobeyed His laws, leading to their exile.[911]

The *djinn* are to Islam what faeries are to Christianity. To Muslims, the *djinn* are capricious, long-lived inhabitants of the Otherworld fond of causing missing time, interfering with children,[912] and coupling with mortals.[913] They eat food best described as rubbish, are long lived,[914] fear both iron and loud noises,[915] and inhabit ruins.[916] Like faeries, their sinister nature has been co-opted by modern culture, which presents them as friendly lamp-dwelling *genies*. Lady Wilde even implied—albeit speciously—that the term "faerie" originated from a Persian term for the *djinn*, "*ferouers.*"[917]

Djinn also abduct children via whirlwinds. Traditionally, both Jews and Muslims in the desert, upon seeing a whirlwind spiraling toward them, shout "Iron! Iron!" to frighten the *djinn* away.[918]

In the Middle East, *djinn* even cause changelings. Any woman in labor is encouraged to repeat, "In the name of Allah" to prevent the *djinn* substituting her child for one of their own. Should this method fail, her culture allows the child to die from neglect. To prevent their abduction after birth, children might be "kept dirty, ragged and unkempt" in public to protect them from the "evil eye." Another page out of the Fairy Faith playbook saw Muslim boys dressed as girls and referred to in the feminine to confound the *djinn*.[919]

In Iran, *djinn* were jealous of babies "during the first ten to forty days," directly paralleled in Slavic belief.[920] As in Europe, Egyptian parents left suspected changelings in cemeteries—though, more humanely, these children were only abandoned for 15-20 minutes, rather than overnight.[921]

Folklorist Hasan M. El-Shamy collected the following Egyptian incident in 1971, which reads like any Irish changeling account:

> My father said that there is a man in our village
> who was married and had a son; it was only forty

days old. His wife had left the little boy in a room by himself and gone off to do something and left him to cry. When she returned, the little boy was sick…The boy's stomach was like an open irrigation canal. He ate everything, and nothing showed on him, neither food nor days [age].

One day his father looked in his mouth and found that [the supposed] forty-day-old infant had teeth! He knew it was a *badal*, changeling. He got his cattle whip and said to it, "Where will it hurt you [most]?" Taaakh! taaakh! taaakh! (hit, hit, hit) until the baby spoke and said to him, "I'll bring your son back." They found their own son in the room, and the other one disappeared in the ground. Of course they [the jinn] (may God make our talk light on them) had exchanged one of their own for the boy![922]

Some rulers of the Middle East proudly wore the title of "changeling." Sargon, who presided over ancient Sumer for 56 years, claimed he was half *djinn*: "Sargon the Mighty King, King of Agade am I," he inscribed. "My mother was a changeling, my father I knew not."[923]

Given Lilith's Mesopotamian origins, it should come as little surprise her fingerprints soil Middle Eastern interpretations of paranormal child theft. In Iran, the *al*, a *djinn* variant, steals the vital organs of women in labor as well as new mothers. They also cause miscarriage and exchange children 40 days after birth. According to Armenian tradition, the first *al*—like Lilith—was Adam's original lover, but the first man could not accept her nature as smokeless fire.[924]

In addition to the *djinn*, Egypt also holds legends of *Abu Rigl Maslukha*, "man with the burnt leg/skin." This entity began life as a human child but failed to obey his parents and became badly burned. Cursed, his sole drive is to kidnap unruly children to his home, where he cooks them.[925]

AFRICA

Surprisingly enough, the African continent boasts robust faerie traditions. The Zulu contend the *abatwa*, "a tiny race of insect-sized cooperative-hunting people," are largely indifferent to humans but occasionally abduct children. Despite this risk, it is considered lucky for children to spot one of these African faeries.[926]

The Yoruba of Nigeria and Benin believe that the *abiku*, a race of elemental spirits, loiter about jungles, footpaths, and dung heaps (the Igbo of southern Nigeria believe in the analogous *ogbanje*).[927] Therefore, pregnant women avoid these spots when the *abiku* are most active—sunrise, sunny afternoons, and dark nights—lest one of these opportunists follow them home, take up residence in their womb, and usurp the fetus to be born in its place.

Before incarnating among mortals, the *abiku* makes a pledge to live a shortened lifespan, usually between a day and several months, though some *abiku* have been known to die in early adulthood. Its foster parents, noticing their child's infirmity, take the *abiku* to a *Babalawo* (faerie doctor) for advice. The *Babalawo*'s magic works for a time, but invariably its potency wears off; the parents, now aware the child is an *abiku*, begin bargaining with the spirit, indicating their willingness to part with any worldly goods in exchange for the life of their child.[928]

This is the *abiku*'s primary goal: to bankrupt its parents before returning to its realm with their worldly wealth. Desperate parents sacrifice livestock, food, clothing, money, etc.[929] Any property or capital lost in the *abiku*'s name directly transfers into its possession.[930]

Like Icelandic changelings, *abiku* stretch to full adult size when unobserved, usually in the dead of night. During this time, they commune with other *abiku*, returning to infant size upon returning home.

Corpses of suspected *abiku* commonly exhibit trauma. Unlike European changeling abuse, however, the worst of these wounds are inflicted post-mortem. According to African folklorist Timothy Mobolade, the intent is for the *abiku* to be "excommunicated from the assembly of its spirit-comrades should it appear to them with any of those marks of ordeal over its body." Should the *abiku* reincarnate into the same family—a common occurrence—its body will exhibit signs of the trauma from its previous visit, e.g. birth marks where burns or lacerations were made to the previous child's corpse.[931]

Abiku could also enter the bodies of newborn children. Early ethnographer A.B. Ellis recorded that any *abiku* distracted with food allowed its mother to fasten "iron rings and small bells to the ankles of the child, and [hang] iron chains round his neck." The ensuing racket and presence of iron kept the spirit bound. Another "cure" involved "making small incisions in the body of the child, and putting therein green peppers or spices, believing that [the mother] will thereby cause pain to the Abiku and make him depart."[932]

Other African cultures feature variations on changeling belief. Mali's Dogon leave "evil" babies in the bush to "turn into snakes and slither away," and the Nuer of southern Sudan and Ethiopia, who interpret disabled infants as hippopotami in disguise, toss them in the river, much as in European tales.[933]

In addition to changelings, contemporary sensationalist reportage from the continent claims a variety of entities still steal children. In 1999, 13-year-old Kwane Afram allegedly disappeared for four days, only returning after a group of shamans performed a series of retrieval rituals. The boy told the presiding sorcerer he had been picking fruit in the fields (berries, perhaps?) when three giants appeared on the road ahead of him. One of the beasts grabbed the boy and took him to a realm populated by goblins, where he performed domestic housework for several days.[934]

SOUTH AMERICA

Of all the entities exported from Europe, *duendes* took full advantage of colonialism. Originating in the Iberian Peninsula, belief in these faeries spread to the Philippines, Mariana Islands, and Latin America.

With them came all the familiar trappings of child abduction. "Their main purpose, or joy, is to steal yet to be baptized babies or unwed young women," wrote Nicaraguan photographer and folklorist Richard Leonardi. "The unwed post-pubescent girl is lured away by hypnotism, little gifts, and sweet words, never to be seen again. *Duendes* can be heard laughing in the deep forest, but also take time out to visit schools and homes of rural villages."[935]

In Paraguay and northeastern Argentina, parents warn their children to stay asleep during siestas, for then *Yasy Yateré* comes calling. This diminutive being entices children into the forest with his enchanting whistle, only to abandon them shortly thereafter. Children taken by *Yasy Yateré* return mute and dazed, a state only remedied by baptism.[936]

Another legend does not explicitly feature child theft but nonetheless touches upon European changeling motifs. Appearing as a large-snakelike creature, the *jaracaca* slinks through the Amazon rainforest in search of nursing mothers. After finding its quarry, the *jaracaca* silences the infant by sticking its tail in the child's mouth like a pacifier. Free to drain the mother's breast, the entity drinks its fill until the baby dies of starvation.[937]

MEXICO & THE CARIBBEAN

Evidence suggests belief in *chaneques*, paranormal dwarfs from Mexico, stretches back to Olmec culture over 3,500 years ago.[938] The superstition perseveres today: several child disappearances in the early 1970s near Veracruz were blamed on these impish spirits. In one infamous example, the uncle of six-year-old Arturo Gutierrez awaited trial for the boy's murder until Arturo safely reappeared; the boy claimed he had been with the *chaneques* for 33 days, eating milk and honey and playing games.[939]

More recently, Mexican parents warn of *la Lechuza*, an immense owl sometimes seen with the face of an old crone. While descriptions and lore surrounding this frightening entity are contradictory, one aspect remains consistent: she loves stealing children, particularly those walking home late at night. One legend states *la Lechuza* is actually a shape-shifting *bruja* (witch) seeking a replacement for her own baby, murdered long ago. Like other paranormal beings, she lures her prey closer by whistling or crying like a baby in distress.[940] (Note that the owl is closely associated with a variety of folkloric entities: the *alf*, a Prussian household faerie;[941] Lilith in Hebrew folklore;[942] *strigoi*, undead entities which feed upon human blood, from Romanian folklore;[943] and—as exemplified by the work of author, experiencer, and researcher Mike Clelland—modern UFO abductions.[944])

The rich Jamaican *duppy* tradition, alluded to in previous chapters, clearly grew out of faerie belief imported during the island's European occupation. These ancestral spirits haunt bedrooms at night; the males among them rape and impregnate sleeping women while female *duppies* lie in wait under the beds of women in labor, ready to kill or kidnap newborns. These are usually the spirits of deceased mothers who disapprove of their grandchild's father.[945] Magical practitioners of *Obeah* might employ *duppies* to target women, assailing them with a variety of afflictions, including inserting animals into the womb—examples include lizards, tadpoles, even cow heads—or, worse yet, causing *false belly*, or miscarriage.[946]

In the wilds of Trinidad and Tobago lurk *douen*, spirits said to be the lost souls of unbaptized children. Doomed to wander the earth, *douen* are known for their pranks and their footprints, which depict backwards feet. Superstitious parents avoid calling the names of their children, lest the *douen* later use the sound to lure them into the forest.[947]

Ole-Higue, a vampire-witch of Guyanese and Jamaican folklore, appears as a normal human in daylight but prowls villages at night, seeking out babies to drain their blood. Villagers can expel *Ole-Higue* by dressing an infant in blue pajamas and leaving a bowl of rice or uncooked asafetida, which it becomes distracted by and counts until dawn. At this time, the parents may enter the room and beat the vampire to death.[948]

UNITED STATES AND CANADA

Despite a separation of 4,000 miles across the Atlantic Ocean, the tribal folklore of North American First Nations reflects the Fairy Faith of the British Isles with a startling specificity.

- Parents among the Catawba of the Carolinas warn children to this day of *yehasuri*, or "Wild Indians" roaming the woods at night.[949] Like European faeries, they are short, live underground, eat rubbish, braid horses' manes, and delight in abducting children. Accounts passed through generations claim some abductees, taken for a full week before returning, perish if they discuss what they ate during their captivity. One victim, brother to informant Margaret Wiley Brown, claimed the *yehasuri* took him to a stump and "sucked the blood out of his arm completely." As with abductees returned by European faeries, the brother gained special abilities—in this case, the Wild Indians "taught him to be a doctor."[950]

- Numerous tribes west of the Mississippi, including the Paiute, Washo, and Cahuilla, believe certain bodies of water are the domain of "water babies," entities appearing as sweet mortal infants but who in fact presage death. To respond to their cries and pick them up invites calamity.[951]

- The *mialuka*, or "wild people" of central and southern Siouan folklore, are commonly described as between one and two feet tall. Sometimes they exhibit wings, or, in the case of the Omaha belief, a single eye. They are known for harming people through witchcraft and abducting children.[952]

- According to the Canadian Innu, diminutive beings known as *apci'lnic* dwell in the mountains of Labrador. They are known for stealing children.[953]

- The Nez Perce of the Pacific Northwest fear "Stick Indians," little people with withered faces crying in the night. A member of the tribe told researcher Barton Nunnelly about a family who briefly locked their baby in the car for safety reasons near Mount Adams, Washington. "While picking berries they heard the baby cry. They went to the car and found that the baby was gone. Then they heard it cry from another direction. They went over there, and there they found it," dropped by the Stick Indians.[954]

- The Shoshone of western Montana are extremely wary of *ninnimbe*, or "little demons." These beings are less than three feet tall and can hex or cause illness with their invisible arrows (similar to elf-shot overseas). In one legend from the Pryor Mountains, these beings kidnapped a boy who fell from his sled, raising him until he obtained supernatural strength.[955]

- Choctaw parents warn of the *Nalusa Chito*, the "Big Black Being," who leaves its subterranean environs to steal women and children.[956]

- According to some, people of the Iroquois Confederacy believe a dark power, known as *otkon*, couples with human woman to produce black-eyed infants with chalky white skin. These children, like changelings of the British Isles, are burned to prevent their resurrection. The *otkon* also possesses any children foolish enough to wander in the woods alone, darkening their eyes and slipping them into a mumbling trance.[957]

- "Beaver Women" allegedly prowl the water's edge at McDermott Lake, Montana. Blackfoot lore says these beautiful creatures appear as human women, though their backs and lower extremities are covered in beaver fur. They not only sing to entice men to their watery doom, but also pluck youth from the shore to raise as their own. In an odd inversion of European faerie belief, they have no use for boys—whom they murder—but instead fold girls into their ranks.[958]

- Several child abductors inhabit modern day Alaska. The Kwakiutl claim *Snanaik* ("timber giants") take any children they encounter and toss them in a basket, while in southern Alaska the Chilkat Tlingit Indians speak of *Goo-teekhl*, a giant who destroys villages and steals youngsters. Far to the north, the Netsilik Inuit warn of the giantess *Amayersuik*, who also kidnapped children by throwing them into a great hole on her back[959] (in a notable parallel, some European legends claimed faeries had no backs, only hollow spaces into which food was tossed).[960]

Historical encounters corroborate First Nations legends. One sensational story comes from a 1915 issue of *The Journal of American*

Folklore. According to Harley Stamp, several hunters camping on Maine's Penobscot River heard a strange rushing sound in the night. During their search the following morning, they happened upon a peculiar wigwam filled with gigantic spoons and a pot cooking on the fire; inside was a dismembered child. They fled the structure, following tiny footprints to an equally miniaturized village—the eldest of the party declared they had stumbled upon the water-faeries, or *warnungmeksooark*. Supposedly, they were captured shortly thereafter by one of these naked creatures. It had

> ... the most beautiful fine long hair; but his face was narrow, with so long a chin that it rested on his breast. His nose was so big and broad that you could see it on each side of his head when his back was toward you. His eyes were very narrow up and down; and his mouth was the shape of a sharp A, the point running up under his nose.[961]

The *warnungmeksooark* took the hunters to their king—dressed in a fashion similar to European faeries—who explained they "saved" children who fell into rivers and lakes, only to feast upon them annually at a great gathering of the twelve faerie tribes.[961]

Alaska Dispatch News picked up a more modern (and credible) encounter in 2008. Nick Andrew Jr. of Marshall claimed to have found a small boy wandering in a field on May 7. He was "disoriented, dazed, confused and scared," and although he had "no concept of time," was not tired, hungry, or thirsty. By the next morning, the lad's memory had returned: he claimed to have been "brought into" Pilcher Mountain where multiple "little beings" interrogated him. Yup'ik folklorists believed the *ircenrraat*, subterranean faeries who loved to disorient and trap travelers, were behind the abduction.[962]

Equally striking are the motivations seen in First Nations stories of the Cannibal Babe, an entity encountered in Montana, Nebraska, and the Dakotas. This gruesome creature draws the attention of some kind soul with its cries, appearing as an abandoned infant in need of a suckle. Placing their nipple or finger into its maw, the victim is stripped boneless, bit-by-bit.[963] While not featuring child abduction, this legend, like the Amazonian *jaracaca* and Yoruba *abiku*, obviously bears similarities to how changelings robbed their parents of their milk, energy, or resources.

Changeling lore is also paralleled in the story of Two Faces, a spirit from Sioux mythology. As its name implies, this hairy giant has two faces, but only one pair of large, elephantine ears, unfurled to capture and digest human beings. In one Two Faces myth, a child's parents watched in horror as the beast snatched their baby; after a grand battle, they finally wrestled the giant to the ground and pried open its ear. Unfortunately, their child had withered away into a mute, hairy creature with two sets of eyes on its grotesquely disfigured face. The child died in short order. One cannot help noting how closely this description—minus the extra eyes—matches some changeling accounts: a hideous creature takes the place of a stolen human child.[964]

BIGHOOTS & THUNDERBIRDS

Other beasts threatened to steal unguarded children in Native American lore. Large owls, alluded to in the *la Lechuza* stories, were feared by First Nations tribes as well—the Apache use "Big Owl Man" to frighten misbehaving children,[965] and Hocąk (Ho-Chunk) speakers warn scamps, "The owls will get you!"[966]

There may be an ornithological precedent for these warnings. Many cryptozoologists (those studying animals believed to be legendary or extinct, otherwise known as cryptids) have proposed First Nations myths of large birds might reference an actual extinct—or extant, but exceptionally well-hidden—species of large raptor.

Mark A. Hall, who exhaustively collected reports of abnormally large birds, dubbed large owls "Bighoots," a humorous play on the term "Bigfoot." Hall saw parallels between modern sightings of large owls and legends of flying, disembodied heads in Iroquois, Wyandot, and Tuscarora legend. These entities, known to various tribes as Flying/Big/Great Heads, possessed sharp talons, fiery eyes, and were noted to travel the landscape in storms, a mode of transportation favored by old world faeries. Like, faeries, they were also "more dangerous and troublesome during rainy, foggy, or misty weather... carried away children; they blighted the tobacco and other crops... Fire was the most potent agency with which to resist them."[967]

In addition to enormous, child-snatching owls, Native American legends also reverently speak of Thunderbirds, enormous raptors fond of human prey, particularly children. The tales are consistent among a great many tribes. Washington's Kathlamet held gigantic birds stole maidens into the sky, while lore from California's Miwok feared the *Yel'-lo-kin*, which was known for taking children as old as 15 years. A Native American folk hero from Massachusetts pursued an enormous bird to its nest in Nantucket, where he found countless bones of children in a great pile.[968]

Rumors of large birds absconding with babies in the modern era fuel cryptozoologists' hopes such creatures might still exist. Most famous among these is the Lawndale, Illinois incident of July 25, 1977. Ten-year-old Marlon Lowe was playing outside when one of "two huge, coal-black birds with long, white-ringed necks, long curled beaks, and wingspans of ten or more feet" allegedly lifted him into the air. It dropped Marlon after a few feet when his mother screamed.[969]

Dozens of newspaper articles from yesteryear describe what appear to be legitimate accounts of children taken by raptors, as compiled by Hall in his 2004 book *Thunderbirds: America's Living Legends of Giant Birds*. Hall found evidence for many credible cases, including a ten-year-old child taken in West Virginia in 1895; a seven-year-old in Quebec, 1888; a one-year-old in New Mexico, 1892. Even American frontiersman Daniel Boone claimed to have witnessed a five-year-old Native American child carried off into the sky by a preternaturally large bird.[970]

Hall met at length with Robert Lyman, Sr., a local historian who penned several books on Pennsylvania folklore. Of special note were several tales from the Black Forest area, a woodland historically plagued by unexplained child disappearances. In addition to this ominous tradition, the area is known for Thunderbird sightings.[971] Reports in the area begin in the 1840s and can be traced to at least as recently as the 1990s.[972]

The motif of raptors absconding with infants is well storied outside North America as well. South African journalist Lawrence Green speculated in his 1967 book *On Wings of Fire* that lammergeyers (bearded vultures) might possibly carry off young children.[973] In New Zealand, Maori legend held *Te Hokioi*, a gigantic bird, once preyed upon babies; paleontologists suspect this may be based upon the Haast eagle, an enormous raptor extinct for 500 years.[974] There is no shortage of pubs in Great Britain named The Eagle and Child, featuring the iconography of an infant in the talons of a gigantic bird.[975] Hall related a practically unimpeachable report from Norway, 1932, where a Gray sea eagle carried four-year-old Svanhild Hansen from the Kvaloyvik bogs to Haga Mountain, 1.2 miles away.

Note also how the concept of youth stolen by Thunderbirds is reflected in Japanese lore, where the child-abducting *tengu* can shapeshift into an enormous bird of prey. A handful of other connections exist between Thunderbirds and the fae folk—their very name evokes associations between the faerie host and storms. Thunderbird legends also underscore the danger inherent in berry picking. Hiram Cranmer, a colorful character of Pennsylvania's Kettle Creek area, claimed to know multiple individuals kidnapped by Thunderbirds, including a four-year-old McKean County girl "who was snatched in 1937 while her family was picking berries."[976]

Berries feature prominently in several Thunderbird legends. According to the Dane-zaa of British Columbia and Alberta, a large spruce tree in the depths of the forest is where the Thunderbirds conceive, a sacred place because of the special berries that grow under its branches.[977] In a cluster of tribal legends collectively entitled "Thunderbird Steals the Wife of Another Bird," the titular victim—typically wife to Woodpecker—is often berry picking when Thunderbird carries her off.[978] In some variants, Woodpecker seeks the wisdom of the Snipe, who suggests a means by which to recover the wives stolen by Thunderbird. From a 1907 retelling:

> "Our warriors," said he, "will change themselves into salmon-berries as soon as they reach the home of the Thunderbird. The women, including the wife of the Woodpecker, will come to pick the salmon-berries and the warriors will assume their proper shapes and carry the women away."[979]

Finally, there seems to be a thread connecting the manner in which Native Americans and those on the British Isles associated certain areas with their respective legends. In the Appalachian Mountains, several distinct barren mountains—known as "balds"—have puzzled botanists and geologists alike for centuries. As opposed to supporting heavy forest growth, these locations instead boast sparse vegetation, leading some botanists to suspect a man-made thinning of the land. This coincides closely with indigenous Cherokee legends, which claim the balds were created by their ancestors in a desperate bid to rid the region of Thunderbirds, burning off the vegetation to deprive the birds of their eyries.[980]

Notably, some English traditions associate barren ground with the fae folk. In Essex tradition, faerie rings were not only circular formations of fungi, but could also refer to a barren circle of ground. "Sometimes they present themselves as circles and curves of bare ground, at other times the barren circle of ground has a rim of luxuriant grass outside," wrote Worthington G. Smith in 1883. "In a perfect fairy circle we have, then, starting from the centre, a ring of barren ground, a ring of rank grass, and a ring of Fungi."[981]

SASQUATCH: A BRIEF INTRODUCTION

Another child-abducting darling of cryptozoology is, of course, Sasquatch. Alleged by some to be a species of relict hominid—*Gigantopithecus blacki* remains the most popular suggestion—roaming the forests of North America, Sasquatch is also commonly known by the modern American slang name, "Bigfoot." First Nations tribes from every region of the continent mention tall, bipedal, hirsute creatures fond of abducting women and children—in fact, some cryptozoologists contend the giant traditions of Alaska mentioned earlier in fact reference Sasquatch.

While Sasquatch is discussed in much greater detail later, a few points are worth mentioning presently in the context of Native American belief. A curious overlap, rarely noted, exists between Sasquatch and witch lore. Both are feared denizens of the forest known for stealing lost children. Like Baba Yaga, *dsonoqua*, the Kwakiutl's hairy "wild woman of the woods," and her southerly cousin, the Lummi's *Ch'eni*,[982] toss their victims into baskets.[983] In the epic saga of Irish folk hero Fionn mac Cumhaill, a witch reaches through a chimney to snatch a sleeping infant; in at least one retelling, her arm is described as long and hairy.[984] Consider that Sasquatch have even been explicitly referred to as "witches"— during the 1978 "Minerva Monster" flap of Ohio, some witnesses referred to the eponymous beast as a "hairy witch."[985]

Regional colloquialisms for Sasquatch also reflect the Fairy Faith, of all things. Various rural Americans speak interchangeably of *boogers* or *wooly boogers* and Bigfoot, particularly in the Southern United States.[986] *Booger* derives from *boogeyman*, which itself comes from faeries like *bugbears* and *boggarts*, and obliquely references their penchant for taking youngsters.[987] (Notably, early settlers to the Ozarks called Hall's Bighoots *booger owls*, suggesting a child-snatching link.[988]) Such details imply perhaps something stranger than an undiscovered wood ape roams America's forests.

Indigenous cultures the world over report remarkably similar themes regarding paranormal child abduction; it should come as no surprise, therefore, that our increasingly connected global society has spawned its own unique folklore surrounding such concerns. Few modern Westerners fear their children will be taken by the fae folk, *yehasuri, duppies, duendes, tengu, Bunian,* or *pmere kwetethe.* No one worries about nursing an *abiku,* or finding a changeling left by faeries or *djinn.*

In today's world, technology has usurped superstition, but the coup is in name only. The same ancient anxieties persist, still keep us awake in the witching hours. In the name of technology and materialism, we have created our own 21st century boogeymen.

Extraterrestrials.

Chapter 11:
"Going but Never Gone—Coming but Never Here"
Modern Modalities of Paranormal Child
Abduction: An Introduction

Here, the Pied Piper doesn't come to town because of something we've done or not done. The Pied Piper came because of what we had.
— Stephen Graham Jones, "Some Wait"

A tale whispered around Las Vegas in the 1940s told of the Senas, a couple who longed for a child but never had one. Returning home from a dance one evening, Mr. Sena heard a baby crying and, looking around, discovered a foundling in a basket. Sena thought of the void in his life and took the child in his arms, but as he started home the infant wailed, "Look, Father, I already have teeth and nails!" After seeing its pointed teeth and claws, Sena dropped the "devil baby," basket and all, and fled home.[989]

This urban legend owes an obvious debt of inspiration to changeling lore. Whenever similar tales surface they are invariably sensational, as reported in a 2005 episode of the Russian television program *Inexplicable, Yet A Fact*. The segment, presented by Sergey Druzhko, claimed every patient in a Rybinsk maternity ward simultaneously went into labor one evening in 1986. When returned to their mothers the following morning, the babies were unrecognizable, bearing odd scars on their heads. One "hybrid" girl, daughter of an Inna Zolotaryeva, allegedly survived into adulthood but suffered nightmares of flying saucers and remained sickly her entire life.[990]

Both yarns are likely hoaxes yet express the same deeply ingrained fears gnawing at parents for centuries; they are fairytales in all but name. Stories resembling the changeling narrative persist into the modern era, but they are rarely attributed to anything other than UFOs and extraterrestrials—regardless of how obstinately the Fairy Faith bleeds into the case files of modern UFOlogy.

What makes extraterrestrials more believable than faeries?

THE LONG GOODBYE

The decline of faerie belief directly parallels their exodus from our mortal realm, a theme common in Celtic literature. All storytellers speak of faeries as a fading race, fewer now than ever. Eyewitnesses have even claimed to watch them marching somberly from their ringforts, destined for places beyond the world of men. (J.R.R. Tolkien incorporated this into *The Lord of the Rings*, with the passing of the Elves across the sea.) Reasons behind this migration vary, but the Industrial Revolution, increasing urbanization, rising scientism, and the spread of Christianity— particularly Protestantism—are all commonly cited.[991]

This protracted goodbye began as early as the 1300s—passages from *The Canterbury Tales* imply as much—and continued well into the 20th century.[992] "However often they may be reported as gone, the fairies still linger," wrote Briggs in 1976, adding that the Fairy Faith remains "part of the normal texture of life" in the British Isles, where anecdotes and sightings still surface.[993]

"The fairies are always going, going—but never gone," said Patrick Harpur. On the other hand, UFOlogists and New Age believers alike swear extraterrestrials "are always coming, coming— but never here."[994] This comparison is echoed in a curious handoff observed circa 1890-1920, where a sharp decline in faerie belief coincided with the growing popularity of a new literary genre: science fiction.

Perhaps one fantasy substituted another.

THE EXTRATERESTRIAL HYPOTHESIS

For millennia humans have observed anomalies in the sky, from bright lights to objects appearing as nonterrestrial structured craft. Though its interpretation shifts depending upon culture and era, the phenomenon itself seems relatively stable.

Despite the prevailing popularity of the Extraterrestrial Hypothesis (ETH)— the notion that flesh-and-blood aliens visit Earth in nuts-and-bolts, physical spacecraft—whatever haunts our clouds remains a mystery. In reality, the ETH is but one of many possible explanations, and a handful of researchers staunchly propose alternative theories: UFOs could be faeries, time travelers, Jungian archetypes, manifestations of psi effects, unexplained natural phenomena, or even top secret human aircraft. Any one explanation may not even explain the entire phenomenon.

Given popular culture's unfortunate assumption that UFOs are evidence of alien visitation, most paranormal researchers of anomalous abduction today predictably gravitate toward the ETH model. In truth, evidence connecting aerial anomalies to bedroom abductions by strange beings is not exceptionally strong; while these two aspects overlap occasionally, one does not always accompany the other. Many "alien abductions" occur in the absence of physical "spacecraft."

The typical alien abduction scenario is no doubt familiar: the victim—driving an isolated roadway, camping in the wilderness, or sleeping in their own bedroom—notices a strange presence nearby, either in the form of a physical being, bright light, or both. They are taken (often levitated, physically or astrally) by this presence to a secondary location, brightly lit and populated by what appear to be non-human entities; in pop culture these are spindly, bulbous headed, large-eyed Grey aliens, although witness descriptions vary wildly, including insectoids, reptilians, hairy dwarfs, robots, Nordic humanoids, and everything in between. Whatever they are, these beings usually perform a sexually-tinged medical examination or procedure upon the abductee. When their time is up, they may give the witness a cryptic or apocalyptic message before "returning them to Earth," often with amnesia of what transpired.

Though skeptics maintain alien abduction is a purely Western problem—fed by media and cinema—the phenomenon, including child abduction, occurs worldwide. In 1931, an Arnhem Land aboriginal elder reported several odd entities descended from the Australian sky and seized a two-year-old toddler.[995] In 1959, residents of Indonesia's Alor Island were besieged by sightings of glowing, oval objects in the sky and short, red humanoids who took at least one child, found later in a daze.[996] Alien abduction is not a Western fantasy, but the rigid interpretation of such through the ETH is certainly endemic to the West.

While the next few chapters filter paranormal child abduction through the lens of modern UFOlogy, the reader is urged to interpret what follows as neither support nor rejection of the ETH, as both are poor approaches to comparativism. One can be highly critical of the ETH while not dismissing it.

That being said, the ETH possesses numerous shortcomings, chiefly how it ignores the "High Strangeness" inherent in so many UFO reports. Aspects of eyewitness testimony regularly shatter precepts of scientific materialism, including reports of telepathy, psi effects, poltergeist phenomena, profoundly improbable synchronicities, and spiritual revelations. While not denying the possibility that extraterrestrial life has visited Earth in the past— or that it may still drop in from time-to-time—these details undermine the notion UFOs are simply advanced scientists from other planets.

HYPNOSIS

Beyond the ETH, mainstream UFOlogy has its own problems, perhaps none greater than its dependence upon hypnotic regression. Though many witnesses clearly recall their experiences without additional aid, it has become common to employ hypnosis when retrieving suppressed or forgotten memories from alleged alien abductees. While an effective tool for behavior modification (e.g. smoking cessation, weight loss, etc.), hypnosis has an extremely spotty reputation as a memory retrieval technique. Too easily can hypnotists—often self-trained—deliberately or accidentally implant ideas while stumbling through the minds of suggestible patients, falsehoods emerging in subsequent testimony as factual recollections. Anyone wishing to fully comprehend the problems with hypnotic regression should consult commentary by Jeffrey Ritzmann and Jack Brewer, particularly Brewer's book *The Greys Have Been Framed*.

In spite of these reservations, the following chapters still cite stories retrieved via hypnotic regression, simply because—as noted before—the motivic consistency across multiple stories is our focus, rather than the veracity of any single account. In the interest of transparency, any testimony obtained via hypnosis is noted as such, provided such information is available.

SPIRITS, BIKERS, & PIED PIPERS

Children of today describe their supernatural kidnappers in a variety of ways. In his book *Abduction: Human Encounters with Aliens*, the late Harvard psychiatrist John Mack talked to multiple victims who, in their childhood, were taken by a smorgasbord of odd entities: an androgynous golden angel; a witch flying by the window inviting children on her broomstick; a white ghost wanting to spirit away a young witness; even a trio of disappearing motorcyclists clad in black.[997]

Despite Mack's earnestness—and the open-mindedness his work exhibited prior to his untimely death—most UFOlogists interpret these accounts as "screen memories," i.e. a self-imposed (or alien-imposed) false memories used to disguise the truthful recollection of events, in this case abductions by extraterrestrials. The approach evokes the old adage, "When all you have is a hammer, everything looks like a nail"—when all you have is a UFOlogist, everything looks like an extraterrestrial.

Perhaps we should throw out the hammer in the face of these baffling encounters. How does one reconcile "Pied Piper" characters with the ETH?

According to paranormal author Tom Slemen, Paul Smith was playing hide-and-seek in his uncle's Liverpool house in 1967 when ice-cold, "pinkish" hands slipped through the window, grabbing his mouth and throat. The hands almost pulled him outside before Paul bit one and screamed. Rushing to the window, Paul's uncle saw him in the clutches of a man with "pink and black patches all over his face and arms, like some unsightly jigsaw pattern of contrasting skin. The patches looked just like the pied markings of a cow or a black and white mongrel dog." The man released Paul and fled into the night.[998]

Martin Jeffrey reported an even more explicit Pied Piper. Several children of Surrey Heath, England, encountered an unsettling figure near the school playground in 1995. Described as tall, red-eyed, and wearing a suit covered in "badges," the figure pointed at children and declared he "wanted" them. He appeared to carry some type of flute.[999]

Are we to believe these are aliens, in spite of their resonance with earlier traditions?

The truth is that multiple phenomena may be at play, or there may be one phenomenon masquerading as many. A majority of paranormal child abduction may indicate extraterrestrial visitation… or the ETH may be wholly incorrect. Perhaps the truth is more akin to worldwide faerie traditions… or perhaps it is so strange, so alien to us, we have not yet even conceptualized its true nature. As ever, we have more questions than answers. The purpose of what follows is to highlight the striking—and oft-overlooked—similarities between thieves in the night, then and now.

Chapter 12:
"A 'Tagged Animal'"
Child Alien Abduction

We wait for a system of signs and signals that shall enable us to correspond with Mars. Yet Mars is further off than the enchanted hills, the canals sound dull compared to the green and purple Hills of Peace where among the Riders of the Shee the boundless deer and roe pass immortal in twos and twos.
> — Lady Archibald Campbell, "The Men of Peace"

September 1965: a seven-year-old girl and her four siblings were staying overnight with their aunt in Litchfield, New Hampshire, when all awoke to a stifling red mist filling the bedroom. Twenty-five years later, the primary witness recalled, under hypnosis, pulling up a chair to peek out the window, where the eyes of a Grey alien stared back. Her next memory was standing in the yard alongside her cousin underneath a hovering, domed disc. Both children were levitated into a brightly lit room inside the craft, paralyzed, and placed upon examination tables. According to a 1990 *MUFON UFO Journal* report, "an entity then performed an undetermined procedure on the girl's lower body" using something like "a long pencil" tipped with a small, needled ball. Afterwards, the two were gently floated back to earth. All the children reported the story to their aunt but were ignored.[1000]

HISTORY

Many erroneously believe alien abductions began in 1961 with the famous New Hampshire "interrupted journey" of Betty and Barney Hill. While most experiencers of the early-to-mid 20th century are certainly better categorized as "contactees"—voluntary guests of pleasant UFOnauts—rather than abductees, there are nonetheless antecedents of involuntary, unpleasant interactions long prior to the Hill Case.

The Hill Case is, however, among the first abductions investigated with hypnotic regression. Psychiatrist Benjamin Simon, who worked with the Hills in 1964,[1001] determined memories retrieved under hypnosis were the couple's "shared delusion."[1002] In 1976, UFOlogist and hypnotist James Harder approached the Hills and extracted a more detailed retelling of their encounter; though Harder and others had employed regression with other witnesses, its use in such a high-profile UFO case cemented its reputation as an investigative tool.[1003]

Reports of child alien abduction didn't truly flourish until the 1980s, boosted by the work of artist-cum-UFOlogist Budd Hopkins. Hopkins followed in Harder's footsteps—as did John Mack, to a less sensational degree—through extensive use of hypnotic regression. While some subjects retained conscious recall of odd occurrences in their lives, elaborate abduction memories largely emerged via hypnosis—real events supposedly occluded by self-repression, alien-induced amnesia, or the march of time (one victim's testimony stretched back to a 1929 childhood encounter).[1004]

Hopkins' books, in particular *Missing Time* and *Intruders*, became mandatory reading for UFOlogists of the era. In the former, he speculated on the prevalence of abduction among children: "How many of these cases, we wondered, might have involved time lapses that a six-year-old girl or a ten-year-old boy, playing alone in the afternoon, would never have noticed?"[1005] Prior to Hopkins, most researchers interpreted childhood UFO sightings as one-off events. After conducting hundreds of interviews, Hopkins perceived a recurring theme: abductions began in adolescence and continued throughout adulthood.[1006]

Virginia Horton's narrative embodied the type of case Hopkins investigated. Shortly before her seventh birthday, Horton experienced an unexplainable event on her grandfather's farm near Lake Superior. In the summer of 1950 she had gone to gather some eggs from the barn, yet her only recollection was regaining consciousness in the yard with a large gash on her leg—underneath her undamaged jeans. A decade later, she disappeared from a family picnic in France in pursuit of an enchanting "mystical" deer in the woods, returning with a bloodied nose. Under regression by Hopkins, Horton revealed these were encounters with grey-skinned entities who regularly examined her, using some sort of probe to implant a tracking or monitoring device up her nostril.[1007]

Though the concept dates back as far as 1957, the notion of alien implants placed into young abductees was popularized in the 1980s and took hold in UFOlogy.[1008] In 1990, researcher John Schuessler wrote of a 12-year-old boy who "claimed that small creatures took him from his bed, stuck a needle into his upper arm and then opened a square patch of skin on the left side of his head."[1009] The motif of a body part implanted with foreign material finds its antecedent in faerie lore, where it might be recalled the faerie blast created lumps and boils filled with detritus.

"The phenomenon almost invariably entails decades-long abductions of the same individuals at irregular intervals," Hopkins concluded. "The abductee becomes, in effect, a 'tagged animal' whose earliest experiences begin in childhood, even as early as the first year of life, and continue afterwards with special frequency in the first ten years or so of adulthood."[1010]

While Harder may have been among the first to notice this trend, Hopkins popularized it. The meme rapidly gained traction in UFOlogy, persisting into the current era.

"An abduction can occur to anyone at anytime," researcher Yvonne Smith said in 1994. "However, research shows that it usually begins in childhood and continues throughout that person's life."[1011] Nearly a decade later, *Flying Saucer Review* suggested "millions of earthlings" were "interfered with since babyhood."[1012]

To be fair, certain individuals seem predisposed to supernatural activity, be they psychics, seers, or simply repeat witnesses. Lifelong alien abductions draw an unappreciated comparison to faerie lore: both feature a longitudinal component. Victims of the faeries were taken once and kept forever; victims of aliens return home but are taken countless times.

SELECTED CASES

Despite the tidy tagged animal narrative promoted by mainstream UFOlogy, no boilerplate account exists. A few examples:

- Around age seven, Próspera Muñoz of Ciudad Real, Spain, was abducted. Though flashes of the incident plagued her for some time, in 1979 she underwent hypnosis and discovered that two entities circa 1945 had emerged from a silver craft and invited her aboard, where they performed a gynecological examination.[1013]

- Lifelong abductee Sandy Nichols consciously recalls his first abduction, which took place at age five. While playing on the porch of his grandmother's home in Nashville, Tennessee, he spied a "round airplane" that came to rest in a nearby field. Shortly thereafter, "two small, strange looking kids" entered the yard and asked him to follow. He was floated to the field and inside the craft, where he was shown three "toys": two flying devices and "a wand with fiber optic tubes attached to it," which drew images in the air. The scenario repeated itself throughout his life, slowly growing more "physically and emotionally invasive."[1014]

- In April 1964, the Lund family began seeing a spinning top-shaped craft over their Missoula, Montana, farm. Three-and-a-half-year-old grandson Kyle regularly conversed with a man—name unpronounceable—near the barn, vanishing "for several hours at a time" before suddenly reappearing.[1015]

- Jenny Randles—herself a childhood experiencer—chronicled numerous child contacts in her 1994 book *Star Children*. One account from a seven-year-old Nottinghamshire, UK, witness in 1967, described football-shaped lights bouncing around her room, followed by levitation into a strange location filled with small, fussy creatures.[1016]

- On October 7, 1979, Canadian brothers aged seven and six found themselves under the care of their 14-year-old cousin. As evening approached, the older brother noticed an escalating hum accompanied by a large disc hovering above the trailer. Blocking the noise with a pillow, the witness and his cousin lost sight of his younger sibling; they looked outside and saw the young boy standing underneath the craft's light. Their next memory was of the saucer drifting away, followed by the mother and aunt's return home. The youngest exhibited evidence of a seizure.[1017]

- According to John Mack, on October 29, 1992, two-year-old Colin began telling his mother of "scary owls with the big eyes" which fell "out of the sky," "attacking" him and making him "eat some food." The young boy regularly declared, "I don't want to go back on the spaceship," adding "I was born there and fell from the stars… I was born on the spaceship and it was dark."[1018]

- "Sam," a witness plagued by nightmares of bright lights and loud noises since age five, began hypnotherapy sessions with Yvonne Smith in the 1990s. Among the recalled events was an incident at age 10 when he levitated from his bed into a brightly lit space. Multiple short entities with "watery" eyes made him disrobe, then inserted a flexible cable into his rectum before returning him home.[1019]

- Three Chilean boys reported their abduction in December 1994. The trio (aged seven, eight, and nine) claimed with six other witnesses an unidentified craft "sucked them up" in a blue light beam. Over the next 72 hours, the boys toured the universe with a silver-haired, shiny "God" who called himself "Lalar" and "scraped [their] faces with a white stick and stuck us in the back with a needle."[1020]

- Circa 1995, researcher John Carpenter interviewed a mother who saw "a thin white being near her one-year-old daughter's crib at the foot of the bed." Under hypnosis, both she and the father independently recalled being paralyzed, helpless to watch as a small being appeared out of a red portal and lifted their baby from its crib.[1021]

- In November 2003, multiple witnesses described female screams near Morehead, Kentucky, coinciding with an emergency services call reporting that a "spaceship" approached "a woman with a baby" on a nearby hill, "taking" her child and prompting the mother's lamentations. Another call several days later complained of a two-year-old toddler ambling down a road in Morehead, "wearing only a diaper."[1022]

Some of the above would not be out-of-place in faerie lore. Consider the last example: a mother atop a hill (geography notable for faerie activity) loses a child abandoned on the roadside (recall the changeling and the whisky distributors). Even the screaming mother herself evokes Irish legends of the *banshee*.

The famous Voronezh, Russia, landing of 1989 warrants special mention. Numerous students and faculty near School No. 33 watched an egg-shaped craft float near the ground on September 27, revealing a trio of neckless, three-eyed beings and a robot. When one boy exclaimed in fear, an entity paralyzed him with a gaze and zapped him with a beam from a wand; the boy vanished, only reappearing after the craft departed. His parents refused to allow interviews.[1023]

The story resembles an October 19, 2000, case where 35 parents and 20 children witnessed a multicolored object descend near a school in San Francisco de Chiu-Chiu, Chile. Accompanied by an odd noise and a burning odor, the craft hovered over the schoolyard and ejected a beam of light onto custodian Fresia Vega and eight-year-old Valentina Rojas Espinoza. Both vanished. They were found nearby, "dazed and shivering." Neither possessed a clear memory of the event.[1024]

TRENDS

UFOs, like faeries before them, are obsessed with children. Open-minded researcher Jenny Randles keenly noted in the late 1970s "the affinity that the UFO phenomenon has for schools and schoolchildren."[1025]

It seems feasible to propose that children are more sensitive to something. If there is a sensitivity involved this is not surprising. Hearing, eyesight, etc., all deteriorate with age. At the age of 10-14 children are at the peak of their sensual faculties and are able coherently to observe and report an incident, hence—perhaps—the number of child witnesses. This is also the time of puberty when psychic researchers have noted that paranormal connections (e.g. poltergeist phenomena) appear to be prevalent.[1026]

The most striking UFO sighting at a school took place on September 16, 1994, in Ruwa, Zimbabwe. Sixty-two children from the Ariel School, aged five to 12, were playing outside when up to five craft were spotted flitting through the skies. One of the craft alit on the edge of the campus, from which two small humanoids emerged.

According to some accounts, the beings had long black hair, large eyes, no nose, and slit-like mouths. Several of the children received telepathic messages conveying the fragility of Earth's environment before the beings took off in their craft.[1027] (The incident bears a passing resemblance to a sighting from the 1940s where a superintendent and around 45 children observed *menehune*—Hawaii's indigenous faeries—playing across the street from their school.[1028])

Most reports suggest alien abductions begin around six or seven years old—though kidnapped infants are not unheard of.[1029]

- On December 31, 1976, the newspaper *La Razon* reported a UFO near Cajabamba, Peru, kidnapped the two-month-old daughter of Candelaria Chilon. Multiple witnesses described a violet saucer appearing as Chilon and the child returned from working in the fields (like so many changeling tales).[1030]

- One of the youngest children ever abducted was the baby of an American witness interviewed by Jenny Randles. The mother, "Sandie," claimed Grey aliens entered her home and took her six-week-old son from his crib for "some tests, before bringing him back again apparently unharmed" (recall the six-week window for faerie abduction in Germany).[1031]

- Another case suggests an *even younger* child was taken: in February 1970, a Peruvian midwife reported her client missing. Some 48 hours later she was found at the base of a mountain near Yungay, claiming small men had brought her into the clouds and taken her baby.[1032]

One challenge when studying child alien abduction is the fluid definition of adulthood in modern society. Our ancestors engaged in cultural institutions such as marriage, war, and work at an age much younger than Westerners do today. As we have pushed the boundaries of childhood older, has the timeframe for child abduction shifted as well?

"The data for ages at which witnesses claim their experiences shows that abductions are a hazard of youth, with children but especially teenagers and young adults the most vulnerable," wrote Eddie Bullard of the phenomenon in 1987. "After a peak in the 20s, instances of abduction decline and the drop is precipitous beyond 40."[1033]

In other words—the previous examples of abducted infants notwithstanding—alien abductions typically begin and continue later than faerie abductions, but still decrease significantly once the societal definition of adulthood is reached. In the modern West, children are generally considered adults when they reach age 18-21; in the British Isles circa 500-1500 A.D., this age was 12-14.[1034] In both examples, the same window for abduction—roughly 14 years—remains intact (alien abduction taking place mostly between ages 7-21, faerie abduction 0-14). Note the significance of this timeframe to faerie lore: many of the stories feature children aged seven; tithes of children were given once every seven years; and the faerie captive Malekin told visitors of Dagworthy she would be released to the mortal realm after 14 years' imprisonment.

(Remember the findings of Andrew Green, who concluded psychic ability peaks in young people around age seven. Consider also the work of University of Virginia School of Medicine psychiatrist Ian Stevenson, whose research into the past-life memories of children found they faded around seven years old. Something is special about this age.[1035])

A fine example of aliens' disinterest in older subjects is the August 12, 1983, account of 77-year-old Englishman Alfred Burtoo, who was ushered inside a landed UFO while fishing. Several beings scanned him with a beam of light before telling him he was "too old and infirm" for their purposes, without further elaborating on exactly what that entailed."[1036]

Compare this dismissal to testimony from a Galway piper more than 75 years earlier: "The fairies never care about old folks. They only *take* babies, and young men and young women."[1037]

Child abductees often behave similarly to children returning from Fairyland. After having seen a UFO while hunting, the Hess family of La Mirada, California, was plagued by nighttime visits from strange figures encircling their beds. On one occasion, they found their five-year-old son "in a trance-like state and spinning like a top"—once he regained consciousness, he begged them not to turn the lights out, "Because when you turn the lights out, the little monsters come."[1038]

Even the simple act of seeing a UFO can put children in a daze, as in the case of an Ithaca, New York, boy who was riding in a car with his mom in December 1967. "At first I observed red lights in the rear-view mirror," the mother told investigators. "The lights passed my car and I saw a large disc about the size of a box-car hovering at an altitude about the height of a telephone pole. It lit up the inside of my car with a blood-red color. It was so eerie; there was no sound. I became hysterical and shouted to my son, but he would not move and seemed to be in a trance."[1039]

Child abductees might also be more phobia-prone. One lifelong abductee, after her first experience at age seven, began bribing her brother to take out the trash after dark. "She always felt like she was being watched," wrote author and experiencer Bret Oldham in 2017. "I was very much like that as a child. All children have some fear of the dark or of being alone. Those who have been visited or taken experience that fear at an entirely different level."[1040]

Data suggests children are treated differently from adults during abductions. The scenario plays out under much less duress, with children largely acting of their own volition. In 2002, researcher Dan Wright reported child abductions differed in several key ways from adult cases: children were controlled less than adults; retained greater awareness of their surroundings; and were more likely to take a tour of the environment with their kidnappers.[1041]

Wright also claimed that although children were physically strapped to examination tables, they did not experience typical paralytic sensations until adulthood abductions.[1042] The character of these differing encounters once more brings to mind faeries, who would blind, beat, rob, or curse adults… but generally treated their young captives kindly.

TALL TALES AND FALSE MEMORIES

Is UFO testimony from children reliable?

On one side, researchers like Raymond Fowler and Deborah Truncale maintained child witnesses could be just as reliable as adults.[1043] Truncale said she rarely saw signs of storytelling— pauses to think, attempts at convincing eye contact—in child testimonies, and they were "generally more animated and [spoke] quickly" compared to those who made up stories.[1044]

John Carpenter felt testimony occasionally carried *greater* weight from children than adults. Asked in 1996 if popular culture contaminated UFO cases, Carpenter cited "emotional accounts from pre-school-age children who could not have read these materials, nor fully understood adult talk shows or movies," arguing in favor of the phenomenon's validity.[1045] Hopkins echoed this sentiment, stating young children were not exposed to the Grey alien image—an argument less defensible today.[1046]

In contrast, Michael Swords astutely noted in 1984 that dissociative hysteria—characterized by estrangement, depersonalization, dream-like states of fantasy, and amnesia—is "fairly common among tense, worried children" and posed "an important psychiatric problem to investigate as an explanation for certain close encounter reports."[1047]

On a more pragmatic note, researcher Ted Bloecher summed up his concerns in 1978:

> The accuracy of children's testimony regarding UFO reports is a difficult thing to determine. On the one hand, children can often exhibit an exhilarating candor and lack of guile in describing something; but they also have rich imaginations that are unconstrained by their limited knowledge and experience with the "real" world. One may hesitatingly conclude (at the risk of appearing to be an adult chauvinist) that UFO reports by children have considerably less probative value than reports by adults. This is not to say that children's reports should be ignored or thrown away.[1048]

Outside UFOlogy, long-dormant claims of physical and sexual abuse quickly spread, becoming part of the cultural landscape of the 1980s and 1990s. Rumors of phantom social workers and Satanic ritual abuse further fueled the fire. So many victims came forward that by the early 1990s psychologists adopted the term "false memory syndrome" (FMS) to explain memories fabricated or altered by outside influences, including recovered-memory-therapy.[1049]

This theory proves a powerful counterargument to claims of abduction obtained via hypnotic regression. Some, like Columbia University psychiatrist Anne Skomorowsky, even suggested traumatic childhood experiences could be integrated into adulthood. Skomorowsky suggested memories of the famous Hill Case came in part from repressed recollections of Barney Hill's childhood tonsillectomy.[1050]

UFOlogists and skeptics alike agree recollections of alien abduction from childhood involve screen memories. But whereas UFOlogists hold mundane imagery stands in for alien contact, skeptics argue abductions mask actual, human-inflicted trauma. The intensity of childhood abuse forces survivors to reinterpret their memories through the alien abduction framework, simply because the truth is too painful. Abusers become all-powerful Grey aliens, their physical and sexual abuse morphing into invasive medical procedures and reproductive examinations.[1051]

Like the medical interpretation of changelings, FMS is a tragic, highly plausible explanation for a great many cases, particularly those retrieved under hypnosis. However, there are a few compelling counterarguments worth addressing.

For one, while FMS has great explicative power regarding the childhood memories of hypnotically regressed adults, it is useless when a young witness recalls an experience from days or weeks earlier.

"The False Memory crusaders... need to account for the *lack* of imagination and diversity in alien encounters that one should expect over thousands of people," Carpenter wrote. "They need to explain how children can report such incidents from the night before."[1052] Moreover, many do not recall abductions exclusively from their childhood, but from throughout their entire lives.[1053]

In 2004, scientists from Stanford University and the University of Oregon discovered a biological mechanism in the human brain specifically designed to repress unwanted memories. "There is a clear neurological basis for motivated forgetting," said professor

Michael Anderson.[1054] While hypnotic regression may not be the best tool to extract these memories, scientific research suggests the concept is not mere fantasy.

Equally problematic is FMS's inability to explain why some victims, even documented survivors of child abuse, remember abusive incidents separately from alien abduction. For example, several women interviewed by Karla Turner for her 1994 book *Taken* reported childhood abuse but, unlike memories of their abductions, these events were never repressed.[1055] As of 1992, abductees reported a higher incidence of sexual assault in childhood than the general population (35% versus 20-25%); some argue this discrepancy precludes abductions as repressed memories of abuse, while others feel it only means the most intense incidents are blocked.[1056]

Finally—unsurprisingly—repressed memories are consistent with faerie lore. Evans Wentz drew parallels between supernatural lapses of time in Fairyland and a "Seeress of Prevorst," who "passed through a period of six years and five months, and then awoke as from a one-night sleep with no memory of what she did during that time; but some time afterwards memory of the period came to her so completely that she recalled all its details. Old people, and some young people too, among the Celts, who go to Fairyland for varying periods of time, sometimes extending over weeks (as in a case I knew in West Ireland), have just such dreams or trance-states as this."[1057]

Alien abduction presents a complicated scenario with a controversial past, numerous data points coalescing into a messy whole. Regardless of whether or not it is as prevalent as UFOlogists would have us believe, or as problematic as skeptics would suggest, we must never lose sight of the fact that, at the center of each case, is a human being.

Chapter 13:
"Children of the Northern Peoples"
Risks, Methods of Abduction, & Destinations

COSMIC KIDNAPING - Indiana Woman Blames Disappearance of Three Year-Old Son on Clouds - Guiler Says She will Search Out of State if Indiana Police Discontinue Their Efforts

— *Close Encounters of the Third Kind* (1977)

Five-year-old Bret Oldham and his siblings had moved into the living room of the family's old two-story farmhouse in an effort to save on the heating bill of a long Illinois winter. One night, a bright light streaming in through the window awakened Oldham. "Something kept calling me inside my head," he later wrote. "It felt calming. It wanted me to come to the window to see something. 'Don't be afraid, don't be afraid,' the voice kept saying. 'I have something special to show you.'"

Oldham peeled back the curtain to find himself face-to-face with a Grey alien. Frozen in fear, he watched three others emerge from the shadows before blacking out.

Oldham awoke naked on an examination table in a brightly lit room. Agitated, he cried out for his mother, prompting each alien to take on the countenance of a human doctor. "At this point in time, the alien beside me, on the right side, leaned over and raised his right hand up to my head. That's the last thing I remember."[1058]

RISKS: BIRTH & GENETICS

This is Oldham's first memory regarding alien abduction. He claims this and other memories, though repressed, were obtained through conscious recall rather than hypnosis. If his story can be believed, Oldham endured countless indignities and horrors over the years, including what amounts to a hypnotic group sex session initiated by his alien captors. Dozens of naked men and women were brought together, zombie-like, to copulate in front of the Greys. Through his addled state, Oldham registered one compelling detail: "I noticed that all of the men in the room had dark hair."[1059]

This detail—an inversion of the faeries' love of fair hair—may be the only example where hair color is cited as a common denominator among abductees. Unlike faerie lore, random circumstances of birth—days of the week, facial features, etc.—are generally not considered risk factors for alien abduction.

After all, UFOlogy is more *scientific*, isn't it? Like the milieu in which it arose, alien abduction is ascribed much more calculated, methodical motivations. It directly reflects our understanding of the world, marching on a spectrum from superstition to science.

Having said that, a probability is associated with certain genetic factors. Primarily, a family history of abduction puts one at risk, at least according to prominent alien abduction researcher David Jacobs. Jacobs, a Temple University historian who has been instrumental in shaping the modern alien abduction narrative, staunchly maintains the phenomenon is inheritable. "If an abductee has children with a nonabductee, the chances are that all their descendants will be abductees," he wrote in *The Threat*. "When those children grow and marry and have children of their own, all of their children, whether they marry an abductee or nonabductee, will be abductees."[1060]

Jacobs—who we return to later—offers many controversial opinions, but anecdotal evidence supports this claim. Beth, an abductee studied by Karla Turner, was startled when her granddaughter mentioned several "mean mushroom men"—later sketched as large-eyed, long-necked beings with "inverted light bulb" heads—who had come into her room and taken her in the middle of the night.[1061] Turner's other subjects experienced similar discussions with their offspring. Jean Moncrief, whose experiences were investigated by Ann Druffel, received some solace when she learned her mother had also experienced bedroom invaders similar to the "electric blue" men who regularly operated upon her.[1062]

While strengthening relationships between parents and children, alien abduction can sometimes generate rifts in marriages. "The abductee's children start having alien abductions, while the non-abductee spouse (or abductee spouse who is in denial) is unbelieving, leaving their marriage partner in emotional isolation," wrote researcher Eve Lorgen.[1063] Of course, this does not happen in every marriage; according to Jacobs, the non-experiencer husband of Reshma Kamal remained "extremely supportive" in light of the experiences of his wife and their five children.[1064]

As with the Kamal children, siblings may experience abductions concurrently. Jonathan (5) and Allison (14), two children of a San Bernardino, California single mother, both consciously recalled highly suggestive experiences circa 1992: bright lights in their bedrooms, strange rushing sounds, and, in Jonathan's case, recollections of beings floating him into a round, levitating craft.[1065] These familial factors echo how certain families were changeling-prone.

A child's heritage may also play a role. It has long been alleged individuals of Celtic or Cherokee ancestry are more likely to be abductees. Whitley Strieber wrote of the letters sent to him and his wife Anne:

> It was not a matter of 10 or 15 percent of the correspondents having recognizably Scots-Irish names. In the random sample we took of five hundred names, it was 55 percent. This kind of ethnic specificity, coupled with the abundant fairy

lore common among the Celtic peoples means something, it must. But what?[1066]

In 2014, Jeff Ritzmann, Jeremy Vaeni, and Drs. D. Ellen K. Tarr, Kimbal E. Cooper, and Tyler A. Kokjohn published findings from Project Core, an ambitious anonymous survey designed to gather information on persons reporting paranormal experiences. The respondents were 57% male, a statistically significant portion calling to mind male vulnerability to faeries, while a preponderance of participants were of Celtic/Irish, German, English, and/or Native American ancestry.[1067]

Each of these ethnic groups has a rich tradition of faerie belief. But—to paraphrase Strieber—what does it mean? A compelling, if enigmatic resonance to Celtic tradition can be found in a cryptic phrase related through abductee Betty Andreasson. During one of her hypnotic regressions, Andreasson lapsed into an unrecognizable tongue, presumably channeled from her extraterrestrial contacts. The language was transcribed phonetically.

A reader of *The Andreasson Affair* reached out to researcher and author Raymond Fowler after parsing the passage. According to the reader, "the language matched remarkably well with old Gaelic," a language family indigenous to the British Isles. "When translated, the message read, 'Children of the northern peoples, you wander in impenetrable darkness. Your mother mourns.'"[1068]

RISKS: HOME LIFE

Harvard psychiatrist John Mack observed: "When I began this work I was struck by how many abductees came from broken homes or had one or more alcoholic parents. There also seems to be a 'poor fit' between some individual experiencers and their parents, and a number of my cases complain about coldness and emotional deprivation within the family."[1069]

Mack's allusion to unsatisfactory home lives certainly calls to mind Munro's hypothesis that changelings were failure to thrive infants. Abuse among modern alien abductees can also be seen in the mistreatment of suspected changelings in centuries past. The dysfunctional nature of abductee families is so prevalent some speculate children are taken *because* they are mistreated.

"Results showed that persons reporting abductions were psychologically indistinguishable from those who had other types of UFO encounters," wrote University of Connecticut psychologist Kenneth Ring of his findings. "However, UFO experiencers in general, while not more fantasy-prone than their controls, reported more sensitivity to non-ordinary realities as children, as well as a higher incidence of child abuse and trauma than controls."[1070]

In most indigenous cultures, shamans—the tribe's intercessors with the Otherworld—are selected because trauma in their childhood brought them into close contact with spirits. During this trauma, they are often brought to the brink of death—a liminal zone, if you will—before encountering entities who escort them into the Otherworld. While there, their bodies are dismembered and reconstituted, with magical crystals implanted inside them as mystical transceivers. Upon recovery they become spiritual leaders, exhibiting psi abilities, facilitating communication with the spirits, healing fellow tribe members, and escorting souls to the afterlife.

The comparison to modern alien abductees, noted at length by Eddie Bullard and others, draws itself.[1071]

Besides abuse, other environmental factors have been claimed but exhibit weaker correlations. Some contend children living near military bases, or those with family members in the armed services, are more susceptible.

"While it is true that most abductees have a family member in the military, that is also true of just about everyone in the country, so that cannot be a significant factor," Turner wrote.[1072]

RISKS: LOCATION

Previous cases illustrate no shortage of children abducted from their bedrooms; like faeries plucking babies from unguarded cradles, aliens are often accused of robbing children directly from their beds.

At the same time, children are often taken from other locales. Schoolyards are surprisingly dangerous, if the Voronezh and San Francisco de Chiu-Chiu cases are to believed (recall how South American *duendes* are said to prowl schools).

Above all, however, the wilderness—once the dwelling of faeries—remains perilous.

- In 1959, David Pelley, then seven, saw a UFO hovering above a circular clearing in Whiting, New Jersey. "I looked up and saw a grayish circular object perhaps 300 feet overhead," he later wrote. The object hummed like "a very high pitch electrical motor," rooting him to the spot. He next recalled his mother calling him home. "It was about 6:00 p.m. and I had missed supper." Thenceforth he experienced strange apparitions, afflictions, and psychic abilities. The clearing, described by Pelley as a "perfect circle" devoid of any small trees or rocks, brought to his mind a UFO landing site—but the resemblance to a faerie ring is equally noteworthy.[1073]

- Summer 1974: a childhood witness and his friend explored a wooded ravine outside Spokane, Washington. Approaching the crest of a hill, they encountered a landed craft and two Greys. The witness's next memory was undergoing a procedure in a "dental chair" before awakening atop the hill, several hours of time elapsed. The witness later visited the spot with his siblings and made "a small circle of stones and boulders in this clearing. It had the distinct shape and feel of a fairy ring."[1074]

- In the early 1990s, Deborah Truncale interviewed Barbara, the nine-year-old daughter of a military man from El Cajon, California. One overcast afternoon Barbara and her friends discovered an abandoned shack in a field they wanted to explore. Unable to enter, they instead began playing, and Barbara shortly noticed "a round silver thing" hovering above the group. Her next memory was of looking at her watch—three hours later.[1075] (Abandoned buildings, particularly mills, were favorite haunts of certain fae folk.[1076])

As with faeries, documented interactions between children and alleged extraterrestrials have taken place in proximity to berry bushes. In Nazi-occupied France, 13-year-old Madeleine Arnoux was returning home from the Le Verger market on her bicycle when she stopped to gather wild berries by the roadside. In spite of the looming clouds and general storminess of the day, Arnoux continued deeper into the forest, plucking berries as she went, until she happened upon something in the thicket: a grey, motionless object the size of an automobile. The object was accompanied by several beings, three feet tall and wearing brown uniforms.[1077]

In a 1972 letter to French UFOlogy magazine *Lumières Dans La Nuit*, Arnoux wrote:

> How much time did this mutual observation last? I cannot say, but I remember the oppressive atmosphere, still worsened by the thundery weather and of my impression to be unable to move... Suddenly I managed to react and wanted to pick up my bicycle again; which lay within a few meters.

The time to bend down and, by looking up at the strange appearance again, there was nothing any more. Only, at this place, the trees were agitated by a violent wind. I did not think of looking up in the air, where I would have undoubtedly still have seen the machine which flew away.[1078]

Note not only the storm—associated with the Good Folk—but also the implied missing time.

Twenty years after Arnoux's encounter, in 1964, five young boys from Conklin, New York, were playing around a field known for its apples and huckleberries when they spied a large, shiny craft shaped like an inverted bowl. Nearby walked a three-foot-tall being in a helmet, which one of the boys thought was after their fruit. After a time, the boys speculated the warm July sun was making the entity thirsty, and left to fetch some water, only to be detained by adults for their absurd—yet consistent—story.[1079]

Wild places are, of course, traditionally places of spiritual awakening, from Jesus' 40 days and 40 nights in the desert to Aboriginal walkabouts. Faerie hills, the very wilderness locations children were advised to avoid, are known for anomalous lights and—perhaps—alien abductions.

In one sensational tale from 1994, a pair of transparent tetrahedrons surmounted by balls of fire approached campers atop Wiltshire's Silbury Hill—considered in some traditions a gateway to Fairyland.[1080] Inside each structure sat a small figure, cross-legged. The tetrahedrons came within 20 feet of the observers before silently exploding and withdrawing from Silbury in a glow of light. The witnesses were left with two hours of missing time and recurring nightmares.[1081]

Any supernatural lapse of time in the wilderness would have been ascribed to faeries or witches in times past, as would any roadside encounter with a nonhuman entity. Journeys are liminal—travelers are neither at their starting point nor their destination, but rather somewhere in-between, making them ripe for supernatural intervention. In the Fairy Faith, travelers were prime targets for becoming pixie led; today alien abductees are often taken from cars.

"Parapsychologists claim that poltergeists always operate in the presence of children, usually a boy or girl at the age of puberty," Keel wrote in 1968. "So contemplate this: in the majority of the cases I have investigated in which low-level objects have closely pursued automobiles there was either a child in the car, or the driver or one of the occupants was a *school teacher*."[1082]

Some examples of children taken from cars:

- Bill, a male witness near Salt Lake City, Utah, noticed a mysterious humming object while changing a tire in June 1969. Inside the car, his female friend and her 2-year-old son began to panic. Bill revealed under hypnosis that the three of them were lifted out of their bodies and into a white, circular room where the beings—white, with large heads and large eyes—sat them in examination chairs and performed some sort of procedure. After returning to their car, the UFO followed them until early morning.[1083]

- One night in 1972, Jack Stevens (pseudonym) and his brother were riding with their mother near Nampa, Idaho, when a large, bright disc appeared, causing the engine to fail. Jack, then 12, recalled going aboard the craft for six hours, leaving the others behind; upon return, they only recalled a crop-duster in the sky and "a strange animal in the road." Jack's mother and brother failed to notice anything amiss, despite arriving home at dawn.[1084]

- August 21, 1980: Megan Elliott and her 18-month-old daughter, Renee, were riding through East Texas when the radio malfunctioned, the lights dimmed, and a piercing noise filled the air. Under hypnosis Megan said her car levitated into a large, metallic object in the sky, where they followed a short, hairless being into an examination room. They disrobed and probes were inserted into Megan's nose and Renee's navel. Though Megan thought the encounter had lasted two weeks, they were returned five miles from home the same evening they left. Shortly thereafter, an earache and rash Renee had prior to the encounter miraculously healed.[1085]

One wonders if perhaps taking multiple generations at once provides some advantage. It certainly brings to mind the manner in which faeries preyed upon mothers and children alike.

LEVITATION

Unlike faeries, aliens rarely seize victims bodily. Granted, there are exceptions to this rule—Virginia Horton, for example, was lifted up by "a humanoid type person" following her elusive deer encounter—but by-and-large, it appears some type of technology, or at least a technique resembling technology, is employed.[1086]

Child abductees regularly report their experiences beginning with the sensation of levitation. This act may be physical or astral (i.e. an out-of-body experience) and is commonly, but not always, accompanied by a shaft of light. Abductees often report the fantastical ability to travel through walls and ceilings while levitated. This key aspect of the alien abduction narrative— alongside astral travel, bright lights, feelings of peace, and a return with newfound psychic abilities—bears a striking resemblance to the Near Death Experience.

"Whitley, this has something to do with what we call death," Anne Strieber reportedly told her author and experiencer husband of the phenomenon. Alien abductees regularly experience what can only be called poltergeist activity in their homes, while some even claim deceased loved ones appear in their abductions, calling to mind the association between faeries and the departed.[1087]

Whatever this levitation technology is—if it can be understood as such—seems far from perfect. In 1937, Australia's *The Northern Miner* carried a story about a Himalayan infant who was "carried away on a beam of light" in the Kangra Valley. Two dozen villagers chased the light for several hundred yards before it extinguished, dropping and killing the baby.[1088]

Levitation was, of course, a favored abduction method of the fae folk. Modern tales of infants misplaced from their cribs evoke descriptions of aborted faerie abductions, where babes were dropped to the floor. A witness told John Carpenter she suffered missing time, vague memories of beings with pear-shaped heads, and anomalous lights in her home; "her six-week old baby went missing from her third-floor bedroom crib, only to be discovered neatly tucked away in the bassinet one floor below." Leaves were left behind in the crib.[1089] Another case, investigated by Ben Moss, saw a baby disappear—from an alarmed, locked home—for three hours in Virginia before reappearing unharmed.[1090]

LURES: VOICES AND PLAY

Like faeries before them, today's aliens are not shy about implementing lures to attract children. One of Hopkins' early hypnotic subjects recalled "an imaginary dog who took me for walks to places where children couldn't go." While Hopkins deemed this a screen memory of a Grey alien, it is interesting to wonder what he would have made of the aforementioned Irish boy lured from his home by a faerie dog.[1091]

One of the more common methods shared by aliens and faeries is the calling of names. Abductees report this their entire lives, beginning in youth. During one of Virginia Horton's episodes, she remembered approaching a bright light in the woods, accompanied by "almost like a whisper, 'Virginia… Virginia,' and I think it was in my head that they were calling me... And I realize that ever since I was a little kid I had this memory... of having my name called, sometimes having my name called in my head."[1092]

"I heard an unfamiliar voice calling my name," Bret Oldham said of another childhood encounter. "As I opened the door from the kitchen to the mudroom, I noticed that the bright light had disappeared, and it was now dark again... I took just a few steps into the mudroom when two of the Grey aliens popped up in the side windows."

The entities told Oldham, "We're not here to hurt you. We are your friends. We want you to come with us for a little while."[1093]

Children are attracted by other sounds as well. In 1984, a young girl walking by a park with her dog in Puerto Rico noticed the sound of children playing. Looking through her binoculars she, and later her sister, observed short Greys who seemed to summon a large sphere of light from the sky. The object hovered over the entities, beaming them aboard one-by-one, before disappearing at high speed.[1094]

What would have happened if the Puerto Rican witness had approached the "children" to play? Like those joining the faerie dance, she would have likely been taken—as other children have.

Adults hear similar sounds—in 1994 a couple storm watching in Davis, California, had their parked automobile buzzed by a white, green, blue, and orange glowing craft. According to their submission to the National UFO Recording Center (NUFORC), they heard what sounded like children giggling as they left the area.[1095]

One American witness prone to missing time recalled playing with "rust-colored beings" on a Brazilian farm in his youth, sometimes supervised by a man and woman of the typical "Nordic" type—entities appearing as beautiful, fit human beings. He told investigator Don Worley that the couple took him underground once to show him "scenes of massive wave destruction."[1096]

In another example, two boys playing behind the family barn in Salem, Oregon recalled mysterious "bald kids" who would play with them in the 1970s. The youngest boy, five, experienced a UFO sighting and missing time.[1097] Besides these general frivolities, aliens also play games: on February 18, 1985, in Tynset, Norway, doll-sized entities in helmets allegedly emerged from a UFO to play hide-and-seek with village children for several hours.[1098]

Hopkins noted this modality of child abduction in 1992.

> In this acquisition procedure, the UFO occupants lure the child or young person away from other children or protecting adults. The child might be playing outside in the daytime with a group of friends and sees a little figure—someone about her size—in the background motioning and waving. The child responds to the presence of this new "playmate." Sometimes she is indoors and notices, through the window, a group of "different-looking children"; she is intrigued and goes outside to play with them.[1099]

More elaborate versions of this ruse include offering abductees toys, or, in the case of an Australian nurse named Sharon, *an entire playground*. Under hypnosis, Sharon remembered regularly entering a large orange globe of light that delivered her to a type of playground, where other children arrived under similar circumstances. The area appeared to be complete with artificial turf and a dome substituting the sky. Sharon felt the area might be "a constructed deception just to make all the children 'feel at home.'" The captives—around 50, all told—were then escorted to a room of tables where examinations were performed by reptilian creatures in white coats, all supervised by tall, silent Grey aliens.[1100]

One need not believe such a fanciful story to find it unsettling. The notion of anything, natural or supernatural, leveraging childlike fun for nefarious purposes is chilling. What are we to make of a 2004 study from the Universities of Washington and Oregon, which determined that 65% of children have imaginary playmates by age seven—the same age most abductees report their first contact?[1101]

DESTINATIONS

Though the answer seems obvious at first, the question of where abductees are taken is not as cut-and-dry as many assume. We have already noted the difficulty in establishing that examination rooms are aboard alien spacecraft.

While alien abductees are not taken to Fairyland, they might as well be. Many accounts describe children taken underground. Patsy Wingate came forward when two Eastern Kentucky youths disappeared near Pikeville, claiming to have seen visions of children locked in cages underneath a local mountain. Wingate, a repeat UFO witness, may have been a crank—but again, the motivic resonance to underground faerie realms cannot be denied.[1102]

Equally resonant (and equally dubious) is the abduction of a mother and her six-year-old son near Cimarron, New Mexico. She claimed they were taken to a subterranean installation—perhaps the famed "underground alien base at Dulce" of UFO mythology—where unpleasant examinations were administered.[1103]

Most abducted children find themselves inside what can be presumed to be, at least among the ETH proponents, spacecraft. Witnesses often report seeing other children, sometimes dozens, in these settings.

- A San Antonio, Texas, abductee reported being taken upwards into a floating object by large head-ed, large-eyed aliens in 1942. Inside a brightly lit two-story room, the witness saw male and female children of every race, nude, frightened, and crying. After a brief medical examination, they took the witness home.[1104]

- In July 1953, twelve-year-old Gerry Armstrong blacked out while skipping school in the English woods. His next memory was of an angry teacher rousing him. Under hypnosis, Armstrong revealed watching a light descend into the forest, followed by two short, grey, large-eyed figures approaching him. A voice in his head urged him to not be afraid. The beings floated Armstrong to the ladder of a landed craft. After boarding, he felt the craft take off and roamed its bright interior, where he saw a large dome full of children. Armstrong's experience ended when a woman in red ripped the cross off his necklace, telling him, "It's not right to worship." Like the queen of the fae folk, she seemed offended by the icon.[1105]

- Six-year-old Alain Duchesne, a future recurring abductee, and friends were playing by Quebec's St. Lawrence River in July 1971 when they noted a multicolored light in the sky. After moments of wondering, the children realized that the light seemed to be collecting them, one-by-one. Duchesne fled, but lost consciousness. He woke up alongside his friends, exhausted and dazed; they had been missing for three hours.[1106]

While the contactee literature of the 1950s and 1960s is peppered with claims of visits to alien worlds, this does not seem to be a strong trend among abducted children. This comes as a surprise—if child abductions are the product of a rich imagination, certainly they would be less mundane.

The few fantastic stories where children claim to have visited alien worlds strain credulity, as in the case of Russian schoolboy Maxim Zhirkov. Zhirkov said that after a tennis match in 1990 two tall, helmeted humanoids in a spherical craft whisked him away to their treeless planet. There were no buildings, but the beings showed Zhirkov "silent people," or the souls of humans who had passed away (shades of the faerie host). The aliens then parachuted Zhirkov back to Earth, where he was found pale and speechless.[1107]

Naturally, such reports are predicated on abductees who have returned. But how many children have been taken by unseen forces and never come home?

On September 3, 1966, Ecuadorian teens Manoel Pereira (14) and José Sotuyo (14) were walking along a mountain path when they spied a saucer shaped light. Waving their flashlight in its direction, the boys signaled "Land, friend, please" in Morse code. The craft allegedly landed, releasing three tiny humanoids. After a pleasant conversation, the boys were invited onboard, but declined. Their parting gift was a device best described as an extraterrestrial flashlight—according to the tale, it was allegedly confiscated by the government shortly thereafter.

A peculiar coda sets the story apart from typical child abductions: Manoel and José disappeared a week before Christmas, never to be seen again.[1108]

Chapter 14:
"It's Time to Take It"
Missing Fetuses

It has given me so much—she has—but did she also take my daughter? If so, then to what end? I sense that my child is out there somewhere, perhaps living a superconscious life, or did she die in abnegation, fodder for some cosmic predator? Or is it that we are all both things?
— Whitley Strieber, *The Super Natural*

In the summer of 1974, the psychiatrist of a 26-year-old woman named Ann—at an impasse to explain her recurring memories of diminutive nighttime invaders—referred her to UFO investigator Barry Taff. Ann told Taff that several small humanoids materialized in her bedroom one night and paralyzed her before taking her to a blindingly bright room. Once there, the Greys telepathically related she would be examined but had nothing to fear and would forget the experience. Ann blacked out when the painful probes entered her every orifice.

The procedure repeated itself a few months later, and this time Ann found herself inexplicably pregnant; not only was she using birth control, but she had not been with a man for months. Several weeks after she told Taff the news, another visit occurred, after which her pregnancy—medically verified—mysteriously ended.[1109]

UNHEALTHY OBSESSIONS

Aliens, like faeries, seem preoccupied with sex and reproduction. Sexuality is an integral component to whatever lies behind the UFO phenomenon. Witnesses see phallic craft, are stripped naked and sexually assaulted—some researchers even claim alien abductees masturbate more than average.[1110]

Even rational arguments mix together UFOs and reproduction. In addition to suggesting alien abductions express latent BDSM desires,[1111] skeptics dismiss abductions as birth memories,[1112] Greys as psychosocial representations of fetuses,[1113] and flying saucers as breast-shaped images from the sexually repressed id.[1114] The whole affair is ironic, given the lack of genitalia in the image of the ubiquitous Grey alien.

The phenomenon's interest focuses primarily upon pregnancy. Expectant mothers have been contacted and observed for decades—as early as 1957, Venusians appeared in the living room of English citizen Cynthia Appleton, accurately predicting the weight, time of birth, and gender of the "space baby" in her womb.[1115] Similar predictions occur through today, an unbroken lineage stretching into antiquity wherein divine beings delivered birth revelations—consider how Mary learned she carried Christ.

Not every mother warmly receives such visitations. On March 8, 1973, Pennsylvania resident Sharyn Stemmel and her son saw a flying saucer covered in red lights from their car. Stemmel, eight months pregnant, warily told investigators she was frightened "they" might be observing her "to find out how all that works."[1116]

Female abductions regularly include gynecological examinations. Even in the 1961 Hill Case, one of the earliest such events, Betty received a painful needle in her navel, later deemed a pregnancy or fertility test.[1117] Pam Owens, five months pregnant at the age of 19 in 1978, remembered a similar procedure under hypnosis after a red light pulled her from her car near Trier, Germany.[1118] According to a NUFORC submission, a Tennessee witness, six months pregnant, suffered an identical experience the same year.[1119] Spacemen are nothing if not consistent in this regard.

Interfering with fetuses—and, as discussed in the next chapter, gathering sperm and ova—is a clear variation on child abduction. This motivic resonance is amplified when children are directly taken from mothers' wombs.

MISCARRIAGES & MISSING FETUSES

Pregnancy complications are blamed on the supernatural in practically every indigenous culture across the globe. In these worldviews, robust spirit ecosystems lurk just beyond sight, constantly poised to steal unborn children. It comes as little surprise we ascribe these powers to aliens today.

Miscarriages in abduction lore are sometimes given the clinical, vaguely offensive name "retrievals."[1120] Regardless of their reality or connection to UFOs, these events are physically and emotionally traumatic for survivors.

A few selections:

- In 1978, the Indiana family of Pamara Johnson experienced three hours' missing time after seeing a UFO on their way home. Vaginal bleeding began that evening. The next day, a doctor who had confirmed Pamara's pregnancy proclaimed her fetus missing. Over time, she slowly, consciously recalled to investigators that "four small aliens" had "used a vibrating wire device to take her fetus."[1121]

- In 1986, Laura awoke to two strange beings waving at her window in Benoni, South Africa. They walked through the wall, bathing the room in golden light. One of the naked, hairless, pear-headed beings, emanating love and peace, told Laura she was its daughter. This occurred three subsequent nights. Laura and her husband, who never roused, were trying to conceive at the time—despite three confirmed pregnancies, each miscarried around three months.[1122]

- Around 1988, Whitley Strieber suffered a night of intense, realistic dreams featuring the hideous blue beings from his earlier encounters. That same evening, Anne, who had withheld the news of her pregnancy, had a miscarriage.[1123]

- Australia, August 7, 1993: After seeing a circle of orange lights in the sky, Kelly and her husband approached a brilliant light in the road. It vanished, leaving the couple with missing time. Kelly noticed a new scar beneath her navel and began menstruating early. After 3 ½ weeks of bleeding, she was hospitalized for a womb infection from a self-terminating pregnancy. Kelly later consciously recalled hearing several tall, red-eyed beings on the road saying, "We mean you no harm. We are a peaceful people."[1124]

A variety of scenarios occur: some specifically recall retrievals, while others simply experience reproductive difficulties. These spontaneous tragedies can occur rapidly and subtly—it is not uncommon for abductees, seeking abortions for medically confirmed pregnancies, to have surgeons inform them that no evidence of fetal tissue can be found.[1125]

UFO witnesses may experience miscarriages even in the absence of explicit abduction memories. In 1982, two pregnant women from Pecém, Brazil, spotting an orange, airborne light, ran half a kilometer before collapsing. One child was born two months premature, the other aborted after only two months' gestation.[1126] Similar events unfolded two years later in the Netherlands where Ine Wagenvoort, four months pregnant, ran from an orange sphere in the sky and lost her baby.[1127]

Naturally, stress and physical exertion can play a role in these cases. Such factors are less likely, however, in the November 2, 1988, case of Joana Rodrigues Ferreira. She and her daughter were taking vegetables to market from their farm in Carnaubinha, Brazil, when they caught an orb "the color of fire" disappearing behind a schoolhouse. When they reached a small stream, the UFO reappeared, filling the air with light and a loud scratching noise. Two short, identical, glowing "men" appeared beside a nearby tree, prompting Ferreira's daughter to drag her to the nearest home for refuge.

"I was five months pregnant, and for seven days after this happened, I was sick with headaches and fever and no energy," Ferreira told investigator Bob Pratt. "Then I went to the hospital in Paraipaba, and I miscarried there."[1128]

The tale contains familiar motifs, including the presence of a child and a school. Had Ferreira been in Papua New Guinea, her proximity to the stream and subsequent miscarriage would likely be interpreted as an interaction with the *wala*.

TRENDS & TECHNIQUES

It is unclear how frequently abductees suffer these complications. Anecdotally, they seem widespread. However, a 1996 study by the Mutual UFO Network (MUFON) claimed that only 34 of 149 female subjects experienced some form of reproductive interference during their encounters, indicating a relatively weak trend.

"The findings do not support an assertion that most captives are subjected to procedures related to reproduction," wrote project manager Dan Wright.[1129]

On balance, a questionnaire implemented by Kathleen Marden and Denise Stoner in 2012 suggested that 69% of female respondents reported gynecological problems, compared to the control group of 33%. The sample consisted of only 18 men and 32 women, again making it difficult to parse the problem's scope.[1130]

Clearer trends suggest abductees who claim miscarriages or missing fetuses are likely to do so more than once—typically three to five times, though higher incidences are recorded.[1131] They are usually reported two to three months into a pregnancy,[1132] a period in which 80% of all natural miscarriages occur.[1133] (Hopkins claimed to have investigated cases where fetuses disappeared as late as the seventh month.[1134]) Abductees living in fear of miscarriages can develop phobias regarding pregnancy, often choosing to not start families.[1135]

Whether consciously or under hypnosis, abductees generally remember the moment of retrieval as a surgical procedure, or at least an event with surgical pageantry. In David Jacobs' *Secret Life*, abductee Lynn Miller recalled a tall, "doctor" Grey poking her in the side and declaring, "It's time to take it." A long, dark instrument tipped with a "cup" was thrust inside her, causing a sucking sensation.

"It feels like he's tearing something inside at first," she told Jacobs under hypnosis. "They're not too gentle. I keep telling them it hurts." The fetus, once extracted, was placed in a liquid-filled container. In another instance, Miller sat in a chair, legs bent, while a Grey alien caught her miscarried fetus in a "little Pyrex thing."[1136]

Another of Jacobs' subjects, Tracy Knapp, related her fetus extraction under hypnosis: "My legs are up, and I'm getting snipped, but internally. Something's snipping... Something burned, burned. A fluid burns me, burns... It's put inside of me." Knapp heard snipping inside her like "cutting threads" with "long, tiny scissors."[1137]

What are we to make of the hundreds of cases where no procedure is recalled, yet mysterious miscarriages occur? Is something else to blame?

Smells and food, oddly enough, may provide clues. Among the most common smells noticed in UFO sightings and alien abductions are the odors of "rotten eggs" (i.e. hydrogen sulfide) and cinnamon. Chronic, low-level exposure to hydrogen sulfide can cause miscarriages and reproductive complications.[1138] Copious consumption of raw cinnamon, on the other hand, is a widespread folk medicine abortifacient.[1139]

While no abduction cases explicitly feature individuals eating cinnamon, plenty of examples exist where a possible birth control may have been administered. In 1975, 16-year-old "Jane Murphy" (pseudonym) claimed several strange entities took her aboard their craft and performed a gynecological examination. After raping her, one of the creatures offered Jane a flavorless "coloured pill" which she took.[1140]

We are still left with UFO witnesses who experience miscarriages in the absence of abductions. Perhaps simple proximity to these objects can cause reproductive complications. In 1988 Michael Persinger noted UFO "flap" areas—locales where a series of sightings take place in a short timeframe—seem to have a disproportionate amount of cancer incidence among their population. Additionally, UFO witnesses experience symptoms consistent with radiation exposure, and field UFOlogists seem more greatly afflicted by cancer.

"Although the link between reproductive problems, such as spontaneous abortions and miscarriages and cancer incidence has not been established, both dysfunctions have been associated with exposures to environmental electromagnetic fields," Persinger wrote. "The sensitivity of the testicles to low frequency electromagnetic fields seems particularly acute."[1141]

Female witnesses experience menstrual difficulties even when not pregnant. On January 6, 1976, Janet Stewart of Bethel, Minnesota, encountered a red, glowing orb with green blinking lights in the sky on her way to pick up a friend. The object continued to follow them for two miles, and the next day both women swore they suffered from severe menstrual cramps and bleeding offset from their normal cycles.[1142] Were low frequency electromagnetic fields to blame?

SKEPTICAL AND SUPERNATURAL EXPLANATIONS

Missing fetus syndrome (MFS) is among the most divisive topics in UFOlogy. Skeptics understandably cite a host of conditions, beyond spontaneous abortion, which can appear as a lost pregnancy. Secondary amenorrhea—a cessation of menstrual bleeding unaccompanied by contraceptives, menopause, or pregnancy—can give patients the impression they are pregnant even though they are not.[1143] Other conditions include blighted ovum, where the embryo is absent from the beginning or quickly degenerates; missed abortions, wherein a fetus dies but is not aborted; hydatidform moles, which cause fertilized eggs to rapidly degenerate; and pseudocyesis, or false pregnancy, a rare condition where individuals show presumptive signs of pregnancy in the absence of a fetus.[1144]

Some conditions result in positive pregnancy tests while others do not, giving each varying degrees of explicative power. In any case, it takes little imagination to see how the UFOlogical narrative could help non-abductees cope with the perceived loss of a pregnancy.

Even UFOlogists must admit many MFS claims can be solved using rational medical investigation. In 1991, Ann Druffel handily solved the case of Morgana Van Klausen, a California witness who claimed four years of UFO entity encounters, including missing time, anomalous lights, and gynecological examinations from a short, white bedroom invader.

On February 28, 1989, Morgana's obstetrician confirmed she was not only unexpectedly pregnant, but it appeared, quote, "healthy." One month later, no heartbeat was detected, and the fetus was deemed dead —a missed abortion, it seemed. Following her procedure, Morgana's surgeon noted "no fetal parts" were found, peculiar for missed abortions.

Distressed, Morgana reached out to Druffel, who organized an in-depth investigation. After conferring with several professionals, Druffel determined the entire affair was a matter of miscommunication. Morgana's "healthy" diagnosis meant developments in her womb were continuing apace, but there was no indicator of a healthy fetus yet. When the surgeon commented "no fetal parts" were found a month later, it referenced a lack of fetal development—even though the fetal pole, or gestational sac, was intact and consistent with a healthy pregnancy.[1145]

While rationality should always be turned to as first resort, the pregnancy complications of other abductees are less easily explained.

Mainstream UFOlogy holds that MFS is part of an ongoing extraterrestrial-human hybridization plan. This particular topic raises numerous questions and considerations addressed in the next chapter; for now, consider the intriguing theory proposed by physicist Hal Puthoff—who in the 1970s investigated remote viewing at the Stanford Research Institute—in an overlooked 1982 letter to the editor of *Flying Saucer Review*:

> Since UFO occupants are often reported to have the appearance of young children, or, more often, foetuses, has anyone ever looked for a correlation between [close encounters of the third kind] and miscarriages or stillborns in the family of contactees?

> The concept I wish to raise is that perhaps "other-dimensionals" begin entry into our realm during the process of birth, and those that abort for some reason or another end up participating in a reality that is closely tied to the physical realm, both with regards to their own personal form, and with regard to the desire to interact with us—sort of "half-made-its," as it were.[1146]

Puthoff's proposal revives Fairy Faith concepts of unbaptized children joining the ranks of the fae folk; one informant told

Evans Wentz "the piskies are the spirits of dead-born children."[1147] Folkloric notions from other parts of the world support Puthoff's theory as well—one type of Australian *pmere kwetethe* is the soul of a child awaiting entrance into the mortal world.[1148]

Do miscarriages plague those touched by the supernatural? Or—conversely—do miscarriages *allow* the supernatural to touch us?

FERTILITY & ANOMALOUS PREGNANCIES

Occasionally abductees experience reproductive difficulties far beyond missing fetuses and miscarriages. Sometimes their fertility is permanently altered.

According to Vladimir Rubtsov, a Ukrainian woman awoke the night of January 25, 1987, to find approximately ten humanlike figures gathered around her bed. Projecting a sensation of joy, the beings extracted a light-colored disc from the witness, telling her, before they faded away, that it was her ovum. From that moment onward, the witness suffered persistent gynecological problems, including an inability to conceive.[1149]

More commonly, infertile witnesses enjoy newfound fertility following their encounters. During her April 1975 abduction, Alice Johnson mentioned to her examiner—a humanlike entity of average height "with a transparent covering over the face"—that she was unable to bear children. The being waved an instrument over her stomach, producing a tingling sensation; she later conceived.[1150] Extreme cases involve abductees experiencing pregnancies well into menopause,[1151] or even after hysterectomies.[1152]

As supporters of the ETH, Jacobs and Hopkins explained these anomalies as the result of "extrauterine gestational sacs," artificial wombs created by aliens and placed inside fertile and infertile abductees alike.[1153] The idea is no longer far-fetched— speculation has become reality, at least among humans. Scientists in 2017 grew sheep in artificial wombs at the Children's Hospital of Philadelphia, but the process is still in its germinal stage. "It's complete science fiction to think that you can take an embryo and get it through the early developmental process and put it on our machine without the mother being the critical element there," said Alan Flake, fetal surgeon and author of the resulting study.[1154]

Even in the face of miraculous scientific advances, non-physical, non-ETH solutions abound to the mystery of spontaneous fertility. The capriciousness with which aliens seem to give and take fertility recalls the manner in which Katherine Briggs referred to faeries as "in the main fertility spirits, [who] could be blamed for hard delivery or barrenness."[1155] Faeries aided not only in the fecundity of the land, but of mankind as well. *Mother Hulda*, the Germanic prototypical "Fairy Godmother," is "associated with the winter snows that invigorate the land's dormant fertility. As queen of the mound people [faeries], she establishes their credentials as fertility spirits."[1156]

In "The Doe in the Woods" by Madame d'Aulnoy—the French writer who coined the term *contes de fees* (fairytales)—an infertile queen makes a pilgrimage to a healing spring, where she encounters a faerie in the guise of a crawfish. The crawfish whisks her to the faerie palace, where it is revealed the queen will soon bear a daughter. While d'Aulnoy was not necessarily a folklorist, her story speaks to the 17th century belief that beings such as faeries could manipulate fertility.[1157]

Returning to the modern era, UFO experiencers often discover their newfound fertility through anomalous pregnancies. Like MFS, they are anecdotally quite common, but hard statistics are lacking. In June 1993, Australian researcher Keith Basterfield found that only nine percent of female abductees became unexpectedly pregnant following their contacts.[1158]

Pregnancies may be unanticipated among abductees for a multitude of reasons. Bret Oldham's wife became pregnant despite their use of birth control.[1159] An Australian witness researched by Jenny Randles experienced a phantom pregnancy at 18, followed by another at 25, complete with miscarriage, even though she swore to have not had intercourse in "many months" in each instance.[1160] In other cases, the husband of a pregnant abductee may be sterile.[1161] Research into anomalous pregnancies is difficult—after all, no foolproof birth control exists, and witnesses can omit details of sexual activity or infidelity.

The next chapter discusses popularly held motives and means behind these anomalous pregnancies, namely the alleged hybridization program between extraterrestrials and humans. Before tackling that sizeable topic, however, it may be enlightening to address oft-ignored quirks tangentially related to MFS.

ALIEN BABY ANIMAL ABDUCTION

Missing fetuses among humans get all the press in UFOlogy— but the practice doesn't stop there. Extraterrestrials exhibit interest in the offspring of species beyond *Homo sapiens*.

Witness testimony occasionally describes a zoo-like environment during abductions, suggesting that UFOs may indeed abduct baby animals. One woman Budd Hopkins interviewed said, "They have baby everythings up here. They have baby babies, they have baby horses, they have baby kangaroos, baby mice, and they have baby-baby-baby—everything's *babies*! God, it's like Universal Motherhood!"

Cattle—whose unexplained mutilations are commonly attributed to UFOs—feature in a number of missing fetus cases. In 1975 a glowing red light appeared over a farmer's barn in Ellsworth, Wisconsin; several days later, a veterinarian told him his cow, long pregnant, had given birth "at least three days ago," though no calf was found.[1162] Cattle mutilations occasionally involve similar instances where pregnant cows are missing fetuses with no obvious miscarriage.[1163]

Certainly, any extraterrestrial race might wish to document every species on our planet—but wouldn't it be more sensible to gather genetic material from a slaughterhouse on one occasion and be finished, rather than perpetrate countless livestock mutilations? On the other hand, Irish farmers, finding their livestock unexpectedly deceased, understood cattle deaths as faerie harvests.[1164] Even in times of famine, these carcasses laid untouched, deemed changelings left by the fae folk that would sicken anyone foolish enough to eat their flesh.[1165]

Credo Mutwa, a South African shaman whose experiences were recorded by John Mack, reported a peculiar amphibious fetus. Mutwa once described "fellows like little dolls" who took him into the bush, paralyzed him, and shoved painful probes up his nose. During this experience, he was shown "a creature like a baby frog, suspended in a purplish liquid." Granted, this may have been a human-alien hybrid, as discussed in the next chapter, but Mutwa's "baby frog" description gives one pause.[1166]

Oddly enough, pregnant rabbits and their kittens are regularly targeted. In the 1970s, Londoner Philip Molava experienced bedroom visitations from hooded entities after four baby rabbits disappeared from his care over the course of three weeks (some rabbits eat their litter, perhaps rendering this mystery not-so-mysterious). [1167] In 1976, a friend of Betty Hill's had all her pregnant female rabbits disappear, while the males and young females were left behind.[1168] Ted Rice, the abductee at the center of Karla Turner's 1994 book *Masquerade of Angels*, reported finding a baby rabbit in his quilt one morning, seemingly from out of thin air.[1169]

Why the extraterrestrial interest in rabbits? No UFOlogical solution springs to mind... but a faerie explanation might.

A Japanese folktale tells how the children of Fairy Mother of the Sky cried to her one night in boredom. Being a sunny day, there were no stars to twinkle and no thunder drums to beat. The Fairy Mother suggested they roll snow into balls and toss them across the sky. As she lit the stars in the sky that evening, the Fairy Mother asked her children why they cried. "Our snowballs all fell through the sky floor. They all fell through the twinkly holes of the stars," said the children. The Fairy Mother threw her torch at the naughty snowballs, scorching their tails and creating rabbits, the faeries' playmates.[1170]

From a broader perspective, the disappearance of baby animals resonates with the calumniated-wife motif found in fairytales. "Here a villain steals a young wife's newborn child, sometimes replacing it with a baby animal, sometimes claiming that the mother cannibalized her own offspring," wrote D.L. Ashliman. "Either way the heroine stands accused of the most horrible breach of motherhood thinkable, but after a period of conflict and suffering, justice prevails."[1171]

THE FETUS IN MAGICAL PRACTICE

Though not explicitly related to UFOlogy, it is impossible not to draw parallels between missing fetuses in abduction lore and the importance of the fetus in magical practice of both antiquity and today. Like many aspects of magical practice, the ritualistic implementation of fetuses can be traced to Egypt, where they were considered magically effective if removed at 14 weeks. This timeframe roughly corresponds with the MFS timeframe of three months in abduction lore.[1172]

Centuries later, Germanic peoples believed thieves' lights—similar to the *Will-O-the-Wisp*—were produced from the fingers of unborn children, which beckoned nighttime travelers astray. Once lost, highwaymen would ambush these victims and steal their belongings. According to folklore, these brigands abducted pregnant serving girls for the express purpose of stealing their children and creating more thieves' lights.[1173]

Fetuses remain central to Thai magical practice. The *kuman thong*—"sanctified young boy"—is a necromantic amulet fashioned from a dead fetus, pulled from its mother's womb. Black magic practitioners believe the souls of these unborn children, captured within the amulets, can be bent to their evil ends. Less nefariously, the *kuman thong* is also utilized among common folk as a household spirit, assisting with daily duties in a manner similar to European faeries.[1174] (Belief from the French Alps, for example, held that the souls of dead, unbaptized children could be procured from the devil as household spirits.[1175]) The practice remains active to this day: in 2012, Chow Hok Kuen was arrested in Bangkok's Chinatown district for *kuman thong* manufacture, covering roasted male fetuses in gold leaf for good luck charms.[1176]

Chapter 15:
"We Need Babies"
Motivation & the Hybridization Theory

ROMAN CASTEVET: Rock him.
ROSEMARY WOODHOUSE: You're trying to get me to be his mother.
ROMAN CASTEVET: Aren't you his mother?
— *Rosemary's Baby* (1968)

If we assume a reality exists behind alien abduction—like faerie kidnappers before them—what motivates their theft of children and unborn babies? Some claim aliens abduct children for food, an idea as sensational as the faeries' *teind* to the devil and equally lacking in supporting evidence.[1177] On the other end of the spectrum, others claim UFOs visit Earth for purely altruistic means, particularly healing children.

At least such proponents have a wealth of evidence to draw upon. UFOlogist Preston Dennett has chronicled many such cases. In one instance, a witness under hypnosis recalled having their genitalia damaged by an abusive uncle in the 1950s, an injury subsequently healed by "little people" in a "spacecraft." Another subject, "Ted" of Santa Clara, California, was diagnosed with a congenital angioma which improved, instead of worsened, at age three; this was due to a childhood abduction where his skull was split open and a laser shrunk the enlargement, he claimed under hypnotic regression. In another example from Dennett, six-year-old Alice Haggerty, unvaccinated by her parents, suffered from diphtheria, but was taken one night by "angels in white robes with silver belts" who waved a "rod-like device" around her body, declaring her "cured and 'cleansed.'"[1178]

Children are often given a mission, charge, or message during their abductions. Unfortunately, most abductees cannot remember specifics and are only left with a vague sense of purpose and urgency. Kevin, the child involved in his parents' 1974 Aveley Abduction, told investigators, "They gave me a lot of things to do when I grow up, but I've forgotten them all."[1179] Similarly, after her childhood abduction, Próspera Muñoz "knew" she was asked to "remember something," but the memory was blocked.[1180]

UFO occupants seem equally interested in the abilities of specific children deemed intelligent or "special." One Louisiana couple happened upon a circular metallic craft landed on their property in 1976. Their three-year-old son ran towards the object's occupants hoping to play with them in spite of their short stature, spindly fingers, and wrinkled skin. The beings communicated to the couple they wished to take the boy away because of his intelligence, but his parents refused.[1181]

In June 1991, a family of five in Puerto Rico experienced car trouble and soon after saw an anomalous light. Several Grey aliens appeared and briefly took the youngest child, a "special baby" with an important task in its future.[1182]

Of course, faeries also took "promising" children,[1183] but modern abduction researchers contend that alien interest in intelligent children stems from their involvement in a long form genetic experiment. The results of this endeavor, we have been assured for nearly four decades, will change our entire existence. For reasons known only to them, Grey aliens contact *Homo sapiens* hoping we might save their dying race, a belief lying at the core of modern UFOlogy. For many abduction proponents, extraterrestrials traverse untold light-years to visit our tiny backwater planet for one purpose: the human-alien hybrid program.

THE HYBRIDIZATION THEORY: AN OVERVIEW

In large part, Budd Hopkins is to thank—or blame—for the human-ET hybridization narrative.

"I was one of the first to point out the aspect of hybrid babies," Hopkins said in 1998. "But the Betty and Barney Hill case involved the taking of sperm/ova samples, so the sexual aspect has been with us a long time. It just wasn't emphasized."[1184]

In truth, UFOlogists were speculating on hybridization within six years of the Hill abduction.[1185] What Hopkins mainly did was codify the concept. Influenced by the testimony of hundreds of subjects, he believed abductees were selected early in life for desirable genetic qualities. The primary goal of abductions was to collect human genetic material—namely gametes—for combination with alien DNA. Over time, abduction researchers like David Jacobs adopted, focused, and expanded upon the hybridization theory.

After Hopkins passed away in 2011, Jacobs became the world's foremost advocate of the hybrid theory, claiming "the focus of the abduction is the production of children" for a surreptitious extraterrestrial plot to takeover of the planet.[1186] In his 2015 book *Walking Among Us: The Alien Plan to Control Humanity*, he speculates the end phase of this invasion is already well underway, with hybrids fully integrated into modern society.[1187]

As far-fetched as the entire notion may be, the hybridization theory has obvious antecedents in folklore. The concept appropriates the primary reason behind faerie abductions, i.e. the incorporation of human beings into the faerie bloodline. As already noted, cultures worldwide have embraced the concept of hybridization with non-human entities, including gods; the collection of sperm and ovum directly reflects the manner in which demonic succubi, incubi, and the devil stole mortal seed (from a practical standpoint, this belief explained away nocturnal emissions, sexual dreams, and sleep paralysis to the concerned early Christian). In medieval belief, these creatures lacked the ability to procreate, hence their need to borrow human semen, which was then used to impregnate witches.[1188] Indeed, incubi were said to have phalluses so large and stiff they inflicted pain upon victims, calling to mind the painful probes used in abductions.[1189] Hybridization theory advocates, of course, suggest these spiritual tales indicate ancient extraterrestrial contact, rather than considering the inverse.

Hybridization themes can be traced to the earliest days of the UFO era. In 1957, South African contactee Elizabeth Klarer claimed to have conceived a child with her extraterrestrial lover, Akon.[1190] That same year, the abduction of Brazilian farmer Antônio Vilas Boas culminated in intercourse with a naked humanoid, who rubbed her stomach and pointed to the sky afterwards.[1191] These traditional means of procreation have been largely supplanted by artificial methods in modern encounters.

Today, the hybridization theory is regarded as *consensus gentium* among UFOlogists, particularly those who see no problem with hypnotic regression. As such, it continuously reinforces itself, growing in popularity. In February 1996, only 18% of abductees reported seeing human-alien hybrids;[1192] two years later, 45% of alien encounters involved hybrids, at least according to Jacobs.[1193]

Entire books are dedicated to the hybridization theory, making it impossible to comprehensively cover the concept. While much of what follows is no doubt familiar to the seasoned UFOlogist, it is necessary to contextualize the hybridization theory within the larger supernatural child abduction framework—aspects of the theory have serious ramifications for our comparison with changeling lore.

WHY HYBRIDIZATION?

According to researchers like Hopkins and Jacobs, children are taken aboard UFOs either to collect their genetic material or because they are human-extraterrestrial hybrids themselves. But what motivates this hybridization in the first place? Obviously, aliens—like faeries—need something from human beings. Something they lack.

Those with a more metaphysical bent claim Greys are trying to attain humanity, or regain emotions like love, by combining their DNA with ours.[1194] Author Nigel Kerner posited Greys are biological robots created by an extinct extraterrestrial civilization and thus lack souls—the hybridization program represents their pursuit to conquer death by acquiring human souls.[1195] In the 1970 abduction of Californian Lori Briggs, her captors told her more or less the opposite: they were spiritual beings of light but hybridized with humans in order to permanently take physical form.[1196]

New Age belief maintains each abductee agrees to participate in the hybrid program in a past life, or before his or her soul incarnates on earth.[1197] In this framework, there seems to be an exchange of souls between our world and the Otherworld—just as in faerie belief. John Mack interviewed individuals who actually claimed to have been Grey aliens in previous lifetimes. In January 1992, he spoke to Peter, "one of the abductees I have worked with who has discovered a dual human/alien identity. In his alien self, he has become aware of having participated willingly in the reported alien-human hybrid breeding program."[1198]

Not only are such claims unfalsifiable, they are borderline offensive when one considers the traumatic nature of many abductions. At the same time, attitudes of consent, right, and ownership bear a certain resemblance to faerie lore. Crofton Croker wrote in 1828, "It seems as if [the Elves] divided among themselves the souls of men, and considered them thenceforth as their property."[1199] Compare this to Charles Fort's conclusion from 1919's *The Book of the Damned:* "I think we're property."[1200]

Equally evocative is an exchange from one of Whitley Strieber's early abductions:

> I remembered my protest to her when she reassured me about the operation not hurting me. The sense of helplessness was an awful thing to contemplate. "You have no right," I had said.

"We do have a right." Five enormous words. Stunning words. *We do have a right.*[1201]

Jacobs, of course, sees all New Age concepts as an attempt to cope with the horror of the situation. In his eyes, the hybridization project is a covert means to take over the planet for... *something*. John Brandenburg endorsed a similar idea in 1990:

> The Reticulians intend that within a century or less, Reticulian-human hybrids will be the only intelligent life form on this planet. Hybrids are used for colonization to avoid biohazard problems. This colonization is to be achieved by treachery, stealth, intimidation and terror rather than open warfare, since such warfare might lead to unpredictable outcomes. Hybrid occupation of the planet is to be exclusive since this is most efficient and humans are too dangerous and territorial to allow a shared existence.[1202]

Equally popular but less alarmist, some hold the Greys are genetically atrophied and have lost the ability to procreate, thus—as with the faeries—they need an infusion of human vitality into their dying race. The reasons behind this vary: a war-ravaged planet, an overreliance on technology for reproduction, etc. Comments related to abductees regularly support this theory. "We need you to propagate our species. We have inbred to a level of sterility," one witness was told.[1203] Another was informed, "We need babies." [1204] An Ohio witness discovered in 1975 that his abductor's species "had trouble bearing male children," echoing the faerie proclivity for abducted boys.[1205]

Compare such statements to commonly-held lore surrounding the *trow*, the troll-like faeries of the Orkney islands: "Legend had it that they were incapable of producing females of their own kind and so, in order to procreate, they needed to impregnate human women," wrote Ceri Houlbrook in *Magical Folk: British and Irish Fairies - 500 AD to the Present*. "However, once the baby trow was born, the human mother would die, and so the trow would require another human woman—a new mother—to nurse his newborn."[1206]

Indeed, one could easily summarize the hybridization theory in terms familiar to a 19th century Fairy Faith adherent: non-human entities, searching for genetic material—faeries need milk, aliens need DNA, both seek breeding stock— take children in the night to bolster their dying race.

THE HYBRIDIZATION PROCESS

Step One: Collection.

Using unknown criteria, aliens select an individual for a lifetime of abductions, typically beginning around seven years old. Because this activity's primary goal is the alleged harvest of sperm and ovum, it is a mystery why men are taken before sexual maturity; women, on the other hand, possess an entire lifetime of eggs from birth.

Harvesting sperm and ovum can be viewed as "pre-birth child abduction," if you will. The method of collecting gametes varies. Typically, aliens clamp a cylindrical device over a male's erect penis, bringing him to orgasm.[1207] One of John Mack's subjects recalled under hypnosis "a faucetlike device was placed on his penis, 'wires' or 'leads' applied to his testicles, and a sperm sample taken as he lay terrified and paralyzed on a table in a UFO."[1208] Female abductees like Shane Kurz, on the other hand, report invasive methods, like the "long tube inserted into her navel."[1209] According to Jacobs, one abductee described the tool as long, flexible, and thin as a "daffodil stem" (there may be some conflation between this method and pregnancy/fertility tests like the one Betty Hill allegedly received).[1210]

Childhood abductions may also be part of a testing or vetting phase, where captors assess the genetic makeup of an abductee.

Hopkins interpreted children's scars as evidence of a "cell-sampling operation."[1211] In light of how non-invasive modern cell collection can be—humans can collect DNA with a swab in the mouth—this method seems exceptionally primitive for any advanced extraterrestrial race.

Step Two: Incubation.

After fertilizing the abductee's ova in vitro with alien genetic material—a process never satisfactorily explained in the literature—the hybrid embryo is placed inside a female abductee's uterus (Jacobs contends artificial wombs facilitate incubation inside sterile experiencers, begging the question why surrogates are needed at all).[1212] In the case of male abductees, aliens presumably place their sperm inside a female alien partner.[1213]

Some suggest, however, both the sperm and ova come from abductees, to which a third non-human constituent is added. A female abductee named Jerry told John Mack she had "been given information from the aliens that they take DNA from a human male—'the sperm could be from my husband' or someone else—and combine it with an egg." Jerry went on to explain how, following the combination of male and female gametes, "the aliens alter the embryo in some way, perhaps adding a genetic principle of their own." Modified embryos are then brought to term within female abductees until retrieval.[1214]

One of Jacobs' female subjects claimed impregnation was accomplished using a "long, rounded instrument" with a projectile inside, carrying the fertilized egg. In other cases, implantation involves procedures similar to the one used for collecting ovum.[1215] Female abductees may experience numerous incubations throughout their lives—in the most extreme example, one prolific witness claimed to have produced 25 fetuses for the hybrid program.[1216]

Despite such sophisticated methods, no shortage of abductees report physical intercourse with non-human entities—consider Elizabeth Klarer, Vilas Boas, or Marlene Travers, an Australian woman who in 1966 encountered a UFO landed in the countryside. Approaching the craft, she saw a tall, handsome man in a green tunic, who telepathically related she was chosen as the first Earthling to bear a child of his race. After having sex, Travers was escorted from the ship but tripped and passed out. She was later confirmed pregnant.[1217]

Step Three: Retrieval.

We have already covered the concept of retrievals at length. Missing fetuses are missing children, another variation on the paranormal child abduction theme. While many of Jacobs' subjects reported the use of special implements, retrievals occasionally feature natural births. Precedent exists for child retrieval in faerie lore—recall the Icelandic tale of Olöf, who had her child taken away by its paternal faerie family.

Step Four: Baby Presentation.

At a later date, aliens abduct the parent with the express purpose of showing him or her their hybrid child. This is known as the child or baby "presentation," and in 1999 Jacobs claimed it appeared in 180 of 700 of his early cases.[1218] Abductees experience this scenario at a variety of ages (the youngest case investigated by Hopkins involved a six-year-old girl, begging the question how a child so young could carry a hybrid baby unnoticed).[1219]

Invariably these reunions involve the experiencer holding, speaking to, or—in the case of female abductees—nursing their hybrid baby.[1220] In 1989, a witness from Adelaide, Australia, claimed her contact culminated in a confrontation with alien Greys who presented an infant to her, which they encouraged her to hold and nurse. "She was then asked by the alien to hold it and nurse the creature," wrote Randles. "This seems to have been the source of some interest for the watching aliens."[1221]

Aliens seem quite adamant about this interaction. Jacobs, who has written more about this aspect than any other abduction researcher, summarized a typical birth presentation in his book

Secret Life:

> The female Being extends her arms with the baby
> in it toward the woman, and the abductee takes
> it. She holds the baby to her chest with the baby's
> head resting on her arm or shoulder. If the abductee
> resists, she may be given a "reason" to force her to
> hold the baby. One woman was told that the baby
> would get sick if she did not hold it, and that it
> would develop a rash or some other sickness if she
> held the baby away from her body. Therefore she
> had to hold the baby against her skin for as long
> as possible. The baby may be naked, or it may be
> wrapped in a "blanket"…
>
> The woman hears another directive: "Nurse the
> baby." "Put the baby to your breast and feed the
> baby." The woman says, "But I do not have any milk."
> The response is, "Put the baby to your breast and
> nurse the baby!" Saying "No" is futile. If she resists,
> the aliens will put the baby to her breast anyway.
> It cups its mouth on her nipple. It has a very weak
> sucking reflex. In many instances, the woman may
> be surprised to find that she is lactating and that
> her breasts are engorged. When that happens the
> baby will partially drain the breast. Often, however,
> nursing the baby is futile but seems to satisfy the
> watchful aliens nonetheless.[1222]

Though infants are most common, these presentations can
also involve hybrids ranging from toddlers through adolescents.
Abductees might interact with their offspring multiple times
throughout their lives.[1223]

HYBRID BABIES, INCUBATORIUMS, AND STAR CHILDREN

The hybrid infants seen in baby presentations consistently appear sickly, listless, and pale; Jacobs described the quintessential hybrid as "lifeless, yet it is not dead. Most women think that there is something terribly wrong with the baby."[1224] Their heads, covered in sparse hair, are often larger than those of their human parent, as are their eyes.[1225]

- Bret Oldham described one of his hybrid children as "hideous looking!... severely deformed, especially the head and facial features... The baby looked very human like except for the head and face."[1226]

- Corrine—a Birmingham abductee whose earliest memory is seeing a "small man" staring through her bedroom window at 18 months old—began having "wise baby dreams" in her late teen years. Corrine's dreams are consistent with other abductees. "In the dreams, she told me in 1988," wrote Randles, "she gives birth to a strange and super-intelligent child. It has wrinkled skin, thin hair and ugly features. The entities whom she has often seen in her life tell her in these vivid nightmares that she is to look after this baby... because they need to test her human emotional response to nurturing this creature."[1227]

- After a hypnotic regression session, Katharina Wilson claimed to be visited again by extraterrestrials on August 7, 1988. In this particular encounter, she recalled giving birth, then being presented with her child. "This isn't right," she journaled. "This isn't our baby." Though encouraged by the beings to accept the infant, Wilson waited until the "Doctor" left and set out to find her actual child, wandering through what appeared to be a hospital. Eventually she found what appeared to be her child, "very, very thin and frail." The child "shook uncontrollably," appearing "severely retarded."[1228]

- Debbie Tomey—whose abductions, under a pseud-onym, formed the basis for Hopkins' *Intruders*— told him under hypnosis that she encountered her adolescent, "sickly unearthly" hybrid. The girl was only a few feet tall, with ivory-white skin. Rest-ing atop her frail body was a large head displaying high cheekbones, her skin completely bare—save the faintest wisp of thin blonde hair.[1229]

Abductees are commonly disgusted at the sight of these hybrids.

"I don't want anything to do with this species, nothing at all," abductee Melissa told Jacobs under hypnosis of the "gross baby" she was presented. "I'll kill it... It's so fucking unnatural. Fucking stupid. Disgusting thing...."[1230]

Wilson recorded a dreamlike memory of giving birth to a hybrid: "No! No! I can't! I don't want it! They are trying to show me my baby... they want me to hold the baby. I'm screaming. No! No! Get it away from me! I don't want to touch it! I don't want to look at it! Get it out!!!"[1231]

Baby presentations can create painful psychological scars. Seeing human infants in public can remind abductees of their hybrid offspring's hideous appearance, or of the trauma associated with the hybridization process.

One abductee described "revulsion and fear" towards small children. "When I was in college, I realized I hated children," she said. "I couldn't stand them! I can't be around them!... Once they get bigger, it's okay."[1232]

Wilson remembered struggling with babysitting as a girl. "To me, babies seemed to be the most deceitful little things on the planet," she wrote. "I didn't dislike them, I just knew I couldn't trust them. I felt extremely uncomfortable with babies until I was twenty-eight years old and my nephew was born."[1233]

During their experiences, abductees may also glimpse "a room filled with containers with light emanating from inside them," as one of Hopkins' subjects put it, with "little embryo-type things in the light."[1234] This facility, known as an "incubatorium," or baby farm, typically features tubes or jars of liquid along the room's walls, each with an embryo or fetus suspended inside. In other configurations, these containers may be symmetrically organized as rows within drawers, akin to a laboratory setting.[1235] They might also be taken to a hybrid nursery of 10-50 babies playing or learning.[1236]

A male abductee named John told Emma Derdak of the Australian UFO Research Network that he was taken by Grey aliens from the side of a Lismore road in 1996. While aboard, he noticed "'baby aliens' in flasks of red, green-orange solution." Inquiring about the flasks, he was told they were alien babies and was asked if he would like to participate in their future. A female alien then approached John, morphing into a human and seducing him. After intercourse he received an anal probe, and a sample of skin was taken from his left hand. Asking about this procedure, the entity told John it was for DNA, since "their planet had blown up and that in order to continue their species and ensure that genetic inbreeding didn't occur that hybrids were the only alternative." John later claimed to father five hybrid sons, one daughter.[1237]

The hybrids in Hopkins' and Jacobs' work usually stayed with their alien brethren, but another school of thought maintains some children—particularly those conceived through intercourse—remain on Earth. Referred to as "Indigo Children" or "Star Children," these youth are said to look like normal humans but possess exceptional intelligence, beauty, empathy, and psychic abilities.[1238] Some theorize that these children are given a special mission by extraterrestrials, or are allowed to live among us to perpetuate a particular lineage, from which viable human mothers can be selected.[1239]

The similarities of hybrid descriptions, baby presentations, baby farms, and Star Children to faerie lore are elaborated in a later chapter.

SKEPTICISM

A great deal of skepticism surrounds the hybridization theory, and for good reason. In addition to the aforementioned problems with hypnotic regression—by which most accounts supporting the theory are obtained—self-proclaimed human-alien hybrids, now grown men and women, regularly appear at UFO conferences yet never consent to DNA testing. Such scientific analysis, proposed for at least thirty years, would do much to support or discredit their extraordinary claims.[1240]

Other critics of the hybridization theory point to the lack of logic behind repeat abductions. "It seems odd, to say the least, that an advanced intelligence capable of spanning star systems should be reduced to the crude gynecological procedures related by most abductees," Dennis Stacy pointed out in 1992. "Any extraterrestrial abductors, in other words, should be able to initiate and maintain a massive genetic hybridization program without the repeated physical kidnapping of individuals."[1241]

Why not abduct someone once and synthesize his or her genetic material on demand? Certainly an advanced alien civilization possesses technology even we lowly humans can anticipate in the near future. If an objective truth lies behind alien abduction, this fact alone suggests something about the *experience*—a variable impossible to replicate, perhaps an emotional response —is more valuable to these beings than human genetic material alone. Oldham recalls Grey aliens forcing him to watch his girlfriend's retrieval, to his terror and anger.

"Looking back now, I'm sure that they found it all very amusing," he wrote. "I was stupid. I had let them win. They wanted me to be upset. The Greys are intensely interested in our human emotions... I knew that they wanted me to observe the procedure they were doing to Denise so that they could monitor my emotional response to it."[1242]

The most compelling counterargument to the hybridization theory of the past several decades has been the basic problem of genetic compatibility.

"Where does the alien sperm used to impregnate human females come from?" wrote Victoria Alexander. "How does a species so different from us, i.e., one without respiratory, digestive or reproductive systems, produce sperm compatible to human biology?"[1243]

To be fair, science has progressed an incredible amount since Alexander's comments in 1994. In early 2017, scientists from the Salk Institute created the first animal-human chimera, combining human and pig DNA at the embryonic level. Like artificial wombs, the technology is still fledgling but shows great promise and makes the hybridization theory a bit more palatable.[1244]

Perhaps UFOlogists interpret reports of a hybridization program too literally. Like shamanic initiation, abduction seems a transformative experience—could hybridization take place on a metaphysical level?

Regarding an acquaintance who regards herself as a hybrid, author and experiencer Mike Clelland said:

> I suspect strongly that if they did a DNA test on her... she would come out as 100% human...
>
> But there's this blurring—when you say "hybrid," is it a physical hybrid, where they were actually born with spliced genes, or the same way we have hybrid strawberries and kiwis in the grocery store?...
>
> It's very murky, and I think that within the UFO lore, there's this kind of echo chamber... where

you say it enough times, and it becomes truth...
So you use the term, "DNA: My DNA has been
upgraded"... and maybe some type of upgrade
has taken place... I don't know if that's true, and I
understand if that's a simple metaphor. It's treated
as a literal truth by a lot of people. I can take a half
step back and say, "Well, maybe, maybe not, but I
understand what you're implying..."

I believe the people who are telling these accounts
are genuine people... They don't seem to have any
malicious intent in what they're saying. They seem
to say it from a point of believing it. This I believe
strongly: that there could be a more spiritual or
more soul-based blending of two separate species,
rather than this physical thing.[1245]

Chapter 16:
"You Are Not Wanted Here!"
Preventing, Thwarting, Confirming, & Resolving Child Alien Abduction

MORGAN: [wearing a tinfoil helmet] So the aliens can't read our minds.
GRAHAM: Oh.
MORGAN: They tell you everything in this book. It says they're probably very small—like my height—because, as their brains developed, there was no use for physical development. It says they're probably vegetarians, because they would have realized the benefits of such a diet.
GRAHAM: Who wrote this book?
MORGAN: Scientists who have been persecuted for their beliefs.
GRAHAM: That means they're unemployed.
— Signs (2002)

In 1998 Ann Druffel released *How to Defend Yourself Against Alien Abduction*, a book dedicated to the techniques discovered by "resisters." These individuals—comprising 70 of Druffel's 250 case studies—claimed to have successfully fended off alien abduction. After carefully examining the testimony of each resister, Druffel proposed nine techniques with the greatest chances of success. Her work—briefly summarized below and highly recommended—forms the backbone of this chapter.

DRUFFEL RESISTANCE TECHNIQUES

In the spring of 1956, Emily Cronin and her five-year-old son were traveling California's Ridge Route overnight with their roommate and driver, Jan Whitley. After pulling off the road for a nap, the travelers were roused by a piercing din and bright light flooding the car. Both women were paralyzed.

Through the terror, Emily—who had similar experiences in the past—began fighting the paralysis by trying to wiggle her finger. After several minutes, her finger began moving ever so slightly, and the sound and lights vanished. Twenty years later, hypnotic regression suggested three dark-clad, flat-faced entities had approached the car, but were foiled by the first of Druffel's proposed techniques: Mental Struggle. Druffel categorizes Mental Struggle as a "strong, internal, silent struggle, directed toward moving one small part of the body, usually a finger or toe."[1246]

Druffel's second method is Physical Struggle, a patently obvious solution if paralysis is not present. Tug-of-war battles between parents and UFOs can be found sporadically throughout history: one famous incident from Manitoba, Canada, involved a UFO and an eight-year-old girl. One Mrs. LeMarquands and several youths testified that her daughter had slowly levitated upward toward a large rectangular object in the sky in June 1967, only to be rescued when a 13-year-old boy nearby grabbed her and threw her bodily to the ground.[1247] Compare this case to tales of children wrested from abducting faeries: "I remember how an old woman pulled me out of a fairy ring to save me from being *taken*," a Scottish minister told Evans Wentz.[1248]

Physical Struggle may also involve violence, or at least the threat of it. Biting, kicking, and punching can do the trick.[1249] Patsy Wingate, an Appalachian witness—part Blackfoot Indian, part Irish—claimed to have killed an alien over an attempted abduction during her pregnancy.

"As the three little Greys approached her across the bedroom floor, she jumped up and grabbed the middle one by its thin neck," a 1997 *Flying Saucer Review* article reported. "She squeezed, and there was a crack, and its head fell back on its spine." The remaining Greys, startled, hastily dragged their wounded companion away.[1250]

If a weapon is at hand, even better—it needn't even be real. In the 1990s an eight-year-old boy named Kevin told Deborah Truncale: "a tall, bald, orange-skinned being, dressed in tight clothing, comes into his room and tries to get him." Kevin's nightly ritual involved pricking the intruder with his toy sword, suggesting that either the intruder was The Universe's Most Flappable Alien... or a holdover of the Fairy Faith, where the mere sight of swords repelled abductors.[1251]

Druffel's third resistance technique is Righteous Anger or, as researcher Rosemary Ellen Guiley calls it, Sovereignty.[1252] Asserting one's sovereignty and directing wrath towards potential abductors is most effective before paralysis sets in. One resister—offended by the invasion of privacy an entity committed by entering her bedroom—began yelling at the alien to leave. The being acted as though climbing an invisible ladder and, upon reaching the ceiling, disappeared, along with the bright light accompanying it.[1253]

Protective Rage is akin to Righteous Anger but employed on the behalf of others, particularly children. Morgana Van Klausen, subject of Druffel's missing fetus investigation, claimed her four-year-old son began discussing "clowns" and "ghosts" coming to his bedroom at night in a saucer-like "airplane." Outraged, Morgana began speaking out loud to the entities over numerous days, saying "Keep out of my house!" and "You are not wanted here!" Eventually, the nighttime visits ceased.[1254]

Druffel also endorses Support from Family Members—seeking advice, help, and comfort from close relatives and friends—and Intuition, where abductions are anticipated before they happen. "The visitors seem to detect that their intended victims are ready to resist and often don't bother to come, knowing that their attempts will meet with failure," Druffel wrote. This suggestion, coupled with her resistance technique of Metaphysical Methods (e.g. envisioning a protective white light around oneself, meditative awareness, etc.), strongly implies a spiritual, or at least non-physical, component to the abduction experience.[1255]

Druffel also encouraged abductees to Appeal to Spiritual Personages, a metaphysical practice lifted directly from faerie lore, which prescribed prayers as protection. "It is perhaps the most powerful technique yet discovered, since it is readily available to a majority of experiencers, and the logic behind it is backed up by all major religions of the world," wrote Druffel.[1256]

Crying out to religious figures like Mohammed the Prophet and Jesus Christ has a track record of proven potency in a variety of paranormal encounters. Near death experiencer Howard Storm was an atheist when a duodenal perforation brought him into a realm of hostile, lascivious pale humanoids who attacked him mercilessly; he recited fragmented Bible verses and called out to Jesus, which ended his visit to what he perceived as Hell. After recovering, Storm—like so many who visit the Otherworld—became a minister.[1257]

Druffel worked at length with a young Iranian man, Timur, who dealt with bedroom visitations from what he perceived as *djinn*. One night in particular, he awoke to a suffocating sensation and thought, "The only hope I have is God," wheezing the last word. Whatever was attacking Timur relented, allowing him to sit up in bed. In the darkness he perceived the welcoming sight of his Koran, as well as "a little figure" with "narrow, elongated eyes" peeking from behind a wall.[1258]

Abduction researcher Joe Jordan has collected a great wealth of cases where abductions have ended—permanently—through appeals to Jesus Christ. In a 2017 episode of the *Conspirinormal* podcast, Jordan told host Adam Sayne of a Florida man whose abduction culminated in "a pole shoved up his rectum." In his terror, the witness called out Jesus' name; the torture ended and he found himself in his bedroom.

On the efficacy of invoking other religious figures, Jordan says:

> There have been next to none [sic] cases reported
> of another [spiritual] personage stopping an
> experience...There's nobody out there documenting
> them, because it isn't happening, but there have been
> a couple that other researchers have reported. But
> the problem in looking at that is I've seen where
> they've recorded that the experience has been able
> to be stopped, but not the phenomenon terminated
> from their life... In other words... [it's] continued
> in their life—they've been able to stop it in that one
> experience....[1259]

Since a paucity of researchers examine this particular niche, it is difficult to verify Jordan's statements. At the same time, given the relationship between the Fairy Faith and Christianity, it would be interesting to see how many alien abductees have been baptized—perhaps old habits are still effective.

UFOlogists ascribe an omnipotence to aliens that would make the fae folk blush; for this reason, little data exists regarding alien repellants. The notion, after all, smacks of superstitions modern UFOlogists consider anathema. To her credit, Druffel drew heavily upon the Fairy Faith for her last resistance technique: Repellants. She spoke with numerous resisters who experienced success using essential oils, aromatherapy, and specific herbs like pennyroyal—used in Ireland to reverse consumptive faerie illness, as documented by Lady Gregory.[1260] Experiencers like Deborah Goodale Marchand have also employed yarrow, "one of the seven herbs that, in Irish belief, nothing natural nor supernatural could injure,"[1261] to reduce abductions.[1262]

Druffel also cited the use of ceiling fans by Morgana Van Klausen to prevent harassing abduction experiences. "Morgana felt that the whirling blades, heavy with metal decorations, possibly prevented the creatures from entering her home," she wrote. This use of metal to ward off entity attacks naturally evokes faerie-repelling iron, as does advice Druffel received from "a top abduction researcher," who claimed "a particular abductee held crossed bar magnets against his chest, and that warded off the greys' approach"[1263] (recall the story where faeries perceived a needle on a child's chest as an immoveable iron bar). Other connections between stopping abductions and iron are addressed shortly.

The faerie-alien connection appears again in Druffel's work. "In the UFO field, a story is currently circulating about one witness who kept her tormentors away by ringing the floor around her bed with salt," she wrote in 1998. The source of the story remains unclear, but it is interesting when taken with findings from Marden and Stoner's 2012 abduction study. "62% of the Abduction Experiencers Group craves salt, whereas only 12% of the Non-Abduction Experiencers Group does," they found. Marden and Stoner go on to speculate about abductee dehydration rates and excited adrenal activity—one can only wonder if perhaps, on some subliminal level, abductees simply crave salt because they know it might keep the Good Folk at bay.[1264]

Above perhaps all else, it should be emphasized that Druffel's resistance techniques mostly rely on the power of belief, implying a strong foothold in a metaphysical reality. If one believes a technique works, it likely will.

MISCELLANY, CLOTHING, AND THE MENKIN HELMET

While Druffel's work remains quite thorough, the literature suggests a few additional methods might aid anyone seeking to avoid alien abduction. Sometimes, it seems, simply being fleet of foot will suffice: in 1973, a copper-colored UFO hovered just over the ground in Tennessee, from which a tall being with its clawlike hands reached out and failed to grab two spritely children.[1265]

The littlest things can thwart abductions. Experiencer and researcher John DeSouza remembers an experience at nine years old when he was lying awake well past his bedtime in his New York bedroom. DeSouza found himself paralyzed and surrounded by diminutive entities, levitating slowly toward the ceiling—which he subsequently hit.

> There were more thuds as they kept trying to push, pull, and force my body through the ceiling that they themselves were easily passing through. They were still trying to do it gently so as not to wake me but their consternation grew. Like floating engineers faced with an unexpected problem, they seemed to stand upon nothing and scratch their heads. Their frustration and the constant bumping of the front of my body against the ceiling dissipated the preternatural drowsiness that had gripped me.[1266]

Fully alert, DeSouza remembers hearing voices in his head: "What's the delay?"

"Something's wrong," a voice replied, followed by, "He's awake." DeSouza then crashed onto his bed.

Alien abductees regularly report their clothing mismatched or inside out.[1267] Many ascribe these irregularities to simple extraterrestrial carelessness—another data point incongruous with their unlimited abilities—but recall how faerie enchantments could be dispelled by the inversion of clothing. Perhaps such wardrobe malfunctions go hand-in-hand with the transition from the Otherworld to our reality—a transition which can, perhaps, be preemptively forced by the inversion of clothing. Unfortunately, no alien abductee has had the presence of mind to try turning their nightclothes inside out on their own.

Another article of clothing said to prevent alien abduction is a do-it-yourself helmet invented by abductee Michael Menkin. According to Menkin, the headgear "scrambles telepathic communication between aliens and humans. Aliens cannot immobilize people wearing thought screens nor can they control their minds or communicate with them using their telepathy. When aliens can't communicate or control humans, they do not take them." Though the headgear is mocked by many, Menkin's website nonetheless has multiple testimonies endorsing the efficacy of the helmet, which can be constructed from a few cheap and simple materials: cloth or plastic tape; any comfortable hat or helmet; and velostat.[1268]

The primary component in Menkin's invention, velostat is a conductive packing material made of polymeric foil impregnated with carbon black, a type of partially combusted petroleum product.[1269] The logic seems that—as a radar absorbing material sometimes used in military aircraft stealth technology—carbon black somehow interferes with the locating and/or retrieval of abductees.[1270]

Carbon black's stealth qualities are rendered more potent when combined on aircraft with ferrite grains… derived from iron.[1271] Another popular stealth material, iron ball paint, "consists of tiny iron particles that are coated with carbonyl iron or ferrite" and functions similarly to the carbon black and ferrite grain coating.[1272]

In case the implications are not clear, both carbon black and iron derivatives are used to block radar—some believe the former can stop alien abductions, while practitioners of the Fairy Faith held the latter could repel faeries.

CONFIRMATION & RESOLUTION

No UFOlogical analogue exists for the elaborate Fairy Faith rituals by which parents confirmed changelings in their midst. Budd Hopkins regularly cited missing time—covered at length, along with its parallels to preternaturally long stays in Fairyland—and unexplained childhood scars as suggestive of alien abduction. In his interpretation, these blemishes were "from an apparent cell-sampling operation carried out when they were abducted as little children," or the result of inserting tracking implants.[1273] "Nothing is more vivid than blood," he wrote. "A childhood accident which causes a wound deep enough to leave a noticeable scar thirty years later should have become a dramatic event in family history."[1274]

Easy ripostes aside—plenty of relatively harmless injuries from childhood can leave behind prominent scars—Hopkins found numerous examples of abductees who could only recall the origin of childhood injuries under hypnosis. In one example, Margaret Bruning (pseudonym) sought out Hopkins because his research resonated strongly with a nightmare from her childhood where three men, accompanied by a loud humming, pinned her to the kitchen table and "pushed a huge needle" into her stomach. She claimed to suffer from an intense nosebleed the following morning.[1275]

In addition to this and other dreams, Bruning had two scars— "right temple 1-2" long, right forearm 4-5" long, for which neither my parents nor I have any explanation."[1276] During her subsequent hypnotic regression, she recalled three bald men in black who carried her to a shining metal object and "'scraped' her wrist, placing the pieces of skin into small, round containers," followed by the needle and another collection at her temple.[1277]

Though longer lasting, a clear parallel can be drawn between these anomalous injuries and the bruises abductees experienced from faerie pinching.[1278] Unlike faeries, however, aliens rarely permanently keep their quarry, rendering resolution of abduction a moot point—or so it seems. Each year, dozens of individuals disappear, both from populated areas and isolated wildernesses. This disturbing implication, and its resonance to the work of David Paulides, is covered in a later chapter.

Now, we find ourselves at the heart of this book: the intersection of changelings, faeries, hybrids, and UFO lore.

Chapter 17:
"Just Out-Of-Frame"
Ufology, Hybrids, Faeries, & Changelings: An Intersection

SPOCK: Not the Nomad we lost from Earth. It took from the other a new directive to replace its own. The other was originally programmed to secure and sterilize soil samples from other planets, probably as a prelude to colonization.
KIRK: A changeling.
SPOCK: I beg your pardon?
KIRK: An ancient Earth legend, Mister Spock. A changeling was a fairy child that was left in place of a human baby. The changeling assumed the identity of the human child. So, it is to sterilize, and for sterilize read kill.

— Star Trek: The Original Series,
Season 2, Episode 8: "The Changeling"

If any past chapters seem overly hostile toward the ETH in favor of a Fairy Faith Hypothesis (FFH), it is only a reaction to how the UFO community has largely downplayed faerie lore as fantasy while advancing its own—nigh-identical—mythology. In reality, both the ETH and FFH are likely incorrect. Though one may be closer to objective reality than the other, both are restricted by superstition, influenced by their respective cultures, and fail to acknowledge that human beings may be wholly incapable of comprehending what seems to be a genuinely alien—in the "unfamiliar" sense of the word—intelligence.

The artwork of Chris Butler provides perhaps the most poignant depiction of these phenomena. For the 2014 reprint of Jacques Vallee's seminal *Passport to Magonia*, Butler provided a cover featuring a stereotypical Grey alien holding three masks: a 1950s space invader, a devil, and a faerie queen. While powerful in its own right, Butler's original concept included the detail of an arm inside the Grey, revealing itself as but a puppet for another, larger force just out-of-frame.

The ETH and FFH are clearly attempts to describe the same set of phenomena. The similarities are undeniable. Whatever its true nature, the UFO-faerie phenomenon constantly recontextualizes itself, adopting culturally-appropriate representations when presenting itself.

Obvious parallels can be drawn between changelings (arguably the most pernicious faerie belief) and modern depictions of human-alien hybrids; the broad strokes are immediately apparent. Hybrid baby presentations are explicit reinventions of the changeling trope: a human child (or fetus) is taken and a grotesque, inhuman infant presented to its parent instead.

These noticeable similarities have been pointed out *ad nauseum* by researchers like Chris Aubeck, Kevin Aspinall, and Graham Hancock. While their work is more than laudable, few truly appreciate the depth of resonance between tales of alien hybrids and faerie changelings. What follows not only compares faerie motifs to the alien hybridization program, but also traces changeling lore through lesser-appreciated dimensions of UFOlogy as a whole.

CLONES

Examples where human beings are replaced by inhuman others are difficult to find in UFO accounts, primarily because the changeling archetype tends to manifest itself motivically rather than literally in modern UFOlogy. When literal substitutions do occur, UFOlogists interpret them as "clones," a view stretching all the way back to Budd Hopkins' earliest subjects: Virginia Horton claimed she was "introduced in the sky house to my sister, who looked exactly like me. She was a clone."[1279] (In his books, Hopkins never satisfactorily explained the motivations behind creating this double.)

In one noteworthy case from 1986, Brazilian investigators revealed the tale of 19-year-old Antônio Álves Ferreira, who regularly claimed interactions with UFOs and their occupants for 11 years. As a child, Ferreira would disappear for hours at a time, returning with tales of large-headed, dark-skinned, slant-eyed entities. Ferreira's contacts allegedly culminated in a 36-hour trip to an alien world, for which they produced an impeccable duplicate left in his stead. "Shortly afterwards, on a screen, he saw this 'double' of his sitting at a table in his house," wrote Irene Granchi in *Flying Saucer Review*. "A few moments later, its head drooped, and it was asleep." When Ferreira's father came in to take him to the hammock for a nap, "he found that the 'boy' had become so heavy that it was impossible for him to carry him alone."[1280]

The story evokes a report from pre-revolutionary Cuba, in which one Arcadia Alvarez spotted a three-foot-tall figure by the side of the road; thinking it was a lost child, she went to pick it up "but was unable to raise it at all, for it seemed to weigh like lead."[1281] Equally reminiscent is the *konakijijii* of Japanese folklore, a baby heard wailing in the woods—anyone hapless enough to pick it up finds it has "the face of an old man... it will suddenly become so heavy that it will crush you."[1282]

Faerie scholars will recall various references to changelings whose weight could rapidly increase. In one Irish tale, a mother wading into a river to toss away a changeling found it growing "heavy as lead," eventually ripping through the quilt as "a heavy stone would through a muslin handkerchief."[1283]

Like changelings of yore, clones afflict adults as well. Extraterrestrials told several of Karla Turner's adult subjects they could be "replaced" by indistinguishable clones if they resisted their abductions. "Similar reports come from other abductees," she wrote, "In one case a man said he saw a room full of inert male and female human bodies, who were beautiful and identical."[1284]

In 2017 Bret Oldham wrote, "I have seen what appeared to be human clones; each one looked like an exact copy of the others. They were white males with an average build and short dark hair."[1285]

Russian researcher Vadim Chernobrov reported this exact tactic. In 1978, art teacher Galina Markovna and her husband were standing at a tram stop when they spied a round object in the winter sky; simultaneously, an old woman approached the couple and said one of her friends, seated on a nearby park bench, needed assistance (shades of both the faerie crone and the "midwife to the faeries" narrative). Galina's husband obliged, saying he would meet her later and leaving her to watch the UFO before returning home.

Well into the evening Galina's husband was nowhere to be found. That evening, a phone call informed her he was taken to a hospital for a heart attack. After his discharge, Galina noticed her husband seemed different, lacking emotion—in essence, a changeling. Less than a week passed before he wasted away and died, leaving his wife convinced aliens had abducted her true husband.[1286]

SOUL SWAPPING

The physicalist explanation of cloning can dovetail with more spiritual substitutions, as in the case of Ted Rice. Rice recalled an overcast, cloudy day from his childhood when a bright light in the sky swallowed him up. Inside a strange room, two Greys stripped him naked and forced him to drink a strange liquid, which somehow separated his soul from his body. His soul was then transferred to an identical body.

"When I was taken and cloned at eight years old, I remembered being returned to the house in a dark, swirling atmosphere, and all of my relatives saw what they thought was a tornado," Rice told

Turner. "They'd been out looking for me because the storm was coming up, and nobody could find me until it blew over. My uncle said that he saw different colored lights inside the funnel cloud, which probably came from the UFO."[1287]

The parallels to faerie lore—the clone as changeling, the storm as abducting faerie whirlwind—are striking. Rice's tale, however fanciful, also supports Evans Wentz's hypotheses that changelings might be explained metaphysically, by Soul-Wandering.

Such notions are not new to UFOlogy. In her book *Star Children*, Jenny Randles told of one woman whose story bears a striking resemblance to changeling tales. The witness— who claimed regular involvement with small, nonhuman entities— told how one day in the garden her nine-month-old daughter suddenly started screaming from her baby carriage. "When the girl grew older it became clear that the child felt that she was somehow 'different,'" Randles wrote. "In fact, she had relinquished her body and allowed an alien entity to take it over during that brief moment in her pram."[1288]

In *The Super Natural*, Whitley Strieber shared a curious soul-swapping changeling vision while visiting an "ill-liked, dishonest" friend from childhood in a hospital. Whitley and his wife were waiting downstairs when he perceived the moment of his friend's passing, followed by a vision of squat, blue entities—likened to *kobolds* of faerie lore—dragging the man through the squalor of an Indian slum.

> Then he was gone and in his place there was a tiny baby girl being held by her father.

> The baby's eyes widened with what seemed to me to be adult recognition, and the infant began screaming terribly, waving its arms and kicking, its eyes practically popping out of its head. The frantic parents tried to comfort it, and then the vision was gone.

The doctor came in and told us that our friend was dead.[1289]

CHANGELINGS *IN UTERO*

Can changelings occur before birth?

One night in Seattle, Washington, a young pregnant woman noticed her dog was whimpering. Moving to its location downstairs, she found her pet cowering in the corner and started searching for the source of its fear. The last thing she remembered was pulling back the curtain and seeing a brightly illuminated shape in the night sky. Troubled by the experience, she later underwent hypnotic regression, where she felt she had stepped outside into a beam of light that took her to a strange tunnel. While there, two vague figures removed and replaced her unborn baby.[1290]

Three years later, pregnant Salina Quail, a British Columbia experiencer, reported an experience with similar overtones. Quail was settling back into sleep after a bathroom visit when she found herself paralyzed by a dark shape alongside her bed. The figure, accompanied by several others, told her she would not be hurt, and that it only wished to "look at" her baby. The figure circled its hand over her abdomen, opening her up and peering inside. After a moment, he repeated the action, sealing the cavity, and the figures disappeared.[1291]

What happens when an unborn baby is examined—or taken from and replaced—inside its mother's womb? If any truth lies behind such stories, it heavily implies some sort of change takes place, and could therefore be understood as a variation upon the changeling myth; after all, perhaps the original fetus is never actually replaced, but instead a substitute left behind.

This concept provides UFOlogy a new framework through which to interpret miscarriages. In these cases, it is largely assumed a hybrid baby has been retrieved—but such cases could equally represent the harvest of a *human child*, with dead fetal tissue left in its place, much as faeries occasionally left behind dead children instead of faerie babies.

Some cases explicitly suggest as much. Pat, an abductee who worked with Karla Turner, delivered a stillborn child after several experiences during her pregnancy. Months later, surrounded by Grey aliens in a quiet room, Pat was asked if she wanted to see her baby—despite the fact she had a productive labor. She declined the offer but still caught sight of the infant. "In that brief glimpse, she saw a tiny, skinny baby with blue, slanted eyes," Turner wrote. "She felt that somehow this baby was a repository for the soul of the child who had died at birth, and she said she felt trusting and thankful toward her friend for showing her that the little boy had, in a sense, survived."[1292]

VANISHING TWIN SYNDROME

A variation upon typical miscarriages is Vanishing Twin Syndrome, or VTS. First medically recognized in 1945, VTS occurs when one unborn child in a multifetal pregnancy seemingly disappears within the womb. Often appearing during the gestation of twins—hence the name—VTS represents the miscarriage of a single child, whose fetal tissue is absorbed either by its siblings, the placenta, or the mother. Since the use of ultrasound, VTS is diagnosed more today than ever; some estimate it occurs in up to 30% of multifetal pregnancies.[1293]

Given the admittedly strange nature of this condition—its cause remains largely unknown—it should come as no surprise that many in the New Age community have taken interest in VTS. In her book *The Millennium Children*, Caryl Dennis describes the experience of a father who lost a child in this fashion:

> There were two umbilical cords: "one freshly cut and one that looked healed over, like an amputee's stump." The doctor had no explanation, except that the baby may have at some point in the pregnancy had a twin. When the daughter was about nine...

he asked her if she knew she was supposed to be a twin. She exclaimed, "Yes Daddy, I know. I know where my twin sister is; she's on the spaceship and I talk to her all the time."[1294]

This interpretation of VTS is common among experiencers and conflates the dead with aliens much in the same way they were once conflated with faeries. Moreover, it reinvents the changeling motif—supernatural forces kidnap an identical version of a child, in this case the vanished twin. From this perspective, the surviving child is the changeling, while its more perfect, idealized double lives carefree in the Otherworld.

Survivors of VTS even behave like changelings. Psychologist Alice Rose holds that in surviving twins, the guilt of taking too much nourishment in their mother's womb engrained in their psyche might render them insatiable. "Surviving twins may sneak food and eat when no one else can discover them," she wrote. "Or they may be secretly greedy about food… They may wolf down food, or be unable to wait to eat."[1295]

Studies also suggest surviving twins are at greater risk for cerebral palsy. An Australian survey found this risk was 15 times greater than among twins where both were live-born and 60 times greater than among singletons.[1296] As noted, cerebral palsy has been proposed as a candidate for explaining changeling behavior.

TOSSING

A Canadian witness—experiencing UFO sightings since the age of eight—told researcher George Filer of a peculiar abduction memory where two insectoid, mantis-like beings ushered him into a dim, round room with "a murky light tone mushroom color." Inside, six smaller beings, which he described as "snowmen," began "tossing me around to each other like a ball… The group appeared to have some type of humor amongst them. I was like a ball in a game."[1297]

This nonsensical behavior has precedent in faerie folklore. The Little *Corrigan*, chronicled by Evans Wentz, allegedly had a beautiful sister who was taken by faeries and "replaced by a little girl babe, so badly deformed that it resembled a ball."[1298] A more explicit parallel comes from the Bros. Grimm:

> [Two lady faeries] took the child away, but upon arriving at the first hill, they began fighting over it, throwing it back and forth at each other like a ball. The child began to cry, which woke up the housemaid. She looked at the underground women's child and realized that an exchange had taken place. She ran to the front of the house, where she found the women arguing about the stolen child. She stepped into the fray and caught the child as they were throwing it back and forth. With the child in her arms she ran home. She placed the changeling outside the door, and the hill-women came and took it back.[1299]

As if this weren't striking enough, a similar story comes from 17th century Japan. A boy who disappeared crossing a field was returned to a rooftop in his village after they engaged in ritualistic drum-beating. Five days of silence followed before he eventually explained that two *tengu*, disguised as hermits, took him to a mountaintop, where one "sang and the others played with the boy as if he was a ball. Then an old priest came and asked them to hand over the boy. At first they took no notice of the priest, but finally they let the child loose."[1300]

RESOLUTIONS

Though there are no clear methods of retrieving children abducted by aliens, certain modern anecdotes reflect historical methods for banishing changelings. Another of abductee Katharine

Wilson's journal entries describes a memory where, once again in the peculiar "hospital" environment, she was given a feeble infant by one of the "nurses."

Handing the child off, Wilson saw "an incinerator... People are putting dead or dying babies into it. Somehow I know that this device doubles as a rejuvenator also. It can also heal babies." After the child was stuffed into the flames, Wilson was relieved to discover it began breathing again, revealed as perfectly healthy.[1301] Recall how parents put changelings into flames or chimneys to bring back their mortal children.

A pregnant woman in Orange County, New York—a locale which saw a large influx of Irish settlers in the 1700s[1302]—blacked out after sighting a series of UFOs in the night sky in October 1977. Upon regaining consciousness, her neck was stiff, and she experienced reproductive bleeding. She spoke with her boyfriend and was shocked to learn he had multiple interactions with short, red-eyed creatures on the property.

Several months later, her doctor informed her, to her surprise, she had miscarried. Following the news, she remembered a directive from her UFO contact: she was to wrap up any miscarried tissue and "put it outside in a certain spot," a directive she followed after passing subsequent material.[1303] While not a live child, this act vaguely echoes the practice of abandoning changelings in the wilderness.

HYBRIDS VS. CHANGELINGS: PHYSICAL DESCRIPTIONS

By far the most obvious and commonly cited point of comparison between changelings and human-alien hybrids is their physical appearance. It takes very little research to find descriptions perfectly matching tales of malformed faerie babies.

- **Stature and body shape.** Abductees interviewed by John Mack described the skin of their hybrid offspring as "dry and scaly and flaky,"[1304] "fleshy" as if covered in "old-age fat."[1305] Their gray bodies,[1306] sometimes big-bellied,[1307] are occasionally "short for their heads."[1308] Hybrids are strikingly tiny—"I couldn't believe that it could live on its own," said one witness[1309]—and are sometimes compared to the size of pears[1310] or grapefruit[1311] (recall Lady Wilde's mushroom-sized changeling). They often appear boneless,[1312] a parallel to the sponginess ascribed to the fae folk by Robert Kirk,[1313] or a changeling described by Asbjørnsen: "I don't think he had any joints at all."[1314]

- **Build and weight.** Hybrids are universally described as scrawny and thin,[1315] often appearing lifeless[1316] or frail.[1317] "I kind of liked holding her, but I was so afraid, she was so fragile-looking," said one of Jacobs' subjects.[1318] Unlike changelings, they are typically lightweight,[1319] though it should be noted faeries themselves were sometimes ascribed a lighter-than-air quality.[1320]

- **Head and eyes.** Like some changelings, hybrids typically have large eyes, sometimes completely black,[1321] sometimes with whites.[1322] Their heads are invariably oversized,[1323] recalling the German *dickkopf.*

- **Limbs.** One witness said his hybrid's "arms are really fragile," a sentiment echoed throughout numerous changeling accounts.[1324] Another described "pencils for arms and legs."[1325]

- **Face.** Hybrids' faces are wrinkled, giving rise to the term "wise babies."[1326] "They scared me when I first looked at them because they looked odd," said abductee Barbara Archer of the hybrids she saw. "They looked kind of old... They don't have much hair... They strike me as being very fragile. I feel like maybe they're what I would think of as premature babies... They don't look healthy to me."[1327] In one account, a hybrid's ears were pointed, calling to mind typical elfin stereotypes.[1328]

Human reactions have remained consistent when confronted with the physical features of these entities; whether changelings or hybrids, they almost always inspire the same revulsion and rejection in their "parents."

HYBRIDS VS. CHANGELINGS: DISPOSITION & BEHAVIOR

Cindy Doraty, whose mother was an abductee, developed a phobia of dolls at age four that continued into adulthood. Working with UFOlogists, Doraty finally pinpointed a moment in her childhood where she was led by a tall, female Grey alien to a room aboard an alien craft packed with "odd-looking children." They reminded her of cancer patients due to their sickly appearance and sparse hair. After one of the children gave her a toothy grin, Doraty began associating her dolls' smiles with the horrific trip, spawning a lifetime of fear.[1329]

The consistency with which hybrids are described as "wasting away, sickly, or phlegmatic" clearly mirrors the lethargy and inability to put on weight noted in so many changeling accounts.

"Abductees universally state that the baby does not have the normal human reactions of a human infant," Jacobs wrote. "It is almost always listless. It does not respond to touch as a normal baby would. It does not squirm; it does not have a grasping reflex with its hands."[1330]

Infirmity complements frequent impressions of old age from

hybrid babies. Recall how some changelings, particularly in Iceland, were regarded as elderly faeries, then consider the hypnotically retrieved memories of Susan Steiner: "It seems like maybe it's about three or four months old but it seems more alert...It seems somehow older and it seems knowledgeable."

Debbie Tomey's hybrid baby was described as appearing "really old." Another "looked like an old man, and he looked so wise... more wise than anybody in the world."[1331] One of Turner's subjects, Polly, described an October 23, 1991, "wise baby" dream:

> Then when he was wanting to nurse, I had this really weird thought, sort of apart from the dream, like standing off a little watching the dream. I thought, *What if he isn't really a baby? What if he is really some midget pervert?* I emphasized this last part because it indicates an awareness that we might be interacting with something less human and less innocent than it seemed.

In summer 1979, recurring witness Karen and her boyfriend Gary were strolling a country lane in Newquay, Cornwall, when they both heard a humming noise and rustling coming from nearby bushes. A blinding light then shot skyward from an adjacent field, leaving the couple with missing time. Soon afterward, Karen discovered she was pregnant and was plagued with birth nightmares. In these recurring dreams, she gave birth to a hyperintelligent baby, devilish and able to speak after delivery. On December 26, she awoke to a miscarriage, though this was not the last of her contacts.[1332]

Listlessness and wizened demeanor aside, hybrids rarely behave like changelings. They seem indifferent to food and on the whole are quite well behaved and quiet—a stark contrast to the endless insatiability and crying of most changelings.[1333] Instead of vocalizing, hybrids "communicate with the abductee through their eyes, as if they were absorbing information from the abductee through neural coupling," Jacobs writes.[1334]

However, this demeanor alters as they grow older. Developing hybrids begin acting more and more like adult changelings as they age. The latest speculation by David Jacobs holds that hybrids get gradually more human with each successive generation, leading to a worldwide sleeper cell of indistinguishable, telepathic "hubrids" now living among us.

The scenario would be frightening if Jacobs didn't describe hubrids as *so incredibly stupid.* "Hubrids represent the end point of the human hybridization plan," he writes, basing his conclusions on his subjects' testimony. "Even after being educated about aspects of Earth living, hubrids are still exceptionally naïve about the complexities of human life, and they require an immense amount of help from abductees."[1335]

In what would make an excellent sitcom, human abductees claim to have been assigned certain hubrids by their alien overlords to show them the proverbial ropes. During the course of these antics, abductees may be tasked with, say, explaining the "rules" of eating an orange to a hubrid: "Where do they come from? How do you get them? How many do you get at one time? How many do you eat?... Do you eat it on your own in private? Do you eat all of it or do you throw part away?" In other examples, an exasperated abductee had to explain canned food could not, in fact, be cooked directly in the can, and furnishings should not all be crammed into one room of a home.[1336]

Setting aside the comedic tone of these dubious encounters, their social ineptitude corresponds to how changelings became dullards if they survived into adulthood: adult changelings were physically disabled, adult hubrids intellectually disabled. In cultures practicing the Fairy Faith, physical ability—to plow, shoe horses, milk cows, etc.—was a prized attribute possessed by contributing members of society. In the modern West, where so few individuals have occupations involving physical labor, intellect has become a more valuable commodity.

Hubrids are also prone to wander, similar to how more mobile changelings roamed the countryside. Like Evans Wentz's Little *Corrigan*, they are fond of nocturnal rambles, needing only a few hours' sleep (in one case, three hubrids visited an abductee in the middle of the night to discuss how iPods operate).

Even in a modern mythology stuffed to bursting with audacious claims, the notion of clueless hubrids on our streets is incredibly difficult to believe as a UFOlogical reality. Perhaps Jacobs' subjects are merely expressing common literary tropes embedded in the collective unconscious. Similar themes stretch back into fiction at least as far as William Henry Frost's 1900 *Fairies and Folk of Ireland*. In this folklore-inspired work, the faerie king becomes jealous of "the wonderful magic that the human people knew so well." The protagonist offers the following solution:

> "You know well," said Naggeneen, "that your people can find out nothing by going out and watching what men do. Now, what you want is to get a human child here, or maybe two of them, and keep them and let them grow up with you here, and then send them out to learn everything that men do, and come back and teach it to your people. Then you'll learn all these things that men do, and you can do the like."[1337]

BABY PRESENTATIONS VS. MIDWIVES & WET NURSES TO THE FAERIES

As noted, baby presentations regularly involve alien abductees nursing their hybrid children—astute readers have already drawn connections to tales of human wet nurses abducted by faeries. Both scenarios involve women taken by mysterious forces to strange environs where they are forced to provide care to inhuman children.

During these rendezvous, female abductees often find themselves spontaneously lactating for no reason—one abductee told Budd Hopkins how she breastfed a hybrid baby at age 12.[1338] In other stories, women are either already lactating as part of another pregnancy or (most curiously) fail to lactate yet are still implored to pantomime nursing. This strongly suggests the *act*, or at least the *intent*, is the most important aspect of these encounters; it is either pure theatre, or a type of metaphysical transfer takes place. In faerie lore, the Good Folk did not actually eat offerings left for them, but rather subsided on the food's essence, or *foyson*— perhaps the intangible essence of milk, or of the mother herself, is the object of desire. [1339]

Both baby presentations and "midwife to the faeries" tales alike end in revulsion; in the former, the sight of the hybrid repulses the woman, while in the latter a daub of ointment dispels glamour, revealing the true squalor of Fairyland. While magical faerie eye ointment fails to show up in baby presentations, Budd Hopkins suggested "the eye socket seems to be a good place to insert implants," after hearing of cases where abductees claimed needles pierced their eyes.[1340]

Ointments and salves of other types do appear in baby presentations, however. For example, one of John Mack's patients saw a hybrid "sponged… with a green liquid, as if to put energy into their bodies."[1341] In another account, a mother refused to breastfeed her child and instead received "a bowl of brown liquid with a 'paintbrush'" to coat the baby with "nourishment"[1342] (recall the Welsh tale of a faerie babe who needed its eye coated in ointment each morning by its mortal foster mother). Minor details such as these—coupled with Jacobs' claim that extraterrestrials consume food through their skin—suggest the entire nursing protocol is a sham. The hybrids are receiving something other than food.

The prevalence of physical touch in these scenarios further supports the concept of energetic nourishment. When baby presentations do not involve nursing, abductees are commonly "required to touch, hold, or hug these offspring," Jacobs wrote. "Apparently it is absolutely essential for the child to have human contact… any physical contact seems to suffice."[1343] One of his subjects, Reshma Kamal, recalled under regression a female alien entreating her to hold a hybrid because "the babies need to be held, otherwise they can't grow."[1344] This need for touch is so great some abductees are even put through baffling "dummy births," where their captors go through the pageantry of labor and present a child—usually much older than an infant—as their own.[1345] Following physical contact, listless hybrids seem slightly more energized and healthier.

Many in the New Age community claim aliens need to learn love from human hands, but more compelling connections can be found in faerie lore. Recall that any faerie woman in labor sought mortal touch, whose ability to heal denizens of the Otherworld was well documented in myth. In an inversion of the typical "midwife to the faeries" trope—where faerie mothers needed mortal midwives to birth their children—fetus retrievals feature mortal abductees in need of alien "midwives" to deliver their hybrid babies.

This clever variation aside, mortals are still called upon to assist in the care of nonhuman infants. In 1989, an elderly lady from Oregon was brought aboard a craft by an egg-headed entity asking for "help" with "the babies."[1346] Though she could not remember any further details, it is unlikely she missed much—the reasons behind these abductions are shockingly mundane.

Jen, the five-year-old daughter of an abductee from Cape Cod, Massachusetts, told her mother "little men with the big black eyes" took her to a playground to show seven other peculiar-looking children "how to play."[1347] This is a common request, alongside showing hybrid children how to dance.

From abductee-cum-researcher Beverly Trout's experience:

> I saw that while in the aliens' custody I'd been approached by a "cowboy" (with blanked-out facial features), then led before a group of "people," all of whom were dressed in country-western clothing. But I instantly knew they weren't dressed right— that their country-western garb was decidedly

inappropriate. For example, instead of cowboy boots, they wore mud boots. Their clothing colors were badly coordinated, and for some reason they were shuffling their feet as they stood in lines before me. They didn't look very lively, and I got the impression they were disadvantaged somehow, that they needed help.

Later, I felt stupid for not instantly recognizing what was happening—these were hybrids, and I was expected to teach them line dancing. I think that the alien scanning my computer later that night was probably going through the dance files stored there.[1348]

Humorous as the image of awkward alien "cowbrids" might be, trace themes from the Fairy Faith can be detected. Playing and dancing were important to faeries and seem important to aliens as well. Just as faeries once needed the help of humans to raise their children, aliens need abductees to aid in socializing and teaching hybrids.

HYBRIDS VS. STOCKS & GLAMOUR

UFOlogists completely overlook parallels between stocks—logs left by faeries in the place of human children—and modern hybrid lore. This oversight is understandable; even though the horticultural practice of using stocks to join plants is a potent metaphor for hybridization, no abductee claims to have been handed an actual log masquerading as an infant (the closest account comes from a Vancouver, Canada abductee who claimed to have been shown "a scaly brown baby" in a sort of cocoon).[1349]

A handful of clues allude to the old stock motif by connecting hybrids with plants. Like inanimate chunks of wood, hybrids seem wholly lifeless and immobile. Descriptions of baby incubatoriums sound akin to hydroponics laboratories, where plants are grown in tubes; the green color of fetuses sometimes reported in these facilities underscores the botanical similarity.[1350] One abductee even claimed the incubatorium was "a large contraption shaped like a Christmas tree, but instead of branches there were incubators filled with babies."[1351]

The most compelling connection between stocks and alien hybridization comes in the form of residual evidence. In 1998, researchers Roger Leir and Derrel Sims provided evidence that markings on the skin of abductees could be revealed under black light (UV-A light).

> They report that the light shows what appear to be fluorescent markings, greenish in color and not easily washed off. They reportedly last from one hour to perhaps ten days, according to Leir and Sims. A variation, reported in regard to women who had held hybrid babies, was red fluorescent markings where the babies contacted their bodies.[1352]

In 2014, Eve Lorgen found similar marks on experiencers visible under UV-A. "Less common types of fluorescence emit in the red-pink (hot pink) region and are found primarily on the hands, fingers, palms and neck region of abductees," she found. "These abductees report handling and cuddling of infant alien/human hybrid creatures."[1353]

In sunlight, chlorophyll—the photosynthesis-generating lifeblood of all plants—absorbs red and blue-violet spectrums and reflects green light. Under UV-A, however, it fluoresces reddish pink.[1354]

To explicitly draw the comparison: changelings in faerie lore were logs-in-disguise, while those touching human-alien hybrids end up covered in a substance resembling tree residue. The folklorist says this is a resurgence of faerie lore in the modern day. The UFOlogist retorts that extraterrestrials must be closely related to plants. The comparative Fortean simply points out the connection.

Faerie glamour was used to cloak rubbish, changing detritus into delicious food and hiding the reality that exchanged infants were, in reality, worthless stocks. If faerie lore is consistently represented in UFOlogy (and it seems to be), we should anticipate accounts where these sacrosanct alien-human hybrids are revealed as insignificant garbage.

"The fetuses, whatever their origin, are not always treated as if they were precious experiments vital to the survival of either our race or the aliens," Turner wrote. "In a few instances, abductees report watching as aliens deliberately destroy fetuses in the 'fetal nursery' scenario."[1355]

Allusions abound to hybrids lacking the essential spark of life. In 1985 Canadian abductee Alvina Scott was told fetuses in the incubatorium "were cloned from the occupants for donor-compatibility, and used for organ transplants" and thusly "contained no essence or spirit."[1356] Reshma Kamal described her hybrid baby as "emotionally empty."[1357] Whitley Strieber described the faces of hybrid fetuses in drawers as "empty," their eyes and mouths agape.[1358] In fact, many get the impression hybrids are wholly artificial: "She doesn't look real," said another of Jacobs' subjects, abductee Janet Demerest, of the child she met. "I don't even think they're real!" agreed an abductee during a regression with Budd Hopkins. "I don't know what they are, but they're not really like babies."[1359]

Do disposable fetuses and soulless hybrids suggest these entities are less than they appear—merely disposable, worthless means to an end, not unlike faerie stocks?

Even if literal glamour is not employed to make hybrids appear important, perhaps simple deception is at play. Hybrids may well be misdirection, distracting witnesses from the true meaning behind baby presentations. "The entire hybrid scenario could be a fantastic cover for an agenda that is completely different than we are being shown," wrote researcher Donna Higbee in 1995.[1360]

Karla Turner embraced this possibility—several of her subjects contended baby presentations were "not to nurture this crossbred infant, not to teach the ETs about emotional love and physical bonding, but to blow our goddamn minds. They use our bodies to get to our minds and emotions... WE care very much, so that is why our bodies are important to them: to get at our caring."

Another abductee maintained, "The hybrid presentation liturgy is not a bonding exercise. In reality it is an act of scrutiny against the mother's measure of courage and understanding. It has a lot to do with mental pain and how the mother deals with it."[1361]

Each testimony implies metaphysical motives behind the hybridization program. In the nearly four decades since such apocalyptic scenarios were first proposed, we have seen zero tangible evidence for the grand schemes espoused by Jacobs and Hopkins. Perhaps the hybrid program is indeed a lifeless, beglamoured sham—but why the theatricality? If world dominance is not the goal, then what motivates this "alien other" to continue interacting with us—and our children?

INDIGO & STAR CHILDREN VS. CHANGELINGS

Fred, an experiencer from New England, claimed regular visits beginning at age three from a tall being with large eyes who wore a silver jumpsuit. On one occasion, the entity "took Fred through the wall" into an alien Otherworld where he was "taken to see his real father," who told him that while his earth parents had been handpicked to raise him, he was not human. Instead, he was one of many children of extraterrestrial parentage who "had tasks to perform and, at some future date when a major event was to occur, all of the star children would suddenly know who they were and would be able to communicate with one another."[1362]

If we draw parallels between hybrids and changelings, the discrepancy with Indigo and Star Children—those hybrids allowed to live among mortal parents—must be addressed. After all, changelings were universally repulsive, while Indigo and Star Children are considered to be "deeply empathic, visionary, intuitive, having a deep sense of mission/purpose, and a very thin veil between the physical and spiritual worlds."[1363] They are also exceedingly healthy, precocious,[1364] "intellectually gifted, resistant to authority," and struggle with "the mundane, non-creative aspects of life—such as the education system."[1365]

Indigo Children are more-or-less interchangeable with Star Children. These youths are touched by the paranormal—usually extraterrestrial intervention—and are sometimes believed to be literal human-alien hybrids living with mortal parents. It is an old trope, paralleling "men of renown," demigods, those born of mortals and deities, from a variety of historical settings: Heracles of Greece, Arjuna of India, even Jesus Christ of Israel.

- According to Brad Steiger, in 1969 Gloria W. of Wisconsin made love to a reptilian that transformed into "the most beautiful man that she had ever seen." Nine months later she gave birth to a son, Ramar, who grew up to be an intelligent chemistry major and athlete with "psychic abilities far beyond the ordinary."[1366]

- In 1979, a Dearborn, Michigan, witness gave birth to a girl who displayed "excessively rapid brain development" and "potential genius ability." She was oddly fascinated by anomalous lights in the sky, which reciprocated her interest with regular appearances.[1367]

- A 1983 *Flying Saucer Review* article told of a Colorado witness who, three years earlier, experienced car trouble, missing time, and a curious abdominal mark. Shortly thereafter, she was surprised to discover she was nearly two months pregnant at the time of her experience; though not carried to full term, the child proved "more developed than was expected and continues to be very healthy and mentally vital and alert, to the point of precociousness."[1368]

- One lifelong abductee told Bret Oldham that her son, pursuing a PhD as of 2017, had "never broken a bone or suffered a sprain even though he was active with baseball, surfing, running and so forth. He skipped grades in school, and his IQ was tested at 204."[1369]

- Beginning at age three, "Art" from Phoenix remembered regular nighttime visits from a peculiar lady. "You have so much to learn and so little time," she once told him. When Art started a family decades later, his son was born two-and-a-half months premature, yet "walked and talked intelligently at the age of nine months." By age four he was receiving visits from his father's Lady. According to Art, the child told him he "had much to learn in so little time."[1370]

The Indigo Children narrative presents a clever inversion of changeling legends: while truly hideous hybrids are kept safely in the Otherworld on alien spacecraft, desirable children are allowed to stay among humans on earth.

"Often children report that they have been told by the aliens that the aliens are their real parents," wrote Rose Hargrove. "Children may grow up with a strong sense that they do not belong there, and that the earth is not their 'real' home, or that one or both of their parents are not biologically related to them."[1371]

In this sense, the *adults* are reframed as horrifying changelings, as the alien other. "A very young abductee is often systematically trained to believe, in effect, that the woman who lives at home, on Earth, is a false mother, an unrelated impostor," said Budd Hopkins. "The young abductee often holds this subtly-imposed concept well on into later life, passively accepting the idea that the woman from whom one was physically delivered after nine months of shared lifeblood, the woman by whom one was nursed and protected and nurtured and loved, is an impostor."[1372]

Indigo variants include youth who acquire superhuman abilities after contact with UFOs, much as abductees like Anne Jeffries did after staying among faeries. In 1973, a three-year-old British witness watched "three large orangey-white lights in a triangle formation only about a metre or so from outside the window," only to find her intellectual development accelerate. "By the time she started school a favourite party trick of the family was to get her to stun visitors by reading articles from the *Bacup Echo* just as she might if she were an adult," Randles wrote.[1373]

In another example, a boy aged 6 from Vancouver, Canada, saw a light "like a shining star" one night in 1986, having had a flying disc sighting a few months before. The boy found he possessed "the ability to read his parents' minds."[1374]

In spite of changelings' undesirability, they nonetheless share certain attributes with Indigos. According to Doreen Virtue, author of *The Care and Feeding of Indigo Children*, Indigos are restless, have short attention spans, and possess "old souls"—qualities certainly in alignment with cantankerous faerie babes. Moreover, they may be exhaustion-prone and ornery, depending upon their diet. Indigos allegedly have a predisposition to hypoglycemia, which can make infants "sweet and fine one minute, and then for no apparent reason... agitated, angry, and irritable the next."[1375]

The preternatural abilities of Indigos also mirror advanced skills displayed by changelings. Changelings showcased musical virtuosity, often playing bagpipes or reeds in infancy, while Indigos exhibit an affinity for the arts at a young age. In much the same manner that changelings rarely displayed these abilities in front of others, "Indigo Children may flunk music classes because they can't memorize musical scales, but after school, they might compose the most beautiful music at home on their musical instruments, using their inner senses," Virtue claims.[1376]

Indigos also share qualities with the children born of mortal-faerie unions. They are headstrong, independent, passionate, and proud;[1377] recall how Lady Wilde said beautiful human-faerie hybrids were bold, reckless, and had "a strange mystic nature," gaining fame through "music and song. They were passionate, revengeful, and not easy to live with."[1378]

EGG SYMBOLISM

Few images repeat themselves as regularly in UFOlogy as the egg. Egg-shaped UFOs are regularly reported, Greys have egg-shaped heads, women have their eggs harvested. Queerly enough, Hopkins' star abductee Virginia Horton even had an egg obsession.

"I remember I always liked eggs, even when l was little," she said. "My grandmother had a porcelain egg for darning and I was very attached to it and I got one for my birthday. I like it. I always like eggs. They had such a nice feeling." Her first abduction, in fact, occurred after gathering eggs from her grandfather's barn.[1379]

The importance of eggs in faerie lore has been addressed, particularly regarding the brewery of eggshells, by which changelings were revealed and removed from homes. Eggs are "a recurring motif in folktales about changelings, and nobody has really explained it, but it's interesting to note how little folklore there is on eggs in general," said Keble College professor Diane Purkiss. "Chickens very rarely get bewitched... so I wonder if the egg has some kind of power derived from being an enclosed but living thing?"[1380] According to some beliefs, "the fairies can take anything but a chicken or an egg."[1381]

Recall how enormous quantities of eggs were often employed in the "brewery of eggshells" method, as well as the manner in which abductions taper off sharply for older women past their sexual prime. A mother could not rid herself of a changeling until she used every last egg in the house; a female abductee is not rid of hybrids until she uses every last egg in her body.

TWILIGHT LANGUAGE

Loren Coleman, one of the foremost contemporary Forteans and cryptozoologists, first introduced the world to the concept of "twilight language" in his 2004 book *The Copycat Effect*. Coleman describes twilight language as exploring "hidden meanings and synchromystic connections via onomatology (study of names) and toponymy (study of place names)."[1382]

Coleman's twilight language approach yields startling coincidences when applied to the field of alien abduction researchers. Consider the two individuals most responsible for popularizing the alien hybridization program: Budd Hopkins and David Jacobs.

Hopkins' surname is of British, Welsh, and Irish origin, derivative of "son of Hob."[1383] In English folklore, "hob was the most common name for rough, hairy creatures of the brownie type, whose work brought prosperity to farms."[1384] Essentially, Budd Hopkins' last name means "faerie child"—fitting for someone whose life work crafted a new changeling mythos.

The name Jacobs, on the other hand, means "supplanting."[1385] This is a reference to Jacob of the Bible, who disguised himself as his brother Esau in order to obtain the birthright blessing from his father. Jacob managed to fool his blind father by covering himself in goatskins, since Esau was covered in hair; in essence, he himself became a changeling, impersonating one of his father's sons for his own advantage. Just like Hopkins, David Jacobs' very namesake echoes the changeling concept.

The parallels between aliens and faeries are remarkable and extend deeply into the lore surrounding paranormal child abduction. The means and motivations behind both phenomena imply a shared ontological reality, but further resonances abound in other realms of Forteana; while only tangentially related at face value, the topics of Sasquatch, "crib creepers," and permanent disappearances warrant investigation before drawing final conclusions about thieves in the night.

Chapter 18:
"Come Out Towards the Woods"
Child Sasquatch Abduction

Every modern male has, lying at the bottom of his psyche, a large, primitive being covered with hair down to his feet.
— Robert Bly, *Iron John*

Recurring abductee Sue Jones (pseudonym) told investigator Don Worley of a relationship she had fostered with her primary Grey handler, Zanna. Jones recalled that Zanna and other entities would "fly her and her sister out of their upstairs bedroom and up to the UFO" as children. Her visitations were not mere childhood fancy, as some alleged landing sites left dead vegetation and damaged telephone poles, as if a large craft had briefly touched down.[1386]

In addition to Zanna, Jones befriended a duo of "para-apes," Teluke and Teleel, who "could shift into her physical dimension or she could sense them in their dimension," Worley wrote. "This wondrous ability acquired from the aliens permitted her to even perceive deceased humans in the other dimension. Also on one occasion, when she played her flute she saw 'Wood Sprites' down in the forest, and a little 'Brownie' came and sat on the cross-piece of her yard swing."[1387]

Jones could well have been mentally ill, though Worley didn't seem to suspect as much. If she was not, her testimony generates an enormous problem for UFOlogists, cryptozoologists, and ghost hunters alike—what are we to make of aliens, Sasquatch, the dead, and faeries intermingling?

GLASS HOUSES

Like UFOs—which are sometimes courteous enough to leave burn marks, as in Jones' case—there is undoubtedly a physical component to the Sasquatch phenomenon. Yet it could be easily argued every other Fortean discipline has "Bigfoot Envy," for a plethora of physical evidence exists supporting the creature's reality (e.g. tracks, hair samples, scat) that so many other phenomena find lacking. There is no denying, both in UFOlogy and cryptozoology, that certain anomalies interact with our material world in measurable ways.

On the other hand, Sasquatch sightings are also akin to UFO experiences in their stubborn unwillingness to yield definitive proof. Many in the cryptozoological community refuse to come to grips with the true High Strangeness surrounding Sasquatch: witnesses report creatures who disappear suddenly, have glowing red eyes, are impervious to gunfire, engage in telepathic "mind speak"—and, of course, are seen in conjunction with UFOs. (Anyone seeking to further explore this last data point is encouraged to consult the work of Stan Gordon, particularly his book *Silent Invasion*.)

These are not the qualities one would expect from an undiscovered population of flesh-and-blood hominids. They are, however, qualities one associates with the fae folk.

Parallels between Sasquatch and faerie lore are substantial and grossly underappreciated. Like aliens and faeries, they purportedly retreat to subterranean spaces; are associated with anomalous lights;[1388] and have been accused of mutilating livestock.[1389] Like faerie folk in the British Isles, First Nations traditions have certain food taboos associated with Sasquatch,[1390] and there is consistent overlap between their horrendous stench and the odors noted in UFO and faerie encounters.[1391] Sasquatch, like the fae folk, are believed to both braid the manes of horses[1392] and suckle milk from cattle.[1393] Faeries and Sasquatch alike have the ability to incapacitate witnesses at a distance—elf-shot from the former, and, according to some, ultra-low frequency infrasound from the latter.[1394] Sightings of Sasquatch map very clearly onto areas in America with the greatest amount of rainfall, while faeries were most active on wet days.[1395] Like faeries and UFOs, Sasquatch are sometimes associated with the dead (for example, the Kwakiutl believe the hairy *buk'wus* presides over drowned ghosts).[1396] They have even caused missing time, as claimed by one witness who allegedly struck a Sasquatch with their car,[1397] and—as elaborated upon shortly—Sasquatch, like faeries, possess an intense interest in human sexuality and hybridity.

A great many faeries were described as covered in hair. Even the tall, hair-covered *Woodwose*, one of the Celtic fae folk otherwise referred to as the Green Man, has a passing resemblance to Sasquatch.[1398] A similar faerie being, the *Ghillie Dhu*, lived a solitary life in the Scottish woods as the quintessential wild man, disheveled and clad in the detritus of the woods.[1399] This appearance provided the name for the shaggy "ghillie suits" used by military personnel today to blend into their surroundings.[1400] The resemblance between the *Ghillie Dhu*, ghillie suits, and Sasquatch is not lost on Australian armed forces, who refer to their ghillie suits as "yowie suits"—named after their continent's own hairy hominid legend.[1401]

The seasoned cryptozoologist no doubt rolls their eyes at these comparisons, firmly of the belief that one day (any day now) a large, undiscovered primate will be bagged by some enterprising hunter and disprove such nonsensical trends. Simultaneously, these individuals forget anyone interested in these fringe topics—be it UFOs, ghosts, Sasquatch, or faeries—lives in a glass house, precluding the throwing of stones. Perhaps the best retort to any cryptozoologist, UFOlogist, or ghost hunter criticizing another area of Fortean research is the old playground mantra: "It takes one to know one."

Every idea should remain on the table until some sort of definitive proof is obtained. As with UFOs, the goal of this discussion is not to reduce all Sasquatch phenomena to faerie activity, but to rather point out the strong points of comparison between the two.

LORE

If Sasquatch is indeed an undiscovered primate, its affinity for abduction is supported by a robust history of apes as child kidnappers. An ex-Ugandan park ranger told Idaho State University anthropologist Jeffrey Meldrum of an incident where "a chimp stole a native baby that had been parked beside the fields while its mother labored"—a loose parallel to children snatched by faeries while mothers worked in Irish fields. In his 2006 book *Sasquatch: Legend Meets Science*, Meldrum cited another example from 1926 where a boy of age 12 was "attacked and badly torn by a chimpanzee" near Sierra Leone. Meldrum was able to verify eight additional accounts of child theft by apes over a 17-year period in Uganda.[1402]

Perhaps this very real threat informed traditional beliefs in child abduction by hairy hominids worldwide. In the rural American south, parents still urge their children to beware tall, hirsute "boogers." "When I was younger, my grandmother always told me, 'Beware of the boogers,'" said one southern witness. "Don't be outside after dark, stay close to the house.'"[1403]

Belief in child abduction by large, hairy man-apes remains a staple in the lore of many First Nations tribes. "A young Native American woman who attended an evening seminar I presented at the Idaho Museum of Natural History..." wrote Meldrum, "remarked afterward that when she was a child, her grandparents had warned her not to venture up certain canyons or the monkey-man would get her." Among the Yokut of central California, children are warned away from rivers or roadways late at night, lest they be taken and eaten by Sasquatch.[1404] Further up America's west coast, Salish mothers ensured "children always slept in the center surrounded by their elders for fear that the *tsiatko* would lift the mats and spirit them away."[1405] In a parallel to European faerie lore, the *asin* of Oregon's Alsean folklore is fond of bewitching huckleberry bushes "so any child who eats its fruit will fall under [its] enchantments and wander off into the woods."[1406]

A Yakima informant told frontiersman L.V. McWhorter of the *Tah-tah-kle'-ah*, or Owl-Woman Monsters, "tall, big women, who lived in a cave" and "hunted children, as better eating":

> The Indians were careful, but the *Tah-tah-kle'-ah* caught one little boy, not to eat, but to raise up and live with them. The boy thought he would be killed, but he was not. The *Tah-tah-kle'-ah* had him several days... [One day], when they were out of sight, the boy hurried away. He ran fast, traveled over rough, wild places, and at last reached his own people... After many years the two *Tah-tah-kle'-ah* were destroyed. None knew how, but perhaps by a higher power. Their cave home became red hot and blew out. The monster-women were never seen again, never more heard of but they have always been talked about as the most dangerous beings on earth. One other of the five sisters was drowned. From her eye, all owls were created. The person or power that killed her said to her, "From now on, your eye will be the only part of you to act. At night it will go to certain birds, the owls."[1407]

Recall the significance of owls to legends of Lilith and *strigoi*.

The work of author Danny Vendramini suggests that ancestral memories of human predation in the distant past by Neanderthals may form the basis for modern Sasquatch stories. In his book *Them and Us: How Neanderthal Predation Created Modern Humans*, Vendramini speculates Neanderthal man "hunted, killed and cannibalized early humans for 50,000 years," sometimes abducting children and raping human females. Alongside this theory, he also contends that modern reconstructions of Neanderthals are grossly inaccurate, humanizing the species far too much; in his artist recreations, Vendramini depicts Neanderthals as much more frightening, apelike, hair-covered beasts.[1408]

DOCUMENTED CHILD SASQUATCH ABDUCTION

Some erroneously claim Sasquatch "seem to appear most often to young children and sexually mature women," disregarding the plentiful number of sightings by adult men, especially including outdoorsmen.[1409] The statement has a kernel of truth however—if one amends that Sasquatch seem to express *great interest* in children and sexually mature women. Indeed, the September 2000 collection of the famed Skookum impression—allegedly depicting a Sasquatch forearm, hip, thigh, and buttocks—was acquired after researchers played recordings of children playing and infants crying.[1410]

Stories abound where Sasquatch is observed closely watching children, seemingly drawn in by sounds of laughter and playing. In the famed "Momo" (Missouri Monster) flap of the early 1970s, a large, hairy hominid was regularly seen in close proximity to children. In one of the earliest sightings—July 11, 1972, near the town of Louisiana—Terry and Wally Harrison, aged eight and five, respectively, were playing in the woods near their house. The boys' older sister, alerted by their screams, looked through the bathroom window and saw a black, six-to-seven-foot tall creature.[1411]

Similar accounts can be found from the UFO-Bigfoot flap that contemporaneously swept Pennsylvania. In one case, a young girl claimed "a big dark hairy man with pointed ears" stared at her through her bedroom window at night.

On September 1, 1973 a mother was visiting a Youngstown cemetery with her toddler when she noticed the sound of a baby crying in the distance. To her surprise, she saw a Sasquatch standing mere feet from her child. "It seemed as though it was when the baby began to cry, the creature started to slowly walk toward the child. The woman ran without hesitation and grabbed her baby, then quickly got into her car." Another mother ran into the creature around the same time and felt the being was somehow tracking her baby's scent.[1412]

Sasquatch's interest in children is reported in some of the earliest encounters. A 1910 account from Wisconsin told of a 10-year old girl who was followed in the woods by "a man-like furry creature."[1413] Given their unfamiliarity with the concept of Sasquatch, these early witnesses often described a variety of primates. In 1913 a young girl playing in a grassy clearing near Labrador, Canada, fled from a "gorilla" that grinned and beckoned to her. A mother in Illinois in the early 1940s saw an enormous "baboon" approaching her home, causing her to take her three children away from the property.[1414]

While these cases certainly suggest intent to abduct, some accounts are more explicit. Multiple children playing in the woods near Pottstown, Pennsylvania, in 1897 told their parents they evaded a wild man in the woods who tried to grab them.[1415] As with faerie abductions, the intervention of guardians can foil these efforts: a Chinese villager claimed an eight-foot-tall hairy hominid grabbed his daughter in 1957, only releasing her once he started beating it with a stick.[1416] Eleven years later a large, hairy beast grabbed a four-year-old child in Kinloch, Missouri; after her aunt screamed and the family dog gave chase, it dropped her.[1417]

Other attempts have met with better success.

- In 1602, 17-year-old Anthoinette Culet disappeared while shepherding near Naves, France. Later that year, lumberjacks near the mouth of a cave claimed to hear Culet's voice from behind a boulder telling them she had been kidnapped by a large, hairy monster.[1418]

- Two-year-old Florence Hughes disappeared from Bradford, Pennsylvania, in July 1888 while playing outdoors. Locals blamed a wild man seen just a few days earlier. "It is now feared the loathsome wretch has spirited the child away to his lair in the hills," the local paper said. A pervasive fog stymied a search party of 200 people, and Florence was never seen again.[1419]

- Twenty-eight witnesses saw Sasquatch near Yankton, Oregon in 1926. The area was allegedly plagued by disappearances of livestock and children.[1420]

- In Thom Powell's book *The Locals*, a lifelong Missouri witness named Dora Bradley recalled a Sasquatch funeral in her youth. "When I was seven years old, I woke up one late summer night. It was a full moon with a breeze. I found that I was lying on a bed made of sticks. I felt chilly because my back touched a cold cave wall. I saw my brother sitting on a stick bed across from me in a small cave. I smelled something unpleasant. I watched very hard and realized it was a dark bigfoot sitting about 5 feet from me. I saw another Bigfoot digging a hole in the dirt. It picked up the small dark body of what might have been a dead infant and put it into the earth." The Sasquatch then picked up her brother and took him away, while another creature nearby pulled her to its chest as she cried. The other Sasquatch returned, retrieved Dora, and dropped her off in the family garden. This was one of at least two similar encounters.[1421]

- In another example of repeated Sasquatch abduction from 1962, a 12-year-old Ohio girl claimed few memories of her kidnappings, only that the events seemed to last the entire night. In one exception, she recalled lying on a slab of rock while all about her Sasquatch were "smiling and laughing." The creatures also regularly harassed her, laughing and slapping her house in the night.[1422] (The slab of rock resembles the tables in alien abduction lore, while the household disturbances echo both poltergeist and faerie activity.)

- On June 14, 1969, six-year-old Dennis Martin disappeared from Spence Field in the Great Smoky Mountains. The ensuing search lasted through September and involved Green Berets flown in from Fort Bragg—an odd reaction to a missing persons case. Several hours later, the Key family, hoping to observe a bear, heard an unearthly scream in an area six miles away. The youngest son pointed out what he thought at first was a bear... only the figure was running upright and carrying something on its shoulder. No trace of Martin was ever found.[1423]

- On May 25, 1990, two boys and a girl were playing hide-and-seek on the banks of a canal in Pakistan when a hair-covered creature ambushed them. The being, described as female, struck the boys and took four-year-old Gul Naz. An enormous search party only yielded his clothing. He was found dead several days later.[1424]

One account worth a closer look was printed in the June 9, 1857, edition of Salem's *Weekly Oregon Statesman*, recently rediscovered by author and researcher Timothy Renner for his book *Bigfoot: West Coast Wild Men*. Because of its depth of resonance with faerie lore, it is reprinted here in its entirety.

Dear Sir — A most wonderful and thrilling adventure has recently occurred in the southern part of this county. A few weeks since, it appears, a man and a boy started in a quest of some lost cattle, and they had traveled a considerable distance from home when night overtook them far away from any human habitation, and building a fire, they lay down to sleep beneath the spreading branches of a stately fir tree. Towards midnight the boy was awakened by a loud plaintive cry that appeared to emanate from a human being in distress not far distant from the spot where he reclined. Springing to his feet with alacrity, and without disturbing his companion, he approached the spot from whence proceeded this, to him, singularly forlorn outcry; he had not advanced many steps however, when he observed an object approaching him that appeared like a man about twelve or fifteen feet high, of athletic proportions, with glaring eyes which had the appearance of liquid balls of fire. The monster drew near to the boy who was unable, from fright, to move a single step, and seizing him by the arm, dragged him forcibly away towards the mountains, over logs, underbrush, swamps, rivers and land with a velocity that seemed to our hero like flying. They had traveled in this manner perhaps an hour and a quarter, when the monster sunk upon the earth apparently exhausted. Our hero then became aware that this creature was indeed a wild man, whose body was completely covered with shaggy brown hair, about four inches in length; some of his teeth protruded from his mouth like tusks, his hands were armed with formidable claws instead of fingers, but his feet, singular to relate, appeared natural, being clothed with moccasins similar to those worn by Indians. Our hero had scarcely made these observations when the "wild man" suddenly started onward as before, never for a moment relaxing his grip on the boy's arm, which had now become painful indeed. They had not proceeded far before they entered an almost impenetrable thicket of logs and undergrowth, when the "wild man" stopped, reclined upon a log, and gave one shriek, terrific and prolonged, the reverberations of which seemed to continue for the space of five minutes; immediately after which the earth opened at their feet, as if a trap door, ingeniously contrived, had just been raised. Entering at once this subterranean abode by a ladder rudely constructed of hazel brush, they proceeded downward, perhaps 150 or 200 feet, when they reached the bottom of a vast cave, which was brilliantly illuminated with a peculiar phosphorescent light, and water trickled from the sides of the cave in minute jets, the appearance of which was indeed singular. Above, the cave seemed slightly arched, the ceiling apparently composed of seashells of every conceivable shape and color; the bottom was, or appeared to be thickly strewn with the bones of many kinds of animals, the sight of which impressed our hero with a fearful presentiment of his own impending fate. As our hero thus closely observed the interior of this awful cave, the "wild man" left him, as if instinctively called away before partaking of his midnight repast of "roasted boy." Presently the huge monster returned by a side door, leading gently by the hand a young and delicate female of almost miraculous grace and beauty, who had doubtless been immured in this dreadful dungeon for years. As they approached our hero, the young lady fell upon her knees, and in some unknown language, in plaintive accents seemed to plead for the privilege of remaining forever in the cave of the "wild man." This singular conduct caused our hero to imagine that the "wild man," conscience stricken, had resolved to set at liberty his lovely victim, by placing her in charge of our hero, whom he had evidently captured for that purpose. As this thought passed through the mind of our hero, his ears were greeted with the strains of the most unearthly music which came from the innermost recesses of the cave. The "wild man" wept piteously as he listened to the sweet voice of the charmer, commingled with the wild music, and sobbing like a child, his handkerchief moist with grief, he raised her very carefully from her recumbent posture, and led her gently away as they had come. A moment afterwards, the damsel returned alone and advancing towards our hero with ladylike modesty and grace, placed in his hands a beautifully embossed card, upon which appeared the following words, traced in the most exquisite hand evidently the lady's own, "Boy, depart hence forthwith, or remain and be devoured." Our hero looked up, but the lady had vanished. However, he acted at once upon the hint implied by these words, and commenced retracing his steps towards the "ladder of hazel brush" which he shortly reached and commenced the ascent. Upon arriving at the top, his horror may be imagined when he found the aperture closed. The cold sweat stood on his brow, his frame quivered with mental agony, when, after a moment, he bethought himself of a small barlow knife (a present from a near relative), he carried in his pocket, with which he instantly commenced picking the earth, being careful not to cut too near the spot where the ladder was made fast, for fear of precipitating himself to the bottom of the cave. After laboring in this manner a short time, he was rejoiced to see daylight through the earth, and he was not much longer in working a hole large enough through which he was enabled to crawl; then, having refreshed himself at a clear running brook close by, he wandered he knew not whither; it was midday when he made his escape from the cave, and he traveled that day and night, and the following day until about half past four o'clock PM, when he encountered a small party of miners prospecting for gold on the headwaters of South Umpqua River, to whom he told the story of his adventure; they listened in silence, evidently disbelieving every word, but as they could not otherwise account for the presence of our hero in that desolate region, they all said nothing, but gave him to eat and to drink.

Our hero reached the house of his father in due time; he related his adventure — the neighbors called in — he told the same story; the circuit preacher called — the story was the same; at first they smiled, then doubted, then believed: and the whole neighborhood are now prepared to make affidavit to the principal facts.

The boy is a mild, modest, moral boy, about thirteen years of age, of fair complexion, and has always borne a character for truthfulness. His parents are moral and religious people, and it is hoped that out of respect to their feelings, the story will not be disbelieved as a general thing, although many parts of it are truly wonderful.[1425]

This story obviously reeks of yellow journalism, yet value may be found in its sensationalism. It is impossible to verify the truth of such accounts, but their thematic consistency with earlier folklore can be clearly perceived. What appears at first blush to be a Bigfoot abduction reveals peculiar resonances with European faerie beliefs. Recall in Celtic lore, faeries preferred abducting male children "of fair complexion," sometimes luring them into the wilderness with strange cries; even more explicitly, the descent of the "wild man" into a subterranean "trap door" is reminiscent of the *souterrains* found in faerie forts. This underground space, with its peculiar indirect illumination, resembles traditional descriptions of Fairyland—as well as, it may be noted, spaces perceived in psychedelic experiences. (The similarities between faerie lore and altered states of consciousness are striking; in this case, the arched, colorful, decorated ceiling is a recurring feature of those who have used DMT, the beauty of which parallels Fairyland). While in this space, the witness allegedly hears "the most unearthly music," another hallmark of faerie lore. Perhaps the most affronting connection between this yarn and European folklore can be found in the wild man's captive: it was not uncommon for those trapped among faeries to encounter fellow mortals, who passed on advice about how to avoid further imprisonment. Finally, the use of a knife in the boy's escape finds antecedent in a Scottish legend, wherein a father keeps the door open to Faerie Land by thrusting his dirk into its threshold.

LURES: MIMICRY AND CRIES

Like faeries and aliens, Sasquatch sometimes employ lures to entice their prey. If accounts are to be believed, their capacity for mimicry is incredible—several witnesses are convinced they have heard their dog's names called from the woods by Sasquatch in an attempt to snag an easy meal. Mike, an Oklahoma witness whose property was plagued by Sasquatch attacks in the infamous "Siege at Honobia" incident, told podcast host Wes Germer:

> "Wes, one time I had left for work and my brother
> and my dad were out there... Every night I call for
> my dogs, to have my dogs come in. My brother and
> my dad are out there, and they hear me calling for
> my dogs out in the woods. They hear my voice, out
> there calling for the dogs..." [Mike's] brother kind
> of felt like it was a little bit of a trap, too, to get
> them to come out towards the woods... it sounded
> just like Mike calling for his dogs.[1426]

It is a small leap from calling the names of dogs to calling
the names of children. The level of sophistication and deception
involved is reminiscent of faeries beckoning children into the
forest. In 1977 Yang Wanchun observed a wild man in China's
Shaanxi province that "uttered 11 or 12 different sounds, which
seemed to imitate a sparrow chirping, dog barking, pony neighing,
leopard growling, and an infant crying."[1427]

The last noise may be a clue to another type of lure: witnesses
to large, hairy hominids worldwide consistently report the sound
of babies crying in their experiences, a fact multiple indigenous
tribes of North America attest to.[1428] Among the Tlingit of Alaska,
the *kushtakaa* is responsible for cries like babies in the night, which
"portend sickness or worse in one's household or among friends"
(parallels to the Irish *banshee*, whose wail presaged death).[1429]

The sound of crying infants might be the most consistent
feature among all Forteana, a trend noted over 40 years ago by Keel.
"The baby crying phenomenon is common not only among UFO
witnesses but among thousands of 'ghost' and monster witnesses as
well," he wrote.[1430] In addition to tales of Sasquatch, UFOs, ghosts,
and anomalous large felines, it is also found in faerie lore.

"When a screaming is heard in the woods and marshes, like
that of crying children... the sounds proceed from their midnight
assemblies, and are made by the vociferous Dwarfs," wrote

Keightley.[1431] In a tale collected by Lady Gregory, a faerie spurned of its milk offering sounded "like the crying of a child."[1432] Rhŷs wrote in 1901 of a faerie-inhabited pool: "Mr. D.E. Davies knows a man, who is still living, and who well remembers the time when the sound of working used to be in the pool, and the voices of children crying somewhere in its depths, but that when people rushed there to see what the matter was, all was profoundly still and quiet."[1433] The phenomenon even extends across the Atlantic—the aforementioned "Wild Indians" of the Catawba tribe were said to make the sound of wailing infants.[1434]

No one has quite determined why things that go bump in the night favor this particular sound. Science, however, suggests an answer. "The sound of a baby cry captures your attention in a way that few other sounds in the environment generally do," said Katie Young, who led a 2012 University of Oxford study that examined how human brains process babies' cries. Sounds of infants in distress generated a more intense reaction in participants' brains compared to similar noises from other animals. For Young, this suggested that baby cries are processed differently than other sounds, "tagged as important even before our brains have had a chance to fully process them" and activating fight-or-flight instincts. Results were the same even in participants who had no experience with children.[1435]

Naturally inquisitive or good-hearted individuals may be drawn to the sound of infant crying. Perhaps Sasquatch uses the same technique as the *merrow-maidens*, the mermaids of Irish folklore, known for luring sailors beneath the waves with their siren song. Of a *merrow*'s voice, Yeats wrote it was "a low mournful cry with just the tender voice of a new-born infant."[1436]

MOTIVATION & HYBRIDITY

Indigenous tradition often brands Sasquatches anthropophages, abducting children for the express purpose of eating them. George M. Eberhart's *Mysterious Creatures: A Guide to Cryptozoology* lists nearly 80 names for "cannibal giants" from North American tribes alone.[1437]

While this is certainly one of the more popular motivations ascribed to Sasquatch, it is not the only one. To the Alaskan Kwakiutl, *dsonoqua* steals and raises young women to help gather salmon berries.[1438] (While obviously dubious, a 2000 *Weekly World News* article claimed a young child was seen in Vancouver, Canada, stealing food for an eight-foot-tall Sasquatch, similar to this Kwakiutl belief.[1439]) This motivation is similar in the Nisqually tradition of Washington, who claim a "race of tall 'wild' Indians" known as *Seatco* keep human children for slaves.[1440]

In Walt Disney's 1967 animated adaptation of Rudyard Kipling's *The Jungle Book,* the orangutan King Louie abducts the young Indian boy Mowgli to learn the secret of "man's red flower," i.e. fire. While erroneous—Louie is not only absent in Kipling's work, but orangutans are indigenous to Indonesia and Malaysia, not India—there is a folkloric basis for this concept. On the Indonesian island of Flores, a race of short, hairy hominids called the *Ebu Gogo* were believed to abduct children with the intent of learning how to harness fire, in this example to use in cooking.[1441] The idea that man-apes kidnap children to learn human skills is also held by the indigenous people of Guatemala, who believe the *Sisemite*, tall man-monkey hybrids, take boys and girls with the intent of learning human speech.[1442]

While it is difficult to corroborate indigenous belief in cannibal behavior—no victim ever returns from *that* abduction—it is a bit easier to find documented reports of young women taken for breeding purposes, even into the modern era.

- A Japanese account from the 19th century described a young girl who disappeared after entering the forest to gather chestnuts. Several years later a hunter encountered her on the slopes of Goyozan Mountain and was told she had been forced to live as the wife of an "immensely tall" man with eyes of "a terrible colour." Though the hunter attempted a rescue, the creature reappeared and seized the girl again.[1443]

- In the early 1900s, Noma Dima, a girl from the Khumbu Himal near Mount Everest, was taken by a *yeti* at age 17 while gathering water from a stream. The creature released her, but not before fathering a child with her. She and the child lived in her village for a time before the populace turned upon them, causing the *yeti* to return for his offspring. When Dima failed to voluntarily relinquish it, the beast tore the child apart.[1444]

- A 1954 article by John W. Burns told the story of a 17-year-old Chehalis girl, Serephine Long, who was walking home when an enormous hairy hand grabbed her and rubbed tree gum in her eyes. Long claimed this young Sasquatch and his parents kept her captive for several years, during which she mothered the creature's child. After pleading to return to her people, the Sasquatch reapplied the tree gum and took her home.[1445] (The detail of the tree gum calls to mind faerie ointment, which sometimes facilitates entrance to Fairyland.)

- A story from Koroška, Slovenia, tells of another young girl kidnapped by a mountain man. After delivering his children, she at last made her escape by crossing a river (shades of evading faeries by traversing flowing water). "The wild man soon stormed in after her, but he could not reach her," wrote Slovenian ethnologist Monika Kropej. "He held one of the children in one hand and in his anger tore him into little pieces."[1446]

"The ape as rapist and kidnapper has been a common theme in the artistic imagination," wrote psychologist Manfred F.R. Kets de Vries. "'The White Monkey,' a story dating back to the Tang dynasty [of China], tells of a woman kidnapped by a white monkey, an affair that ends with the conception of a child."[1447]

Breeding with denizens of the Otherworld has remained a pernicious theme throughout this book. It also begs the question of other intersections between Sasquatch and changeling lore.

CHANGELING PARALLELS

While Sasquatch and changelings initially seem to share little in common, certain motifs appear in oblique ways. For example, the term "changeling" among the Chuckchi of the Russian Arctic applies to humans carried off by the wind who become *tery'ky*, hairy carnivorous man-beasts.[1448]

A more elegant blending of themes is the story of St. Onuphrius, a fourth century hermit venerated in the Roman and Eastern Catholic Churches. Like a handful of other Christian saints, Onuphrius's origins are steeped in changeling tradition. "According to legend, he was the son of a pagan ruler or, by some accounts, of an Abyssinian nomadic chieftain, born while his father was on campaign," wrote Timothy Husband in *The Wild Man: Medieval Myth and Symbolism.* "Upon his return, Onuphrius's father determined to test the child's legitimacy by fire; if the child were legitimate he would not be consumed. When the child miraculously survived the test, an angel appeared and ordered the father to baptize the child."[1449]

Following his christening, Onuphrius lived with Egyptian monks until adulthood, when he set out to live as a hermit in a wilderness cave, (traditionally on Abu Tor near Israel's Valley of Hinnom). Over the years, his clothes fell away and he developed a thick layer of body hair, including a beard "so long that it reached the ground."[1450]

St. Onuphrius's legend blends changeling lore with the wild

man archetype. There are also UFOlogical undertones; some might argue the "angel" of Onuphrius's story who administered communion to him each Sunday represented extraterrestrial intervention.[1451] Moreover, the Valley of Hinnom—otherwise known as Gehenna, site of hell-on-earth in Hebrew tradition—provides an oblique demonological connection.[1452]

The fingerprints of changelings are more visible in the offspring from alleged human-Sasquatch couplings. Like changelings and alien hybrids, they universally appear in poor health—Serephine Long's child only survived a few hours.[1453] An old Nanaimo woman told researcher J. Robert Alley her grandmother had been taken by *squee'noos* in the early 1900s. When she returned, she gave birth to a stillborn and "sadly malformed" hybrid. Another woman from the tribe returned after her time among the *squee'noos* with a "not right, very strange" baby who died within its first year.[1454]

When they survive, Sasquatch hybrids have an appearance that roughly coincides with both changelings and alien hybrids, albeit with more hair. According to local legend, hirsute giants from the Solomon Islands abducted a villager named Mango and held her captive for years before she was found again, rendered insane and feral. During her time with her monstrous husband, Mango birthed a "hideous-looking child."[1455] The boy lived in the village for five years before his uncle killed him.[1456]

Another apocryphal tale from the 1920s tells of a young shepherd girl abducted while washing laundry by a stream near Spain's Sierra Morena Mountains. After repeated rapes by her ape-like captor, she delivered Anica, "the daughter of the orangutan," who possessed a hairy body, long arms, and an "ape-like mouth."[1457] Similarly, Noma Dima's baby had long arms, short legs, the face of a monkey, and was covered head-to-toe in hair.[1458]

Some changelings had excessively long limbs and short legs. The faces of apes, like changelings and human-alien hybrids, uniformly appear wrinkled and wizened, even in adolescence. In another simian connection, some stories described changelings as excessively hairy—recall the French *poulpican* changeling—

or boasting prodigious beards. The changeling of one Irish tale produced "a strong growth of hair on forehead, cheeks, lips and chin... At the end of a fortnight a full grown beard appeared all over the child's face."[1459]

The experiences alleged by Marion, North Carolina, resident Thomas K. Burnette are much more motivically resonant with changeling lore. Over the course of a decade, Burnette claimed to have numerous dramatic encounters with Sasquatch on his property, interactions which began mundanely enough before escalating into more and more bizarre territory, including strange mists, government agents, shady trespassers, and flying machines sighted in the sky. The strangeness of Burnette's encounters reached a fever pitch after an intensely realistic dream on December 31, 1993.

Burnette dreamed he was examining a set of tracks when a Middle Eastern man appeared alongside several Bigfoot. The visitor himself morphed into a Sasquatch, the environment transforming to the interior of a strange room. Nearby, a young girl appeared to be in childbirth. Each Sasquatch came to shake Burnette's hand, scraping skin off with their sharp claws. One approached Burnette with a long syringe, which was plunged into his heart. After losing consciousness, Burnette came to and saw the girl had given birth to a beautiful baby boy, one he intuitively knew was his child. Upon awakening from this dream, Burnette had strange marks on his hand.

Clearly, Burnette's dream carries all the fingerprints of alien abduction and subsequent baby presentation. His experiences further echoed the changeling narrative when, some years later, he discovered what he claimed was a Sasquatch child in his driveway. The child appeared unwell and, in a desperate attempt to return it to its family, Burnette abandoned the infant Sasquatch in the woods.

Just as in changeling stories, Burnette believed "his" child could be found in the Otherworld, while a sickly child of the Otherworld was brought and left with him. Similarly, Burnette's actions following the appearance of the Sasquatch baby—specifically abandoning it in the woods—directly parallels the manner in which mothers of the British Isles would dispose of changelings.[1460]

Unbelievably, shades of the faerie stock tradition can be found in modern Sasquatch accounts. A great many sightings, particularly those unnoticed at the time but later captured in photographs, are attributable to misidentification of large tree stumps. Even more interesting, some witnesses claim Sasquatch have the ability to *appear as* stumps, logs, and trees, explaining the manner in which they seemingly disappear.

Germer described the moments prior to an East Texas hunter's Sasquatch sighting:

> He was sitting down and he was kind of taking a break, and he looks up and here's this stump... He said it was probably about 50 feet from him... He couldn't quite figure out what was odd about it... Something wasn't right, and he kind of looked away and went back and looked at it... He said all he saw was big, black eyes... As he starts getting up, he said this stump stood up and looked at him, and that's when he realized, "Oh crap, it's not a stump."[1461]

Bob Strain of the North American Wood Ape Conservancy (NAWAC) experienced this phenomenon during an investigation in the south central United States. Searching for Sasquatch, Strain poked his head into a thicket but saw nothing out of the ordinary, just a few large logs on the ground. The next day, the same area was searched, but the logs were missing.[1462]

"It's our belief that the logs were actually apes that were prone, that were laying there, pretending to be logs," said Brian Brown of the NAWAC. "We have a slogan: shoot all the logs," he jokingly added. "Stopping and freezing and pretending to be a tree... not moving, is something that has been observed time-and-again."[1463]

This type of camouflage, which undoubtedly requires a change in visible texture, is demonstrable in cephalopods but unprecedented among mammals. The ability to become wholly inanimate—as a log no less—calls to mind both stocks and faerie glamour.

An unbelievable (yet highly resonant story) from Washington further underscores this connection. In his 2017 update of *The Inhumanoids: Real Encounters with Beings That Can't Exist!*, Barton Nunnelly tells of a woman who spotted a Sasquatch standing outside her home. After she started approaching it, "the creature abruptly walked a short distance into the woods, lay down on the ground, and, in full view, *turned into a log*." Humorously, the witness "dragged the log back into her home" where she "has used it as a coffee table for years."[1464]

Claiming your living room furniture is a disguised Sasquatch is absurd. At the same time, claiming your kitchen utensil is a changeling is equally unbelievable—yet it may be recalled this is exactly what happened in the changeling tale "Mind da Crooked Finger," where the husband repurposed his wife's stock as a chopping block.

Chapter 19:
"As a Baby in My Crib"
The Crib Creepers

I don't know what hovers over this house, but it was strong enough to punch a hole into this world and take your daughter away from you. It keeps Carol Anne very close to it and away from the spectral light. It lies to her, it tells her things only a child could understand. It has been using her to restrain the others. To her, it simply is another child. To us, it is the Beast.

— Poltergeist (1982)

It is said King Charles I of England was incredibly irritable in his infancy. According to legend, the reason for this peevishness could be traced to a specific incident. Late one night, the stillness of Dunfermline Palace was shattered by the cries of Charles' nurse, rousing his father, King James. The nurse told James, "There was one like an auld man came into the room and threw his cloak owre the prince's cradle and syne drew it till him again, as if he had taken cradle, bairn and a'away wi' him. I'm feared it was the thing that's no canny." Some suspected Charles of being a changeling from that moment on.[1465]

This 17th century account might be the earliest example of an unsettling subset of bedroom intruders we shall call "crib creepers"—entities lurking in the bedrooms of children. Though these intruders might appear to only *observe* young boys and girls, their mere presence suggests child abduction; six out of nine lifelong experiencers told UFO researcher Joseph Nyman in 1989 they recalled "being infants in their cribs or bassinets with their special entity looking down at them."[1466]

Crib creepers rarely frighten infants. Most often, babies are oblivious to these intruders… or find them amusing. One couple told UFO British Columbia founder Graham Conway they heard laughing and chattering after putting their son down for the night. Upon investigation, they found the child "standing in his crib apparently happily conversing with someone or something that was not visible to them."[1467]

Because she was believed in some traditions to target smiling infants, Lilith was fond of tickling her victims' feet. Thus, mothers were encouraged to hit their children three times on the nose, should they be found giggling or smiling in their sleep.[1468]

Some examples of crib creepers through the centuries:

- In the late 1800s, an entire dinner party at Delaware's Kensey John Homestead witnessed "a pale-looking woman" comforting and rocking a baby in its crib. "The woman wore a white silk dress, with a pearl comb in her hair and soft-leather slippers on her feet," wrote author Dennis William Hauck. The mysterious, silent woman joined the guests for dinner before slipping away, never seen again.[1469] (The tale calls to mind mothers held captive by the fae folk who returned to nurse their infants.)

- One night in 1974 a babysitter from Wauwatosa, Wisconsin, received a sudden urge to check on her ward. As she approached the nursery, she noticed a dim glow coming from inside: some type of gnome—two feet tall and clad in britches, suspenders, and a vest—seemed to be dancing by the bedside. Keeping an eye on the intruder, the witness slowly approached the crib, collected the baby, and backed out of the room.[1470]

- According to UFO researcher Jorge Martín, a Puerto Rican family reported numerous home invasions by a trio of short, green humanoids in December 1979. On at least one occasion they were caught staring at a baby in its crib, only to disappear when confronted.[1471]

- A Derbyshire witness told faerie researcher Marjorie Johnson she saw "a tiny man with a pointed beard, a tunic with a belt, and a little hat turned over on one side" by her daughter's cot. "He appeared startled as he grasped the curtains, and he turned his bright little eyes and looked at me, then scrambled up the curtains and out of the window like quicksilver."[1472]

- In the aforementioned case of Salina Quail, the witness saw a dark figure lurking by her daughter's playpen in the middle of a cold March 1981 night—despite Quail's protestations that the being "could not have her," she was told, "She is part of us."[1473]

- Shortly following a UFO sighting in the early hours of July 15, 1989, in an Addingham, UK, neighborhood, a six-year-old girl told her parents a small figure had climbed the stairs to her bedroom. She described it as having a "thin white face and unusual 'angry' eyes." Later that night, the figure returned with a "female companion" in tow—on both occasions, they did nothing but stare for a while then disappear.[1474] (It should be noted there is an

Iron Age settlement—a faerie ringfort—just outside town.)

- In September 1994, a woman from Tres Piedras,
  New Mexico, claimed three Greys stood by her
  baby before "shuffling out of the bedroom" and de-
  parting in "a silver disc-shaped ship."[1475]

- UFO researcher Albert Rosales interviewed a Sydney, Australia, witness who claimed in late 1996
  to have seen a "large-headed, insect eyed" creature
  with small limbs staring directly at her son on his
  nearby cot. "As she looked at the being it seemed
  to realize that she could see it." It then promptly
  vanished.[1476]

PURPOSE

Certainly such tales imply child kidnapping, or at least
reconnaissance for future abductions. They might indicate a
recently returned abductee, or a foiled abduction attempt—in one
case collected by anomalist Vladimir Rubtsov, a young man from
Voronezh, Russia, was visiting his nephew on October 3, 1963,
when he saw a peculiar, small, hairless head peer out of the infant's
room. Once the head retreated inside, the witness heard his
nephew crying and rushed to the doorway. A dark shape flashed
out of the room, leaving the baby behind, nude on the floor but
unharmed.[1477]

According to some experiencers, crib creepers can enhance
children's mental capacity. UFOlogist Marilyn Henry Childs
claimed her earliest memories "began as a baby in my crib," where
an "imaginary" playmate taught her astronomy, math, and advanced
languages.[1478]

In addition to full-bodied entities, a great many abductees
recall nightly visitation from orbs of light in their youth. These

encounters, typically beginning between ages two and six, take place in children's bedrooms and are playful, involving behavior perceived as "games." The orbs "are very specific in appearance and behavior," wrote Randles. "They are balls of light—between tennis-ball and basketball in size—which enter the bedroom of the youngster and quite often start to 'play' with them."[1479]

Based on this trend, Randles formulated the "Psychic Toy" theory. "Just as children use toys or dolls to develop social or motor skills, so these balls of light were stretching their mind and their acceptance of paranormal phenomena," Randles theorized. "They may even have been training the youngster in psychic abilities—since it was clear that, whatever alien contacts prove to be, they involve parapsychological forms of contact."[1480]

DEATH & LIFE: PSYCHOPOMPS

Traditionally, crib creepers were perceived as bad omens, spreading illness and death. In 1767, an outbreak of Scarlet Fever swept through an Eton, Berkshire boarding school. Among the quarantined boys was one Francis Humberston Mackenzie, who described an old hag with a wallet hanging about her neck, moving from bed-to-bed in the middle of the night.

"The first [bed] she had passed but, reaching the second, she had paused, from the wallet removing a mallet and a peg," wrote author Stuart Gordon in *The Book of Curses*. "In his delirium, Mackenzie had seen her use the mallet to drive the peg into the boy's forehead." She repeated this process, passing some children while pegging others. When Mackenzie alerted the attending nurse, she scoffed at the tale—but his testimony accurately predicted the death of each pegged boy.[1481]

The archetype of death-bringing crib creepers is found worldwide. An analogue to Mackenzie's hag is found in the *acheri* of India, the ghost of a little girl who brings disease to sleeping children "by casting its shadow over victims."[1482] (As in faerie lore, a red thread tied about the neck could avert this fate.) Witches were feared throughout Europe for their ability to silently kill infants in cradles.[1483] Popular depictions of cats as witches' familiars—coupled with the belief Lilith herself turned into *El Broosha*, a large black cat—are likely origins for old wives' tales of felines sucking the breath out of newborn babes.[1484]

The motif of killing an infant through its breath can be found in representations of "Murder," a headless demon from the *Testament of Solomon* who attacks babies, particularly those born premature, at night. If one 10 days old cries after sunset, Murder "rushes in and attacks it through its voice."[1485]

Crib creepers presage death among children in contemporary accounts. The son of famed UFO contactee Howard Menger died from a brain tumor at age 12, telling family members the light phenomena glimpsed around his death bed were "from the planet Orion" and there "to take me away"; in short, they were psychopomps.[1486]

In Greek, the term "psychopomp" literally means the "guide of souls." Cultures worldwide speak of intercessor entities charged with escorting the dead to the afterlife—in Animistic societies, these were animals like owls, ravens, deer, etc., while more codified cosmologies listed specific deities (Anubis of Egyptian practice, Charon of Greek legend, or Visnudutas and Yamadutas of Hinduism).[1487] For other cultures, earthbound shamans might serve this same role.[1488] In addition to guiding souls through the barrier between life and death, psychopomps may also serve as guides at other major, liminal life transitions.[1489]

Rather than thinking of crib creepers—or perhaps psychopomps—strictly as harbingers of death, perhaps they are better understood as having dominion over death *and* life—consider the rich history of children healed by UFOs and their occupants. If shamans intercede in the spirit world on the behalf of humans, psychopomps intercede in the human world on the behalf of spirits.

Lecouteux described this exact relationship regarding the role of the blessed departed: "The good dead individual becomes, among other things, a conduit between the living and the higher powers."[1490] Given the connection between those who have passed on and faerie lore, it seems but a little stretch to frame the Good Folk as psychompomps. On September 20, 1909, Biddy Grant told Evans Wentz of the Good Folk she saw in Ireland:

> I saw *them* once as plain as can be—big, little, old, and young. I was in bed at the time, and a boy whom I had reared since he was born was lying ill beside me. Two of *them* came and looked at him; then came in three of *them*. One of *them* seemed to have something like a book, and he put his hand to the boy's mouth; then he went away, while others appeared, opening the back window to make an avenue through the house; and through this avenue came great crowds. At this I shook the boy, and said to him, "Do you see anything?" "No," he said; but as I made him look a second time he said, "I do." After that he got well.[1491]

Chapter 20:
"Storm Child"
Missing 411

Here in Derry children disappear unexplained and unfound at the rate of forty to sixty a year. Most are teenagers. They are assumed to be runaways. I suppose some of them even are.

— Stephen King, *It*

In September 1880, on a small farm in Sumner County, Tennessee, David Lang disappeared without a trace. The event happened in full view of Lang's wife and multiple other witnesses— he simply vanished mid-stride. Rumor had it a large, circular depression in the grass appeared at the site. Anyone standing within it claimed Lang's voice could be heard faintly drifting on the wind.[1492]

It is a compelling account. Unfortunately, the tale of David Lang and its variants— the boy Oliver Lerch, Larch Thomas, Oliver Larch, Oliver Thomas, etc.—are likely hoaxes. Consensus holds these yarns are modeled on the work of Ambrose Bierce, specifically his 1888 short story "The Difficulty of Crossing a Field,"[1493] which features "a planter named Williamson" who disappears from his Selma, Alabama, field in July 1854. (In an ironic twist, a composer named David Lang wrote an opera based on Bierce's story in 2002.[1494])

Cases from roughly the same era resembling Bierce's story are regularly presented as fact. For example, on Christmas Eve 1909, a Welsh boy was supposedly "levitated from snow-covered ground," his footprints ending near a well.[1495] This is not to say permanent disappearances do not happen—Bierce himself vanished in Mexico in 1914—but accounts of similar aspect within a quarter century of his story's publication should be viewed with skepticism.[1496]

A more recent Russian story contains an interesting detail. One afternoon in January 1959, Alescha Sorkin (10) and his sister, Karya (12), failed to return after leaving the house to play in the freshly fallen snow around Moscow. Their parents were shocked to discover the children's footprints stopped 20 feet from the front door. Though authorities closely surveyed the surrounding property, they found no trace of the missing siblings. The tracks simply ended.[1497]

Note how this disappearance was preceded by a snowstorm—a seemingly insignificant factor that may, in reality, provide an important clue.

THE FOG

The Crow Nation of the western United States tells the legend of the "Storm Child." During an unusually violent midwinter storm, a thick black cloud covered a mountaintop, from which "two long arms... deposited an infant on the earth." This child disappeared again into the cloud, but not before "an old squaw, who had not borne children for several years... felt herself seized with violent labour pains, and was delivered of a female child, perfectly green, like grass." The Crow felt this was the same baby brought by the cloud, and she named it the "Storm Child."[1498]

Inclement weather and anomalies go hand-in-hand; the case is no different for mysterious disappearances. Many cases of missing children involve strange mists or fogs.

- According to Ukrainian researcher Andrew Zabava, a family cabin in Russia was approached in

1914 by an unnatural fog that alit in a nearby field. The owners were shocked when they realized this was the exact location their son and daughter were playing moments before. The children were never seen again—their parents believed they had been taken by "wood goblins."[1499]

- In 1968, 11-year-old Graciela del Lourdes Giménez was playing outside in a suburb of Cordoba, Argentina, when "a white cloud, like mist, appeared on the front path. It gradually came towards where I was, and then I could no longer see the other houses and I couldn't move or call out to Mummy." Her next memory was finding herself in the Plaza España in the heart of Cordoba. Afterward, she suffered from cold chills and uncontrollable sobbing.[1500]

- The aunt and grandmother of Rubén Walter Rusin, aged 11, were readying to go downstairs when the boy was enveloped in a dark cloud in the corridor. He was missing for two and a half hours before they found him in the corridor once more. "His flesh was unnaturally warm, and on each cheek of his face... there was a strange pale red circle," according to an article published in 1997 in *Flying Saucer Review*. Rubén recalled being paralyzed and placed onto "something soft and warm, like a mattress," where something invisible touched him and yelled, "Talk! Talk!"[1501]

"The storm overtaking the traveller to the Otherworld is... by no means always a snowstorm," wrote literature researcher Martin Puhvel, referring to instances of transportive snow and mist in "Sir Gawain and the Green Knight." "At times it is a question of a wind-, rain-, or hail-storm accompanied by thunder... the passage through the magic storm 'seems to be another form of the motif of a dive through the water of a spring or lake which in many Irish stories... is the mode of entrance to the Other World.'"[1502]

Mist and fog are not only associated with fae folk (as noted *ad nauseum*), but they also appear in modern alien abduction accounts. These anomalous fogs regularly surround cars, as in the October 27, 1974, case of John Day, who, along with his wife and three children, spotted a UFO near Aveley, England—"soon a greenish fog swallowed the car," causing missing time and, if hypnotic regression is to believed, an alien abduction.[1503] UFO interiors are commonly reported as misty or foggy—some even claim extraterrestrial spacecraft can take the form of smoke.

One trucker recalled seeing a thick cloud of smoke on the roadway with no discernable source: "The following morning... the memory of the cloud was more troubling, because he didn't think it had been smoke and he didn't think it had been fog," wrote journalist C.D.B. Bryan. "And when, as he began to dress, he noticed what appeared to be a couple of scoop marks on the big toe of his right foot, 'I began to weave things together... my suspicions began to grow.'"[1504]

MISSING 411

In early 2012, retired police officer David Paulides released the first book in his now-widely-popular Missing 411 series. After discovering that the United States National Park Service shockingly *does not* keep a running list of visitors who have disappeared within their confines, Paulides uncovered a disturbing trend of geographical clusters involving missing people.[1505]

A familiarity with Paulides's work, arguably the most popular topic in Forteana today, is recommended. While his body of research is too extensive to cover in depth here—as of writing, he has authored six books on the subject—several recurring factors noticed by Paulides are worth mentioning.

Over the course of several years, Paulides discovered that certain areas of the world (particularly national parks) seem prone to disappearances, inexplicable deaths, and missing time among those reported missing. In most cases, individuals simply vanish without a trace. Whenever victims' bodies are recovered, they show signs of strange behavior prior to death and often appear in difficult-to-access areas. On the rare occasion someone is found alive after being reported missing in these areas, they are frequently at a loss to describe where they have been while friends, family, and law enforcement searched for them.

"Inclement weather is often associated with the disappearance," Paulides wrote.[1506] These storms typically manifest during or just after disappearances and hinder search efforts. For example, the 1957 disappearance of one Lowell Linn was followed by a storm which "dumped 48 inches of snow in the search area" on Mount Rainier.[1507] In another case from 1941, a four-year-old boy's search was hampered by a major storm that raised creeks and rivers in Camp Sacramento, California.[1508]

According to Paulides, whenever victims are found alive, they are "often times found in creeks or riverbeds, or swamps... they are often unconscious or semi-conscious and cannot remember details when they were missing. Many times victims are located with missing shoes or clothing. Missing victims are often times discovered in an area previously searched. Berries and swamps are inextricably associated with many of the missing cases. An unusual number of the victims are found to climb thousands of feet uphill or travel many miles further than any Search and Rescue guidelines indicate is normal."[1509]

Additional trends include the refusal of dogs to track,[1510] disappearances near boulder fields,[1511] victims with exceptionally high intelligence or disabilities, a preponderance of male victims[1512] of German descent,[1513] and brightly colored clothing worn by the missing.[1514] When found deceased, authorities have difficulty determining cause of death.[1515]

Corpses of the missing are also commonly found face down

in the dirt in various stages of undress. In the most peculiar cases, their clothes are neatly folded beside their bodies.[1516] In 1964, two-year-old Kenneth Edwards was found dead seven miles from his parent's California camp, sans jacket and sweatshirt, "face down in a nap-like sprawl near the top of a sand and rock covered slope."[1517]

A few cases exemplifying this trend:

- On April 10, 1952, two-year-old Keith Parkins was visiting grandparents in Ritter, Oregon, when he disappeared. He was found alive 19 hours later, face down, a dozen miles away (commonly Search and Rescue guidelines hold toddlers are typically found no more than two miles away). He remembered nothing of the experience and was treated for exposure.[1518]

- The body of two-year-old David Allen Scott was found in a boulder field after disappearing near Mono Village, California, in July 13, 1957. He wore only a t-shirt and a sock on one foot. He had traveled 3,000 feet higher than the elevation where he was last seen.[1519]

- Mentally disabled Jimmy Duffy, aged two, went missing in 1973 near Washington's Wenatchee Lake. His parents had left him and his infant sister, Natalie, asleep in the camper while the father hunted nearby and the mother went on a short walk, keeping them roughly within eyesight. Fifteen minutes later, the father returned to check on the children, then met his wife around 150 yards from the camper. Moments later they heard an unearthly scream and hurried back to find the camper door open—Natalie and the family's two cats were still asleep, but Jimmy was nowhere to be seen.

No footprints, tracks, or sign of anything could be found by authorities, who searched every camper in the region. The father said the sound from the camper sounded similar to a baby crying. The child was never found. [1520]

- In July 1976, two-year-old Hector González Portas disappeared from his bed in northwest Spain. Eleven hours later he was found high in the mountains eight kilometers from home. "A doctor who examined him declared that the child definitely had not walked there." Despite having put them under the bed at home, Hector was wearing his sandals. [1521]

- Lee Littlejohn, 18-months-old, and his two-year-old cousin disappeared from their aunt's Redding, California, home in the middle of a heavy rainstorm on December 23, 1977. Searchers were unable to track the children in the heavy downpour, but Lee's cousin was found after an hour of searching—she was unable to tell them where he had gone. By noon the next day, Lee's body was found three-quarters of a mile up a steep hill, missing his shoes and socks. [1522]

Paulides has chronicled hundreds of similar cases, all with similar themes. His work has captured the imagination of paranormalists the world over, prompting the obvious question: "What could be responsible for this?"

The Missing 411 phenomenon has become something of a paranormal Rorschach test: UFOlogists blame aliens, cryptozoologists blame Sasquatch, conspiracy theorists blame the government, true crime buffs blame a serial killer. In truth, none of these satisfactorily explain the Missing 411 trends—can Sasquatch control the weather? Do aliens prowl berry bushes? Why does the government take victims' clothing? What serial killer spree spans centuries?

There is a possible answer. But it has been overlooked.

In 1935, a young girl was out for a walk when she found herself unable to leave a hilltop. "When she tried to leave one way, she would find herself walking in the opposite direction," wrote J. Mark Buehring. "She then tried to get out the way she got in, and found her way blocked by an 'invisible wall' which was 'so solid she could follow it round with her hands.'" Later that evening, she saw a search party not 20 yards away, but they were unable to see or hear her. She patiently waited until, for no apparent reason, the barrier dissipated.[1523]

The girl was in Ireland's County Mayo. Faerie country.

MISSING FAE ONE ONE

The only extant tradition satisfying all of Paulides's Missing 411 criteria is faerie lore.

The connections to inclement weather (an abduction method favored by faeries) are obvious, as are victims' proximity to boulder fields and water (typical faerie environs). We have discussed at length the faerie-related pitfalls of berry picking, as well as the manner in which those taken to Fairyland return in a trance. It is established lore that the fae folk preferred taking boys; many of Paulides's victims are male.

In Missing 411 cases, animals, particularly dogs, refuse to venture into the woods. Trained bloodhounds, for example, simply lay down at the forest's edge and will not venture further. This behavior is not only reflected in faerie lore—which holds that dogs both saw and feared faeries[1524]—but also in modern sightings. Massachusetts resident William Russo claimed to have seen a *pukwudgie*—a short, hairy faerie from Wampanoag lore—while walking his dog near Raynham in the early 1990s. "Russo went on to claim that he and his dog were frozen with fear and failed to get within less than ten feet of the creature," wrote documentarian Aaron Cadieux.[1525]

Many point to the vast distances traveled by Missing 411 victims, or the manner in which they are suddenly found in areas previously searched, as evidence of levitation by UFOs. (A frantic cellphone call placed by adult victim Todd Geib, which sounded as though he was rushing through the air, is a favorite to argue.[1526]) But many faeries could levitate both themselves and their victims, including the Welsh faeries of the Isle of Anglesey: "As aerial beings the *Tylwyth Teg* could fly and move about in the air at will."[1527]

Mirroring the tendency for intellectuals to disappear in Paulides's cases, Evans Wentz was told that the fae "take the whole body and soul of young and intellectual people who are interesting, transmuting the body to a body like their own. I asked them once if they ever died, and they said, 'No; we are always kept young.'"[1528]

The details surrounding clothing in Missing 411 cases are especially compelling. Many victims are wearing brightly colored clothing when they disappear (red is especially common)—recall how specific colors of clothing could offend the fae folk. Moreover, it has already been noted that a remedy for becoming pixie led— when faeries lead one astray in the wilderness—was to invert an article of clothing. Many of the Missing 411 victims are found with their clothing removed.

Compare the detail of corpses found naked, face down in the dirt to an excerpt from Katharine Luomala's "Phantom Marchers in the Hawaiian Islands," an article that appeared in the Fall 1983 edition of *Pacific Studies*. In Luomala's retelling, two limpet pickers ran across a procession of "night marchers," a spectral army closely associated with the *menehune*, Hawaii's faeries:

> We looked toward Ka-wai-hae side and then we saw it. It looked like a procession. At first we saw a line of torches in the distance. The procession was moving along the coastline. The conch shell blew again.
>
> I took out my knife and Keoki got the rifle. We went seaward and laid down on the lava rock. We

knew about night marchers from other fishermen. We knew you aren't supposed to look upon the marchers and to lay on the ground face down. We did this. The marchers passed about fifty yards in front of us on the sand path. As they passed we could hear the sound of a drum pounding beat by beat. We didn't look up until they were farther down the coast. All we could see now was the line of torches, and all we could hear was the far away sound of the conch shell.[1529]

Luomala describes this behavior as part of a larger set of Hawaiian beliefs regarding the procession of royalty:

A herald often accompanied a dignitary in order to command people to get off the road and, if the principal marcher was of very high rank, to prostate themselves (*kapu moe*), or, if of lower rank, to squat down (*kapu noho*). The herald might also require the onlooker to close his eyes or to remove all or part of his clothing....[1530]

Night marchers seen during daylight are thought to be escorting the souls of the dead—like European faeries, they serve a psychopompic role.

None of this is necessarily to say fae folk are perpetrating the cases studied by Paulides. It is apparent, however, that whatever the Fairy Faith *describes* may well be the same phenomenon behind the Missing 411 disappearances.

Most surprisingly, some Missing 411 cases reveal changeling motifs. The most fanciful account covered by Paulides was that of a three-year-old boy who vanished on the slopes of Mount Shasta, California, only to be found five hours later on a regularly trafficked path. The boy claimed a double of his grandmother appeared and took him to a "cave or dungeon." The boy believed this doppelgänger was "a robot," one of many "other robots in the cave that never moved." His grandmother's double "placed a piece of sticky paper on the ground and told him that she wanted him to poop on the paper. He said that he didn't have to." Nonplussed, robo-granny brought him aboveground and placed him under a bush, directing him to stay put.[1531] Though farfetched, the presence of doubles, an underground setting, and abandonment beneath a bush all evoke changeling lore.

The French tale of Pauline Picard is not found in Paulides's files, but it is even more resonant. Picard, only two years old, disappeared from her family's farm in Goas Al Ludu, Brittany in April 1922. No trace was found until several weeks later, when a toddler matching Pauline's description was seen wandering the streets of Cherbourg—300 miles away. Her parents were notified, and they traveled to see the girl but were greeted with fear; despite looking exactly like Pauline, she did not seem to recognize her family. "On top of this, she also allegedly had an entirely different personality, mannerisms, and remained mute throughout, not saying a word to anyone," wrote author Brent Swancer. Ascribing her behavior to the trauma of separation, the Picards took her home, where she nonetheless remained aloof—it even seemed as though she neither understood nor spoke the Breton dialect.

Shortly thereafter, "a local came across the severely decomposed naked body of a little girl with a neatly folded pile of clothes next to her not far from the Picard farm." Stab wounds indicated the girl had been viciously murdered. "Adding to the whole mystery was that the ravaged body was found in a place that had been searched before, and locals claimed that they had passed by there frequently without anyone ever noticing anything amiss, leading to the idea that the body had been placed there rather recently." The girl's clothes matched what Pauline wore the day she disappeared.

Despite her uncanny resemblance to their daughter, the Picards relocated the Cherbourg child to an orphanage. The circumstances surrounding Pauline's death—and the origins of her changeling—remain a mystery to this day.[1532]

Chapter 21:
"We Need Shamans"
Seeking Answers

As to the nature of that change, we can tell you very little. We do not know how it is produced—what trigger impulse the Overmind employs when it judges that the time is ripe. All we have discovered is that it starts with a single individual—always a child—and then spreads explosively, like the formation of crystals round the first nucleus in a saturated solution. Adults will not be affected, for their minds are already set in an unalterable mould.
— Arthur C. Clarke, *Childhood's End*

If the material gathered here is any indication, paranormal child abduction is a broad, complex topic manifesting in a variety of modalities. It is naïve to assume any single solution could possibly account for the nuance embedded in these cases, yet there most certainly is a common thread weaving through these cases, particularly in the Fairy Faith and UFOlogy.

Many of the kidnappings in this book represent what at least *seem to be* physical encounters. While not discounting physicalist interpretations of faerie and alien abduction, the body of evidence simply has too much of a spiritual mouthfeel to ignore metaphysical solutions. Recall, for instance, the manner in which those taken by faeries were often described in a sort of trance, rather than being bodily absent. Even in the physical disappearances described in faerie lore, Missing 411 cases, and modern UFOlogical literature, victims are dazed after their rescue. While this is largely assumed to be a byproduct of their bodily abduction, the opposite is just as possible—that an altered state of consciousness spurs these individuals to wander off, similar to those experiencing dissociative fugue states.

This esoteric suggestion is dogged by the undeniable explanation of what changelings are in hard-science, strictly materialist terms. While there is a metaphysical component to the lore surrounding paranormal child abduction, there is also a tragic link to developmental disability.

Perhaps a middle road exists, combining materialist realities and metaphysical probabilities into a single model. Like any good synthesis, such speculation must account for the shortcomings of both strictly scientific *and* strictly esoteric interpretations, hopefully using the strengths of one approach to compensate for weaknesses inherent in the other.

Appropriately enough… a *hybrid* approach may prove most useful.

WHAT WE KNOW

Before diving into conjecture, it is important to review a few key trends established over the course of this presentation. We have already reiterated the prevalence of altered states of consciousness (i.e. trances) in paranormal child abductions, as well as the links between developmental disabilities—especially autism—and tales of faerie changelings. Recall also the regularity with which the developmentally disabled disappear in David Paulides's Missing 411 research.

As seen in numerous cases, children returning from visits among the fae folk often returned with special, supernormal abilities and rekindled spirituality, traits still seen in modern alien abductions. Recall that these qualities also manifest in the claims made by alleged human-alien hybrids and Star/Indigo Children.

Finally, recall the manner in which inhabitants of the Otherworld seem in dire need of something human beings possess. What they seek is a mystery, but the reliance of supernatural beings upon the human world for their well-being is consistently documented across the world and across time (faeries needed milk and human vigor, aliens need human genetic material, witches need babies for spells, etc.).

The Dogon, an ethnic group indigenous to Mali, contend that human-Otherworld interaction occurs for a simple, symbiotic reason. According to researcher Laird Scranton, the Dogon believe:

> ... universes form in pairs... our material universe has a twin universe that is nonmaterial, and that we don't readily perceive... The nonmaterial universe is characterized by having perfect knowledge, but an inability to act, whereas the material universe has imperfect knowledge and full ability to act... In that mindset, there's sort of this cosmic game of charades going on, where the nonmaterial side is able to give little clues to the material side, to try to induce particular actions that it can't take for itself, and on the material side, these play out in the form of vivid dreams, things that look like coincidences, unusual behavior of animals, divination, clairvoyance, and things like that. So on the material side—for the people who pick up on certain of these seeming coincidences not being coincidences, or who pick up on a vivid image of a dream as something they should follow up on— those people become progressively more aware of the existence of this nonmaterial twin. Other people who don't pick up on those things don't.[1533]

Supernatural kidnappers need us to act. Or, specifically, they need our children.

WHY CHILDREN?

Though it has become something of a cliché, the minds of children are demonstrably more malleable than those of adults. Compared to the average adult, the brain of a two-year-old child contains twice as many synaptic connections between brain cells.[1534] Wright State University Professor of Early Childhood William Mosier wrote:

> The first three years of human life is a critical period for brain development. It is a period of rapid synapse formation that can facilitate functional nerve cell connections. Although the brain continues to develop after the first three years of life, it does so, typically, by eliminating synaptic connections, not by forming new ones. During the first three years of life, an adequately stimulating environment can have its strongest and most lasting effect on brain development... by the end of the fourth year of human life, the pace of learning slows... By the time most young children become "language competent" (around age three), the architecture of the brain has essentially completed its basic formation. From that time until adolescence, the brain remains eager to learn with occasional growth spurts, but it will never again attain the incredible pace of learning that occurs during the first three years of life.[1535]

It is likely that childhood paranormal abductions deliberately target this critical developmental period—their malleable minds are simply more receptive to the fantastic, while adults may doubt their very sanity, or at least their interpretation of events. Deborah Truncale held that children, by virtue of this formative state, are able to more readily assimilate encounters with the Otherworld into their perception of reality.[1536]

But to what end are these malleable intellects needed?

We find a possible answer in shamanic traditions worldwide. The similarities between shamanic awakening and alien abduction (and, by extension, faerie abduction) have already been noted—childhood trauma, the primary factor in instigating this spiritual enlightenment, is seen both in the lives of many alien abductees and in changeling lore. Could the act of shamanic awakening, on a metaphysical level, essentially "hybridize" humans with the Otherworld?

Consider the insightful observation of experiencer Mike Clelland. "In our modern world, we simply can't tolerate the idea of a child falling into their own deeper selves," he wrote in his 2015 book *The Messengers: Owls, Synchronicity, and the UFO Abductee.* "It is never considered that this turn inward could prove vitally important to the greater community. The idea of *shaman sickness* is well understood in indigenous cultures, but westerners have no reference point and treat it as mental illness."[1537]

Clelland adds a quote from his conversation with author Joe Lewels, who said: "The people who have these experiences [alien abductions] are, many times rather unwillingly, being dragged into a shamanic apprenticeship. The people having these experiences are being taught how to heal, their consciousness is being elevated, they are being given opportunities to help people... *We need shamans, and if society doesn't provide it, the universe will.*"[1538]

Forteans ignore this comparison at their peril—it is simply too parsimonious to discount. Of Whitley Strieber's work, Jeffrey Kripal wrote:

> The entire drama of *Communion*, for example, can be seen as a kind of initiatory trial or illness. His famous owls and wolves can be seen to function as power animals or guiding totemic spirits. His proclivity for trance, out-of-body travel and visionary experience are patently obvious to anyone who cares to look at his books with an open mind...

As support for such a reading, consider the simple fact that much of his initial abduction experience as recounted in *Communion* revolved around a single word uttered by the almond-eyed female visitor: She told him that he had been "chosen."[1539]

HYPOTHESIS

In modern media, there exists the problematic trope of the "Inspirationally Disadvantaged." This familiar plot device employs disability to either highlight a disabled character's inspirational personality or, more germane to the discussion at hand, grant them supernatural abilities beyond typical human capacity. Notable examples include John Coffey from *The Green Mile*, Chance the Gardener from *Being There*, Christian Wolff in *The Accountant*, or, to a more realistic degree, the titular savant of *Rain Man*. Among critics it is now regarded as a hackneyed plot device, in some cases for good reason.[1540]

As tired as the trope may be, autistic savants do exist in our world. Their conditions no doubt have underlying physical, medical causes—yet may also have concomitant metaphysical sources, begging the question whether or not *spiritual* savants exist.

While the following hypothesis posits a supernatural origin for these conditions *in some cases*, we should stress that *not all cases* involve a metaphysical component, even if the concept is somehow true. Undoubtedly there is no "greater reason" for how some individuals are born other than genetics or random chance—anyone can be afflicted with lifelong disability by a roll of the cosmic dice. Developmental disabilities are not generally regarded as a blessing, and sufferers deserve our respect, compassion, and assistance.

To reiterate: developmental disabilities are not superpowers... but they may, in select cases, put individuals in contact with the spirit world.

What if changelings were simultaneously autistic, shamans, and abductees to the Otherworld? What if autism and similar disabilities are related to interaction with entities beyond the physical plane, an interaction fundamentally altering the consciousness of the percipient in our reality? We see this alteration as autism in certain cases, but perhaps it is only a symptom of contact with non-human intelligences.

A possible—highly explicative, yet equally flawed and problematic—framework emerges:

> **Some force outside human perception (the Other), having little ability to act within our physical realm, desires contact with humanity. In order to facilitate this communication, a shaman is required; in cultures without a shamanic tradition, the Other selects an individual, typically a youth with a malleable mind, sometimes with a history of trauma or abuse.**

> **The Other, or psychopomps acting on its behalf, reaches out to the selected youth via an altered state of consciousness. The youth may manifest a developmental disability (e.g. autism) as a result of contact with the Otherworld—whether the disability is a conduit for or a byproduct of this communion is unclear. In some cases, this communication and/or disability prompts a fugue state and physical retreat into the wilderness, a locale universally regarded as a place of spiritual awakening (excepting those with limited mobility, including infants). This bodily absence gives the appearance of physical abduction by supernatural forces.**

> **Upon return, the youth is notably different. Physiological reactions differ depending on a**

> **variety of factors—mental stability, the intensity of contact, etc. In those strong enough to weather contact with the Other, they return in a daze but there is little change in mental condition, save perhaps a burst in creativity, intuition, spirituality, or psychic effects. In others, this contact presents as disability of varying severity. In extreme cases, it may result in death or a permanent, physical absence from our reality.**

Regarding this last point, consider common religious beliefs delineating the dangers of theophany, beholding the divine. Gods can be lethal to witness in their true forms. In Greek myth, Semele, mortal consort of Zeus, died when Hera tricked her into seeing her lover in all his divine glory.[1541] Numerous references in Abrahamic tradition suggest that looking upon God can kill—for example, in Exodus 33:20 it is written: "But He said, 'You cannot see My face, for no man can see Me and live!" In the Bhagavad Gita, the god Krishna reveals his true form to Arjuna, who, while not perishing, finds "neither peace nor courage" in the sight, stating his "mind is tortured with fear." Arjuna remains inconsolable until Krishna takes on the more humble form of his four-armed avatar. This, of course, represents only a small portion of theophany in world religions; countless other witnesses to the divine escape with their lives, yet carry profound new spiritual insight.

What is this Divinity, this Other? Anyone's guess is as good as another. The God of the Old Testament, the collective human unconsciousness, extraterrestrials, the fae folk, an ecology of spirits, time travelers—all answers, if we are honest, remain on the table.

A story recently investigated by Clelland in his 2018 book *Stories from the Messengers: Owls, UFOs and a Deeper Reality* strongly suggests there may be some basis to our hypothesis—even though it involves a slightly older witness. Shortly before the 2012 autumn equinox, North Carolina resident Allison (pseudonym) participated in several Native American ceremonies, including a sweat lodge ritual and fasting. A few days later, she was hiking with her boyfriend, Eric, in the mountains when something compelled her to take several steps off the trail and into a small meadow. Once there, Allison began to hear the hooting of multiple owls—perhaps as many as five—all around her as she developed the curious sensation of, in her words, "blipping off the map." For reasons unknown to her, she began to disrobe and sat in the clearing, naked, watching as four to five cloudy, spherical, ringed UFOs began swirling in the air above.[1542]

"Just like the hooting owls in the surrounding trees, she felt these formless craft were communicating with her," Clelland wrote. "She was told that they knew she was there, and they had been looking for her. She described a clear telepathic message telling her they were making changes to accelerate a spiritual awakening."[1543]

During this time, Eric was frantically searching for his girlfriend. A team of rescuers and dogs were brought to the area. When she was finally discovered over five hours later, Allison was in the same clearing, despite Eric having checked it numerous times during the search. She was not cold, though the ambient temperature sat in the low-60s, and was convinced she couldn't have possibly spent so much time there alone.[1544]

Following her brief disappearance, Allison was blessed with newfound enthusiasm and aptitude for her musical career. When she received a bipolar disorder diagnosis several years later, she began to question the reality of her experience, attributing it to "some kind of psychosis at the time." Whether or not she was actually bipolar prior to her disappearance remains unclear.[1545]

"Allison is a performer and musician, and after the event she began playing music with a heightened intensity and passion," Clelland wrote. "There is something joyous within the creative process, and it's heartening that this would be elevated after her experience. But this same fervor could be interpreted as some sort of mania—and a symptom of mental illness. Also, in the aftermath she said she'd developed perfect pitch, and this seems magical to me—something akin to the gifts of a savant."[1546]

Allison's experience seems to directly correspond with our hypothesis—but it remains a mystery as to *what* she experienced. Was it an alien abduction? A trip to Fairlyand? A Missing 411 case? An encounter with psychopomps in the form of owls and UFOs? An altered state of consciousness? A shamanic awakening?

Or all of the above?

CRITICISMS

As explicative as this proposed conclusion may be, it is not without substantial shortcomings. As noted, certain disorders are devastating to not only sufferers but also friends and family, and seemingly serve no higher purpose. The idea that developmental disorders may be divinely ordained is undoubtedly offensive to some. There is also no shortage of abductees who return from their experiences *without* extrasensory abilities, or abductees taken late in life, as opposed to during childhood.

Moreover, critics may find that the hypothesis poorly accounts for bodily abductions, something seen in all stripes of paranormal child abduction. On balance, nothing about the hypothesis suggests the Other lacks the ability to manifest physically to some degree, or at the very least present an illusion of physicality in the perception of the observer. Perhaps, much in the same way that Hindu gods took on avatars masking their true form, the Other and its psychopomps can project images in our collective mind's eye. Certainly these phenomena have a physical component—it is impossible to otherwise explain away burn marks left by UFOs, scratches left on abductees, hair left by Sasquatch, etc.

Psychic phenomena present a suitable allegory for this Other. Like the Other, these abilities are wholly intangible, yet—in a variety of experiments and anecdotes—possess the capacity to act upon our physical environment. For example, the act of moving objects by mental force alone, known as psychokinesis, has been claimed for centuries (and arguably *proven* in laboratories).[1547] Regarding such abilities, the possibility exists that those with developmental conditions—particularly autism spectrum disorder (ASD)—may exhibit psychic talents with greater regularity than the average human being.

ALIENS, AUTISM, & SHAMANISM

The antiquated practice of calling an individual with developmental disabilities "touched" or "touched in the head" comes directly from the sense they have made contact with nonhuman consciousness.[1548] Like certain disorders, paranormal child abduction appears to have an inheritable component. If communion with the Otherworld can contribute to these conditions, autism is a natural candidate—it is arguably the most liminal of developmental disabilities, a condition of degrees, placed upon a spectrum describing a wide range of disorders. Like contact with the supernatural, there is no shortage of researchers who see a correlation between autism and abuse, even at the epigenetic level. One recent study suggested women abused in childhood are more likely to have autistic children.[1549]

While the connections between developmental disability and changelings are well established, some in UFOlogy maintain a connection exists between autism and alien abduction. Michael Menkin—inventor of the much derided "thought screen helmet"—maintains an entire second website contending that recent increases in autism rates are directly connected to extraterrestrial interference.[1550] According to experiencer Donna Lynn, extraterrestrials wishing to help humanity volunteered to "incarnate into bodies that could not speak. Some of your nonverbal autistic children are such."[1551] Betsey, one of David Jacobs' subjects, described an older human-alien hybrid as akin to "an autistic person. The social aspects are just off. The intelligence is there, but the social part is just not."[1552] In another example, a child named Henry from Pennsylvania developed "symptoms of autism" at age nine, despite having no prior history; this occurred shortly after visits from "little gray men" with "big eyes" who took him out his window into a spaceship.[1553] Of course, these are far from unimpeachable sources—*caveat emptor*—but they are intriguing clues nonetheless.

While autistic savants (not unlike some alien abductees) exhibit a capacity for mathematics, musicianship, memory, and art far exceeding the abilities of average human beings, evidence suggests that some possess abilities beyond the grasp of modern science. Professor Anne M. Donnellan and Paul Haskew discussed telepathy among autistic children and their caretakers at length. "Shortly after facilitation begins… facilitators often report that their communicators have an uncanny ability to know thoughts in their facilitators' minds," they wrote. "Exploration usually reveals that communicators have a well-developed 'sixth sense' that allows them both to understand what others think, feel, or know, and to transmit their own thoughts to nonverbal acquaintances, and sometimes to their facilitators… Among experienced facilitators [telepathy's] occurrence is no longer controversial."[1554]

While some dismiss these claims as pseudoscience based solely upon anecdotes, other researchers are exploring the possibility in a more scientific manner. Psychiatrist Diane Powell, a graduate of Johns Hopkins University School of Medicine, has been collecting evidence of psi abilities among autistic savants. Powell logically hypothesized that "the people that would be the most likely to exhibit [telepathy] would be nonverbal autistic children." In one of her experiments, Haley, a ten-year-old girl with nonverbal autism, revealed an astounding level of accuracy. As her therapist asked her to "read her mind" on the other side of a visual barrier, Haley "pointed with her wooden pencil inside characters on stencils with her right hand to select them, then entered them with her left into a device that converts text to speech."[1555] The results were astounding.

"You'll also notice that her answer is 100% accurate on 18 out of 18 digits," Powell said in a video presentation of Haley accurately transcribing mathematical formulae. "This is just one of ten equations that she did in a ten minute period, with accuracy above 90% each time." A time-stamped video feed revealed no evidence of deception. Powell has experienced similar results with several other nonverbal autistic children.[1556]

For some time, advocates have suggested the idea that certain disabilities represent an evolution of human consciousness. Author William Stillman believes that children with ASDs "have a unique openness to the subtle realms," claiming to have viewed their psi abilities firsthand.[1557] In a 2000 lecture, Scottish comic book author, artist, and magician Grant Morrison championed the notion that multiple personality disorder is a more humanizing way of looking at the world, by abandoning the destructive ego.

> The more I looked into it, the more I began to see that we have these mutants living among us, right now... If you lived in... Tunguska two hundred years ago, and you were an epileptic, you would be a shaman. There was a context for you. In this society, you're an epileptic. It's quite simple; it's a disease, and nothing you say is of any worth because it's considered pathology.
>
> If, on the other hand, you look at these people, who are the "mutants"... and what do they call it? Multiple Personality Disorder...
>
> So what I'm suggesting is that we start working with that. Abandon the personality; abandon the individual; abandon the "I" because it's a lie, and it has held us down; it's been like a weight round our necks...
>
> And I think what we should do is walk away from the crap of the 21st century, and start thinking about what we've been experiencing.[1558]

More articulate are the sentiments of Jason Horsley (aka Aeolus Kephas), self-described "autist" and experiencer. In an October 13, 2013, interview on the *Expanding Mind* podcast, Horsley said:

> Even low low-functioning, nonverbal [autists], which in the past and still today are assumed to be "retarded" or just mentally absent, more and more evidence suggests—proving, really—that they're not absent at all... They're absolutely present, they're absolutely sentient, but their way of communicating and their way of behaving is so foreign that we're not able to recognize it... So it is almost like they are embodying an unconscious aspect of ourselves, and by definition we can't actually recognize it, or identify it because it doesn't fit with our idea about what being human is, or what being sentient is, or what intelligence is...
>
> We've become so habituated to a certain way of perceiving our environment and interacting with it that we've actually isolated ourselves from a whole other portion of experience. I think autism is, in a sense, picking up the slack for the species there.[1559]

Morrison and Horsley seem to vaguely suggest that what is generally called the "autism epidemic" may represent some new stage of human development. For decades, researchers held roughly one in 2,500 individuals suffered from ASD.[1560] Then—perhaps beginning with an underestimation of rates in the 1970s—diagnoses began to climb.[1561]

"The data for PDDs [Pervasive Developmental Disorders, a type of ASD] point to roughly a 10-fold increase for all ASDs from the 1970s to the early-to-mid 1990s," Mark F. Blaxill wrote in *Public Health Reports*.[1562] During that period, the rate steadily climbed through the 1980s (2.5-16 per 10,000 births) and 1990s (5-31 per 10,000 births) until today.[1563] In the brief time between 1993 and 2003, the rate ballooned over 657% in America alone,[1564] with the Centers for Disease Control and Prevention most recently estimating in 2017 that one in 68 children has been identified with some form of ASD.[1565]

Certainly diagnostic measures have improved detection rates and the spectrum has broadened, encompassing personality types not previously associated with autism—but this only partially explains the increased incidence, according to a 2015 report from the *American Journal of Medical Genetics*.[1566] "For years, we've known that a proportion of the increase in autism prevalence is attributable to increased awareness of autism and changes in diagnostic criteria," elaborated Michael Rosanoff, epidemiologist and Director of Public Health Research for Autism Speaks. "However, these factors alone don't account for the entire increase in autism prevalence..."[1567]

Some may counter that those with autism spectrum disorder aren't fulfilling any evolutionary or shamanic role in our society—after all, they aren't healing others, telling us where to hunt, or communicating messages from the Otherworld—but perhaps those in the West in the 21st century simply aren't listening to them, for the reasons outlined by Horsley. Imelda Almqvist, mother of two autistic children, takes the time to ask them what they experience while "stimming" ("self-stimulating behaviors such as spinning, flapping, humming, or head-banging"). According to their answers, Almqvist believes her children are "shamanic journeying or talking to spirit."[1568]

Evidence of a link between autism spectrum disorder and holy figures can be found in the historical record. There is growing suspicion among the psychological community that many Indian ascetics, including the saint Ramakrishna Paramahamsa, were autistic. As a child, Ramakrishna avoided social contact, spending his days cremating the dead and transfixed for hours by clay statues. He also was averse to touch and possessed linguistic disfluency.[1569]

In the west, Catholic scholars have speculated that several holy figures were autistic. Brother Juniper, follower of Saint Francis of Assisi, had great difficulty with social cues; French nun Léonie Martin was "undisciplined" and "mentally undeveloped" as a child, stuttering as an adult; Saint Joseph of Cupertino "was very absent-minded, awkward and extremely sensitive to his surroundings."[1570] Even in our modern world, some Jewish sects believe that those with autism spectrum disorder can contact the Otherworld. In the 1990s, ultra-orthodox Haredi Jews "began staging large public gatherings in which autistic children moved an adult facilitator's fingers to computer or typewriter keys in response to questions from rabbis."[1571]

To bring this discussion full circle, recall that alien abductees—like those touched by deities—often emerge from their experiences with a mission, quest, or charge, much like religious saints. When remembered, this is almost uniformly a message of utmost importance pertaining to mankind's stewardship of the planet, warning against such threats as nuclear proliferation and pollution.

THE TRUE THIEF IN THE NIGHT

"Traditionally shamanism was used to maintain a mutually healthy equilibrium between people and their environment," wrote Christina Pratt in *An Encyclopedia of Shamanism*. "The shaman guided the restoration of balance between the community and the animal world, spirit world, or the natural environment by creating necessary rituals as guided by their helping spirits." [1572]

While vestiges of the concept have existed since time immemorial, it comes as little surprise the alien hybrid craze blossomed in the late 1970s and early 1980s, when an overreliance on technology and a disinterest toward our neighbors began insidiously taking root. Simultaneously, undeniable turmoil began unfolding worldwide, the sewn seeds being reaped today: record-setting hurricanes in the Atlantic, climbing temperatures, seething societal unrest, political upheaval. If contact with the Other is indeed a call—back to Earth, back to spirit, back to soul—it should be heeded.

Few compelling arguments could be raised that humans have not become exponentially more divorced from reality in the past 50 years. The rate is unprecedented; though the Roman Empire may have collapsed in an implosion of decadence and apathy, there was still reliance upon face-to-face human interaction. The supply chain for food was shorter. Our dependence upon the planet was understood.

Today, as empires fall, we simple do not care—we are all Neros, fiddling away while Rome burns. We are drowning in data, tethered to smartphones and distracted by the bread and circuses of entertainment. We can live without walking barefoot on the grass; we cannot live without the internet. There is an extreme disconnect between mankind and our environment when water— an element essential to life and literally covering 70% of the planet—can destroy a majority of the technology in our homes. This is the Dogon mirror universe we have created: a separate, walled-off reality that is wholly unsustainable.

Perhaps we have stumbled upon the reason for the alarming rise in global autism rates. Recall the sudden onset of the epidemic post-1970; though their roots certainly begin earlier, alien abductions as understood in their current incarnation took off as a UFOlogical meme in the 1970s, reaching a fever pitch in the 1980s and 1990s. The coincidence of rising autism diagnoses with this phenomenon may indeed be just that—coincidental—but what if it isn't?

At some point in our deep past, trafficking with the spirit world was understood as a natural aspect of life, helping maintain balance between the physical and nonphysical realms. Communication between mankind and the Other was open and frequent, facilitated by those in shamanic roles, those selected by the Other. As humanity wandered from this spiritual dialogue— led astray by mechanization, urbanization, physical materialism, and the like—this essential interaction declined.

The faeries left. But centuries later the conversation was forced upon us once more, during our spiritual nadir. The aliens arrived.

The Other first presented itself as benignly encouraging Space Brothers, then—as our stubbornness and inability to listen grew more apparent—maliciously assertive Grey aliens. Perhaps the escalation of visitations in the modern era—forceful and non-consensual, a tonal contrast to the *laissez-faire* interactions from the contactee era of the 1950s and 1960s—represents this attempt to bridge the gap between humanity and the Otherworld.

Is the Other becoming increasingly desperate to contact us? Do we need shamans more than ever to reconnect us to spirituality, to ground us to Mother Earth? To remind us of our duty to our neighbors? To avert our impending self-destruction?

Apocalyptic lamentations come easy to authors but take a backseat in our daily lives. Understandably so; amidst this turmoil, we must somehow find a way to simply *exist* in the societal cages we have constructed. We have no choice but to pay the rent, feed the dog, service our automobiles, and mow our lawns.

Parents have no choice but to parent. But that is a blessing.

Paranormal child abduction reminds us of the supremacy of the Other, the unnamable forces to which every knee must bend. If it wants us, it takes us. While there is no shortage of existential fear in the concept, it is also comforting to know things are beyond our control.

Though folklore tells us there are many things in the shadows to fear—faeries, aliens, Sasquatch—there is a more pernicious danger to our children than the boogeymen coiled in our nightmares. The biggest threat to the wellbeing of our children is the world we leave behind: environmentally, socially, politically.

Spiritually.

This is the true thief in the night: a future of increasing disconnect between ourselves and our neighbors, between ourselves and the Earth, robbing us of the truly miraculous, magical reality that is our birthright. Our gift—nay, our *obligation*—to future generations is, as magician Gordon White puts it, to "re-enchant the world." Even if there is no objective reality to faeries, the possibility of their existence imbues every tree with the mystery, majesty, and respect it deserves. Even if extraterrestrials are not visiting Earth, the idea makes our skies more enigmatic, our existence more humble. These concepts allow us to appreciate the wonder inherent in our natural world, inherent in life.

Regardless of what lies behind the Other—benign or malevolent—its steadfast defiance in the face of narrow-minded rationality and unemotional scientism serves as a reminder that our reality is stranger than we realize. Stranger, and more wonderful.

For millennia mankind has fretted about what paranormal thieves in the night are taking from us.

Perhaps it is time we considered what they have given humanity.

Acknowledgements

It takes a village to raise a Fortean, and I am no exception. While there are countless influences, friends, and fans to thank for their help, a few deserve special attention (and apologies for any of you I forgot!).

A very special thanks to Sam Shearon for providing some truly outstanding (and unsettling) cover art!

Thanks to Kelsie Skye, Adam Loyal, Jeff Ritzmann, Mike Clelland, and Timothy Renner for suggesting various leads and topics to examine. A very special debt of gratitude to Dr. Simon Young for his advice on several faerie and folklore related topics. Both Robert Smith and Robert Bartholomew deserve thanks for helping me track down some hard-to-find journal articles. I am also thankful for the Irish folklore expertise of Michael Quinlan and M. Heavey.

I could not have accomplished this without the help of dear friends. Aaron Gulyas, Patrick Huyghe, Wren Collier, my parents, and my wife Sarah were angels in the editing process, providing valuable feedback, corrections, and insight on how to handle sensitive subjects.

Finally, two dear groups always deserve special mention for their perennial place in my heart: my ParaManiacs (including, but not exclusive to, Greg Bishop, Tim Binnall, Miguel Romero, and Smiles Lewis) and Seriah Azkath and the *Where Did the Road Go?* extended podcast family.

Endnotes

1   Swords, M.D. (2005). *Grassroots UFOs: Case Reports from the Center for UFO Studies.* San Antonio, TX: Anomalist Books. (Original work published by The Fund for UFO Research)

2   Guiley, R.E. (2007). *The Encyclopedia of Ghosts and Spirits* (3ʳᵈ ed). New York, NY: Facts on File, Inc. (Original work published 1992)

3   Guiley 2007.

4   Rees, D. (1979, March). Floating Entity at Reddish. *Flying Saucer Review 25(2)*, pp. 29-31.

5   Keel, J. (1971). *Our Haunted Planet.* London, UK: Neville Spearman, Ltd.

6   Vallee, J., & Aubeck, C. (2009). *Wonders in the Sky: Unexplained Aerial Objects from Antiquity to Modern Times.* New York, NY: Jeremy P. Tarcher/Penguin.

7   Rickard, B., & Michell, J. (2007). *Unexplained Phenomena: A Rough Guide Special* (2ⁿᵈ ed.). London, UK: Rough Guides, Ltd.

8   Sedlak, A.J., Finkelhor, D., Hammer, H., & Schultz, D.J. (2002, October). *National Estimates of Missing Children: An Overview.* In Flores, J.R. (Ed.), *NISMART: National Incidence Studies of Missing, Abducted, Runaway, and Thrownaway Children.* Washington, DC: U.S. Department of Justice.

9   Keel, J. (1976). *The Mothman Prophecies.* New York, NY: Signet Books.

10   White, G. (2017, March 1). *Rune Soup: Talking Worldviews, Culture and Comparison with Dr. Jeff Kripal.* Retrieved May 30, 2017 from https://runesoup.com/2017/03/talking-worldviews-culture-and-comparison-with-dr-jeff-kripal

11   Jozuka, E. (2016, September 22). *Aboriginal Australians are Earth's oldest civilization: DNA study.* Retrieved May 30, 2017 from http://www.cnn.com/2016/09/22/asia/indigenous-australians-earths-oldest-civilization/

12   Purkiss, D. (2000). *Troublesome Things: A History of Fairies and Fairy Stories.* London, UK: The Penguin Group.

13   Schwartz, H. (2004). *Tree of Souls: The Mythology of Judaism.* New York, NY: Oxford University Press, Inc.

14   Koltuv, B.B. (1986). *The Book of Lilith.* York Beach, ME: Nicolas-Hays, Inc.

15   Purkiss 2000.

16   Spence, L. (1920). *An Encyclopaedia of Occultism.* New York, NY: Dodd, Mead & Company.

17   Guiley, R.E. (2009). *The Encyclopedia of Demons & Demonology.* New York, NY: Facts on File, Inc.

18   Schwartz 2004.

19   Guiley 2009.

20   Schwartz 2004.

21   Guiley 2009.

22   Schwartz 2004.

23   Schachter-Shalomi, Z., & Miles-Yepez, N. (2009). *A Heart Afire: Stories and Teachings of the Early Hasidic Masters.* Philadelphia, PA: The Jewish Publication Society.

24   Bergmann, M.S. (1992). *In the Shadow of Moloch: The Sacrifice of Children and Its Impact on Western Religions.* New York, NY: Columbia University Press.

25   Heider, G.C. (1985). *The Cult of Molek: A Reassessment.* Sheffield, England: University of Sheffield Department of Biblical Studies.

26   BBC. (2016, January 20). Fairy tales origins thousands of years old, researchers say. Retrieved May 30, 2017 from http://www.bbc.com/news/uk-35358487

27   Scutts, J. (2015). *The Pied Piper of Hamelin at the Crossroads of History, Religion, and Literature.* Raleigh, NC: Lulu.

28   Harpur, P. (2003). *Daimonic Reality: A Field Guide to the Otherworld.* Ravensdale, WA: Pure Winds Press.

29   Redfern, N. (2017, March 24). The Mystery of the U.K.'s "Phantom" Social Workers. Retrieved September 6, 2017 from http://mysteriousuniverse.org/2017/03/the-mystery-of-the-u-k-s-phantom-social-workers/

30   Gabler, E. (2014, June 2). Charges detail Waukesha pre-teens' attempt to kill classmate. Retrieved May 30, 2017 from http://archive.jsonline.com/news/crime/waukesha-police-2-12-year-old-girls-plotted-for-months-to-kill-friend-b99282655z1-261534171.html

31   Sikes, W. (1880). *British Goblins: Welsh Folklore, Fairy Mythology, Legends and Traditions.* London, UK: Sampson Low, Marston, Searle, & Rivington (2nd ed.).

32   Briggs, K. (1976). *An Encyclopedia of Fairies: Hobgoblins, Brownies, Bogies, and Other Supernatural Creatures.* New York, NY: Pantheon Books.

33   Briggs 1976.

34   Briggs 1976.

35   Evans Wentz, W.Y. (1911). *The Fairy-Faith in Celtic Countries.* London, UK: Henry Frowde.

36   Yeats, W.B. (Ed.). (1890). *Fairy and Folk Tales of the Irish Peasantry.* New York, NY: The Walter Scott Publishing Co., Ltd.

37   Silver, C.G. (1999). *Strange and Secret Peoples: Fairies and Victorian Consciousness.* New York, NY: Oxford University Press, Inc.

38   Lecouteux, C. (2013). *The Tradition of Household Spirits.* (J.E. Graham, Trans.). Rochester, VT: Inner Traditions. (Original work published 2000)

39   Briggs, K. (2002). *The Fairies in Tradition and Literature.* London, UK: Routledge (Original work published 1967)

40   Martin, K., Walker, J. (Producers), & Walker, J. (Director). (2000). *The Fairy Faith* (motion picture). Canada: National Film Board of Canada.

41   Árnason, J. (1864). *Icelandic Legends.* (G.E.J. Powell & E. Magnússon, Trans.). London, UK: Richard Bentley.

42   Bane 2013.

43   Mack, C.K., & Mack, D. (1998). *A Field Guide to Demons, Fairies, Fallen Angels, and Other Subversive Spirits.* New York, NY: Henry Holt and Company, LLC.

44   Sikes 1880.

45   Yeats 1890.

46   Wilde, J. (1887). *Ancient Legends, Mystic Charms, and Superstitions of Ireland.* London, UK: Ticknor and Co.

47   Bane, T. (2013). *Encyclopedia of Fairies in World Folklore and Mythology.* Jefferson, NC: McFarland & Company, Inc.

48   Butler, J. (2017). The *Sídhe* and Fairy Forts. In S. Young & C. Houlbrook (Eds.), *Magical Folk: British and Irish Fairies: 500 AD to the Present* (Kindle Edition). London, UK; Gibson Square.

49   Lecouteux, C. (2015). *Demons and Spirits of the Land.* (J.E. Graham, Trans.). Rochester, VT: Inner Traditions. (Original work published 1995)

50   Silver 1999.

51   Wilde 1887.

52   Coulson, L. (2017). Trows and Trownie Wives. In S. Young & C. Houlbrook (Eds.), *Magical Folk: British and Irish Fairies: 500 AD to the Present* (Kindle Edition).

53   Randles, J. (1988). *Abduction: Over 200 Documented UFO Kidnappings Exhaustively Investigated.* London, UK: Robert Hale Ltd.

54   Casteel, S. (2008). Fairies and Aliens. In T.G. Beckley (Ed.), *UFOs, Time Slips, Other Realms, and the Science of Fairies* (pp. 9-19) New Brunswick, N.J.: Timothy Green Beckley (Global Communications/Conspiracy Journal).

55   Bogart (n.d.). *Oxford Living Dictionaries.* Retrieved May 31, 2017, from https://en.oxforddictionaries.com/definition/bogart

56   Bane 2013.

57   Guiney, L.I. (1888). *Brownies and Bogles.* Boston, MA: D. Lothrop Company.

58   Silver 1999.

59   Campbell, J.G. (1910, July). The Origin of the Fairy Creed. *The Scottish Historical Review 7(28),* pp. 364-376.

60   Bug. (n.d.). *Merriam-Webster.* Retrieved June 3, 2017 from https://www.merriam-webster.com/dictionary/bug

61   Evans Wentz 1911.

62   Guiney 1888.

63   Keightley, T. (1828). *The Fairy Mythology.* London, UK: William Harrison Ainsworth.

64   Evans Wentz 1911.

65   Guiney 1888.

66   Norman, M., & Hickey-Hall, J. (2017). Pixies and Pixy Rocks. In S. Young & C.

Houlbrook (Eds.), *Magical Folk: British and Irish Fairies: 500 AD to the Present* (Kindle Edition). London, UK; Gibson Square.

67 Woodyard, C. . (2017). Banshees and Changelings. In S. Young & C. Houlbrook (Eds.), *Magical Folk: British and Irish Fairies: 500 AD to the Present* (Kindle Edition). London, UK; Gibson Square.

68 Narváez, P. (1997). Newfoundland Berry Pickers "In the Fairies." In P. Narváez (Ed.), *The Good People: New Fairylore Essays* (pp. 336-368). Lexington, KY: The University Press of Kentucky.

69 Von Sydow, C.W. (1948). The Manhardian Theories about the Last Sheaf and the Fertility Demons from a Modern Critical Point of View. *Selected Papers on Folklore 4.* Copenhagen, DK.

70 Crookshank, M. (1909, September 30). Old-Time Survivals in Remote Norwegian Dales. *Folklore 20(3),* pp. 313-336.

71 Croker, T.C. (1828). *Fairy Legends & Traditions of the South of Ireland Part III.* London, UK: John Murray.

72 Kroth, J. (2017). *Extraterrestrial Contacts: Roswell Foil, UFOs, and How They Alter Our Understanding of the Modern World.* Santa Clara, CA: Genotype.

73 Croker 1828 *Part III.*

74 Strieber, W. (1997). *Transformation.* New York, NY: Avon Books.

75 Árnason 1864.

76 Alexander, M. (2006). *Sutton Companion to British Folklore, Myths & Legends.* Stroud, UK: The History Press. (Original work published 2002)

77 Evans Wentz 1911.

78 Sikes 1880.

79 Wilde 1887.

80 Keightley 1828.

81 Aspinall, K. (1995, Summer). "Alien Abductions" and "Fairy Abductions": A Comparison. *Flying Saucer Review 40(2),* pp. 9-11.

82 Ashliman, D.L. (2005, December 17). German Changeling Legends. Retrieved June 2, 2017 from http://www.pitt.edu/~dash/gerchange.html

83 Kropej, M. (2012). *Supernatural Beings from Slovenian Myth and Folktales.* Ljubljana, SI: Scientific Research Centre of the Slovenian Academy of Sciences and Arts.

84 Jenkins, R.P. (1997). Witches and Fairies: Supernatural Aggression and Deviance Among the Irish Peasantry. In P. Narváez (Ed.), *The Good People: New Fairylore Essays* (pp. 302-335). Lexington, KY: The University Press of Kentucky.

85 Franklin, R. (2005). *Baby Lore: Superstitions & Old Wives Tales from the World Over.* West Sussex, UK: Diggory Press.

86 Fleming, M. (2002). *Not of This World: Creatures of the Supernatural in Scotland.* Edinburgh, UK: Mercat Press Ltd.

87 Hickey, E.M. (1938). Medical Superstitions in Ireland. *Ulster Medical Journal 7,* pp. 268-270.

88   Hartland, E.S. (1891). *The Science of Fairytales: An Inquiry into Fairy Mythology.* London, UK: Walter Scott.

89   Lysaght, P. (1997). Fairylore from the Midlands of Ireland. In P. Narváez (Ed.), *The Good People: New Fairylore Essays* (pp. 22-46). Lexington, KY: The University Press of Kentucky.

90   Silver 1999.

91   Wilde 1887.

92   Guiley 2007.

93   Guiney 1888.

94   Miss Dempster. (1888). The Folk-Lore of Sutherland-Shire [Continued]. *The Folk-Lore Journal 6(4)*, pp. 215-252.

95   Wilde 1887.

96   Silver 1999.

97   MacGregor, A. (1901). *Highland Superstitions.* London, UK: Gibbings & Company, Ltd.

98   Evans Wentz 1911.

99   Evans Wentz 1911.

100   Wilde 1887.

101   Wilde 1887.

102   Wilde 1887.

103   Wilde 1887.

104   Wilde 1887.

105   Owen, E. (1887). *Welsh Folklore.* Owestry & Wrexham, UK: Woodall, Minshall, and Co.

106   Yeats 1890.

107   Jenkins 1997.

108   No author. (2009, July 10). John Keel (Obituary). Retrieved June 8, 2017 from http://www.telegraph.co.uk/news/obituaries/science-obituaries/5797746/John-Keel.html

109   Evans Wentz 1911

110   Evans Wentz 1911.

111   Rhŷs, J. (1901). *Celtic Folklore: Welsh and Manx, Vol. I.* Oxford, UK: Clarendon Press.

112   Lecouteux 2015.

113   Briggs 1976.

114   Monaghan, P. (2004). *The Encyclopedia of Celtic Mythology and Folklore.* New York, NY: Facts on File, Inc.

115   Seifert, M. (2002). *Rewriting Newfoundland Mythology: The Works of Tom Dawe.*

Glienicke, DE: Galda & Wilch Verlag.

116   Kennedy, P. (1866). *Legendary Fictions of the Irish Celts*. London, UK: Macmillan and Co.

117   Guiney 1888.

118   Evans Wentz 1911.

119   MacGregor 1901.

120   Hartland 1891.

121   Keightley 1828.

122   Briggs 2002.

123   Hartland 1891.

124   Skjelbred, A.H.B. (1997). Rites of Passage as Meeting Place: Christianity and Fairylore in Connection with the Unclean Woman and the Unchristened Child. In P. Narváez (Ed.), *The Good People: New Fairylore Essays* (pp. 215-223). Lexington, KY: The University Press of Kentucky.

125   Hartland 1891.

126   Bloch, A.R. (2013). The Two Fonts of the Florence Baptistery and the Evolution of the Baptismal Rite in Florence, ca. 1200-1500. In H.M. Sonne de Torrens & M.A. Torrens (Eds.), *The Visual Culture of Baptism in the Middle Ages* (pp. 77-104) Surrey, UK: Ashgate Publishing Limited.

127   Buccola, R. (2006). *Fairies, Fractious Women, and the Old Faith: Fairy Lore in Early Modern British Drama and Culture*. Selinsgrove, PA: Susquehanna University Press.

128   O'Hanlon, J. (1870). *Irish Folk Lore: Traditions and Superstitions of the Country; with Humorous Tales*. Glasgow, UK: Cameron & Ferguson.

129   Evans Wentz 1911.

130   Evans Wentz 1911.

131   Kirby, E.J. (2014, June 20). Why Icelanders are wary of elves living beneath the rocks. Retrieved September 25, 2017 from http://www.bbc.com/news/magazine-27907358

132   Lecouteux 2015.

133   Bane 2013.

134   Heavey, M. (2017, September 28). Food, Folklore and Fairies. [Live lecture].

135   Guiney 1888.

136   Harper, D. (2017). Online Etymology Dictionary: Panic. Retrieved September 19, 2017 from http://www.etymonline.com/index.php?term=panic

137   Guiney 1888.

138   Harte, J. (2017). Fairy Barrows and Cunning Folk. In S. Young & C. Houlbrook (Eds.), *Magical Folk: British and Irish Fairies: 500 AD to the Present* (Kindle Edition). London, UK; Gibson Square.

139   Ashliman 2005.

140   Wright, E.M. (1913). *Rustic Speech and Folk-Lore.* Oxford, UK: Humphrey Milford, Oxford University Press.

141   Lecouteux 2015.

142   Sikes 1880.

143   Sikes 1880.

144   Evans Wentz 1911.

145   Breatnach, D. (1993). *Chugat an Púca.* Dundalk, IE: Dundalgan Press.

146   Narváez 1997.

147   Bane 2013.

148   Power, M. (2017). A Changeling Story. Retrieved July 2, 2017 from http://www.duchas.ie/en/cbes/5080332/4879042

149   Ashliman 2005.

150   Evans Wentz 1911.

151   Lady Gregory (1920). *Visions and Beliefs in the West of Ireland Collected and Arranged by Lady Gregory, First Series.* New York, NY: The Knickerbocker Press.

152   Ashliman, D.L. (2013). Changeling Legends from the British Isles. Retrieved June 8, 2017 from http://www.pitt.edu/~dash/britchange.html

153   Hazlitt, W.C. (1905). *Brand's Popular Antiquities of Great Britain, Vol. I.* In J. Brand & H. Ellis (Eds.). London, UK: Reeves and Turner.

154   Ashliman 2013.

155   Wilde 1887.

156   Latham, M.W. (1930). *The Elizabethan Fairies.* New York, NY: Columbia University Press.

157   Young, S. (2017, May 10). Personal communication.

158   Ashliman 2005.

159   Sikes 1880.

160   Suggett, R. (2017). The Fair Folk and Enchanters. In S. Young & C. Houlbrook (Eds.), *Magical Folk: British and Irish Fairies: 500 AD to the Present* (Kindle Edition). London, UK; Gibson Square.

161   Guiley 2007.

162   Briggs 1976.

163   White, C. (2005). *A History of Irish Fairies.* New York, NY: Carrol & Graf Publishers. (Original work published 1976)

164   Hunt, B. (1912). *Folk Tales of Breffny.* London, UK: Macmillan.

165   Wilde 1887.

166   Dunican, I. (2017). Changelings (continued). Retrieved June 8, 2017 from http://www.duchas.ie/en/cbes/4921674/4889287

167   Yeats 1892.

168   Young, S. (2017). Fairy Bread and Fairy Squalls. In S. Young & C. Houlbrook (Eds.), *Magical Folk: British and Irish Fairies: 500 AD to the Present* (Kindle Edition). London, UK; Gibson Square.

169   Guiley 2007.

170   Benjamin, S. (2009). Chapter One: Blue Like Me. In V.G.J. Rajan & S. Bahun-Radunović (Eds.), *From Myth to Canvas: Appropriations of Myth in Women's Aesthetic Production*, pp. 11-22. Newcastle, UK: Cambridge Scholars Publishing.

171   Parsons, P.T. (1939). *Pueblo Indian Religion, Vol. I.* Chicago, IL: University of Chicago Press.

172   Briggs 1976.

173   Ankarloo, B., Clark, S., & Monter, W. (2002). *Witchcraft and Magic in Europe: Volume 4 - The Period of the Witch Trials.* London, UK: The Athlone Press.

174   Lady Gregory 1920, *First Series.*

175   Umbarger, M. (2011). *Harp Song: The Golden Thread with Selected Arrangements for the Folk Harp.* Pacific, MO: Mel Bay Publications.

176   Sikes 1880.

177   Hewlett, M. (1913). *Lore of Prosperine.* New York, NY: Charles Scribner's Sons.

178   Hunt, R. (1871). *Popular Romances of the West of England: The Drolls, Traditions, and Superstitions of Old Cornwall.* London, UK: John Camden Hotten (2nd ed.).

179   Hall, A. (2007). *Elves in Anglo-Saxon England: Matters of Belief, Health, Gender and Identity.* Rochester, NY: Boydell & Brewer.

180   Sikes 1880.

181   Rhŷs 1901.

182   Wilde 1887.

183   Yeats 1892.

184   Sikes 1880.

185   Sugg, R. (2017, August 23). Child abduction, poltergeist sightings, crop failure and haunted building sites blamed on sinister work of fairies. Retrieved September 1, 2017 from http://www.mirror.co.uk/news/weird-news/child-abduction-poltergeist-sightings-crop-11036934

186   Guiley, R.E. (2010). *Mysteries, Legends, and Unexplained Phenomena: Fairies.* New York, NY: Chelsea House.

187   Lysaght 1997.

188   Murray, U. (2017). Old Stories – A Changeling. Retrieved June 9, 2017 from http://www.duchas.ie/en/cbes/5009032/4979185/5115813

189   Nunnelly, B.M. (2011). *The Inhumanoids: Real Encounters with Beings That Can't Exist.* Woolsery, UK: CFZ Press.

190   Lang, C.R. (2002, October). Psychic/Spiritual Awakenings. *MUFON UFO Journal 414*, pp. 8-10.

191   Sveinsson, E.Ó. (2003). *The Folk-Stories of Iceland.* (B. Benedikz, Trans.). E.G.

Pétursson (Ed.). Exeter, UK: Short Run Press Limited.

192   Árnason 1866.

193   Bruford, A. (1997). Trolls, Hillfolk, Finns, and Picts: The Identity of the Good Neighbors in Orkney and Shetland. In P. Narváez (Ed.), *The Good People: New Fairylore Essays* (pp. 116-141). Lexington, KY: The University Press of Kentucky.

194   Evans Wentz 1911.

195   Holloway, V. (2017, June 15). Fairy Folklore: Come Away, O Human Child. Retrieved December 13, 2017 from http://folklorethursday.com/legends/come-away-o-human-child/#sthash.xXRJkDNb.h2HjS5Lf.dpbs

196   Quinn, R. (2006). *Little People*. Lakeville, MN: Galde Press, Inc.

197   Nunnelly 2011.

198   Ashliman, D.L. (2012, December 22). The Origin of Underground People. Retrieved June 12, 2017 from http://www.pitt.edu/~dash/originunder.html

199   Silver 1999.

200   Roberts, J. (2016). *The Sacred Mythological Centres of Ireland*. IE: Bandia Publishing.

201   Evans Wentz 1911.

202   Croker, T.C. (1825). *Fairy Legends & Traditions of the South of Ireland Part I*. London, UK: John Murray.

203   Smith, C. (2005, September). The Land of the Hidden People. *Fortean Times 201*, pp. 42-47.

204   Harpur 2003.

205   Croker 1828 *Part III*.

206   Evans Wentz 1911.

207   Evans Wentz 1911.

208   Briggs 1976.

209   MacDougall, J. (1910). *Folk Tales and Fairy Lore in Gaelic and English*. G. Calder (Ed.). Edinburgh, UK: John Grant.

210   Evans Wentz 1911.

211   Briggs 1976.

212   Rhŷs 1901.

213   Croker 1828 *Part III*.

214   Ey, A. (1862). *Harzmärchenbuch; oder, Sagen und Märchen aus dem Oberharze*. Stade, DE: Verlag von Fr. Steudel.

215   MacDougall 1910.

216   Ashliman 2005.

217   Wilde 1887.

218   Sikes 1880.

219   Henderson, L., & Cowan, E.J. (2001). *Scottish Fairy Belief.* East Lothian, UK: Tuckwell Press.

220   Bagshawe, T.W., & Coote Lake, E.F. (1949, March). Folk Life and Traditions. *Folklore 60(1)*, pp. 245-248.

221   Guiney 1888.

222   Kvideland, R., & Sehmsdorf, H.K. (Eds.). (1988). *Scandinavian Folk Belief and Legend.* Minneapolis, MN: University of Minnesota Press.

223   Lawing, S.B. (2013, Summer). The Place of Evil: Infant Abandonment in Old Norse Society. *Scandinavian Studies 85(2)*, pp. 133-150.

224   Keightley 1828.

225   Hooykaas, J (1960). The Changeling in Balinese Folklore and Religion. *Bijdragen tot de Taal-, Land- en Volkenkunder 116(4)*, pp. 424-426.

226   Grimm, J. (2003). *Deutsche Mythologie.* Wiesbaden, DE: Fourier Verlag. (Original work published 1835)

227   Ashliman 2005.

228   Lindow, J. (1978). *Swedish Legends and Folktales.* Berkeley and Los Angeles, CA: University of California Press.

229   Rajchel, D. (2016). Crop Lore: When the Plants Talked Back. In E. Day & L. Heineman (Eds.), *Llewellyn's 2017 Herbal Almanac*, pp. 275-280. Woodbury, MN: Llewellyn Worldwide Ltd.

230   Bane 2013.

231   Kropej 2012.

232   Dworski, L. (2015, October 29). Slavic Mythology from Poland (Part 4): BOGIN-KI. Retrieved June 2, 2017 from https://lamusdworski.wordpress.com/2015/10/29/polish-mythology-boginki

233   Jestice, P.G. (2000). *Encyclopedia of Irish Spirituality.* Santa Barabara, CA: ABC-CLIO, Inc.

234   Doniger, W., & Spinner, G. (1998, Winter). Misconceptions: Female Imaginations and Male Fantasies in Parental Imprinting. *Daedalus 127(1)*, pp. 97-129.

235   Doniger & Spinner 1998.

236   Goodey, C.F., & Stainton, T. (2001, June). Intellectual Disability and the Myth of the Changeling Myth. *Journal of the History of the Behavioral Sciences 37(3)*, pp. 223-240.

237   Goodey & Stainton 2001.

238   Green, R.F. (2016). *Elf Queens and Holy Friars: Fairy Beliefs and the Medieval Church.* Philadelphia, PA: University of Pennsylvania Press.

239   Ashliman 2005.

240   Henderson & Cowan 2001.

241   Buccola 2006.

242   Forbes, T.R. (1962, April). Midwifery and Witchcraft. *Journal of the History of Medicine and Allied Sciences 17(2)*, pp. 264-283.

243   Silver 1999.

244   American Folklore Society. (1889, January-March). Notices of the Folk-Lore of Other Continents. *The Journal of American Folklore 2(4)*, pp. 80-82.

245   Clark, J. (2006, July). "Small, Vulnerable ETs": The Green Children of Woolpit. *Science Fiction Studies 33(2)*, pp. 209-229.

246   Munro, J.U. (1997). The Invisible Made Visible: The Fairy Changeling as a Folk Articulation of Failure to Thrive in Infants and Children. In P. Narváez (Ed.), *The Good People: New Fairylore Essays* (pp. 251-283). Lexington, KY: The University Press of Kentucky.

247   Asbjørnsen, P.C. (1883). *Folk and Fairy Tales.* (H.L. Braekstad, Trans.). New York, NY: A.C. Armstrong & Son (7th ed.).

248   Ashliman 1997.

249   Evans Wentz 1911.

250   Wilde 1887.

251   Hartland 1891.

252   M'Manus, L. (1914, September 30). Folk-Tales from Western Ireland. *Folklore 25(3)*, pp. 324-341.

253   Evans Wentz 1911.

254   Skjelbred 1997.

255   MacGregor 1901.

256   M'Manus 1914.

257   Sprenger, J. (2016). *Malleus Maleficarum – The Witch Hammer.* (M. Summers, Trans.). North Charleston, SC: Createspace. (Original work published 1489)

258   Guiley 2009.

259   Stainton, T. (2006). Changeling. In G.L. Abrecht, S.L. Snyder, D.T. Mitchell (Eds.), *Encyclopedia of Disability* (pp. 235-236). Thousand Oaks, CA: SAGE Publications.

260   Ashliman 2005.

261   Yeats, W.B. (Ed.). (1892). *Irish Fairy Tales.* London, UK: T. Fisher Unwin.

262   Bottrell, W. (1873). *Traditions and Hearthside Stories of West Cornwall, Vol. 2.* Penzance, UK: Beare and Son.

263   Guiney 1888.

264   Lawing 2013.

265   Coulson 2017.

266   Yeats 1892.

267   Rolfe, W.J. (Ed.). (1895). *Fairy Tales in Prose and Verse.* New York, NY: Harper & Bros.

268   Hartland 1891.

269   Stainton 2006.

270   Evans Wentz 1911.

271   Mooney, J. (1887, January). The Medical Mythology of Ireland. *Proceedings of the American Philosophical Society 24(125)*, pp. 136-166.

272   Árnason, J. (1866). *Icelandic Legends: Second Series.* (G.E.J. Powell & E. Magnússon, Trans.). London, UK: Longmans, Green, and Co.

273   Yeats 1892.

274   Tangherlini, T.K. (1995, Winter). From Trolls to Turks: Continuity and Change in Danish Legend Tradition. *Scandinavian Studies 61(1)*, pp. 32-62.

275   Mac Suibhné, A. (2017). Páiste Shiobhain Cuimín - A Changeling. Retrieved June 4, 2017 from http://www.duchas.ie/en/cbes/4921674/4889287

276   Westropp, T.J. (1921). A Study of Folklore on the Coasts of Connacht, Ireland. *Folk-Lore: A Quarterly Review 32*, pp. 103-105.

277   Banks, G. & Blackhall, S. (2015). *Scottish Urban Myths and Ancient Legends.* Stroud, UK: The History Press.

278   Croker 1828 *Part III.*

279   Hartland 1891.

280   Mooney 1887.

281   Monaghan 2004.

282   Briggs 1976.

283   Guiney 1888.

284   Thompson, C.J.S. (1927). *The Mysteries and Secrets of Magic.* London, UK: John Lane, The Bodley Head Ltd.

285   Eberly, S.S. (1988). Fairies and the Folklore of Disability: Changelings, Hybrids and the Solitary Fairy. *Folklore 99 (1)*, pp. 58-77.

286   O'Hanlon 1870.

287   Evans Wentz 1911.

288   Beachcombing. (2015, April 24). Manx Judge and Manx Fairies, 1932. Retrieved June 4, 2017 from http://www.strangehistory.net/2015/04/24/manx-judge-manx-fair-ies-1932

289   Lady Gregory 1920, *First Series.*

290   Sikes 1880.

291   O'Hanlon 1870.

292   Keightley 1828.

293   Bane 2013.

294   Croker 1828 *Part III.*

295   Campbell, J.F. (1890). *Popular Tales of the West Highlands Vol. II.* London, UK: Alexander Gardner & Paisley.

296   Wilde 1887.

297   Evans Wentz 1911.

298   Morrison, S. (1911). *Manx Fairy Tales*. London, UK: David Nutt.

299   O'Hanlon 1870.

300   Asbjørnsen 1883.

301   Briggs 1976

302   Keightley 1828.

303   Kennedy 1866.

304   Thompson 1927.

305   Martin, M. (2000). *A Description of the Western Islands of Scotland*. Edinburgh, UK: Birlinn Ltd. (Original work published 1703)

306   Bane 2013.

307   Owen 1887.

308   Hartland 1891.

309   Kennedy 1866.

310   Evans Wentz 1911.

311   Lady Gregory 1920, *First Series*.

312   Wilde 1887.

313   Evans Wentz 1911.

314   Silver 1999.

315   Lady Gregory (1920). *Visions and Beliefs in the West of Ireland Collected and Arranged by Lady Gregory, Second Series*. New York, NY: The Knickerbocker Press.

316   Árnason 1866.

317   Simpson, J. (2004). *Icelandic Folktales & Legends*. Stroud, UK: The History Press. (Original work published 1972)

318   Thomas, W.J. (1907). *The Welsh Fairy Book*. London, UK: Fisher Unwin.

319   Arrowsmith, N. (2009). *Field Guide to the Little People: A Curious Journey into the Hidden Realm of Elves, Faeries, Hobgoblins & Other Not-So-Mythical Creatures*. Woodbury, Minnesota: Llewellyn Publications. (Original work published 1977)

320   Owen 1887.

321   Yeats 1890.

322   Hunt 1871.

323   Briggs 1976.

324   Briggs 1976.

325   Cutchin, J. (2015). *A Trojan Feast: The Food and Drink Offerings of Aliens, Faeries, and Sasquatch*. San Antonio, TX: Anomalist Books.

326   Henderson & Cowan 2001.

327   Yeats 1890.

328   Ashliman, D.L. (1997). Changelings. Retrieved June 6, 2017 from http://www.pitt.edu/~dash/changeling.html

329   Briggs 1976.

330   Evans Wentz 1911.

331   Keightley 1828.

332   Narváez, P. (1997). Physical Disorders: Changelings and the Blast. In P. Narváez (Ed.), *The Good People: New Fairylore Essays* (pp. 225-226). Lexington, KY: The University Press of Kentucky.

333   Wilde 1887.

334   Wilde 1887.

335   Hartland 1891.

336   Henderson, W. (1879). *Notes of the Folk-Lore of the Northern Countries of England and the Borders*. London, UK: Folk-Lore Society.

337   Cameron, I. (1928). *A Highland Chapbook*. Stirling, UK: Observer Press.

338   Rickard, B., & Michell, J. (2000). *Unexplained Phenomena: A Rough Guide Special*. London, UK: Rough Guides, Ltd.

339   Fleming 2002.

340   Lewis, D.G. (2010). *Welsh-English English-Welsh Dictionary*. Glasgow, UK: The Gresham Publishing Company Ltd.

341   Fetch. (n.d.). *Oxford Living Dictionaries*. Retrieved June 6, 2017 from https://en.oxforddictionaries.com/definition/fetch

342   Kennedy 1866.

343   Yeats 1890.

344   Guiley 2007.

345   Stock. (n.d.). *Oxford Living Dictionaries*. Retrieved June 6, 2017 from https://en.oxforddictionaries.com/definition/stock

346   Lewis, W.J., & Alexander, D.McE. (2008). *Grafting and Budding: A Practical Guide for Fruit and Nut Plants and Ornamentals*. Collingwood, AU: Landlinks Press (2nd ed.).

347   Briggs 1976.

348   Briggs, K. (1979). *Abbey Lubbers, Banshees & Boggarts*. New York, NY: Pantheon Books.

349   Evans Wentz 1911.

350   Hartland 1891.

351   Miss Dempster 1888.

352   Sikes 1880.

353   Briggs 1976.

354   Bane 2013.

355   Campbell, J.G. (1900). *Superstitions of the Highlands and Islands of Scotland.* Glasgow, UK: James Maclehose & Sons.

356   Guiney 1888.

357   Spence 1920.

358   Wilde 1887.

359   Vicente, X.X.S. & Valle, X.C. (2003). *El Gran Libro de la Mitología Asturiana.* Oviedo, ES: Ediciones Trabe.

360   Keightley 1828.

361   Rolfe 1895.

362   Ashliman 2005.

363   Evans Wentz 1911.

364   Silver 1999.

365   Beachcombing. (2017, January 9). Fairy Vampires #1: Spence Speaks. Retrieved June 13, 2017 from http://www.strangehistory.net/2017/01/09/fairy-vampires-1-spence-speaks

366   Árnason 1866.

367   Briggs 1976.

368   Briggs 2002.

369   Ashliman 2005.

370   Silver 1999.

371   Guiney 1888.

372   Bane 2013.

373   Rolfe 1895.

374   Evans Wentz 1911.

375   Wilde 1887.

376   Frankel V.E. (2015). *The Symbolism and Sources of Outlander: The Scottish Fairies, Folklore, Ballads, Magic and Meaning That Inspired the Series.* Jefferson, NC: McFarland & Company, Inc.

377   Wilde 1887.

378   Green 2016.

379   Hancock, G. (2007). *Supernatural.* New York, NY: The Disinformation Company, Ltd.

380   Sayce, R.U. (1934, June). The Origins and Development of the Belief in Fairies. *Folklore 45(2)*, pp. 99-143.

381   Hancock 2007.

382   Mott, W.M. (2011). *Caverns, Cauldron, and Concealed Creatures* (3rd ed.). Nashville, TN: Grave Distractions Publications.

383   Hancock 2007.

384   Guiley 2009.

385   Sparks, H.F.D. (Ed.). (1984). *The Apocryphal Old Testament*. Oxford, UK: Oxford University Press.

386   Briggs 1976.

387   Briggs 2002.

388   MacDougall 1910.

389   Árnason 1864.

390   Fleming 2002.

391   Briggs 1976.

392   Hartland 1891.

393   Evans Wentz 1911.

394   Leland, C.G. (1891). *Gypsy Sorcery and Fortune Telling*. New York, NY: C. Scribner's Sons.

395   Silver 1999.

396   Arrowsmith 2009.

397   Keightley 1828.

398   Hancock 2007.

399   Bronson, B.H. (1959). *The Traditional Tunes of the Child Ballads, Vol. I*. Princeton, NJ: Princeton University Press.

400   Hartland 1891.

401   Kirk, R. (1893). *The Secret Commonwealth of Elves, Fauns, & Fairies*. London, UK: D. Nutt.

402   Yeats 1892.

403   Lady Gregory 1920, *First Series*.

404   Lady Gregory 1920, *First Series*.

405   Henderson & Cowan 2001.

406   Hartland 1891.

407   Wilde 1887.

408   Lady Gregory 1920, *First Series*.

409   Lady Gregory 1920, *First Series*.

410   Briggs 1976.

411   Sikes 1880.

412   Hartland 1891.

413   Briggs 1976.

414   Sveinsson 2003.

415   Cárthaigh, C.M. (1988, June). *Midwife to the Fairies: A Migratory Legend*. (mas-

ter's thesis). The National University of Ireland, Dublin, IE.

416   Harpur 2003.

417   Hartland 1891.

418   Briggs 1976.

419   Hartland 1891.

420   Croker 1828 *Part III.*

421   Briggs 1976.

422   Briggs 1976.

423   Rhŷs 1901.

424   Gwyndaf, R. (1997). Fairylore: Memorates and Legends from the Welsh Oral Tradition. In P. Narváez (Ed.), *The Good People: New Fairylore Essays* (pp. 155-195). Lexington, KY: The University Press of Kentucky.

425   Briggs 1976.

426   Briggs 1976.

427   Rodway, A. (1981). *Fairies.* New York, NY: G.P. Putnam's Sons.

428   Pepper, W., & Wilcock, J. (2000). *Magical and Mystical Sites: Europe and the British Isles.* Grand Rapids, MI: Phanes Press.

429   Westropp 1921.

430   Bourke, A. (1995, Autumn). Reading a Woman's Death: Colonial Text and Oral Tradition in Nineteenth-Century Ireland. *Feminist Studies 21(3),* pp. 553-586.

431   Sikes 1880.

432   Evans Wentz 1911.

433   Guiney 1888.

434   Thomas 1907.

435   Bane 2013.

436   Collier, A.L. (2016). *Lilith: The Legend of the First Woman.* Woodstock, ON: Devoted Publishing.

437   Aspinall 1995.

438   Hofberg, H. (1893). *Swedish Fairy Tales.* (W.H. Myers, Trans.). Chicago, IL: W.B. Conkey Company.

439   Duncan, L.L., Whelan, B., Wheln, A., Lynch, M., McVittle, E., & Drumkeeran. (1896, June). Fairy Beliefs and Other Folklore Notes from County Leitrim. *Folklore 7(2),* pp. 161-183.

440   Duncan, Whelan, Wheln, Lynch, McVittle, & Drumkeeran 1896.

441   Beachcombing. (2018, April 28). Beware Fairy Home Invasion! Retrieved May 9, 2018 from http://www.strangehistory.net/2018/04/28/beware-fairy-home-invasion/

442   Rodway 1981.

443   Beachcombing. (2013, August 21). Fairy Knick Knacks: The Five Strangest.

Retrieved July 4, 2017 from http://www.strangehistory.net/2013/08/21/fairy-knick-knacks-the-five-strangest/

444   Lecouteux 2013.

445   Dean, C. (2012). The Boo Hag. Retrieved June 26, 2017 from http://www.carolinaconjure.com/the-boo-hag.html

446   Hansen, W. (2002). *Ariadne's Thread: A Guide to International Tales Found in Classical Literature*. Ithaca, NY: Cornell University Press.

447   Butler, G.R. (1997). The *Lutin* Tradition in French-Newfoundland Culture. In P. Narváez (Ed.), *The Good People: New Fairylore Essays* (pp. 5-21). Lexington, KY: The University Press of Kentucky.

448   Duncan, Whelan, Wheln, Lynch, McVittle, & Drumkeeran 1896.

449   Aspinall 1995.

450   MacGregor 1901.

451   Lecouteux 2015.

452   Aspinall 1995.

453   Hartland 1891.

454   Hartland 1891.

455   Aspinall 1995.

456   Ashliman 2005.

457   Briggs 1976.

458   Ankarloo, Clark, & Monter 2002.

459   Kirk 1893.

460   Fleming 2002.

461   Briggs 1976.

462   Evans Wentz 1911.

463   M'Manus 1914.

464   Guiley 2009.

465   Henderson & Cowan 2001.

466   Evans Wentz 1911.

467   O'Hanlon 1870.

468   Evans Wentz 1911.

469   Watts, D.C. (2007). *Elsevier's Dictionary of Plant Lore*. Burlington, MA: Academic Press.

470   Sikes 1880.

471   Ballard, L.M. (1997). Fairies and the Supernatural on Reachrai. In P. Narváez (Ed.), *The Good People: New Fairylore Essays* (pp. 47-93). Lexington, KY: The University Press of Kentucky.

472   Lecouteux 2013.

473   Hartland 1891.

474   Sobo, E.J. (1996). Cultural Explanations for Pregnancy Loss in Rural Jamaica. In R. Cecil (Ed.), *The Anthropology of Pregnancy Loss* (pp. 39-58). Oxford, UK: Berg.

475   Rhind, J.P. (2014). *Fragrance and Wellbeing: Plant Aromatics and Their Influence of the Psyche.* London, UK: Singing Dragon.

476   Evans Wentz 1911.

477   Watts 2007.

478   Wilde 1887.

479   Carbery, M. (2010). *The Farm by Lough Gur: The Story of Mary Fogarty (Sissy O'Brien).* The Lilliput Press. (Original work published 1937)

480   Briggs 1976.

481   Watts 2007.

482   Briggs 1976.

483   Evans Wentz 1911.

484   Cockayne, T.O. (1865). *Leechdoms, Wortcunnning, and Starcraft of Early England, Vol. 2.* London, UK: Longman, Green, Longman, Roberts, and Green.

485   Evans Wentz 1911.

486   Watts 2007.

487   Ashliman 2013.

488   Briggs 1976.

489   Wilde 1887.

490   Wilde 1887.

491   Watts 2007.

492   Watts 2007.

493   Briggs 1976.

494   Watts 2007.

495   Rodway 1981.

496   Watts 2007.

497   Aspinall 1995.

498   Hartland 1891.

499   Sikes 1880.

500   Fleming 2002.

501   Guiney 1888.

502   Hartland 1891.

503   Hartland 1891.

504   Evans Wentz 1911.

505   Silver 1999.

506   Jenkins 1997.

507   Croker 1828 *Part III.*

508   Ballard 1997.

509   Wilde 1887.

510   Croker 1828 *Part III.*

511   Sobo 1996.

512   Thompson 1927.

513   Lysaght 1997.

514   Lecouteux 2013.

515   Kelly. (2015). Weird Spiritual Practices: What's Up With The Red String? Retrieved June 26, 2017 from http://blog.sivanaspirit.com/spiritual-red-string/

516   Hartland 1891.

517   Lysaght 1997.

518   Bruford 1997.

519   Henderson 1879.

520   Monaghan 2004.

521   Lecouteux 2013.

522   Ballard 1997.

523   Sikes 1880.

524   Briggs 1976.

525   Thompson 1927.

526   Nahachewsky, A. (2012). *Ukranian Dance: A Cross-Cultural Approach.* Jefferson, NC: McFarland & Company, Inc.

527   Lewis, J.R. (2001). *Satanism Today.* Santa Barbara, CA: ABC-CLIO.

528   Norman & Hickey-Hall 2017.

529   Sikes 1880.

530   Courtney, M.A. (1887). Cornish Folk Lore Part III [Continued]. *The Folk-Lore Journal 5(3),* pp. 177-220.

531   Árnason 1866.

532   Courtney 1887.

533   Hartland 1891.

534   Briggs 1976.

535   Sveinsson 2003.

536   Simpson 2004.

537 Croker 1828 *Part III.*

538 Evans Wentz 1911.

539 Hartland 1891.

540 Hartland 1891.

541 Hartland 1891.

542 Briggs 1976.

543 Butler 1997.

544 Sikes 1880.

545 Briggs 1976.

546 Rodway 1981.

547 MacGregor 1901.

548 Ross, A. (2011). *Folklore of the Scottish Highlands.* Stroud, UK: The History Press. (Original work published in 2000)

549 Evans Wentz 1911.

550 Holland, E. (2006). *Holland's grimoire of Magickal Correspondences.* Franklin Lakes, NJ: New Page Books.

551 Guiley 2009.

552 Mooney 1887.

553 Butler 2017.

554 Briggs 1976.

555 Briggs 1976.

556 Gordon, S. (1997). *The Book of Curses: True Tales of Voodoo, Hoodoo and Hex.* Leicester, UK: Brockhampton Press. (Original work published 1994)

557 Butler 2017.

558 Evans Wentz 1911.

559 Sikes 1880.

560 Lady Gregory 1920, *Second Series.*

561 Thomas 1907.

562 Campbell 1910.

563 Campbell 1910.

564 Aspinall 1995.

565 Lady Gregory 1920, *First Series.*

566 Guiney 1888.

567 Henderson 1879.

568 Hewlett 1913.

569 Bane 2013.

570   Kassinger, R. (2003). *Iron and Steel: From Thor's Hammer to the Space Shuttle.* Brookfield, CT: Twenty-First Century Books.

571   Barron, J.R. (1929, Winter). Shetland Fairies. *Prairie Schooner 3(1)*, pp. 47-53.

572   Briggs 1976.

573   Campbell 1890.

574   Duncan, Whelan, Wheln, Lynch, McVittle, & Drumkeeran 1896.

575   Guiley 2007.

576   Lecouteux 2013.

577   Vaughan, J.D. (1879). *The Manners and Customs of the Chinese of the Straits Settlements.* Singapore: Mission Press.

578   Guiley 2007.

579   Conway, D.J. (2009). *A Witch's Travel Guide to Astral Realms.* Woodbury, MN: Llewellyn Publications. (Original work published 1995)

580   Lvcifer [Screen name]. (2011, February 15). Iron in Folklore – Superstitions Explained. Retrieved June 28, 2017 from https://diabolicalconfusions.wordpress.com/2011/02/15/iron-in-folklore-superstitions-explained/

581   Sharp, A. (1899, May 5). The Design of Wheels and Pulleys. *Practical Engineer and Engineer's Gazette 19-20*, pp. 424-425.

582   Kassinger 2003.

583   Kassinger 2003.

584   Weeks, M.E. (1956). *Discovery of the Elements* (6th ed.).. Leicester, H.M., & Dains, F.B. (Eds.). Easton, PA: Journal of Chemical Education.

585   David, A. (2017, March 23). Charm the Water: Episode 34 – Gordon White. Retrieved June 29, 2017 from http://www.charmthewater.com/podcast/2017/3/23/episode-34-gordon-white

586   Gary & Ruth. (2017, May 1). Celtic Myth Podshow Special 43: *Folklore, Fairies, Cold Iron of Sussex and Puck of Pook's Hill.* Retrieved June 29, 2017 from http://celticmythpodshow.com/Shownotes/episodeSP43.php

587   Renner, T. (2017, June 29). Episode 11: Iron and the Supernatural, part 2: The Blacksmith. Retrieved June 29, 2017 from http://strangefamiliars.darkhollerarts.com/episode-11-iron-supernatural-part-2-blacksmith/

588   Hartland 1891.

589   Campbell 1910.

590   Guiney 1888.

591   Lady Gregory 1920, *Second Series.*

592   Wilde 1887.

593   Butler 2017.

594   Bord, J. (2014). *Fairies: Real Encounters with Little People* [Kindle edition]. London, UK: Michael O'Mara Books. (Original work published 1998)

595   Guiley, R.E. (2008). *The Encyclopedia of Witches, Witchcraft, and Wicca* (3rd ed). New York, NY: Facts on File, Inc. (Original work published 1992).

596   Beachcombing. (2017, March 8). Fairy Wind Rescue Spell. Retrieved June 29, 2017 from http://www.strangehistory.net/2017/03/08/fairy-wind-rescue-spell/

597   Ashliman 2005.

598   Evans Wentz 1911.

599   Lady Gregory 1920, *First Series.*

600   Hofberg 1893.

601   Kennedy 1866.

602   Rhŷs 1901.

603   Hartland 1891.

604   Briggs 2002.

605   Lindow, J. (1995, Winter). Supernatural Others and Ethnic Others: A Millennium of World View. *Scandinavian Studies 67(1)*, pp. 8-31.

606   Rolfe 1895.

607   Guiney 1888.

608   Ashliman 2005.

609   Hartland 1891.

610   Denham, M.A. (1895). *The Denham Tracts: A Collection of Folklore by Michael Aislabie Denham.* J. Hardy (Ed.). London, UK: The Folklore Society.

611   Silver 1999.

612   Hartland 1891.

613   Hartland 1891.

614   Silver 1999.

615   Rhŷs 1901.

616   Ashliman 2013.

617   Silver 1999.

618   Briggs 1976.

619   Croker 1825

620   Grimm, J., & Grimm, W. (1812). *Kinder- und Hausmärchen.* Stuttgart, DE: Deutsche Verlags-Anstalt.

621   Jacobs, J. (Ed.). (1892). *Celtic Fairy Tales.* London, UK: David Nutt.

622   Guiney 1888.

623   MacDougall 1910.

624   Croker 1825.

625   Kennedy 1866.

626   Rolfe 1895.

627   Hartland 1891.

628   Hartland 1891.

629   Bane 2013.

630   Ey 1862.

631   Hartland 1891.

632   Ey 1862.

633   Gallaher. (2017). The Changeling (continued). Retrieved July 3, 2017 from http://www.duchas.ie/en/cbes/5009189/4996096/5104919

634   Lecouteux 2013.

635   Asbjørnsen 1883.

636   Waldron, G. (1744). *The History and Description of the Isle of Man*. London, UK: W. Bickerton (2nd ed.).

637   Purkiss 2000.

638   Beachcombing. (2011, October 26). Eggs, Mermaids and Fairies. Retrieved July 3, 2017 from http://www.strangehistory.net/2011/10/26/eggs-mermaids-and-fairies/

639   Árnason 1864.

640   Asbjørnsen 1883.

641   Keightley 1828.

642   Paine, R. (1944, Summer). Night Village and the Coming of Men of the Word: The Supernatural as a Source of Meaning among Coastal Saami. *The Journal of American Folklore 107(425)*, pp. 343-363.

643   Ashton, A. (1975). *Saints & Changelings: Folk-Tales of Brittany*. Glasgow, UK: Blackie and Son Limited.

644   Ashliman 2005.

645   Stewart, S. (2003, Summer). Genres of Work: The Folktale and "Silas Marner." *New Literary History 34(3)*, pp. 513-533.

646   Westropp, T.J. (1920, June). The Marriages of the Gods at the Sanctuary of Tailltu. *Folklore: A Quarterly Review 31*, pp. 109-141.

647   Mooney 1887.

648   Rhŷs 1901.

649   Lysaght 1997.

650   Sikes 1880.

651   Ballard 1997.

652   Hartland 1891.

653   Dempster 1888.

654   Bronson 1959.

655   Lawrence, R.M. (1898). *The Magic of the Horse-Shoe*. Boston, MA: Houghton, Mifflin, and Company.

656   Silver 1999.

657   Hartland 1891.

658   Henderson & Cowan 2001.

659   Williamson, R. (2006). The Fisherman's Son and the *Gruagach* of Tricks. On *Four Gruagach Tales* [CD]. Cambridge, UK: Gottdiscs Limited.

660   Murray, B. (2017). Story – A Changeling. Retrieved July 4, 2017 from http://www.duchas.ie/en/cbes/5009102/4986879/5122047

661   Schmitt, J.C. (1983). *The Holy Greyhound: Guinefort, Healer of Children Since the Thirteenth Century*. Cambridge, UK: Cambridge University Press (Original work published 1979)

662   Green 2016.

663   Evans Wentz 1911.

664   Wood, J. (2005, December). Folk Narrative Research in Wales at the Beginning of the Twentieth Century: The Influence of John Rhŷs (1840-1916). *Folklore 116(3)*, pp. 325-341.

665   Silver 1999.

666   Rhŷs 1901.

667   Thomas 1907.

668   Rhŷs 1901.

669   Thomas 1907.

670   Evans Wentz 1911.

671   Kennedy 1866.

672   Barron 1929.

673   Croker 1828 *Part III*.

674   Hartland 1891.

675   Lawing 2013.

676   Sugg, R. (2016, May). The Fairy Menace. *BBC History Magazine* pp. 60-63.

677   Silver 1999.

678   Thomas 1907.

679   Hartland 1891.

680   Wilde 1887.

681   Croker 1828 *Part III*.

682   Gregor, W. (1881). *Notes on the Folk-Lore of the North-East of Scotland*. London, UK: Folk-Lore Society.

683   Silver 1999.

684   Evans Wentz 1911.

685   Hartland 1891

686   Mooney 1887.

687   Thomas 1907.

688   Wilde 1887.

689   Ross 2011.

690   Wilde 1887.

691   Bane 2013.

692   Lady Gregory 1920, *First Series.*

693   O'Hanlon 1870.

694   Conaill, M.Ó. (2017). A Changeling. Retrieved July 5, 2017 from http://www. duchas.ie/en/cbes/4758565/4754979

695   Evans Wentz 1911.

696   Sikes 1880.

697   Reid, K. (2017). A Funny Story. Retrieved July 5, 2017 from http://www.duchas. ie/en/cbes/5009285/5004673

698   Thomas 1907.

699   Munro 1997.

700   Evans Wentz 1911.

701   Guiney 1888.

702   Ashliman 2005.

703   Feindt, C.W. (2010). *UFOs and Water: Physical Effects of UFOs on Water Through Accounts by Eyewitnesses.* Bloomington, IN: Xlibris Corporation.

704   Heavey 2017.

705   Kennedy 1866.

706   Arrowsmith 2009.

707   Hartland 1891.

708   Leland 1891.

709   Hickey 1938.

710   Mooney 1887.

711   Munro 1997.

712   Jacobs, J. (1894). *More English Fairy Tales.* London, UK: G. Putnam's Sons.

713   Mooney 1887.

714   Hartland 1891.

715   Gay, D.E. (1988). Anglo-Saxon Metrical Charm 3 Against a Dwarf: A Charm Against Witch-Riding? *Folklore 99(2),* pp. 174-177.

716   Lagerlöf, S. (1915). *Troll och människor.* Stockholm, SE: Albert Bonniers Boktryckeri.

717   McVeigh, J. (2017). The Changeling. Retrieved July 5, 2017 from http://www.duchas.ie/en/cbes/4427871/4352542/4436965

718   Beachcombing. (2014, February 25). The Most Beautiful Folk Cure: An Epilepsy Ring. Retrieved July 5, 2017 from http://www.strangehistory.net/2014/02/25/the-most-beautiful-folk-cure-an-epilepsy-ring/

719   Spence 1920.

720   Evans Wentz 1911.

721   Courtney 1887.

722   Lady Gregory 1920, *First Series.*

723   Asbjørnsen 1883.

724   Ashliman 2005.

725   Hartland 1891.

726   Lady Gregory 1920, *Second Series.*

727   Silver 1999.

728   No author. (1889, January-March). Notices of the Folk-Lore of Other Continents. *The Journal of American Folklore 2(4)*, pp. 80-82.

729   Sugg 2016.

730   Sikes 1880.

731   Duncan, Whelan, Wheln, Lynch, McVittle, & Drumkeeran 1896.

732   Curran, B. (2004). *Celtic Lore and Legend.* Franklin Lakes, NJ: The Career Press, Inc.

733   Mooney 1887.

734   Briggs 1976.

735   Evans Wentz 1911.

736   Hartland 1891.

737   Wilde 1887.

738   Wilde 1887.

739   Hartland 1891.

740   Wilde 1887.

741   Breen, R. (1980, Spring/Summer). The Ritual Expression of Inter Household Relationships in Ireland. *The Cambridge Journal of Anthropology 6(1/2 – Double Issue)*, pp. 33-59.

742   Kennedy 1866.

743   Evans Wentz 1911.

744   Sikes 1880.

745 Sikes 1880.

746 Hartland 1891.

747 Farrell, E. (2013). *A Most Diabolical Deed': Infanticide and Irish Society, 1850-1900.* Manchester, UK: Manchester University Press.

748 MacGregor 1901.

749 Spence 1920.

750 Hartland 1891.

751 Hartland 1891.

752 Bechstein, L. (1853). *Deutsches Sagenbuch.* Leipzig, DE: G. Wigand.

753 Hartland 1891.

754 Beachcombing. (2016, February 4). Red Fairies #3: Do NOT Use the Chimney. Retrieved July 6, 2017 from http://www.strangehistory.net/2016/02/04/red-fairies-3-do-not-use-the-chimney/

755 Hartland 1891.

756 Wilde 1887.

757 Lecouteux 2013.

758 Lecouteux 2013.

759 Quinlan, M. (2017, October 4). Personal communication.

760 Rhŷs 1901.

761 No author. (1895, March 30). Black Witchcraft. *The British Medical Journal* 1(1,787), pp. 717-718.

762 Breen 1980.

763 Trial by fire. (n.d.). Dictionary.com. Retrieved July 7, 2017 from http://www.dictionary.com/browse/trial-by-fire

764 Farrell 2013.

765 Eberly 1988.

766 Buccola 2006.

767 Pontolillo, J. (1993). *INFO Occasional Paper No.2: Demons, Doctors, and Aliens: An Exploration into the Relationships Among Witch Trial Evidence, Sexual-Medical Traditions, and Alien Abductions.* Arlington, VA: RDM Publications.

768 Farrell 2013.

769 Croker, T.C. (1828). *Fairy Legends & Traditions of the South of Ireland Part II.* London, UK: John Murray.

770 Beachcombing. (2016, June 17). The Baby and the Fairy Bush. Retrieved July 7, 2017 from http://www.strangehistory.net/2016/06/17/baby-fairy-bush/

771 Fleming 2002.

772 Klintberg, B.A. (1972). *Svenska Folksägner.* Stockholm, SE: Norstedts.

773 Beachcombing. (2012, February 18). Irish Changeling in New York. Retrieved

July 7, 2017 from http://www.strangehistory.net/2012/02/18/irish-changeling-in-new-york/

774   Topping, A. (2012, March 1). Accusations of witchcraft are part of growing pattern of child abuse in UK. Retrieved July 7, 2017 from https://www.theguardian.com/uk/2012/mar/01/accusations-witchcraft-pattern-child-abuse

775   Evans Wentz 1911.

776   Altmann, A.E. (2006). *The Seven Swabians, and Other German Folktales*. Westport, CT: Libraries Unlimited.

777   Bane 2013.

778   Evans Wentz 1911.

779   Mooney 1887.

780   Silver 1999.

781   Yeats 1890.

782   Beachcombing. (2012, March 30). Handlist of Adult Changelings. Retrieved July 7, 2017 from http://www.strangehistory.net/2012/03/30/handlist-of-adult-changelings/

783   M'Manus 1914.

784   Sikes 1880.

785   Evans Wentz 1911.

786   Kaftal, G. (1943, June). An Apocryphal Legend Relating to the Birth of Several Saints. *Folklore 54(2)*, pp. 308-309.

787   Hartland, E.S. (1886). The Outcast Child. *The Folk-Lore Journal 4(4)*, pp. 308-349.

788   Russell, J.B. (1984). *Lucifer: The Devil in the Middle Ages*. Ithaca, NY: Cornell University Press.

789   Rojcewicz, P.M. (1997). Fairies, UFOs, and Problems of Knowledge. In P. Narváez (Ed.), *The Good People: New Fairylore Essays* (pp. 479-514). Lexington, KY: The University Press of Kentucky.

790   Cressy, J. (1996). Mysticism and the Near-Death Experience. In L.W. Bailey & J. Yates (Eds.), *The Near-Death Experience: A Reader* (pp. 369-384). Abingdon, UK: Routledge.

791   Hunt, R. (1903). *Popular Romances of the West of England: The Drolls, Traditions, and Superstitions of Old Cornwall*. London, UK: Chatto and Windus (3rd ed.).

792   Briggs 1976.

793   Gwyndaf 1997.

794   Fleming 2002.

795   Buccola 2006.

796   Silver 1999.

797   Wilde 1887.

798   Evans Wentz 1911.

799   Wilde 1887.

800   Lady Gregory 1920, *First Series.*

801   Suggett 2017.

802   Ashliman 2005.

803   Bottrell 1873.

804   Tangherlini 1995.

805   Rhŷs 1901.

806   Wilde 1887.

807   Bane 2013.

808   Evans Wentz 1911.

809   Rhŷs 1901.

810   Bottrell 1873.

811   Yeats 1892.

812   Ashliman 2005.

813   Hartland 1891.

814   Skjelbred 1997.

815   Bottrell 1873.

816   Simpson, J. (2011, April). On the Ambiguity of Elves [1]. *Folklore 122(1)*, pp. 76-83.

817   Rhŷs 1901

818   Wilde 1887.

819   Bane 2013.

820   Rhŷs 1901

821   Richardson, M.A. (1846). *The Borderer's Table Book: Or, Gatherings of the Local History and Romance of the English and Scottish Border.* Newcastle upon Tyne, UK: Printed for the author.

822   Evans Wentz 1911.

823   House of Commons and Commande. (1863, February 5-July 28). *The Census of Ireland for the Year 1861: Part III – Vital Statistics, Vol. I: Reports and Tables Relating to the Status of Disease.* Dublin, IE: Alexander Thom.

824   Mooney 1887.

825   Eberly 1988.

826   Sayce 1934.

827   Locke, J. (1906). *Locke's Essay Concerning Human Understanding: Books II & IV.* M.W. Clakins, Ed. Chicago, IL: The Open Court Publishing Company (2nd ed., original work published 1690)

828   Vickery, R. (1988). Linnaeus and the Changeling. *Folklore 99(2)*, p. 250.

829   Guiley 2009.

830   Briggs 1976.

831   Hunt 1903.

832   Silver 1999.

833   Vickery 1988.

834   Silver 1999.

835   Eberly 1988.

836   Eberly 1988.

837   Eberly 1988.

838   DeLuke, D.M., & Haug, R.H. (Eds.). (2014, September). *Clinical Review Articles - Atlas of the Oral and Maxillofacial Surgery Clinics of North America: Syndromes of the Head and Neck*. Philadelphia, PA: Elsevier.

839   Sternberg, S. (2003, April 16). Gene found for rapid aging disease in children. Retrieved July 11, 2017 from https://usatoday30.usatoday.com/news/science/2003-04-16-agin-gene_x.htm

840   Silver 1999.

841   DeLuke & Haug 2014.

842   Eberly 1988.

843   Mason, T.B.A., Arens, R., Sharman, J., Bintliff-Janisak, B., Schultz, B. Walters, A.S., Cater, J.R., Kaplan, P., Pack, A.I. (2011, October 12). Sleep in Children with Williams Syndrome. *Sleep Medicine 12*(9), pp. 892-897.

844   Lenhoff, H.M. (1999). A Real-World Source for the "Little People": A Comparison of Fairies to Individuals with Williams Syndrome. In G. Westfahl & G. Slusser (Eds.), *Nursery Realms: Children in the Worlds of Science Fiction, Fantasy, and Horror* (pp. 150-160). Athens, GA: University of Georgia Press.

845   Williams Syndrome Association. (2014). Adult Medical Issues. Retrieved July 10, 2017 from https://williams-syndrome.org/doctor/adult-medical-issues

846   Purcell, C. (2005, February 25). Fairytales tell of autistic children. Retrieved July 10, 2017 from http://www.abc.net.au/science/articles/2005/02/25/1309455.htm

847   Leask, J., Leask, A., & Silove, N. (2005, March) Evidence for Autism in Folklore? *Archives of Disease in Childhood 90*(3), p. 271.

848   Eberly 1988.

849   Nazeer, K. (2006). *Send in the Idiots: Stories from the Other Side of Autism*. London, UK: Bloomsbury Publishing.

850   Chen, I. (2015, October 7). Wide Awake: Why children with autism struggle with sleep. Retrieved December 7, 2017 from https://spectrumnews.org/features/deep-dive/wide-awake-why-children-with-autism-struggle-with-sleep/

851   Centers for Disease Control and Prevention. (2017, March 10). Autism Spectrum Disorder (ASD): Data & Statistics. Retrieved February 21, 2018 from https://www.cdc.gov/ncbddd/autism/data.html

852   Ball, J. (2008). *Early Intervention & Autism*. Arlington, TX: Future Horizons, Inc.

853   Munro 1997.

854   Feinberg, T.E., & Roane, D.M. (2001). Visual Aspects of Anosognosia, Confabulation and Misidentification. In F. Boller, J. Grafman, & M. Behrmann (Eds.), *Handbook of Neuropsychology 2nd Edition: Volume 4 – Disorders of Visual Behavior* (pp. 143-158). Amsterdam, NEL Elsevier Science B.V.

855   Evans Wentz 1911.

856   Croker 1825.

857   Metzler, I. (2013, October 10). Disability, Witches and the Middle Ages: Some Mythbusting. Retrieved July 11, 2017 from https://irinametzler.org/2013/10/10/disability-witches-and-the-middle-ages-some-mythbusting/

858   Eberly, S. (1997). Fairies and the Folklore of Disability: Changelings, Hybrids and the Solitary Fairy. In P. Narváez (Ed.), *The Good People: New Fairylore Essays* (pp. 227-250). Lexington, KY: The University Press of Kentucky.

859   Cefalo, A. (2013, March 25). Cleft Lip in the Middle Ages. Retrieved July 11, 2017 from https://andreacefalo.com/2013/03/25/cleft-lip-in-the-middle-ages/

860   Goodey & Stainton 2001.

861   Skjelbred 1997.

862   Rhŷs 1901.

863   Silver 1999.

864   Mooney 1887.

865   Henderson & Cowan 2001.

866   Ashliman 1997.

867   Silver 1999.

868   Lysaght 1997.

869   Lindahl, C. (1986, April). Psychic Ambiguity at the Legend Core. *Journal of Folklore Research 23(1)*, pp. 1-21.

870   Silver 1999.

871   Bird, S. (2017). *A Cross-Cultural Look at Child-Stealing Witches*. Tucson, AZ: University of Arizona Linguistics Circle.

872   Spence 1920.

873   Hartland 1891.

874   Guiley 2007.

875   Thompson 1927.

876   Victor, J.S. (1993). *Satanic Panic: The Creation of a Contemporary Legend*. Chicago, IL: Open Court.

877   Tralins, R. (1969). *Children of the Supernatural*. New York, NY: Lancer Books, Inc.

878   Tabies, A.C. (1980). *Abordaje al Caleuche*. Santiago, CL: Nascimento.

879   Bird 2017.

880   Guiley 2009.

881   Briggs 2002.

882   Harpur 2003.

883   Thompson 1927.

884   Hartland 1891.

885   Guiley, R.E. (2006). *The Encyclopedia of Magic and Alchemy*. New York, NY: Facts On File, Inc.

886   Pontolillo 1993.

887   Rickard & Michell 2000.

888   Winkvist, A. (1996). Water Spirits, Medicine-men and Witches: Avenues to Successful Reproduction among the Abelam, Papua New Guinea. In R. Cecil (Ed.), *The Anthropology of Pregnancy Loss* (pp. 59-74). Oxford, UK: Berg.

889   Bane, T. (2016). *Encyclopedia of Beasts and Mosters in Myth, Legend and Folklore*. Jefferson, NC: McFarland & Company, Inc.

890   Kenny, A. (2004, June). Western Arrernte Pmere Kwetethe Spirits. *Oceania 74(4)*, pp. 276-288.

891   MidWeek Staff. (2010, October 13). Green Lady Lurking in Spooky Wahiawa Park. Retrieved October 17, 2017 from http://archives.midweek.com/content/zones/central_news_article/green_lady_lurking_in_spooky_wahiawa_park/

892   Spence 1920.

893   Hooykaas 1960.

894   Bane, T. (2012). *Encyclopedia of Demons in World Religions and Cultures*. Jefferson, NC: McFarland & Company, Inc.

895   Woods, D.L. (2006). *The Philippines: A Global Studies Handbook*. Santa Barbara, CA: ABC CLIO.

896   Bartholomew, R.E., & Jamaludin, A. (2000). Contemporary Malaysian Close Encounters with Fairies and Aliens. *Australian Folklore 15*, pp. 178-199.

897   Bartholomew & Jamaludin 2000.

898   Bartholomew & Jamaludin 2000.

899   Bartholomew & Jamaludin 2000.

900   Bartholomew & Jamaludin 2000.

901   Bartlett, S. (2014). *Guide to the World's Supernatural Places*. Washington, D.C.: The National Geographic Society.

902   Bartlett 2014.

903   Blacker, C. (1967). Supernatural Abductions in Japanese Folklore. *Asian Folklore Studies 26(2)*, pp. 111-147.

904   Blacker 1967.

905   Dorson, R.W. (1962). *Folk Legends of Japan*. Tokyo, JP: Charles E. Tuttle Co.

906   Blacker 1967.

907   Foster, M.D. (1998). The Metamorphosis of the Kappa: Transformation of Folklore to Folklorism in Japan. *Asian Folklore Studies 57(1)*, pp. 1-24.

908   De Visser, M.W. (1908). The Tengu. *Transactions of the Asiatic Society of Japan XXXVI (Part II)*, pp. 25-99. London, UK: Kegan Paul, Truebner & Co., Ltd.

909   De Visser 1908.

910   Blacker 1967.

911   Guiley, R.E. (2013). *The Djinn Connection.* New Milford, CT: Visionary Living, Inc.

912   Guiley 2013.

913   Druffel, A. (1998). *How to Defend Yourself Against Alien Abduction.* New York, NY: Three Rivers Press.

914   Guiley, R.E., & Imbrogno, P. J. (2011). *The Vengeful Djinn.* Woodbury, MN: Llewellyn Publications.

915   Guiley 2013.

916   Guiley 2009.

917   Wilde 1887.

918   Levy, I.J., & Zumwalt, R.L. (2013). Folk Belief. In R. Patai & H. Bar-Itzhak (Eds.), *Encyclopedia of Jewish Folklore and Traditions* (pp. 159-161). Abingdon, UK: Routledge.

919   Shiloh, A. (1961, Summer). The System of Medicine in Middle East Culture. *Middle East Journal 15(3)*, pp. 277-288.

920   Lancy, D.F. (2015). *The Anthropology of Childhood.* Cambridge, UK: Cambridge University Press.

921   El-Shamy, H.M. (1980). *Folktales of Egypt.* Chicago, IL: The University of Chicago Press.

922   El-Shamy 1980.

923   Lebling, R. (2010). *Legends of the Fire Spirits: Jinn and Genies from Arabia to Zanzibar.* New York, NY: I.B. Tauris & Co. Ltd.

924   Astarian, G. (2001). Āl Reconsidered. *Iran & the Caucasus 5*, pp. 149-156.

925   Bane, T. (2016). *Encyclopedia of Giants and Humanoids in Myth, Legend, and Folklore.* Jefferson, NC: McFarland.

926   Bane 2016.

927   McCabe, D. (2002, Spring). Histories of Errancy: Oral Yoruba Àbíkú Texts and Soyinka's "Abiku." *Research in African Literatures 33(1)*, pp. 45-74.

928   Mobolade, T. (1973, Autumn). The Concept of Abiku. *African Arts 7(1)*, pp. 62-64.

929   McCabe 2002.

930   Mobolade 1973.

931   Mobolade 1973.

932   Ellis, A.B. (1894). *Yoruba-Speaking Peoples of the Slave Coast of West Africa.* London, UK: Chapman and Hall, Ltd.

933   Lancy 2015.

934   Hale, R. (n.d.). Case 84. In A. Rosales (Ed.), *1999 Humanoid Sighting Reports.* Retrieved February 5, 2014 from http://www.ufoinfo.com/humanoid/humanoid-1999.pdf

935   Bartholomew, R.E., & Rickard, B. (2014). *Mass Hysteria in Schools: Worldwide Histroy Since 1566.* Jefferson, NC: McFarland & Company, Inc.

936   Blache, M. (1999). Guaranitic Storytelling. In M.R. MacDonald, J.H. McDowell, L. Dégh, & B. Toelken (Eds.), *Traditional Storytelling Today: An International Sourcebook* (pp. 490-493). Chicago, IL: Fitzroy Dearborn Publishers.

937   Bartlett 2014.

938   Varner, G.R. (2007). *Creatures in the Mist: Little People, Wild Men, and Spirit Beings Around the World.* New York, NY: Algora Publishing.

939   Lopez, R.A.P. & Bound, R.F. (1974, November). Chaneques: Mexican Gnomes or Interplanetary Visitors? *Fate 27*, pp. 51-57.

940   Bitto, R. (2016, June 27). The Lechuza. Retrieved July 20, 2017 from http://mexicounexplained.com/the-lechuza/

941   Lecouteux 2013.

942   Clelland 2015.

943   Gaffiot, F. (1934). *Dictionnaire Latin Français.* Paris, FR: Hachette.

944   Clelland, M. (2015). *The Messengers: Owls, Synchronicity and the UFO Abductee.* New York: Richard Dolan Press.

945   Sobo 1996.

946   Sobo 1996.

947   Pemberton, J. (2013). *Myths and Legends from Cherokee Dances to Voodoo Trances.* Eastbourne, UK: Canary Press.

948   Bane 2016.

949   Redish, L. (2015). Legendary Native American Figures: Yehasuri (Wild Indians). Retrieved July 18, 2017 from http://www.native-languages.org/morelegends/yehasuri.htm

950   Blumer, T.J. (1985, Spring). Wild Indians and the Devil: The Contemporary Catawba Indian Spirit World. *American Indian Quarterly 9(2)*, pp. 149-168.

951   Redish, L. (2015). Native American Legends: Water Babies. Retrieved July 18, 2017 from http://www.native-languages.org/water-babies.htm

952   Redish, L. (2015). Legendary Native American Figures: Wild People (Mialuka). Retrieved July 18, 2017 from http://www.native-languages.org/morelegends/wild-people.htm

953   Bane 2013.

954   Nunnelly 2011.

955   Lawrence, E. & Ober, M. (2016). *Montana Myths and Legends: The True Stories*

Behind History's Mysteries. Helena, MT: Twodot.

956   Mott 2011.

957   Vasey, G.M. (2017). *The Chilling, True Terror of the Black-Eyed Kids.* Asteroth's Books.

958   Blackman, W.H. (1998). *The Field Guide to North American Monsters.* New York, NY: Three Rivers Press.

959   Varner 2007.

960   Mack & Mack 1998.

961   Stamp, H. (1915). The Water-Fairies. *The Journal of American Folklore 28(109),* pp. 310-316.

962   Dunham, M. (May 31, 2008). 'Little people' e-mail zips through rural Alaska. Retrieved July 18, 2017 from https://groups.yahoo.com/neo/groups/mythfolk/conversations/messages/4626 (original article posted to http://www.adn.com/life/story/422883.html)

963   Blackman 1998.

964   Blackman 1998.

965   Redish, L. (2015). Native American Legends: Big Owl Man. Retrieved July 20, 2017 from http://www.native-languages.org/big-owl.htm

966   Clelland 2015.

967   Hall, M.A. (2004). *Thunderbirds: America's Living Legends of Giant Birds.* New York, NY: Paraview Press.

968   Hall 2004.

969   Coleman, L. & Clark, J. (1999). *Cryptozoology A to Z.* New York, NY: Fireside.

970   Hall 2004.

971   Hall 2004.

972   Coleman, L. (2002). *Mothman and Other Curious Encounters.* New York, NY: Paraview Press (3rd ed.).

973   Green, L.G. (1967). *On Wings of Fire.* Cape Town, SA: Howard Timmins.

974   Eveleth, R. (2013, June 3). Legendary Human-Eating Bird Was Real, Probably Could Have Eaten People. Retrieved February 23, 2018 from https://www.smithsonianmag.com/smart-news/legendary-human-eating-bird-was-real-probably-could-have-eaten-people-89257268/

975   Beachcombing. (2010, November 5). Baby-Eating Eagles. Retrieved February 23, 2018 from http://www.strangehistory.net/2010/11/05/baby-eating-eagles/

976   Hall 2004.

977   Oker, G. (2014). Recreating Cultural Literacy: A Dane-zaa Knowledge Perspective. *The Canadian Journal For Teacher Research 1(1),* pp. 9-18.

978   Boas, F. (1916). Tsimshian Mythology. *Thirty-First Annual Report of the Bureau of American Ethnology to the Secretary of the Smithsonian Institution: 1909-1910,* pp. 27-1037. Washington, DC: Government Printing Office.

979   Sands, H. (1907). The Woodpecker's Revenge. *The Canadian Magazine of Politics, Science, Art and Literature 28,* pp. 550-552. Toronto, ON: The Ontario Publishing Co., Limited.

980   Hall 2004.

981   Smith, W.G. (1883, June). On Fairy Rings. *Transaction of the Essex Field Club III(7),* pp. 69-73. Buckhurst Hill, UK: Essex Field Club.

982   Bird 2017.

983   Alley, J.R. (2007). *Raincoast Sasquatch.* Blaine, WA: Hancock House. (Original work published 2003)

984   Kennedy 1866.

985   Megargle, A., Morgan, J., Newcomer, N., Taylor, K. (Producers), & Breedlove, S. (Director). (2015). *Minerva Monster* (motion picture). United States of America: Small Town Monsters.

986   Daegling, D.J. (2004). *Bigfoot Exposed: An Anthropologist Examines America's Enduring Legend.* Walnut Creek, CA: Altamira Press.

987   Booger. (n.d.). *Merriam-Webster.* Retrieved February 27, 2018 from https://www.merriam-webster.com/dictionary/booger

988   Hall 2004.

989   Harmeyer, A.J. (1947, March). Devil Stories from Las Vegas, New Mexico. *Hoosier Folklore 6(1),* pp. 37-39.

990   Druzhko, S. (2005). Case 33. In A. Rosales (Ed.), *1986 Humanoid Sighting Reports.* Retrieved February 5, 2014 from http://www.ufoinfo.com/humanoid/humanoid-1986.pdf

991   Sikes 1880.

992   Silver 1999.

993   Briggs 1976.

994   Harpur 2003.

995   Chalker, B. (1996). *The Oz Files.* Potts Point, AU: Duffey and Snellgrove.

996   Salatun, J. (1982). *UFO: Salah Satu Masalah Dunia Masa Kini.* Jakarta, ID: Yayasan Idayu.

997   Mack, J.E. (1994). *Abduction: Human Encounters with Aliens.* New York, NY: Charles Scribner's Sons.

998   Slemen, T. (2010). The Full Moon Prowler. Retrieved August 3, 2017 from http://www.slemen.com/fullmoonprowler.html

999   Jeffrey, M. (n.d.). Case 266. In A. Rosales (Ed.), *1995 Humanoid Sighting Reports.* Retrieved February 5, 2014 from http://www.ufoinfo.com/humanoid/humanoid-1995.pdf

1000   Wright, D. (1990, October). Current Case Log. *MUFON UFO Journal 270,* pp. 17-18, 23.

1001   Chalker, B. (2005). *Hair of the Alien.* New York, NY: Paraview.

1002   Bader, C.D. (1995, April). The UFO Contact Movement form the 1950s to the Present. *Studies in Popular Culture 17*(2), pp. 73-90.

1003   Friedman, S., & Marden, K. (2015). *True Stories of Alien Abduction*. New York, NY: The Rosen Publishing Group.

1004   Hopkins, B. (1981, February). Probable Childhood Abduction. *MUFON UFO Journal 156*, pp. 4-6.

1005   Hopkins, B. (1981). *Missing Time*. New York, NY: Richard Marek Publishers.

1006   Hopkins 1981.

1007   Hopkins 1981.

1008   Rogerson, P. (1993, June). Fairyland's Hunters: Notes Towards a Revisionist History of Abductions. Part One. Retrieved May 7, 2018 from http://magoniamagazine. blogspot.com/2013/11/notes-towards-revisionist-history-of.html

1009   Schuessler, J. (1990, June). The Implant Enigma. *MUFON UFO Journal 266*, pp. 18, 23.

1010   Clark, J. (1990). *UFOs in the 1980s* (Vol. 1). Detroit, MI: Apogee Books.

1011   Stacy, D. (1994, August). The 1994 MUFON UFO Symposium. *MUFON UFO Journal 316*, pp. 3-10.

1012   Buckingham, M.R. (2003, Spring). Aliens – Their Hidden Agenda. *Flying Saucers Review 48*(1), pp. 2-5.

1013   Creighton, G. (1984, Spring). Spanish Woman Recalls Abduction 36 Years Ago. *Flying Saucer Review 29*(4), pp. 8-9.

1014   Oldham, B. (2017). *The Baby Takers*. J. Smith (Ed.). Henderson, NV: Halo House Publishing.

1015   Gribble, B. (1989, April). Looking Back. *MUFON UFO Journal 252*, pp. 27-28.

1016   Randles, J. (1994). *Star Children*. London, UK: Robert Hale Limited.

1017   NUFORC (n.d.). Case 281. In A. Rosales (Ed.), *1979 Humanoid Sighting Reports*. Retrieved February 5, 2014 from http://www.ufoinfo.com/humanoid/humanoid-1979.pdf

1018   Mack 1994.

1019   Smith, Y.R. (2014). *Coronado: The President, The Secret Service, and Alien Abductions* [Kindle edition].

1020   Creighton, G. (1995, Autumn). Three Boys Abducted in Argentina (1994). *Flying Saucer Review 40*(3), pp. 18-19.

1021   Carpenter, J. (1995, July). Abduction Notes. *MUFON UFO Journal 327*, pp. 18-19.

1022   Young, K. (2004, January). Report of "Screaming Woman" Evolves Into Possible Abduction Case in Ohio. *MUFON UFO Journal* 429, pp. 7-9.

1023   Creighton, G. (1990) The UFO Landings at Voronezh. In T. Good (Ed.), *The UFO Report 1991* (pp. 64-79). London, UK: Sidgwick & Jackson, Ltd.

1024   Trainor, J. (2001, February). UFO Reportedly Abducts Two in Northern Chile.

MUFON UFO Journal 393, p. 9.

1025   Randles, J. (1977, Winter). Strange Object Near Childrens' Home. *Flying Saucer Review* 23(4), pp. 31-32.

1026   Randles, J. (1981, Spring). Repeater Witnesses. *Flying Saucer Review 26*(6), pp. 26-30.

1027   Rutkowski, C. (2008). *A World of UFOs*. Toronto, ON: Dundurn Press.

1028   Coleman, L., & Huyghe, P. (2006). *The Field Guide to Bigfoot and Other Mystery Primates*. San Antonio, TS: Anomalist Books.

1029   Hopkins 1981.

1030   Bowen, C. (Ed.). (1978, February). World Round-Up. *Flying Saucer Review 23*(5), pp. 32-33.

1031   Randles 1994.

1032   Silva, C. (1993). Case 62. In A. Rosales (Ed.), *1970 Humanoid Sighting Reports*. Retrieved February 5, 2014 from http://www.ufoinfo.com/humanoid/humanoid-1970.pdf

1033   Bullard, T. (1987). *UFO Abductions: The Measure of A Mystery* (Vol. 1). Mount Rainier, MD: Fund for UFO Research.

1034   Orme, N. (2005). Childhood of Medieval England, *c.* 500-1500. Retrieved August 7, 2017 from http://www.representingchildhood.pitt.edu/medieval_child.htm

1035   Stevenson, I. (2001). *Children Who Remember Previous Lives: A Question of Reincarnation – Revised Edition*. Jefferson, NC: McFarland & Company, Inc.

1036   Bullard 1987 Vol. 1.

1037   Evans Wentz 1911.

1038   Casteel, S. (1995, December). Ron Felber of "Searchers." *MUFON UFO Journal 332*, pp. 19-20.

1039   Gribble, B. (1987, December). Looking Back. *MUFON UFO Journal 236*, pp. 17-18.

1040   Oldham 2017.

1041   Connelly, D. (Ed.). (2002, August). Speakers Cover Wide Range of Topics. *MUFON UFO Journal 412*, pp. 3-12.

1042   Wright, D. (1996, June). Sorting Entities. *MUFON UFO Journal 338*, pp. 3-6.

1043   Fowler, R.E. (1981). *Casebook of a UFO Investigator*. Upper Saddle River, NJ: Prentice Hall Trade.

1044   Truncale, D.B. (1994). Alien/UFO Experiences of Children. In A. Pritchard, D.E. Pritchard, J.E. Mack, P. Kasey, & C. Yapp (Eds.), *Alien Discussions: Proceedings of the Abduction Study Conference* (pp. 116-126). Cambridge, UK: North Cambridge Press.

1045   Stacy, D. (1996, August). MUFON's 27th Annual Symposium. *MUFON UFO Journal 340*, pp. 3-13.

1046   Hopkins, B. (1994). The Hopkins Image Recognition Test (HIRT) for Children. In A. Pritchard, D.E. Pritchard, J.E. Mack, P. Kasey, & C. Yapp (Eds.), *Alien Discus-*

sions: Proceedings of the Abduction Study Conference (pp. 127-134). Cambridge, UK: North Cambridge Press.

1047   Swords, M.D. (1984, October). UFO Reports and Dissociative Hysteria. *MU-FON UFO Journal 198*, pp. 10-12.

1048   Bloecher, T. (1978, February). CE-III Report from Montvale, NJ: Preliminary Report. *MUFON UFO Journal 123*, pp. 4-7.

1049   Mollon, P. (2000). *Freud and False Memory Syndrome*. London, UK: Icon Books

1050   Marden, K. (2015 ,January). Accidental Awareness or Alien Abduction? *MU-FON UFO Journal 561*, pp. 8-9.

1051   Newman, L.S., & Baumeister, R.F. (1996). Toward and Explanation of the UFO Abduction Phenomenon: Hypnotic Elaboration, Extraterrestrial Sadomasochism, and Spurious Memories. *Psychological Inquiry 7*(2), 99-126.

1052   Carpenter, J. (1994, November). False Memories and Imagination. *MUFON UFO Journal 319*, pp. 17-18.

1053   Jacobs, D.M. (1999). *The Threat*. New York, NY: Fireside. (Original work published 1998)

1054   Trei, L. (2004, January 8). Psychologists Offer Proof of Brain's Ability to Suppress Memories. Retrieved August 7, 2017 from http://news.stanford.edu/news/2004/january14/memory-114.html

1055   Turner, K. (1994). *Taken: Inside the Alien-Human Abduction Agenda*. Tallahassee, FL: Rose Printing Company, Inc.

1056   Bryan, C.D.B. (1995). *Close Encounters of the Fourth Kind*. New York, NY: Penguin Group (Arkana).

1057   Evans Wentz 1911.

1058   Oldham, B. (2013). *Children of the Greys*. Murfreesboro, TN: House of Halo.

1059   Oldham 2013.

1060   Jacobs 1999.

1061   Turner 1994.

1062   Druffel 1998.

1063   Lorgen, E.F. (1999, January). 'The Love Bite': Alien-instigated human bonding dramas, relationship manipulations, and love obsessions. *MUFON UFO Journal 369*, pp. 9-11.

1064   Jacobs 1999.

1065   Truncale 1994.

1066   Strieber, W., & Kripal, J.J. (2016). *The Super Natural*. New York, NY: Jeremy P. Tarcher.

1067   Ritzmann, J., Vaeni, J., Tar, D.E.K., Cooper,, K.E., & Kokjohn, T.A. (2014). Project Core Anonymous Survey Synopsis of Results. Retrieved August 8, 2017 from http://paratopiaoculus.com/wp-content/uploads/2016/08/Project-Core-Anonymous-Survey-Synopsis-of-Results.pdf

1068   Turner, K. (1992). *Into the Fringe.* New York, NY: Berkley Books.

1069   Mack 1994.

1070   Stacy, D. (1991, February). The UFO Press: Journal of UFO Studies, New Series, Vol. 2. *MUFON UFO Journal*, p. 18.

1071   Harvey, S.B. (2000, December). Shamanism and Alien Abduction: A Comparative Study. (Unpublished Master's Thesis). Edith Cowan University, Perth, AU.

1072   Turner 1994.

1073   Webb, W.N. (1989, June). The Pelley Time-Lapse UFO Encounter. *MUFON UFO Journal 254*, pp. 11-13.

1074   Jasek, M. (n.d.). A Similar Encounter by Jonah. Retrieved August 9, 2017 from http://www.ufobc.ca/Beyond/asimilarencounter.htm

1075   Truncale 1994.

1076   Briggs 2002.

1077   Gross, P. (2009, October 21). URECAT - UFO Related Entities Catalog: Summer 1944, Toulon-Sur-Arroux, Saone-Et-Loire, France, Madeleine Arnoux. Retrieved October 24, 2017 from https://ufologie.patrickgross.org/ce3/1944-france-toulonsurarroux.htm#ma1

1078   Gross 2009.

1079   Rutkowski, C.A. (2009). *I Saw It Too! Real UFO Sightings.* Toronto, ON: Dundurn Press.

1080   Newcomb, J., & Geddes-Ward, A. (2007). *A Faerie Treasury.* London, UK: Hay House.

1081   Collins, A. (2012). *LightQuest: Your Guide to Seeing and Interacting with UFOs, Mystery Lights, and Plasma Intelligences.* Memphis, TN: Eagle Wing Books, Inc.

1082   Keel, J. E. (1968, May/June). A New Approach to UFO Witnesses. *Flying Saucer Review 14*(3), pp. 23-24.

1083   Bullard, T. (1987). *UFO Abductions: The Measure of A Mystery* (Vol. 2). Mount Rainier, MD: Fund for UFO Research.

1084   Dennett, P. (2001, November). Why Abductees Don't Talk. *MUFON UFO Journal 403*, pp. 18-20.

1085   Willis, L. (1982, January). Mother and Child Texas Abduction Case. *MUFON UFO Journal 167*, pp. 3-7.

1086   Hopkins 1981.

1087   Strieber, W. (2015, January 8). Anne: Lady in Autumn. Retrieved August 3, 2017 from http://www.unknowncountry.com/journal/anne-lady-autumn

1088   No author. (1937, September 27). Baby Carried on Beam of Light! *The Northern Miner*, p. 2.

1089   Carpenter, J. (1993, October). Abduction Notes. *MUFON UFO Journal 306*, pp. 14-16.

1090   Nicholas, C. (2015, February). One-on-One: Virginia Chief Investigator Ben

Moss. *MUFON UFO Journal 562*, p. 20.

1091   Bryan 1995.

1092   Hopkins 1981.

1093   Oldham 2013.

1094   Martin, J. (1994). Case 154. In A. Rosales (Ed.), *1984 Humanoid Sighting Reports*. Retrieved February 5, 2014 from http://www.ufoinfo.com/humanoid/humanoid-1984.pdf

1095   NUFORC. (n.d.). Case 137. In A. Rosales (Ed.), *1994 Humanoid Sighting Reports*. Retrieved February 5, 2014 from http://www.ufoinfo.com/humanoid/humanoid-1994.pdf

1096   Worley, D. (2000, Summer). Researching "Nordic-Type" Alien Experiencer Cases. *Flying Saucer Review 45*(2), pp. 12-15.

1097   Vike, B. (n.d.). Case 43. In A. Rosales (Ed.), *1970 Humanoid Sighting Reports*. Retrieved February 5, 2014 from http://www.ufoinfo.com/humanoid/humanoid-1970.pdf

1098   Randles, J. (1997). *Alien Contact: The First Fifty Years*. New York, NY: Barnes & Noble Books.

1099   Hopkins, B. (1994). The Abduction Experience: Acquisition. In A. Pritchard, D.E. Pritchard, J.E. Mack, P. Kasey, & C. Yapp (Eds.), *Alien Discussions: Proceedings of the Abduction Study Conference* (pp. 49-52). Cambridge, UK: North Cambridge Press.

1100   Carpenter, J. (1997, February). Abduction Notes. *MUFON UFO Journal 346*, pp. 15-16.

1101   Schwarz, J. (2004, December 9). Imaginary friends: Most kids have one (or more). Retrieved August 10, 2017 from http://www.washington.edu/news/2004/12/09/imaginary-friends-most-kids-have-one-or-more/

1102   Nunnelly 2011.

1103   Aggen, Jr., E.A. (1990, July). Desert Secrets. *MUFON UFO Journal 267*, pp. 8-10.

1104   Clear, C. (1999). *Reaching for Reality: Seven Incredible True Stories of Alien Abduction*. San Antonio, TX: Consciousness Now, Inc.

1105   Nagaitis, C., & Mantle, P. (1994). *Without Consent*. Upper Saddle River, NJ: Prentice Hall.

1106   Cyr, D. (2009, August 3). Abduction de masse! Retrieved August 10, 2017 from https://donald059.wordpress.com/2009/08/03/abduction-de-masse/

1107   Lenin's Way Newspaper. (1990, December 4). Case 552. In A. Rosales (Ed.), *1990 Humanoid Sighting Reports*. Retrieved February 5, 2014 from http://www.ufoinfo.com/humanoid/humanoid-1990.pdf

1108   Tralins 1969.

1109   Taff, B.E. (1991, May). Close, But No Saucer. *MUFON UFO Journal 277*, pp. 3-7.

1110   Turner, K. (1998, Winter). Alien Aftershock: Compulsions in the Aftermath of

Alien Abduction Experiences. *Flying Saucer Review 43*(4), pp. 21-24.

1111   Newman & Baumeister 1996.

1112   Clore, D. (2015). Flying Saucers Stink: Alien Odors and Supernatural Smells. In D. Clore, *The Unspeakable and Others*. Odense, Denmark: H. Harksen Productions, pp. 293-309.

1113   Flaherty, R.P. (2010, November). "These Art They": ET-Human Hybridization and the New Daemonology. *Nova Religio: The Journal of Alternative and Emergent Religions 14*(2), pp. 84-105.

1114   Hynek, J.A. (1970, March/April). Commentary on the AAAS Symposium. *Flying Saucer Review 16*(2), pp. 3-5.

1115   Trench, B.L.P (1959, September-October). Baby Almost As Forecast. *Flying Saucer Review 5*(5), p. 5.

1116   Herbstritt, M.R. (1973, May). Pennsylvania Housewives Report UFO. *Skylook 66*, p. 14.

1117   Connelly, D. (2001, September). September 19th Marks 40th Anniversary of the Classic Betty & Barney Hill Case. *MUFON UFO Journal 401*, pp. 3-6.

1118   Bartholomew, R.E., & Howard, G.S. (1998). *UFOs and Alien Contacts: Two Centuries of Mystery*. New York, NY: Prometheus Books.

1119   NUFORC (n.d.). Case 278. In A. Rosales (Ed.), *1978 Humanoid Sighting Reports*. Retrieved February 5, 2014 from http://www.ufoinfo.com/humanoid/humanoid-1978.pdf

1120   Fowler, O. (2003, Autumn). An Alien Base in Siberia & Alien Contact. *Flying Saucer Review 48*(3), pp. 16-17.

1121   Worley, D. (2004, September). While Blue Book Slept. *MUFON UFO Journal 437*, pp. 5-6.

1122   Hind, C. (Ed.). (January 1997). The Unexplained! *UFO Afrinews 15*, pp. 28-30.

1123   Strieber & Kripal 2016.

1124   Basterfield, K. (1995, January). Abducted: An Independently Witnessed Event? Part 1. *MUFON UFO Journal 321*, pp. 10-12.

1125   Turner 1994.

1126   Pratt, B. (1989, March). An Extraordinary Field-Investigation Trip to Brazil (1986). *Flying Saucer Review 34*(1), pp. 7-12.

1127   UFO Workgroup - The Netherlands. (1995). Case 150. In A. Rosales (Ed.), *1984 Humanoid Sighting Reports*. Retrieved February 5, 2014 from http://www.ufoinfo.com/humanoid/humanoid-1984.pdf

1128   Pratt, B. (1996). *UFO Danger Zone: Terror and Death in Brazil – Where Next?* Blue River, WI: Horus House Press.

1129   Wright 1996.

1130   Marden, K. (2012, December). Abduction Study Complete. *MUFON UFO Journal 536*, pp. 1, 4-5, 6.

1131   Anthony, S. (2014, November). Arizona Case Revisited: Drive-In Movie UFO

Encounter. *MUFON UFO Journal 559*, p. 1, 11-13.

1132   Connelly 2002.

1133   Curtis, M.G., Linares, S.T., & Antoniewics, L. (2014). *Glass' Office Gynecology* (7ᵗʰ ed). Philadelphia, PA: Wolter Kluwer Health.

1134   Hopkins, B. & Rainey, C. (2003). *Sight Unseen*. New York, NY: Atria Books.

1135   Turner 1998.

1136   Jacobs, D. (1993). *Secret Life*. New York, NY: Simon and Schuster.

1137   Jacobs 1993.

1138   Cutchin, J. (2016). *The Brimstone Deceit*. San Antonio, TX: Anomalist Books.

1139   Johari, H. (2000). *Ayurvedic Healing Cuisine: 200 Vegetarian Recipes for health, Balance, and Longevity*. Rochester, VT: Healing Arts Press. (Original work published in 1994)

1140   Cutchin 2015.

1141   Persinger, M.A. (1988, August). Possible Increased Cancer and Depression Risk Among UFO Field Researchers and Populations Near "Flap" Areas. *MUFON UFO Journal 244*, pp. 3-6.

1142   Stringfield, L.H. (1977, January). The Stanford, Kentucky Abduction. *MUFON UFO Journal 110*, pp. 5-15.

1143   Curtis, Linares, & Antoniewics 2014.

1144   Bryan 1995.

1145   Druffel, A. (1991, November). "Missing Fetus" Case Solved. *MUFON UFO Journal 283*, pp. 8-12.

1146   Puthoff, H.A. (1982, January). Mail Bag: Birth of a New Theory? *Flying Saucer Review 27*(4), p. 23.

1147   Evans Wentz 1911.

1148   Kenny 2004.

1149   Rubtsov, V.V. (1994). Alien Contacts and Abduction Experiences: A Look From the C.I.S. In W.H. Andrus, Jr. (Ed.)., *MUFON 1994 International UFO Symposium Proceedings* (pp. 137-152). Seguin, TX: Mutual UFO Network.

1150   Bullard 1987 Vol. 2.

1151   Jacobs 1999.

1152   Coddington, R.H. (1997, May). The UFO Press. *MUFON UFO Journal 349*, p. 15-16.

1153   Jacobs 1999.

1154   Becker, R. (2017, April 25). An artificial womb successfully grew baby sheep—and humans could be next. Retrieved August 14, 2017 from https://www.theverge.com/2017/4/25/15421734/artificial-womb-fetus-biobag-uterus-lamb-sheep-birth-premie-preterm-infant

1155   Briggs 1976.

1156   Bois, GJ.C. (2010). *Jersey Folklore & Superstitions, Vol. 2*. Milton Keynes, UK: AuthorHouse UK Ltd.

1157   Tucker, H. (2003). *Pregnant Fictions: Childbirth and the Fairy Tale in Early-Modern France*. Detroit, MI: Wayne State University Press.

1158   Randles 1994.

1159   Oldham 2013.

1160   Randles 1994.

1161   Conway, G. (1989, March). Report from British Columbia, Canada: An Emerging Epidemic? *Flying Saucer Review 34*(1), pp. 1-4.

1162   Gribble, B. (1990, March). Looking Back. *MUFON UFO Journal 263*, pp. 21-22.

1163   Connelly, D. (2000, August). Symposium Speakers Cover Diverse Topics. *MUFON UFO Journal 388*, pp. 3-7.

1164   Banks, M.M. (1940, June). Fairies' Methods of Securing Good Stock. *Folklore 51*(2), pp. 113-114.

1165   Monaghan, P. (2010). Calamity Meat and Cows of Abundance. *Anthropological Journal of Eurooean Cultures 19*(2), pp. 44-61.

1166   Wilson, C. (1998). *Alien Dawn: An Investigation into the Contact Experience*. New York, NY: Fromm International Publishing Corporation.

1167   Bord, J., & Bord, C. (1978, November). A Case of Rabbit Snatching? *Flying Saucer Review 24*(3), pp. 16-17.

1168   Schwarz, B.E. (1977, October). Talks with Betty Hill: 2 – The Things That Happen Around Her. *Flying Saucer Review 23*(3), pp. 11-14, 31.

1169   Turner, K. (1994). *Masquerade of Angels*. Roland, AR: Kelt Works.

1170   Williston, T.P. (1911). *Japanese Fairy Tales, Second Series*. Chicago, IL: Rand McNally & Co.

1171   Ashliman, D.L. (2004). *Folk and Fairy Tales*. Westport, CT: Greenwood Press.

1172   Frankfurter, D. (2006). Fetus Magic and Sorcery Fears in Roman Egypt. *Greek, Roman, and Byzantine Studies 46*, pp. 37-62.

1173   Guiley 2006.

1174   White, G. (January 12, 2017). *Rune Soup: Talking Thai Animism and Sorcery with Jenx*. Retrieved August 15, 2017 from https://runesoup.com/2017/01/talking-thai-animism-and-sorcery-with-jenx/

1175   Lecouteux 2013.

1176   MacKinnon, I. (2012, May 18). Briton Arrested with Roasted Human Foetuses fro Use in Black Magic Ritual. Retrieved August 15, 2017 from http://www.telegraph.co.uk/news/worldnews/asia/thailand/9274106/Briton-arrested-with-roasted-human-foetuses-for-use-in-black-magic-ritual.html

1177   Hopkins, B. (1990, March). Thoughts On Psychiatrists & UFO Investigators. *MUFON UFO Journal 263*, pp. 13-14, 17.

1178   Dennett, P. (1996, October). UFO Healings. *MUFON UFO Journal 342*, pp. 3-9.

1179   Collins, A. (1978, June). The Aveley Abduction: Part 3. *Flying Saucer Review* *24*(1), pp. 5-15.

1180   Ribera, A. (1984, August). Do Abductees Fit Into A Certain Pattern? Some Reflections and Findings About an Intriguing Phenomenon. *Flying Saucer Review 29*(6), pp. 20-21.

1181   Ring, K. (1992). *The Omega Project.* New York, NY: William Morrow & Co.

1182   Martin, J. (n.d.). Case 205. In A. Rosales (Ed.), *1991 Humanoid Sighting Reports.* Retrieved February 5, 2014 from http://www.ufoinfo.com/humanoid/humanoid-1991.pdf

1183   Mooney 1887.

1184   Connelly, D. (1998, July). UFOlogy Profile: Budd Hopkins. *MUFON UFO Journal 363*, pp. 10-11.

1185   Bowen, C. (Ed.). (1967, July-August). Mail Bag. *Flying Saucer Review 13*(4), pp. 18-20.

1186   Mack, J. (1992, March). Secret Life: A Foreward. *MUFON UFO Journal 287*, pp. 8-9.

1187   Jacobs, D. (2015). *Walking Among Us: The Alien Plan to Control Humanity.* San Francisco, CA: Disinformation Books.

1188   Ankarloo, Clark, & Monter 2002.

1189   Guiley 2009.

1190   Klarer, E. (2009). *Beyond the Light Barrier: The Autobiography of Elizabeth Klarer.* Flagstaff, AZ: Light Technology Publishing. (Original work published 1980)

1191   Creighton, G. (1965, January). The Most Amazing Case of All: Part I – A Brazilian Farmer's Story. *Flying Saucer Review 11*(1), pp. 13-17.

1192   Wright, D. (1996, February). Sexuality, Aliens, Hybrids and Abductions. *MUFON UFO Journal 334*, pp. 11-12.

1193   Sandow, G. (1998, April). The UFO Press. *MUFON UFO Journal 360*, pp. 10-12, 13.

1194   Clancy, S.A. (2005). *Abducted: How People Come to Believe They Were Kidnapped by Aliens.* Cambridge, MA: Harvard University Press.

1195   Kerner, N. (2010). *Grey Aliens and the Harvesting of Souls.* Rochester, VT: Bear & Company.

1196   Hancock 2007.

1197   Emmons, C.F. (1997). *At the Threshold: UFOs, Science, and the New Age.* Leland, NC: Wild Flower Press.

1198   Mack 1994.

1199   Croker 1828 *Part III.*

1200   Fort, C. (1919). *The Book of the Damned.* New York, NY: Boni and Liveright.

1201   Strieber, W. (1987). *Communion.* New York, NY: Avon Books.

1202   Brandenburg, J.E. (1990, September). A Hypothesis of Reticulian Intentions and the Fallacy of Human Insignificance. *MUFON UFO Journal 269*, pp. 11-13.

1203   Crawford, F. (1991, December). The Revealing Science of Ufology: An Anatomy of Abduction Correlations. *MUFON UFO Journal 284*, pp. 10-15.

1204   Dennett, P. (2003, July). Conversations with Extraterrestrials. *MUFON UFO Journal 423*, pp. 3-6.

1205   Jones, B. (1977, June). New Ohio Abduction Case. *MUFON UFO Journal 115*, pp. 9-10.

1206   Houlbrook, C. (2017). The Seelie and Unseelie Courts. In S. Young & C. Houlbrook (Eds.), *Magical Folk: British and Irish Fairies: 500 AD to the Present* (Kindle Edition).

1207   Oldham 2013.

1208   Mack 1994

1209   Randles 1997.

1210   Jacobs 1993.

1211   Hopkins, B. (1987, March). Intruders: UFO Abductions. *MUFON UFO Journal 227*, pp. 3-4.

1212   Jacobs 1999.

1213   Mack 1994.

1214   Mack 1994.

1215   Jacobs 1993.

1216   Worley, D. (1999, Spring). A World Under Assault. *Flying Saucer Review 44*(1), pp. 21-22.

1217   Holzer, H. (1976). *The UFOnauts*. New York, NY: Fawcett Books.

1218   Jacobs 1999.

1219   Hopkins 1994 HIRT.

1220   Jacobs 1999.

1221   Randles 1994.

1222   Jacobs 1993.

1223   Jacobs, D. (1994). Subsequent Procedures. In A. Pritchard, D.E. Pritchard, J.E. Mack, P. Kasey, & C. Yapp (Eds.), *Alien Discussions: Proceedings of the Abduction Study Conference* (pp. 64-68). Cambridge, UK: North Cambridge Press.

1224   Jacobs 1993.

1225   Hancock 2007.

1226   Oldham 2013.

1227   Randles 1994.

1228   Wilson, K. (1993). *The Alien Jigsaw*. Portland, OR: Puzzle Publishing.

1229   Schnabel, J. (1994). *Dark White*. London, UK: Hamish Hamilton.

1230   Jacobs 1993.

1231   Wilson 1993.

1232   Bryan 1995.

1233   Wilson 1993.

1234   Bryan 1995.

1235   Jacobs 1994.

1236   Jacobs 1994.

1237   Frola, R. (2002, April). AUFORN Complied Sighting Reports – Issue 27. Retrieved August 18, 2017 from http://www.ufoinfo.com/ufoicq/auforn27.shtml

1238   Randles 1994.

1239   Oldham 2017.

1240   Lacas, V. (1992, February). Laibow Visits Russia Plans New Treat. *MUFON UFO Journal 286*, p. 14.

1241   Stacy, D. (1992, May). Japanese Create Aritifical Womb! *MUFON UFO Journal 289*, p. 5.

1242   Oldham 2017.

1243   Alexander, V. (1994, September). The Alexander UFO Religious Crisis Survey. *MUFON UFO Journal 317*, pp. 3-7, 13.

1244   Blakemore, E. (2017, January 26). Human-Pig Hybrids Created in the Lab—Here Are the Facts. Retrieved August 17, 2017 from http://news.nationalgeographic.com/2017/01/human-pig-hybrid-embryo-chimera-organs-health-science/

1245   Azkath, S. (2017, February 11). UFO History: Part 11 - with Mike Clelland and Aaron Gulyas. Retrieved August 18, 2017 from http://www.wheredidtheroadgo.com/show-archive/2017/item/361-ufo-history-part-11-with-mike-clelland-and-aaron-gulyas-feb-11-2017

1246   Druffel 1998.

1247   Crain, T.S. (1985, October). UFO Lifting Power. *MUFON UFO Journal 210*, 3-4, 16.

1248   Evans Wentz 1911.

1249   Druffel 1998.

1250   Worley, D. (1997, Summer). Some Denizens of the "Black Nether-World" and Their Abductee Victims. *Flying Saucer Review 42*(2), pp. 7-11.

1251   Truncale 1994.

1252   Guiley 2013.

1253   Druffel 1998.

1254   Druffel 1998.

1255   Druffel 1998.

1256   Druffel 1998.

1257   Storm, H. (2008). *My Descent Into Death: And the Message of Love Which Brought Me Back.* Forest Row, UK: Clairview Books. (Original work published 2000)

1258   Druffel 1998.

1259   Sayne, A. (2017, April 24). Conspirinormal Episode 160 – Joe Jordan (CE4 Research and Stopping Alien Abductions). Retrieved June 27, 2017 from https://www.podomatic.com/podcasts/conspirinormal/episodes/2017-04-23T20_06_18-07_00

1260   Druffel 1998.

1261   Watts 2007.

1262   Druffel 1998.

1263   Druffel 1998.

1264   Marden, K., & Stoner, D. (2012). The Marden-Stoner Study on Commonalities Among Abduction Experiencers. Retrieved August 24, 2017 from http://www.kathleen-marden.com/commonalities-study-final-report.php

1265   Webb, D. (1976). *1973, Year of the Humanoids: An Analysis of the Fall UFO/Humanoid Wave.* Evanston, IL: Center for UFO Studies.

1266   DeSouza, J. (2016). *The Extra-Dimensionals: True Tales And Concepts of Alien Visitors.* Oro Valley, AZ: TAMA Publishing.

1267   Lewis, B. (2012). *Angels, Aliens, and Prophecy: The Connection.* Bloomington, IL: AuthorHouse.

1268   Menkin, M. (2008). Stop Alien Abductions. Retrieved August 24, 2017 from http://www.stopabductions.com/

1269   Drake, N. (1996, October). *Polymeric Materials for Electrostatic Applications.* London, UK: Rapra Technology.

1270   Kumar, N. & Vadera, S.R. (2017). Stealth Materials and Technology for Airborne Systems. In N.E. Prasad & R.J.H. Wanhill (Eds.), *Aerospace Materials and Material Technologies – Volume 1: Aerospace Materials* (pp. 519-538). Singapore: Springer Nature.

1271   Kumar & Vadera 2017.

1272   Engineering 360. (2017). Radar Absorbing Materials Information. Retrieved August 24, 2017 from http://www.globalspec.com/learnmore/materials_chemicals_adhesives/electrical_optical_specialty_materials/radar_absorbing_materials_structures_ram_ras

1273   Hopkins 1987.

1274   Hopkins 1981.

1275   Hopkins, B. (1986, February). A Childhood Abduction? *MUFON UFO Journal 214,* pp. 15-16.

1276   Hopkins 1986.

1277   Hopkins, B. (1986, March). A Childhood Abduction? Part II. *MUFON UFO Journal, 215,* pp. 14-15.

1278   Amano, Y. (2012). *Fairies.* (C. Nieh, Trans.). Milwaukie, OR: Dark Horse Books.

1279   Bryan 1995.

1280   Granchi, I. (1986, January). The Case of Antônio Álves Ferreira – Physical Experiences, and Eleven Alleged Trips to a Strange Planet! *Flying Saucer Review 31*(2), pp.

6-12.

1281   Martín, J. (1999, Autumn). UFOs and Humanoids in Neighboring Cuba. (G. Creighton, Trans.). *Flying Saucer Review 44*(3), pp. 19-21.

1282   Guiley 2007.

1283   Kennedy 1866.

1284   Turner 1994.

1285   Oldham 2017.

1286   Chernobrov, V. (2003). Case 392. Retrieved In A. Rosales (Ed.), *1978 Humanoid Sighting Reports*. Retrieved February 5, 2014 from http://www.ufoinfo.com/humanoid/ humanoid-1978.pdf

1287   Turner 1994, *Masquerade of Angels*.

1288   Randles 1994.

1289   Strieber & Kripal 2016.

1290   Edwards, A. (1988). *On the UFO Road Again*. Seattle, WA.: UFO Contact Center International.

1291   Conway, G. (n.d.). Case 175. Retrieved In A. Rosales (Ed.), *1980 Humanoid Sighting Reports*. Retrieved February 5, 2014 from http://www.ufoinfo.com/humanoid/ humanoid-1980.pdf

1292   Turner 1994.

1293   American Pregnancy Association. (2016, September 2). Vanishing Twin Syndrome. Retrieved August 25, 2017 from http://americanpregnancy.org/multiples/vanishing-twin-syndrome/

1294   Dennis, C., & Whitman, P. (1997). *The Millennium Children*. Clearwater, FL: Rainbows Unlimited.

1295   Dennis & Whitman 1997.

1296   Pinborg, A. (2017). Vanishing Twin Syndrome and Long-Term Outcome. In R.G. Farquharson & M.D. Stephenson (Eds.), *Early Pregnancy* (pp. 262-271). Cambridge, UK: Cambridge University Press (2nd ed.).

1297   Church of Ufology. (2011, June 19). Scarborough, Ontario, Canada. Retrieved August 27, 2017 from http://thechurchofufology.blogspot.com/2011/06/scarborough-ontario-canada.html

1298   Evans Wentz 1911.

1299   Ashliman 2005.

1300   Visser 1908.

1301   Wilson 1993.

1302   Ford, H.J. (1915). *The Scotch-Irish in America*. Princeton, NJ: Princeton University Press.

1303   MUFON CMS. (n.d.) In A. Rosales (Ed.), *1977 Humanoid Sighting Reports*. Retrieved February 5, 2014 from http://www.ufoinfo.com/humanoid/humanoid-1977.pdf

1304　　Mack, J. (1999). *Passport to the Cosmos*. New York, NY: Three Rivers Press.

1305　　Mack 1994

1306　　Nagaitis & Mantle 1994.

1307　　Mack 1994.

1308　　Mack 1999.

1309　　Dennett, P. (1999). *UFOs Over Topanga Canyon*. St. Paul, MN: Llewellyn Publications.

1310　　Bryan 1995.

1311　　Jacobs 1999.

1312　　Jacobs 1993.

1313　　Kirk 1893.

1314　　Asbjørnsen 1883.

1315　　Turner 1994.

1316　　Bryan 1995.

1317　　Nagaitis & Mantle 1994.

1318　　Jacobs 1993.

1319　　Jacobs 1993.

1320　　Hewlett 1913.

1321　　Kolomiets, I. (2003). Case 326. In A. Rosales (Ed.), *1968 Humanoid Sighting Reports*. Retrieved February 5, 2014 from http://www.ufoinfo.com/humanoid/humanoid-1968.pdf

1322　　Jacobs 1993.

1323　　Mack 1999.

1324　　Mack 1994.

1325　　Avery, G. (n.d.) In A. Rosales (Ed.), *1990 Humanoid Sighting Reports*. Retrieved February 5, 2014 from http://www.ufoinfo.com/humanoid/humanoid-1990.pdf

1326　　Wilson 1993.

1327　　Jacobs 1993

1328　　Bullard 1987 Vol. 2.

1329　　Carpenter, J. (1994, June). Abduction Notes. *MUFON UFO Journal 314*, pp. 12-13.

1330　　Jacobs 1993.

1331　　Harpur 2003.

1332　　Randles 1997.

1333　　Jacobs 1993.

1334　　Jacobs 1999.

1335   Jacobs 2015.

1336   Jacobs 2015.

1337   Frost, W.H. (1900). *Fairies and Folk of Ireland.* New York, NY: Charles Scribner's Sons.

1338   Bryan 1995.

1339   Cutchin 2015.

1340   Connelly, D. (Ed.). (2004, August). 2004 MUFON Symposium Speakers Explore the Technological Evidence. *MUFON UFO Journal 436*, pp. 8-11.

1341   Mack 1995.

1342   Jacobs 1999.

1343   Jacobs 1993.

1344   Jacobs 1999.

1345   Jacobs 1993.

1346   Swords 2005.

1347   Hopkins & Rainey 2003.

1348   Connelly, D. (1999, February). Ufology Profile: Beverly Trout Wears Two Hats: Investigator And..... *MUFON UFO Journal 370*, pp. 14-16.

1349   Conway 1989.

1350   Bilodeaux, J. (2004, October). Raechel's Eyes - The Strange Case of an Apparent Hybrid: Part 2. *MUFON UFO Journal 438*, pp. 5-7.

1351   Dennett 2003.

1352   Connelly, D. (1998, May). Editor's Note to "Buzz, Buzz, Who's There?" by D. Bahor. *MUFON UFO Journal 361*, p. 6.

1353   Lorgen, E. (2014, June 17). Evidence for Alien Abduction: Fluorescence Body Marks. Retrieved August 31, 2017 from http://evelorgen.com/wp/news/evidence-for-alien-abduction-fluorescence-body-marks/

1354   Buschmann, C., Langsdorf, G., & Lichtenthaller, H.K. (2009). Blue, Green, Red, and Far-Red Fluorescence Signatures of Plant Tissues, Their Multicolor Fluorescence Imaging, and Application for Agrofood Assessment. In M. Zude (Ed.), *Optical Monitoring of Fresh and Processed Agricultural Crops* (pp. 272-318). Boca Raton, FL: CRC Press.

1355   Turner, K. (1994, December). Genetic Agenda A Double-Cross? *MUFON UFO Journal* 320, pp. 13-14.

1356   Goldfader, L. (1992, Summer). The Traumatic Abduction Story of Alvina Scott (Canada), and Another Foetus Mystery! *Flying Saucer Review 37*(2), pp. 22-23.

1357   Jacobs 1999.

1358   Strieber 1997.

1359   Bryan 1995.

1360   Higbee, D. (1995, September). Abductee Brainwashing. *MUFON UFO Journal* 329, pp. 10-12.

1361   Turner 1994.

1362   Randles 1994.

1363   Lang, C.R. (2004, February). The Indigo Hypothesis: Is This a Goal of the Visitors' Agenda(s). *MUFON UFO Journal 430*, pp. 9-11.

1364   Bullard 1987 Vol. 2.

1365   Lang 2004.

1366   Steiger, B. (1988). *The UFO Abductors*. New York, NY: The Berkley Publishing Group.

1367   Steiger 1988.

1368   Sigismond, R. (1983, December). CE-IIIs: New Dimensions in Investigations. *Flying Saucer Review 29*(2), pp. 21-26.

1369   Oldham 2017.

1370   Steiger 1988.

1371   Hargrove, R. (2000, January). Post Abduction Syndrome (PAS) Includes Cluster of Symptoms. *MUFON UFO Journal 381*, pp. 6-8.

1372   Hopkins, B. (1996, Winter). Abduction and Deception. *Flying Saucer Review 41*(4), pp. 12-15.

1373   Randles 1994.

1374   Conway, G. (1987, June). Another "Observing Eye" in the House? *Flying Saucer Review 32*(4), p. 28.

1375   Virtue, D. (2001). *The Care and Feeding of Indigo Children*. Carlsbad, CA: Hay House, Inc.

1376   Virtue 2001.

1377   Virtue 2001.

1378   Wilde 1887.

1379   Hopkins 1981.

1380   Beachcombing 2011, October 26.

1381   Mooney 1887.

1382   Coleman, L. (2013). Twilight Language. Retrieved September 1, 2017 from http://copycateffect.blogspot.com/

1383   Norman, T. (1999). *Names Through the Ages*. New York, NY: Berkley Books.

1384   Simpson, J., & Roud, S. (2000). *A Dictionary of English Folklore*. Oxford, UK: Oxford University Press.

1385   Norman 1999.

1386   Worley, D. (1996, Autumn). Alien Abduction—The Ominous Truth of Our Day. *Flying Saucer Review 41*(3), pp. 1-4.

1387   Worley, D. (1996, Winter). Examining the Mystery of the "Para-Apes." *Flying Saucer Review 41*(4), pp. 20-22.

1388 Redfern, N. (2016). *The Bigfoot Book: The Encyclopedia of Sasquatch, Yeti and Cryptid Primates.* Canton, MI: Visible Ink Press.

1389 Kelleher, C.A. & Knapp, G. (2005). *Hunt for the Skinwalker: Science Confronts the Unexplained at a Remote Ranch.* New York, NY: Paraview Pocket Books.

1390 Cutchin 2015.

1391 Cutchin 2016.

1392 Redfern 2016.

1393 Renner, T. (2017). *Bigfoot in Pennsylvania.* Charleston, SC: CreateSpace Independent Publishing Platform.

1394 Redfern 2016.

1395 Cowley, S., & Cox, G. (2012). *Searching for Bigfoot.* New York, NY: The Rosen Publishing Group.

1396 Redish, L. (2015). Native Languages of the Americas: Kwakiutl Indian Legends (Kwakwaka'wakw). Retrieved September 11, 2017 from http://www.native-languages.org/kwakiutl-legends.htm

1397 Shiel, L.A. (2012). *Top Secret Sasquatch: Forbidden Bigfoot, Part Two.* USA: Jacobsville Books.

1398 Redfern 2016.

1399 Bane 2013.

1400 Glenn, J., & Larsen, E.F. (2015). *Unbored Adventure.* New York, NY: Bloomsbury USA.

1401 Wahlert, G., & Linwood, R. (2014). *One Shot Kills: A History of Australian Army Sniping.* Sydney, AU: Big Sky Publishing.

1402 Meldrum, J. (2006). *Sasquatch: Legend Meets Science.* New York, NY: Forge Books.

1403 Germer, W. (2017, June 7). Sasquatch Chronicles Radio // SC EP: 273 The Eyeshine. Retrieved September 5, 2017 from https://www.youtube.com/watch?v=3U9DtCapSZc

1404 Meldrum 2006.

1405 Rennard, A. (2000, June 18). Pre-Columbian and Early American Legends of Bigfoot-like Beings. Retrieved September 5, 2017 from http://www.bfro.net/legends/salish.htm

1406 Bane 2016.

1407 Rennard 2000.

1408 Vendramini, D. (2011). *Them and Us: How Neanderthal Predation Created Modern Humans.* Armidale, AU: Kardoorair Press.

1409 Lewis, M.A. (1984, January). 'Earth-Based' UFOs. *MUFON UFO Journal 191*, pp. 16-18.

1410 Meldrum 2006.

1411 Coleman, L. (2003). *Bigfoot! The True Story of Apes in America.* New York, NY: Paraview Pocket Books.

1412   Gordon, S. (2010). *Silent Invasion: The Pennsylvania UFO-Bigfoot Casebook*. R. Marsh (Ed.). Greensburg, PA: Stan Gordon Productions.

1413   Bord, J., & Bord, C. (1989). *Unexplained Mysteries of the 20th Century*. Lincolnwood, IL: Contemporary Books.

1414   Bord, J., & Bord, C. (2006). *Bigfoot Casebook Updated: Sightings and Encounters from 1818 to 2004*. Enumclaw, WA: Pinewinds Press.

1415   Renner 2017.

1416   Swancer, B. (2016, September 23). Truly Strange Cases of People Kidnapped by Bigfoot. Retrieved September 5, 2017 from http://mysteriousuniverse.org/2016/09/truly-strange-cases-of-people-kidnapped-by-bigfoot/

1417   Keel, J. (2002). *The Complete Guide to Mysterious Beings*. New York, NY: Tom Doherty Associates, LLC. (Original work published 1970 as *Strange Creatures from Time and Space*)

1418   Swancer 2016.

1419   Renner 2017.

1420   Keel 2002.

1421   Powell, T. (2003). *The Locals*. Surrey, CA: Hancock House Publishers Ltd.

1422   Swancer 2016.

1423   Swancer, B. (2017, June 9). Some Very Strange Information on the Bizarre Vanishing of Dennis Martin. Retrieved September 5, 2017 from http://mysteriousuniverse.org/2017/06/some-very-strange-information-on-the-bizarre-vanishing-of-dennis-martin/

1424   Magraner, J. (1991). *Les Hominides reliques d'Asie Centrale*. Valence, FR: Association Troglodytes.

1425   Renner, T. (2018). *Bigfoot: West Coast Wild Men*. Charleston, SC: CreateSpace Independent Publishing Platform.

1426   Germer, W. (2017, February 22). Sasquatch Chronicles Radio // SC EP: 11 The 'Siege' at Honobia. Retrieved September 5, 2017 from https://www.youtube.com/watch?v=s_izA6N4x-A

1427   Bord & Bord 1989.

1428   Meldrum 2006.

1429   Alley 2007.

1430   Keel, J. (2016). *Anomaly: An Irregular Newsletter Edited by John Keel*. Martinez, CA: Paranoia Publishing. (Original works published 1969-1974)

1431   Keightley 1828.

1432   Lady Gregory 1920, *Second Series*.

1433   Rhŷs 1901.

1434   Blumer 1985.

1435   Jha, A. (2012, October 17). Why Crying Babies are So Hard to Ignore. Retrieved September 5, 2017 from https://www.theguardian.com/science/2012/oct/17/

crying-babies-hard-ignore

1436   Yeats 1892.

1437   Eberhart, G.M. (2002). *Mysterious Creatures: A Guide to Cryptozoology*. Santa Barbara, CA: ABC-CLIO, Inc.

1438   Alley 2007.

1439   Foster, M. (2000, May 23). Bigfoot Roaming the Wilds—With A Human Child! *Weekly World News*, p. 31.

1440   Cutler, C.L. (2002). *Tracks that Speak: The Legacy of Native American Words in North American Culture*. Boston, MA: Houghton Mifflin Company.

1441   Forth, G. (2008). *Images of the Wildman in Southeast Asia: An Anthropological Perspective*. Abingdon, UK: Routledge.

1442   Redfern 2016.

1443   Blacker 1967.

1444   Childress, D.H. (2010). *Yetis, Sasquatch, & Hairy Giants*. Gardena, CA: SCB Distributors.

1445   Burns, J.W. (1954, December). "My Search for B.C.'s Giant Indians." *Liberty Magazine*, pp. 38-39.

1446   Kropej 2012.

1447   Kets de Vries, M.F.R. (2014). *Talking to the Shaman Within: Musings On Hunting*. Bloomington, IN: iUniverse.

1448   Rytkheu, Y. (2011). *The Chuckchi Bible*. (I.Y. Chavasse, Trans.). New York, NY: Archipelago Books.

1449   Husband, T., & Gilmore-House, G. (1980). *The Wild Man: Medieval Myth and Symbolism*. New York, NY: The Metropolitan Museum of Art.

1450   Millgram, A.E. (1990). *Jerusalem Curiosities*. Philadelphia, PA: The Jewish Publication Society.

1451   Husband & Gilmore-House 1980.

1452   Cutchin 2016.

1453   Burns 1954.

1454   Alley 2007.

1455   Redfern 2016.

1456   Boirayon, M. (2009) *Solomon Islands Mysteries*. Kempton, IL: Adventures Unlimited Press.

1457   Swancer 2016.

1458   Childress 2010.

1459   Dubhthaigh, P.Ó. (2017). A Folk-Tale of Ballyboden Rathfarnham – The Year Following the Famine. Retrieved September 7, 2017 from https://www.duchas.ie/en/cbes/4428228/4387366/4458585

1460   Burnette, T.K. (1999). *Nature's Secret Agents*. Marion, NC: Tom Burnette Publishing.

1461   Germer, W. (2017, July 23). Sasquatch Chronicles Radio // SC EP: 345 A Hunter's Encounter. Retrieved September 7, 2017 from https://www.youtube.com/watch?v=_cseD8Ohqso

1462   Breedlove, S. (2015, June 7). Episode 52: with Daryl Colyer and Brian Brown. Retrieved September 8, 2017 from http://saswhat.podbean.com/e/episode-52-with-daryl-colyer-and-brian-brown/

1463   Breedlove 2015.

1464   Nunnelly, B. (2017). *The Inhumanoids: Real Encounters with Beings That Can't Exist!* US: Triangulum Publishing (2nd ed.).

1465   Buccola 2006.

1466   Nyman, J. (1989, March). The Familiar Entity and Dual Reference in the Latent Encounter. *MUFON UFO Journal 251*, pp. 10-12.

1467   Conway, G. (2002, June). Not a Fairy Story. Retrieved September 14, 2017 from http://www.ufobc.ca/Experiencer/fairy_v2.htm

1468   Monaghan, P. (2014). *Encyclopedia of Goddesses & Heroines: Revised Edition.* Novato, CA: New World Library.

1469   Hauck, D.W. (2002). *Haunted Places: The National Directory.* New York, NY: Penguin Books.

1470   Jarvis, S. (Ed.). (1992). *Dark Zones.* New York, NY: Warner Books.

1471   Martín, J. (n.d.). Case 318. In A. Rosales (Ed.), *1979 Humanoid Sighting Reports.* Retrieved February 5, 2014 from http://www.ufoinfo.com/humanoid/humanoid-1979.pdf

1472   Johnson, M.T. (2014). *Seeing Fairies: From the Lost Archives of the Fairy Investigation Society, Authentic Reports of Fairies in Modern Times.* San Antonio, TX: Anomalist Books.

1473   Conway, G. (n.d.). Case 61. Retrieved In A. Rosales (Ed.), *1981 Humanoid Sighting Reports.* Retrieved February 5, 2014 from http://www.ufoinfo.com/humanoid/humanoid-1981.pdf

1474   Randles 1994.

1475   O'Brien, C. (1995). *The Mysterious Valley.* New York, NY: St. Martin's Press.

1476   Rosales, A. (n.d.). Case 345. In A. Rosales (Ed.), *1996 Humanoid Sighting Reports.* Retrieved February 5, 2014 from http://www.ufoinfo.com/humanoid/humanoid-1996.pdf

1477   Rubtsov 1994.

1478   Childs, M.H. (2008, January). Women in Ufology: Marilyn Henry Childs, PhD. *MUFON UFO Journal 477*, p. 8.

1479   Randles 1994.

1480   Randles 1994.

1481   Gordon 1997.

1482   Guiley 2007.

1483   Ankarloo, Clark, & Monter 2002.

1484   Allred, A.P. (2005). *Cats' Most Wanted.* Washington, D.C.: Potomac Books.

1485   Guiley 2009.

1486   Raynes, B. (1982, February). UFOs or "Soul Ships?" *MUFON UFO Journal 168*, pp. 15-17.

1487   GardenStone. (2011). *The Mercury-Woden Complex.* Norderstedt, DE: Books on Demand GmbH.

1488   Kowalewski, D. (2015). *Death Walker: Shamanic Psychopomps, Earthbound Ghosts, and Helping Spirits in the Afterlife Realm.* Bloomington, IN: iUniverse.

1489   Strong, L. (2016). What is a Psychopomp? Retrieved September 14, 2017 from http://www.psychopomps.org/what-is-a-psychopomp.html

1490   Lecouteux 2015.

1491   Evans Wentz 1911.

1492   Fanthorpe, L., & Fanthorpe, P. (1997). *The World's Greatest Unsolved Mysteries.* Toronto, CA: Hounslow Press.

1493   Castle of Spirits. (2001). Strange Disappearances. Retrieved September 13, 2017 from http://www.castleofspirits.com/strangediss.html

1494   McCutchan, A. (1999). *Muse That Sings: Composers Speak About the Creative Process.* Oxford, UK: Oxford University Press.

1495   Phillips, T. (2005, December). Physical Traces. *MUFON UFO Journal 452*, pp. 18-19.

1496   Rickard & Michell 2000.

1497   Tralins 1969.

1498   Dorman, R.M. (1881). *The Origin of Primitive Superstitions and Their Development into the Worship of Spirits and Doctrine of Spiritual Agency Among the Aborigines of America.* Philadelphia, PA: Lippincott & Co.

1499   Zabava, A. (n.d.). Case 1. In A. Rosales (Ed.), *1910-1919 Humanoid Sighting Reports.* Retrieved February 5, 2014 from http://www.ufoinfo.com/humanoid/humanoid-1919.pdf

1500   Keel 1971.

1501   Guma, J. (1997, Spring). Highlights from Large Batches of Spanish-American Press Clippings Received from Jane Guma (Jane Thomas) in November 1994, and June 1995. (G. Creighton, Trans.). *Flying Saucer Review 42*(1), pp. 8-12.

1502   Puhvel, M. (1978). Snow and Mist in "Sir Gawain and the Green Knight": Portents of the Otherworld? *Folklore 89*(2), pp. 224-228.

1503   Bullard 1987 Vol. 1.

1504   Bryan 1995.

1505   Paulides, D. (2011). *Missing 411 – Eastern United States.* Charleston, SC: CreateSpace.

1506   Paulides, D. (2013, October). Missing Persons May Be Tied to UFO Cases. *MUFON UFO Journal 546*, pp. 1, 7-9.

1507   Paulides, D. (2012). *Missing 411 – North America and Beyond*. Charleston, SC: CreateSpace.

1508   Paulides 2012.

1509   Paulides 2013.

1510   MacIsaac, T. (2016, June 18). Retired Police Detective Identifies Mysterious Patterns Across Thousands of Missing Persons Cases. Retrieved September 13, 2017 from http://www.theepochtimes.com/n3/2093486-retired-police-detective-identifies-mysterious-patterns-across-thousands-of-missing-persons-cases/

1511   Paulides, D. (2011). *Missing 411 – Western United States and Canada*. Charleston, SC: CreateSpace.

1512   Occult Museum. (2017). Missing 411: Why are So Many People Going Missing in America's National Parks? Retrieved September 13, 2017 from http://www.theoccultmuseum.com/missing-411-many-people-going-missing-americas-national-parks/

1513   Paulides, D. (2015). *Missing 411 – A Sobering Coincidence*. Charleston, SC: CreateSpace.

1514   Paulides 2011 *Eastern United States.*

1515   Billman, J. (2017, March 13). How 1,600 People Went Missing from Our Public Lands Without a Trace. Retrieved September 13, 2017 from https://www.outsideonline.com/2164446/leave-no-trace

1516   Paulides 2011 *Eastern United States.*

1517   Paulides 2012.

1518   Paulides 2011 *Western United States.*

1519   Paulides 2011 *Western United States.*

1520   Paulides, D. (2016). *Missing 411 – Hunters (Volume 1)*. Charleston, SC: CreateSpace.

1521   Creighton, G. (Ed.). (1977, April). Some Recent Spanish Reports. (G. Creighton, Ed.). *Flying Saucer Review 22*(6), pp. 27-29.

1522   Paulides 2012.

1523   Buehring, J.M. (1984, June). Invisible Barriers. *Flying Saucer Review 29*(5), pp. 19-22.

1524   Silver 1999.

1525   Cadieux, A. (2013, December 23). "The Bridgewater Triangle" vs "Monsters and Mysteries in America." Retrieved September 13, 2017 from http://thebridgewatertriangledocumentary.com/the-bridgewater-triangle-vs-monsters-and-mysteries-in-america/

1526   Knapp, G. (2015, September 12). Missing 411: Urban Disappearances. Part 2 of 4. Retrieved September 13, 2017 from https://www.youtube.com/watch?v=2Cs8r8RTrew&feature=youtu.be&t=2234

1527   Evans Wentz 1911.

1528   Evans Wentz 1911.

1529   Luomala, K. (1983, Fall). Phantom Marchers in the Hawaiian Islands. *Pacific Studies* 7(1), pp. 1-33.

1530   Luomala 1983.

1531   Paulides 2012.

1532   Swancer, B. (2017, June 29). Bizarre Vanishings, Baffling Clues, and Strange Imposters. Retrieved September 13, 2017 from http://mysteriousuniverse.org/2017/06/bizarre-vanishings-baffling-clues-and-strange-imposters/

1533   Azkath, S. (2016, December 24). Laird Scranton on Skara Brae, the Dogon, Egypt, and More... Retrieved September 19, 2017 from http://www.wheredidtheroadgo.com/itemlist/tag/Laird%20Scranton

1534   Mosier, W.A. (2013). Addressing the Affective Domain: What Neuroscience Says About Social/Emotional Development in Early Childhood. In L.H. Wasserman & D. Zambo (Eds.), *Educating the Young Child 7: Advances in Theory and Research, Implications for Practice - Early Childhood and Neuroscience – Links to Development and Learning* (pp. 77-104). Heidelberg, DE: Springer Science.

1535   Mosier 2013.

1536   Truncale 1994.

1537   Clelland 2015.

1538   Clelland 2015.

1539   Strieber & Kripal 2016.

1540   TVTropes. (n.d.). Inspirationally Disadvantaged. Retrieved September 19, 2017 from http://tvtropes.org/pmwiki/pmwiki.php/Main/InspirationallyDisadvantaged

1541   Van der Toorn, K., Becking, B., & Van der Horst, P. (1999). *Dictionary of Deities and Demons in the Bible.* Leiden, NL: Koninklijke Brill NV (2nd ed.).

1542   Clelland, M. (2018). *Stories from the Messengers: Owls, UFOs and a Deeper Reality.* New York: Richard Dolan Press.

1543   Clelland 2018.

1544   Clelland 2018.

1545   Clelland 2018.

1546   Clelland 2018.

1547   Schmidt, H. (1974). *Psychic Exploration: A Challenge for Science.* New York, NY: G.P. Putnam's Sons.

1548   Dodds, E.R. (1951). *The Greeks and the Irrational.* Los Angeles, CA: Berkeley.

1549   Roberts, A.L., Lyall, K., Rich-Edwards, J.W., Ascherio, A., & Weisskopf, M.G. (2013, May). Maternal exposure to childhood abuse is associated with elevated risk of autism. *JAMA Psychiatry* 70(5), pp. 508-515.

1550   Menkin, M. (2013). Aliens and Children. Retrieved September 20, 2017 from http://aliensandchildren.org/

1551   Lynn, D. (2016). *From Fear to Love.* Huntsville, AR: Ozark Mountain Publishing.

1552   Jacobs 2015.

1553   Wilson, P.A. (2011). *UFOs in Pennsylvania: Encounters with Extraterrestrials in the Keystone State.* Mechanicsburg, PA: Stackpole Books.

1554   Haskew, P., & Donnellan, A.M. (1993). *Emotional Maturity and Well-Being: Psychological Lessons of Facilitated Communication.* Madison, WI: DRI Press.

1555   Powell, D. (2014, Novemeber 25). Telepathy Project with non-verbal autistics children DEBUNKS skeptics. Retrieved September 20, 2017 from https://www.youtube.com/watch?v=BBGwkk8vp3w

1556   Powell 2014.

1557   Mauro, C. (2015). *Spiritual Telepathy.* Wheaton, IL: Quest Books.

1558   Morrison, G. (2000). Grant Morrison Disinfo Con Lecture Magick Terence Mckenna. Retrieved September 21, 2017 from https://www.youtube.com/watch?v=1-cxBuRU09w

1559   Davis, E. (2013, October 13). Expanding Mind – Autistic Imagination. Retrieved September 21, 2017 from http://expandingmind.podbean.com/2013/10/13/expanding-mind-autistic-imagination-101313/

1560   Arkowitz, H., & Lilienfield, S.O. (2012, August 1). Is There Really an Autism Epidemic? Retrieved February 21, 2018 from https://www.scientificamerican.com/article/is-there-really-an-autism-epidemic/

1561   Heussler, H., Polnay, L., Marder, E., Standen, P., Lyn U, C., & Butler, N. (2001, September 15). Prevalence of autism in early 1970s may have been underestimated. *British Medical Journal 323*(7313), p. 633.

1562   Blaxill, M.F. (November-December 2004). What's Going On? The Question of Time Trends in Autism. *Public Health Reports 119*, pp. 536-551.

1563   Schreibman, L. (2005). *The Science and Fiction of Autism.* Cambridge, MA: Harvard University Press.

1564   Arkowitz & Lilienfield 2012.

1565   Centers for Disease Control and Prevention 2017.

1566   Autism Speaks. (2015, July 23). Shift in diagnosis only partly explains rise in autism prevalence. Retrieved February 21, 2018 from https://www.autismspeaks.org/science/science-news/shift-diagnosis-only-partly-explains-rise-autism-prevalence

1567   Autism Speaks 2015.

1568   Almqvist, I. (2016). *Natural Born Shamans.* New Alresford, UK: Moon Books.

1569   McCauley, R.N. (2017, March 3). An Autistic Saint? Retrieved September 21, 2017 from https://www.psychologytoday.com/blog/why-religion-is-natural-and-science-is-not/201703/autistic-saint

1570   Kosloski, P. (2017, February 2017). 3 Saints Who May Have Had Autism Spectrum Disorder. Retrieved September 21, 2017 from https://aleteia.org/2017/02/08/3-saints-who-may-have-had-autism-spectrum-disorder/

1571   Grinker, R.R. (2007). *Unstrange Minds: Remapping the World of Autism.* Philadelphia, PA: Basic Books.

1572   Pratt, C. (2007). *An Encyclopedia of Shamanism: Volume One – A-M*. New York, NY: The Rosen Publishing Group, Inc.

Bibliography

Aggen, Jr., E.A. (1990, July). Desert Secrets. *MUFON UFO Journal 267*, pp. 8-10.

Alexander, M. (2006). *Sutton Companion to British Folklore, Myths & Legends*. Stroud, UK: The History Press. (Original work published 2002)

Alexander, V. (1994, September). The Alexander UFO Religious Crisis Survey. *MUFON UFO Journal 317*, pp. 3-7, 13.

Alley, J.R. (2007). *Raincoast Sasquatch*. Blaine, WA: Hancock House. (Original work published 2003)

Allred, A.P. (2005). *Cats' Most Wanted*. Washington, D.C.: Potomac Books.

Almqvist, I. (2016). *Natural Born Shamans*. New Alresford, UK: Moon Books.

Altmann, A.E. (2006). *The Seven Swabians, and Other German Folktales*. Westport, CT: Libraries Unlimited.

Amano, Y. (2012). *Fairies*. (C. Nieh, Trans.). Milwaukie, OR: Dark Horse Books.

American Folklore Society. (1889, January-March). Notices of the Folk-Lore of Other Continents. *The Journal of American Folklore 2(4)*, pp. 80-82.

American Pregnancy Association. (2016, September 2). Vanishing Twin Syndrome. Retrieved August 25, 2017 from http://americanpregnancy.org/multiples/vanishing-twin-syndrome/

Ankarloo, B., Clark, S., & Monter, W. (2002). *Witchcraft and Magic in Europe: Volume 4 - The Period of the Witch Trials*. London, UK: The Athlone Press.

Anthony, S. (2014, November). Arizona Case Revisited: Drive-In Movie UFO Encounter. *MUFON UFO Journal 559*, p. 1, 11-13.

Arkowitz, H., & Lilienfeld, S.O. (2012, August 1). Is There Really an Autism Epidemic? Retrieved February 21, 2018 from https://www.scientificamerican.com/article/is-there-really-an-autism-epidemic/

Árnason, J. (1864). *Icelandic Legends*. (G.E.J. Powell & E. Magnússon, Trans.). London, UK: Richard Bentley.

Árnason, J. (1866). *Icelandic Legends: Second Series*. (G.E.J. Powell & E. Magnússon, Trans.). London, UK: Longmans, Green, and Co.

Arrowsmith, N. (2009). *Field Guide to the Little People: A Curious Journey into the Hidden Realm of Elves, Faeries, Hobgoblins & Other Not-So-Mythical Creatures.* Woodbury, Minnesota: Llewellyn Publications. (Original work published 1977)

Asbjørnsen, P.C. (1883). *Folk and Fairy Tales.* (H.L. Braekstad, Trans.). New York, NY: A.C. Armstrong & Son (7th ed.).

Ashliman, D.L. (1997). Changelings. Retrieved June 6, 2017 from http://www.pitt.edu/~dash/changeling.html

Ashliman, D.L. (2004). *Folk and Fairy Tales.* Westport, CT: Greenwood Press.

Ashliman, D.L. (2005, December 17). German Changeling Legends. Retrieved June 2, 2017 from http://www.pitt.edu/~dash/gerchange.html

Ashliman, D.L. (2012, December 22). The Origin of Underground People. Retrieved June 12, 2017 from http://www.pitt.edu/~dash/originunder.html

Ashliman, D.L. (2013). Changeling Legends from the British Isles. Retrieved June 8, 2017 from http://www.pitt.edu/~dash/britchange.html

Ashton, A. (1975). *Saints & Changelings: Folk-Tales of Brittany.* Glasgow, UK: Blackie and Son Limited.

Aspinall, K. (1995, Summer). "Alien Abductions" and "Fairy Abductions": A Comparison. *Flying Saucer Review 40(2),* pp. 9-11.

Astarian, G. (2001). Āl Reconsidered. *Iran & the Caucasus 5,* pp. 149-156.

Autism Speaks. (2015, July 23). Shift in diagnosis only partly explains rise in autism prevalence. Retrieved February 21, 2018 from https://www.autismspeaks.org/science/science-news/shift-diagnosis-only-partly-explains-rise-autism-prevalence

Avery, G. (n.d.) In A. Rosales (Ed.), *1990 Humanoid Sighting Reports.* Retrieved February 5, 2014 from http://www.ufoinfo.com/humanoid/humanoid-1990.pdf

Azkath, S. (2016, December 24). Laird Scranton on Skara Brae, the Dogon, Egypt, and More... Retrieved September 19, 2017 from http://www.wheredidtheroadgo.com/itemlist/tag/Laird%20Scranton

Azkath, S. (2017, February 11). UFO History: Part 11 - with Mike Clelland and Aaron Gulyas. Retrieved August 18, 2017 from http://www.wheredidtheroadgo.com/show-archive/2017/item/361-ufo-history-part-11-with-mike-clelland-and-aaron-gulyas-feb-11-2017

Bader, C.D. (1995, April). The UFO Contact Movement form the 1950s to the Present. *Studies in Popular Culture 17*(2), pp. 73-90.

Bagshawe, T.W., & Coote Lake, E.F. (1949, March). Folk Life and Traditions. *Folklore 60(1),* pp. 245-248.

Ball, J. (2008). *Early Intervention & Autism*. Arlington, TX: Future Horizons, Inc.

Ballard, L.M. (1997). Fairies and the Supernatural on Reachrai. In P. Narváez (Ed.), *The Good People: New Fairylore Essays* (pp. 47-93). Lexington, KY: The University Press of Kentucky.

Bane, T. (2012). *Encyclopedia of Demons in World Religions and Cultures*. Jefferson, NC: McFarland & Company, Inc.

Bane, T. (2013). *Encyclopedia of Fairies in World Folklore and Mythology*. Jefferson, NC: McFarland & Company, Inc.

Bane, T. (2016). *Encyclopedia of Beasts and Mosters in Myth, Legend and Folklore*. Jefferson, NC: McFarland & Company, Inc.

Banks, G. & Blackhall, S. (2015). *Scottish Urban Myths and Ancient Legends*. Stroud, UK: The History Press.

Banks, M.M. (1940, June). Fairies' Methods of Securing Good Stock. *Folklore 51*(2), pp. 113-114.

Barron, J.R. (1929, Winter). Shetland Fairies. *Prairie Schooner 3(1)*, pp. 47-53.

Bartholomew, R.E., & Howard, G.S. (1998). *UFOs and Alien Contacts: Two Centuries of Mystery*. New York, NY: Prometheus Books.

Bartholomew, R.E., & Jamaludin, A. (2000). Contemporary Malaysian Close Encounters with Fairies and Aliens. *Australian Folklore 15*, pp. 178-199.

Bartholomew, R.E., & Rickard, B. (2014). *Mass Hysteria in Schools: Worldwide Histroy Since 1566*. Jefferson, NC: McFarland & Company, Inc.

Bartlett, S. (2014). *Guide to the World's Supernatural Places*. Washington, D.C.: The National Geographic Society.

Basterfield, K. (1995, January). Abducted: An Independently Witnessed Event? Part 1. *MUFON UFO Journal 321*, pp. 10-12.

BBC. (2016, January 20). Fairy tales origins thousands of years old, researchers say. Retrieved May 30, 2017 from http://www.bbc.com/news/uk-35358487

Beachcombing. (2010, November 5). Baby-Eating Eagles. Retrieved February 23, 2018 from http://www.strangehistory.net/2010/11/05/baby-eating-eagles/

Beachcombing. (2011, October 26). Eggs, Mermaids and Fairies. Retrieved July 3, 2017 from http://www.strangehistory.net/2011/10/26/eggs-mermaids-and-fairies/

Beachcombing. (2012, February 18). Irish Changeling in New York. Retrieved July 7, 2017 from http://www.strangehistory.net/2012/02/18/irish-changeling-in-new-york/

Beachcombing. (2012, March 30). Handlist of Adult Changelings. Retrieved July 7, 2017 from http://www.strangehistory.net/2012/03/30/handlist-of-adult-changelings/

Beachcombing. (2013, August 21). Fairy Knick Knacks: The Five Strangest. Retrieved July 4, 2017 from http://www.strangehistory.net/2013/08/21/fairy-knick-knacks-the-five-strangest/

Beachcombing. (2014, February 25). The Most Beautiful Folk Cure: An Epilepsy Ring. Retrieved July 5, 2017 from http://www.strangehistory.net/2014/02/25/the-most-beautiful-folk-cure-an-epilepsy-ring/

Beachcombing. (2015, April 24). Manx Judge and Manx Fairies, 1932. Retrieved June 4, 2017 from http://www.strangehistory.net/2015/04/24/manx-judge-manx-fairies-1932

Beachcombing. (2016, February 4). Red Fairies #3: Do NOT Use the Chimney. Retrieved July 6, 2017 from http://www.strangehistory.net/2016/02/04/red-fairies-3-do-not-use-the-chimney/

Beachcombing. (2016, June 17). The Baby and the Fairy Bush. Retrieved July 7, 2017 from http://www.strangehistory.net/2016/06/17/baby-fairy-bush/

Beachcombing. (2017, January 9). Fairy Vampires #1: Spence Speaks. Retrieved June 13, 2017 from http://www.strangehistory.net/2017/01/09/fairy-vampires-1-spence-speaks

Beachcombing. (2017, March 8). Fairy Wind Rescue Spell. Retrieved June 29, 2017 from http://www.strangehistory.net/2017/03/08/fairy-wind-rescue-spell/

Beachcombing. (2018, April 28). Beware Fairy Home Invasion! Retrieved May 9, 2018 from http://www.strangehistory.net/2018/04/28/beware-fairy-home-invasion/

Bechstein, L. (1853). *Deutsches Sagenbuch*. Leipzig, DE: G. Wigand.

Becker, R. (2017, April 25). An artificial womb successfully grew baby sheep—and humans could be next. Retrieved August 14, 2017 from https://www.theverge.com/2017/4/25/15421734/artificial-womb-fetus-biobag-uterus-lamb-sheep-birth-premie-preterm-infant

Benjamin, S. (2009). Chapter One: Blue Like Me. In V.G.J. Rajan & S. Bahun-Radunović (Eds.), *From Myth to Canvas: Appropriations of Myth in Women's Aesthetic Production*, pp. 11-22. Newcastle, UK: Cambridge Scholars Publishing.

Bergmann, M.S. (1992). *In the Shadow of Moloch: The Sacrifice of Children and Its Impact on Western Religions*. New York, NY: Columbia University Press.

Billman, J. (2017, March 13). How 1,600 People Went Missing from Our Public Lands Without a Trace. Retrieved September 13, 2017 from https://www.outsideonline.com/2164446/leave-no-trace

Bilodeaux, J. (2004, October). Raechel's Eyes - The Strange Case of an Apparent Hybrid: Part 2. *MUFON UFO Journal 438*, pp. 5-7.

Bird, S. (2017). *A Cross-Cultural Look at Child-Stealing Witches.* Tucson, AZ: University of Arizona Linguistics Circle.

Bitto, R. (2016, June 27). The Lechuza. Retrieved July 20, 2017 from http://mexicounexplained.com/the-lechuza/

Blache, M. (1999). Guaranitic Storytelling. In M.R. MacDonald, J.H. McDowell, L. Dégh, & B. Toelken (Eds.), *Traditional Storytelling Today: An International Sourcebook* (pp. 490-493). Chicago, IL: Fitzroy Dearborn Publishers.

Blacker, C. (1967). Supernatural Abductions in Japanese Folklore. *Asian Folklore Studies 26(2)*, pp. 111-147.

Blackman, W.H. (1998). *The Field Guide to North American Monsters.* New York, NY: Three Rivers Press.

Blakemore, E. (2017, January 26). Human-Pig Hybrids Created in the Lab—Here Are the Facts. Retrieved August 17, 2017 from http://news.nationalgeographic.com/2017/01/human-pig-hybrid-embryo-chimera-organs-health-science/

Blaxill, M.F. (November-December 2004). What's Going On? The Question of Time Trends in Autism. *Public Health Reports 119*, pp. 536-551.

Bloch, A.R. (2013). The Two Fonts of the Florence Baptistery and the Evolution of the Baptismal Rite in Florence, ca. 1200-1500. In H.M. Sonne de Torrens & M.A. Torrens (Eds.), *The Visual Culture of Baptism in the Middle Ages* (pp. 77-104) Surrey, UK: Ashgate Publishing Limited.

Bloecher, T. (1978, February). CE-III Report from Montvale, NJ: Preliminary Report. *MUFON UFO Journal 123*, pp. 4-7.

Blumer, T.J. (1985, Spring). Wild Indians and the Devil: The Contemporary Catawba Indian Spirit World. *American Indian Quarterly 9(2)*, pp. 149-168.

Boas, F. (1916). Tsimshian Mythology. *Thirty-First Annual Report of the Bureau of American Ethnology to the Secretary of the Smithsonian Institution: 1909-1910*, pp. 27-1037. Washington, DC: Government Printing Office.

Bogart (n.d.). *Oxford Living Dictionaries.* Retrieved May 31, 2017, from https://en.oxforddictionaries.com/definition/bogart

Boirayon, M. (2009) *Solomon Islands Mysteries.* Kempton, IL: Adventures Unlimited Press.

Bois, GJ.C. (2010). *Jersey Folklore & Superstitions, Vol. 2.* Milton Keynes, UK: AuthorHouse UK Ltd.

Booger. (n.d.). *Merriam-Webster*. Retrieved February 27, 2018 from https://www. merriam-webster.com/dictionary/booger

Bord, J. (2014). *Fairies: Real Encounters with Little People* [Kindle edition]. London, UK: Michael O'Mara Books. (Original work published 1998)

Bord, J., & Bord, C. (1978, November). A Case of Rabbit Snatching? *Flying Saucer Review 24*(3), pp. 16-17.

Bord, J., & Bord, C. (1989). *Unexplained Mysteries of the 20th Century*. Lincolnwood, IL: Contemporary Books.

Bord, J., & Bord, C. (2006). *Bigfoot Casebook Updated: Sightings and Encounters from 1818 to 2004*. Enumclaw, WA: Pinewinds Press.

Bottrell, W. (1873). *Traditions and Hearthside Stories of West Cornwall, Vol. 2*. Penzance, UK: Beare and Son.

Bourke, A. (1995, Autumn). Reading a Woman's Death: Colonial Text and Oral Tradition in Nineteenth-Century Ireland. *Feminist Studies 21(3)*, pp. 553-586.

Bowen, C. (Ed.). (1967, July-August). Mail Bag. *Flying Saucer Review 13*(4), pp. 18-20.

Bowen, C. (Ed.). (1978, February). World Round-Up. *Flying Saucer Review 23*(5), pp. 32-33.

Brandenburg, J.E. (1990, September). A Hypothesis of Reticulian Intentions and the Fallacy of Human Insignificance. *MUFON UFO Journal 269*, pp. 11-13.

Breatnach, D. (1993). *Chugat an Púca*. Dundalk, IE: Dundalgan Press.

Breedlove, S. (2015, June 7). Episode 52: with Daryl Colyer and Brian Brown. Retrieved September 8, 2017 from http://saswhat.podbean.com/e/episode-52-with-daryl-colyer-and-brian-brown/

Breen, R. (1980, Spring/Summer). The Ritual Expression of Inter Household Relationships in Ireland. *The Cambridge Journal of Anthropology 6(1/2 – Double Issue)*, pp. 33-59.

Briggs, K. (1976). *An Encyclopedia of Fairies: Hobgoblins, Brownies, Bogies, and Other Supernatural Creatures*. New York, NY: Pantheon Books.

Briggs, K. (1979). *Abbey Lubbers, Banshees & Boggarts*. New York, NY: Pantheon Books.

Briggs, K. (2002). *The Fairies in Tradition and Literature*. London, UK: Routledge. (Original work published 1967)

Bronson, B.H. (1959). *The Traditional Tunes of the Child Ballads, Vol. I*. Princeton, NJ: Princeton University Press.

Bruford, A. (1997). Trolls, Hillfolk, Finns, and Picts: The Identity of the Good Neighbors in Orkney and Shetland. In P. Narváez (Ed.), *The Good People: New Fairylore Essays* (pp. 116-141). Lexington, KY: The University Press of Kentucky.

Bryan, C.D.B. (1995). *Close Encounters of the Fourth Kind.* New York, NY: Penguin Group (Arkana).

Buccola, R. (2006). *Fairies, Fractious Women, and the Old Faith: Fairy Lore in Early Modern British Drama and Culture.* Selinsgrove, PA: Susquehanna University Press.

Buckingham, M.R. (2003, Spring). Aliens – Their Hidden Agenda. *Flying Saucers Review 48*(1), pp. 2-5.

Buehring, J.M. (1984, June). Invisible Barriers. *Flying Saucer Review 29*(5), pp. 19-22.

Bug. (n.d.). *Merriam-Webster.* Retrieved June 3, 2017 from https://www.merriam-webster.com/dictionary/bug

Bullard, T. (1987). *UFO Abductions: The Measure of A Mystery* (Vol. 1). Mount Rainier, MD: Fund for UFO Research.

Bullard, T. (1987). *UFO Abductions: The Measure of A Mystery* (Vol. 2). Mount Rainier, MD: Fund for UFO Research.

Burnette, T.K. (1999). *Nature's Secret Agents.* Marion, NC: Tom Burnette Publishing.

Burns, J.W. (1954, December). "My Search for B.C.'s Giant Indians." *Liberty Magazine,* pp. 38-39.

Buschmann, C., Langsdorf, G., & Lichtenthaller, H.K. (2009). Blue, Green, Red, and Far-Red Fluorescence Signatures of Plant Tissues, Their Multicolor Fluorescence Imaging, and Application for Agrofood Assessment. In M. Zude (Ed.), *Optical Monitoring of Fresh and Processed Agricultural Crops* (pp. 272-318). Boca Raton, FL: CRC Press.

Butler, G.R. (1997). The *Lutin* Tradition in French-Newfoundland Culture. In P. Narváez (Ed.), *The Good People: New Fairylore Essays* (pp. 5-21). Lexington, KY: The University Press of Kentucky.

Butler, J. (2017). The *Sídhe* and Fairy Forts. In S. Young & C. Houlbrook (Eds.), *Magical Folk: British and Irish Fairies: 500 AD to the Present* (Kindle Edition).

Cadieux, A. (2013, December 23). "The Bridgewater Triangle" vs "Monsters and Mysteries in America." Retrieved September 13, 2017 from http://thebridgewatertriangledocumentary.com/the-bridgewater-triangle-vs-monsters-and-mysteries-in-america/

Cameron, I. (1928). *A Highland Chapbook.* Stirling, UK: Observer Press.

Campbell, J.F. (1890). *Popular Tales of the West Highlands Vol. II.* London, UK: Alexander Gardner & Paisley.

Campbell, J.G. (1900). *Superstitions of the Highlands and Islands of Scotland.* Glasgow, UK: James Maclehose & Sons.

Campbell, J.G. (1910, July). The Origin of the Fairy Creed. *The Scottish Historical Review 7(28)*, pp. 364-376.

Carbery, M. (2010). *The Farm by Lough Gur: The Story of Mary Fogarty (Sissy O'Brien).* The Lilliput Press. (Original work published 1937)

Carpenter, J. (1993, October). Abduction Notes. *MUFON UFO Journal 306*, pp. 14-16.

Carpenter, J. (1994, June). Abduction Notes. *MUFON UFO Journal 314*, pp. 12-13.

Carpenter, J. (1994, November). False Memories and Imagination. *MUFON UFO Journal 319*, pp. 17-18.

Carpenter, J. (1995, July). Abduction Notes. *MUFON UFO Journal 327*, pp. 18-19.

Carpenter, J. (1997, February). Abduction Notes. *MUFON UFO Journal 346*, pp. 15-16.

Casteel, S. (1995, December). Ron Felber of "Searchers." *MUFON UFO Journal 332*, pp. 19-20.

Casteel, S. (2008). Fairies and Aliens. In T.G. Beckley (Ed.), *UFOs, Time Slips, Other Realms, and the Science of Fairies* (pp. 9-19) New Brunswick, N.J.: Timothy Green Beckley (Global Communications/Conspiracy Journal).

Castle of Spirits. (2001). Strange Disappearances. Retrieved September 13, 2017 from http://www.castleofspirits.com/strangediss.html

Cárthaigh, C.M. (1988, June). *Midwife to the Fairies: A Migratory Legend.* (master's thesis). The National University of Ireland, Dublin, IE.

Cefalo, A. (2013, March 25). Cleft Lip in the Middle Ages. Retrieved July 11, 2017 from https://andreacefalo.com/2013/03/25/cleft-lip-in-the-middle-ages/

Centers for Disease Control and Prevention. (2017, March 10). Autism Spectrum Disorder (ASD): Data & Statistics. Retrieved February 21, 2018 from https://www.cdc.gov/ncbddd/autism/data.html

Chalker, B. (1996). *The Oz Files.* Potts Point, AU: Duffey and Snellgrove.

Chalker, B. (2005). *Hair of the Alien.* New York, NY: Paraview.

Chen, I. (2015, October 7). Wide Awake: Why children with autism struggle with sleep. Retrieved December 7, 2017 from https://spectrumnews.org/features/deep-dive/wide-awake-why-children-with-autism-struggle-with-sleep/

Chernobrov, V. (2003). Case 392. Retrieved In A. Rosales (Ed.), *1978 Humanoid Sighting Reports.* Retrieved February 5, 2014 from http://www.ufoinfo.com/humanoid/humanoid-1978.pdf

Childress, D.H. (2010). *Yetis, Sasquatch, & Hairy Giants.* Gardena, CA: SCB Distributors.

Childs, M.H. (2008, January). Women in Ufology: Marilyn Henry Childs, PhD. *MUFON UFO Journal 477,* p. 8.

The Church of Ufology. (2011, June 19). Scarborough, Ontario, Canada. Retrieved August 27, 2017 from http://thechurchofufology.blogspot.com/2011/06/scarborough-ontario-canada.html

Clancy, S.A. (2005). *Abducted: How People Come to Believe They Were Kidnapped by Aliens.* Cambridge, MA: Harvard University Press.

Clark, J. (1990). *UFOs in the 1980s* (Vol. 1). Detroit, MI: Apogee Books.

Clark, J. (2006, July). "Small, Vulnerable ETs": The Green Children of Woolpit. *Science Fiction Studies 33(2),* pp. 209-229.

Clear, C. (1999). *Reaching for Reality: Seven Incredible True Stories of Alien Abduction.* San Antonio, TX: Consciousness Now, Inc.

Clelland, M. (2015). *The Messengers: Owls, Synchronicity and the UFO Abductee.* New York: Richard Dolan Press.

Clelland, M. (2018). *Stories from the Messengers: Owls, UFOs and a Deeper Reality.* New York: Richard Dolan Press.

Clore, D. (2015). Flying Saucers Stink: Alien Odors and Supernatural Smells. In D. Clore, *The Unspeakable and Others.* Odense, Denmark: H. Harksen Productions, pp. 293-309.

CNN Library. (2017, April 23). *Missing Children Fast Facts.* Retrieved May 30, 2017 from http://www.cnn.com/2013/10/22/us/missing-children-fast-facts

Cockayne, T.O. (1865). *Leechdoms, Wortcunnning, and Starcraft of Early England, Vol. 2.* London, UK: Longman, Green, Longman, Roberts, and Green.

Coddington, R.H. (1997, May). The UFO Press. *MUFON UFO Journal 349,* p. 15-16.

Coleman, L. & Clark, J. (1999). *Cryptozoology A to Z.* New York, NY: Fireside.

Coleman, L., & Huyghe, P. (2006). *The Field Guide to Bigfoot and Other Mystery Primates.* San Antonio, TS: Anomalist Books.

Coleman, L. (2003). *Bigfoot! The True Story of Apes in America.* New York, NY: Paraview Pocket Books.

Coleman, L. (2002). *Mothman and Other Curious Encounters*. New York, NY: Paraview Press (3rd ed.).

Coleman, L. (2013). Twilight Language. Retrieved September 1, 2017 from http://copycateffect.blogspot.com/

Collier, A.L. (2016). *Lilith: The Legend of the First Woman*. Woodstock, ON: Devoted Publishing.

Collins, A. (1978, June). The Aveley Abduction: Part 3. *Flying Saucer Review 24*(1), pp. 5-15.

Collins, A. (2012). *LightQuest: Your Guide to Seeing and Interacting with UFOs, Mystery Lights, and Plasma Intelligences*. Memphis, TN: Eagle Wing Books, Inc.

Conaill, M.Ó. (2017). A Changeling. Retrieved July 5, 2017 from http://www.duchas.ie/en/cbes/4758565/4754979

Connelly, D. (1998, May). Editor's Note to "Buzz, Buzz, Who's There?" by D. Bahor. *MUFON UFO Journal 361*, p. 6.

Connelly, D. (1998, July). Ufology Profile: Budd Hopkins. *MUFON UFO Journal 363*, pp. 10-11.

Connelly, D. (1999, February). Ufology Profile: Beverly Trout Wears Two Hats: Investigator And..... *MUFON UFO Journal 370*, pp. 14-16.

Connelly, D. (2000, August). Symposium Speakers Cover Diverse Topics. *MUFON UFO Journal 388*, pp. 3-7.

Connelly, D. (2001, September). September 19th Marks 40th Anniversary of the Classic Betty & Barney Hill Case. *MUFON UFO Journal 401*, pp. 3-6.

Connelly, D. (Ed.). (2002, August). Speakers Cover Wide Range of Topics. *MUFON UFO Journal 412*, pp. 3-12.

Connelly, D. (Ed.). (2004, August). 2004 MUFON Symposium Speakers Explore the Technological Evidence. *MUFON UFO Journal 436*, pp. 8-11.

Conway, D.J. (2009). *A Witch's Travel Guide to Astral Realms*. Woodbury, MN: Llewellyn Publications. (Original work published 1995)

Conway, G. (n.d.). Case 61. Retrieved In A. Rosales (Ed.), *1981 Humanoid Sighting Reports*. Retrieved February 5, 2014 from http://www.ufoinfo.com/humanoid/humanoid-1981.pdf

Conway, G. (n.d.). Case 175. Retrieved In A. Rosales (Ed.), *1980 Humanoid Sighting Reports*. Retrieved February 5, 2014 from http://www.ufoinfo.com/humanoid/humanoid-1980.pdf

Conway, G. (1987, June). Another "Observing Eye" in the House? *Flying Saucer Review 32*(4), p. 28.

Conway, G. (1989, March). Report from British Columbia, Canada: An Emerging Epidemic? *Flying Saucer Review 34*(1), pp. 1-4.

Conway, G. (2002, June). Not a Fairy Story. Retrieved September 14, 2017 from http://www.ufobc.ca/Experiencer/fairy_v2.htm

Coulson, L. (2017). Trows and Trownie Wives. In S. Young & C. Houlbrook (Eds.), *Magical Folk: British and Irish Fairies: 500 AD to the Present* (Kindle Edition).

Courtney, M.A. (1887). Cornish Folk Lore Part III [Continued]. *The Folk-Lore Journal 5(3)*, pp. 177-220.

Cowley, S., & Cox, G. (2012). *Searching for Bigfoot*. New York, NY: The Rosen Publishing Group.

Crawford, F. (1991, December). The Revealing Science of Ufology: An Anatomy of Abduction Correlations. *MUFON UFO Journal 284*, pp. 10-15.

Crain, T.S. (1985, October). UFO Lifting Power. *MUFON UFO Journal 210*, 3-4, 16.

Creighton, G. (1965, January). The Most Amazing Case of All: Part I – A Brazilian Farmer's Story. *Flying Saucer Review 11*(1), pp. 13-17.

Creighton, G. (Ed.). (1977, April). Some Recent Spanish Reports. (G. Creighton, Ed.). *Flying Saucer Review 22*(6), pp. 27-29.

Creighton, G. (1984, Spring). Spanish Woman Recalls Abduction 36 Years Ago. *Flying Saucer Review 29*(4), pp. 8-9.

Creighton, G. (1990) The UFO Landings at Voronezh. In T. Good (Ed.), *The UFO Report 1991* (pp. 64-79). London, UK: Sidgwick & Jackson, Ltd.

Creighton, G. (1995, Autumn). Three Boys Abducted in Argentina (1994). *Flying Saucer Review 40*(3), pp. 18-19.

Cressy, J. (1996). Mysticism and the Near-Death Experience. In L.W. Bailey & J. Yates (Eds.), *The Near-Death Experience: A Reader* (pp. 369-384). Abingdon, UK: Routledge.

Croker, T.C. (1825). *Fairy Legends & Traditions of the South of Ireland Part I*. London, UK: John Murray.

Croker, T.C. (1828). *Fairy Legends & Traditions of the South of Ireland Part II*. London, UK: John Murray.

Croker, T.C. (1828). *Fairy Legends & Traditions of the South of Ireland Part III*. London, UK: John Murray.

Crookshank, M. (1909, September 30). Old-Time Survivals in Remote Norwegian Dales. *Folklore 20(3)*, pp. 313-336.

Curran, B. (2004). *Celtic Lore and Legend.* Franklin Lakes, NJ: The Career Press, Inc.

Curtis, M.G., Linares, S.T., & Antoniewics, L. (2014). *Glass' Office Gynecology* (7th ed). Philadelphia, PA: Wolter Kluwer Health.

Cutchin, J. (2015). *A Trojan Feast: The Food and Drink Offerings of Aliens, Faeries, and Sasquatch.* San Antonio, TX: Anomalist Books.

Cutchin, J. (2016). *The Brimstone Deceit.* San Antonio, TX: Anomalist Books.

Cutler, C.L. (2002). *Tracks that Speak: The Legacy of Native American Words in North American Culture.* Boston, MA: Houghton Mifflin Company.

Cyr, D. (2009, August 3). Abduction de masse! Retrieved August 10, 2017 from https://donald059.wordpress.com/2009/08/03/abduction-de-masse/

Daegling, D.J. (2004). *Bigfoot Exposed: An Anthropologist Examines America's Enduring Legend.* Walnut Creek, CA: Altamira Press.

David, A. (2017, March 23). Charm the Water: Episode 34 – Gordon White. Retrieved June 29, 2017 from http://www.charmthewater.com/podcast/2017/3/23/episode-34-gordon-white

Davis, E. (2013, October 13). Expanding Mind – Autistic Imagination. Retrieved September 21, 2017 from http://expandingmind.podbean.com/2013/10/13/expanding-mind-autistic-imagination-101313/

Dean, C. (2012). The Boo Hag. Retrieved June 26, 2017 from http://www.carolinaconjure.com/the-boo-hag.html

DeLuke, D.M., & Haug, R.H. (Eds.). (2014, September). *Clinical Review Articles - Atlas of the Oral and Maxillofacial Surgery Clinics of North America: Syndromes of the Head and Neck.* Philadelphia, PA: Elsevier.

Denham, M.A. (1895). *The Denham Tracts: A Collection of Folklore by Michael Aislabie Denham.* J. Hardy (Ed.). London, UK: The Folklore Society.

Dennett, P. (1996, October). UFO Healings. *MUFON UFO Journal 342*, pp. 3-9.

Dennett, P. (1999). *UFOs Over Topanga Canyon.* St. Paul, MN: Llewellyn Publications.

Dennett, P. (2001, November). Why Abductees Don't Talk. *MUFON UFO Journal 403*, pp. 18-20.

Dennett, P. (2003, July). Conversations with Extraterrestrials. *MUFON UFO Journal 423*, pp. 3-6.

Dennis, C., & Whitman, P. (1997). *The Millennium Children.* Clearwater, FL: Rainbows Unlimited.

DeSouza, J. (2016). *The Extra-Dimensionals: True Tales And Concepts of Alien Visitors.* Oro Valley, AZ: TAMA Publishing.

De Visser, M.W. (1908). The Tengu. *Transactions of the Asiatic Society of Japan XXXVI (Part II)*, pp. 25-99. London, UK: Kegan Paul, Truebner & Co., Ltd.

Dodds, E.R. (1951). *The Greeks and the Irrational.* Los Angeles, CA: Berkeley.

Doniger, W., & Spinner, G. (1998, Winter). Misconceptions: Female Imaginations and Male Fantasies in Parental Imprinting. *Daedalus 127(1)*, pp. 97-129.

Dorman, R.M. (1881). *The Origin of Primitive Superstitions and Their Development into the Worship of Spirits and Doctrine of Spiritual Agency Among the Aborigines of America.* Philadelphia, PA: Lippincott & Co.

Dorson, R.W. (1962). *Folk Legends of Japan.* Tokyo, JP: Charles E. Tuttle Co.

Drake, N. (1996, October). *Polymeric Materials for Electrostatic Applications.* London, UK: Rapra Technology.

Druffel, A. (1991, November). "Missing Fetus" Case Solved. *MUFON UFO Journal 283*, pp. 8-12.

Druffel, A. (1998). *How to Defend Yourself Against Alien Abduction.* New York, NY: Three Rivers Press.

Druzhko, S. (2005). Case 33. In A. Rosales (Ed.), *1986 Humanoid Sighting Reports.* Retrieved February 5, 2014 from http://www.ufoinfo.com/humanoid/humanoid-1986.pdf

Dubhthaigh, P.Ó. (2017). A Folk-Tale of Ballyboden Rathfarnham – The Year Following the Famine. Retrieved September 7, 2017 from https://www.duchas.ie/en/cbes/4428228/4387366/4458585

Duncan, L.L., Whelan, B., Wheln, A., Lynch, M., McVittle, E., & Drumkeeran. (1896, June). Fairy Beliefs and Other Folklore Notes from County Leitrim. *Folklore 7(2)*, pp. 161-183.

Dunham, M. (May 31, 2008). 'Little people' e-mail zips through rural Alaska. Retrieved July 18, 2017 from https://groups.yahoo.com/neo/groups/mythfolk/conversations/messages/4626 (original article posted to http://www.adn.com/life/story/422883.html)

Dunican, I. (2017). Changelings (continued). Retrieved June 8, 2017 from http://www.duchas.ie/en/cbes/4921674/4889287

Dworski, L. (2015, October 29). Slavic Mythology from Poland (Part 4): BOGINKI. Retrieved June 2, 2017 from https://lamusdworski.wordpress.com/2015/10/29/polish-mythology-boginki

Eberhart, G.M. (2002). *Mysterious Creatures: A Guide to Cryptozoology.* Santa Barbara, CA: ABC-CLIO, Inc.

Eberly, S. (1997). Fairies and the Folklore of Disability: Changelings, Hybrids and the Solitary Fairy. In P. Narváez (Ed.), *The Good People: New Fairylore Essays* (pp. 227-250). Lexington, KY: The University Press of Kentucky.

Eberly, S.S. (1988). Fairies and the Folklore of Disability: Changelings, Hybrids and the Solitary Fairy. *Folklore 99 (1)*, pp. 58-77.

Edwards, A. (1988). *On the UFO Road Again.* Seattle, WA.: UFO Contact Center International.

Ellis, A.B. (1894). *Yoruba-Speaking Peoples of the Slave Coast of West Africa.* London, UK: Chapman and Hall, Ltd.

El-Shamy, H.M. (1980). *Folktales of Egypt.* Chicago, IL: The University of Chicago Press.

Emmons, C.F. (1997). *At the Threshold: UFOs, Science, and the New Age.* Leland, NC: Wild Flower Press.

Engineering 360. (2017). Radar Absorbing Materials Information. Retrieved August 24, 2017 from http://www.globalspec.com/learnmore/materials_chemicals_adhesives/electrical_optical_specialty_materials/radar_absorbing_materials_structures_ram_ras

Evans Wentz, W.Y. (1911). *The Fairy-Faith in Celtic Countries.* London, UK: Henry Frowde.

Eveleth, R. (2013, June 3). Legendary Human-Eating Bird Was Real, Probably Could Have Eaten People. Retrieved February 23, 2018 from https://www.smithsonianmag.com/smart-news/legendary-human-eating-bird-was-real-probably-could-have-eaten-people-89257268/

Ey, A. (1862). *Harzmärchenbuch; oder, Sagen und Märchen aus dem Oberharze.* Stade, DE: Verlag von Fr. Steudel.

Fanthorpe, L., & Fanthorpe, P. (1997). *The World's Greatest Unsolved Mysteries.* Toronto, CA: Hounslow Press.

Farrell, E. (2013). *'A Most Diabolical Deed': Infanticide and Irish Society, 1850-1900.* Manchester, UK: Manchester University Press.

Flaherty, R.P. (2010, November). "These Art They": ET-Human Hybridization and the New Daemonology. *Nova Religio: The Journal of Alternative and Emergent Religions 14*(2), pp. 84-105.

Frankel V.E. (2015). *The Symbolism and Sources of Outlander: The Scottish Fairies, Folklore, Ballads, Magic and Meaning That Inspired the Series.* Jefferson, NC: McFarland & Company, Inc.

Feinberg, T.E., & Roane, D.M. (2001). Visual Aspects of Anosognosia, Confabulation and Misidentification. In F. Boller, J. Grafman, & M. Behrmann (Eds.), *Handbook of Neuropsychology 2nd Edition: Volume 4 – Disorders of Visual Behavior* (pp. 143-158). Amsterdam, NEL Elsevier Science B.V.

Feindt, C.W. (2010). *UFOs and Water: Physical Effects of UFOs on Water Through Accounts by Eyewitnesses.* Bloomington, IN: Xlibris Corporation.

Fetch. (n.d.). *Oxford Living Dictionaries.* Retrieved June 6, 2017 from https://en.oxforddictionaries.com/definition/fetch

Fleming, M. (2002). *Not of This World: Creatures of the Supernatural in Scotland.* Edinburgh, UK: Mercat Press Ltd.

Forbes, T.R. (1962, April). Midwifery and Witchcraft. *Journal of the History of Medicine and Allied Sciences 17(2),* pp. 264-283.

Ford, H.J. (1915). *The Scotch-Irish in America.* Princeton, NJ: Princeton University Press.

Fort, C. (1919). *The Book of the Damned.* New York, NY: Boni and Liveright.

Forth, G. (2008). *Images of the Wildman in Southeast Asia: An Anthropological Perspective.* Abingdon, UK: Routledge.

Foster, M. (2000, May 23). Bigfoot Roaming the Wilds—With A Human Child! *Weekly World News,* p. 31.

Foster, M.D. (1998). The Metamorphosis of the Kappa: Transformation of Folklore to Folklorism in Japan. *Asian Folklore Studies 57(1),* pp. 1-24.

Fowler, O. (2003, Autumn). An Alien Base in Siberia & Alien Contact. *Flying Saucer Review 48*(3), pp. 16-17.

Fowler, R.E. (1981). *Casebook of a UFO Investigator.* Upper Saddle River, NJ: Prentice Hall Trade.

Frankfurter, D. (2006). Fetus Magic and Sorcery Fears in Roman Egypt. *Greek, Roman, and Byzantine Studies 46,* pp. 37-62.

Franklin, R. (2005). *Baby Lore: Superstitions & Old Wives Tales from the World Over.* West Sussex, UK: Diggory Press.

Friedman, S., & Marden, K. (2015). *True Stories of Alien Abduction.* New York, NY: The Rosen Publishing Group.

Frola, R. (2002, April). AUFORN Complied Sighting Reports – Issue 27. Retrieved August 18, 2017 from http://www.ufoinfo.com/ufoicq/auforn27.shtml

Frost, W.H. (1900). *Fairies and Folk of Ireland.* New York, NY: Charles Scribner's Sons.

Gabler, E. (2014, June 2). Charges detail Waukesha pre-teens' attempt to kill classmate. Retrieved May 30, 2017 from http://archive.jsonline.com/news/crime/waukesha-police-2-12-year-old-girls-plotted-for-months-to-kill-friend-b99282655z1-261534171.html

Gaffiot, F. (1934). *Dictionnaire Latin Français.* Paris, FR: Hachette.

Gallaher. (2017). The Changeling (continued). Retrieved July 3, 2017 from http://www.duchas.ie/en/cbes/5009189/4996096/5104919

GardenStone. (2011). *The Mercury-Woden Complex.* Norderstedt, DE: Books on Demand GmbH.

Gary & Ruth. (2017, May 1). Celtic Myth Podshow Special 43: *Folklore, Fairies, Cold Iron of Sussex and Puck of Pook's Hill.* Retrieved June 29, 2017 from http://celticmythpodshow.com/Shownotes/episodeSP43.php

Gay, D.E. (1988). Anglo-Saxon Metrical Charm 3 Against a Dwarf: A Charm Against Witch-Riding? *Folklore 99(2),* pp. 174-177.

Germer, W. (2017, February 22). Sasquatch Chronicles Radio // SC EP: 11 The 'Siege' at Honobia. Retrieved September 5, 2017 from https://www.youtube.com/watch?v=s_izA6N4x-A

Germer, W. (2017, June 7). Sasquatch Chronicles Radio // SC EP: 273 The Eyeshine. Retrieved September 5, 2017 from https://www.youtube.com/watch?v=3U9DtCapSZc

Germer, W. (2017, July 23). Sasquatch Chronicles Radio // SC EP: 345 A Hunter's Encounter. Retrieved September 7, 2017 from https://www.youtube.com/watch?v=_cseD8Ohqso

Glenn, J., & Larsen, E.F. (2015). *Unbored Adventure.* New York, NY: Bloomsbury USA.

Goldfader, L. (1992, Summer). The Traumatic Abduction Story of Alvina Scott (Canada), and Another Foetus Mystery! *Flying Saucer Review 37(2),* pp. 22-23.

Goodey, C.F., & Stainton, T. (2001, June). Intellectual Disability and the Myth of the Changeling Myth. *Journal of the History of the Behavioral Sciences* 37(3), pp. 223-240.

Gordon, S. (1997). *The Book of Curses: True Tales of Voodoo, Hoodoo and Hex.* Leicester, UK: Brockhampton Press. (Original work published 1994)

Gordon, S. (2010). *Silent Invasion: The Pennsylvania UFO-Bigfoot Casebook.* R. Marsh (Ed.). Greensburg, PA: Stan Gordon Productions.

Green, R.F. (2016). *Elf Queens and Holy Friars: Fairy Beliefs and the Medieval Church.* Philadelphia, PA: University of Pennsylvania Press.

Granchi, I. (1986, January). The Case of Antônio Álves Ferreira – Physical Experiences, and Eleven Alleged Trips to a Strange Planet! *Flying Saucer Review 31*(2), pp. 6-12.

Green, L.G. (1967). *On Wings of Fire.* Cape Town, SA: Howard Timmins.

Gregor, W. (1881). *Notes on the Folk-Lore of the North-East of Scotland.* London, UK: Folk-Lore Society.

Gribble, B. (1987, December). Looking Back. *MUFON UFO Journal 236*, pp. 17-18.

Gribble, B. (1989, April). Looking Back. *MUFON UFO Journal 252*, pp. 27-28.

Gribble, B. (1990, March). Looking Back. *MUFON UFO Journal 263*, pp. 21-22.

Grimm, J. (2003). *Deutsche Mythologie.* Wiesbaden, DE: Fourier Verlag. (Original work published 1835)

Grimm, J., & Grimm, W. (1812). *Kinder- und Hausmärchen.* Stuttgart, DE: Deutsche Verlags-Anstalt.

Grinker, R.R. (2007). *Unstrange Minds: Remapping the World of Autism.* Philadelphia, PA: Basic Books.

Gross, P. (2009, October 21). URECAT - UFO Related Entities Catalog: Summer 1944, Toulon-Sur-Arroux, Saone-Et-Loire, France, Madeleine Arnoux. Retrieved October 24, 2017 from https://ufologie.patrickgross.org/ce3/1944-france-toulonsurarroux.htm#ma1

Guiley, R.E. (2006). *The Encyclopedia of Magic and Alchemy.* New York, NY: Facts On File, Inc.

Guiley, R.E. (2007). *The Encyclopedia of Ghosts and Spirits* (3rd ed). New York, NY: Facts on File, Inc. (Original work published 1992)

Guiley, R.E. (2009). *The Encyclopedia of Demons & Demonology.* New York, NY: Facts on File, Inc.

Guiley, R.E. (2008). *The Encyclopedia of Witches, Witchcraft, and Wicca* (3rd ed). New York, NY: Facts on File, Inc. (Original work published 1992).

Guiley, R.E. (2010). *Mysteries, Legends, and Unexplained Phenomena: Fairies.* New York, NY: Chelsea House.

Guiley, R.E., & Imbrogno, P.J. (2011). *The Vengeful Djinn.* Woodbury, MN: Llewellyn Publications.

Guiley, R.E. (2013). *The Djinn Connection.* New Milford, CT: Visionary Living, Inc.

Guiney, L.I. (1888). *Brownies and Bogles.* Boston, MA: D. Lothrop Company.

Guma, J. (1997, Spring). Highlights from Large Batches of Spanish-American Press Clippings Received from Jane Guma (Jane Thomas) in November 1994, and June 1995. (G. Creighton, Trans.). *Flying Saucer Review 42*(1), pp. 8-12.

Gwyndaf, R. (1997). Fairylore: Memorates and Legends from the Welsh Oral Tradition. In P. Narváez (Ed.), *The Good People: New Fairylore Essays* (pp. 155-195). Lexington, KY: The University Press of Kentucky.

Hale, R. (n.d.). Case 84. In A. Rosales (Ed.), *1999 Humanoid Sighting Reports.* Retrieved February 5, 2014 from http://www.ufoinfo.com/humanoid/humanoid-1999.pdf

Hall, A. (2007). *Elves in Anglo-Saxon England: Matters of Belief, Health, Gender and Identity.* Rochester, NY: Boydell & Brewer.

Hall, M.A. (2004). *Thunderbirds: America's Living Legends of Giant Birds.* New York, NY: Paraview Press.

Hancock, G. (2007). *Supernatural.* New York, NY: The Disinformation Company, Ltd.

Hansen, W. (2002). *Ariadne's Thread: A Guide to International Tales Found in Classical Literature.* Ithaca, NY: Cornell University Press.

Harmeyer, A.J. (1947, March). Devil Stories from Las Vegas, New Mexico. *Hoosier Folklore 6(1)*, pp. 37-39.

Harper, D. (2017). Online Etymology Dictionary: Panic. Retrieved September 19, 2017 from http://www.etymonline.com/index.php?term=panic

Harpur, P. (2003). *Daimonic Reality: A Field Guide to the Otherworld.* Ravensdale, WA: Pure Winds Press.

Harte, J. (2017). Fairy Barrows and Cunning Folk. In S. Young & C. Houlbrook (Eds.), *Magical Folk: British and Irish Fairies: 500 AD to the Present* (Kindle Edition). London, UK; Gibson Square.

Hartland, E.S. (1886). The Outcast Child. *The Folk-Lore Journal 4(4)*, pp. 308-349.

Hartland, E.S. (1891). *The Science of Fairytales: An Inquiry into Fairy Mythology.* London, UK: Walter Scott.

Harvey, S.B. (2000, December). Shamanism and Alien Abduction: A Comparative Study. (Unpublished Master's Thesis). Edith Cowan University, Perth, AU.

Haskew, P., & Donnellan, A.M. (1993). *Emotional Maturity and Well-Being: Psychological Lessons of Facilitated Communication.* Madison, WI: DRI Press.

Hauck, D.W. (2002). *Haunted Places: The National Directory*. New York, NY: Penguin Books.

Hazlitt, W.C. (1905). *Brand's Popular Antiquities of Great Britain, Vol. I*. In J. Brand & H. Ellis (Eds.). London, UK: Reeves and Turner.

Heavey, M. (2017, September 28). Food, Folklore and Fairies. [Live lecture].

Heider, G.C. (1985). *The Cult of Molek: A Reassessment*. Sheffield, England: University of Sheffield Department of Biblical Studies.

Henderson, L., & Cowan, E.J. (2001). *Scottish Fairy Belief*. East Lothian, UK: Tuckwell Press.

Henderson, W. (1879). *Notes of the Folk-Lore of the Northern Countries of England and the Borders*. London, UK: Folk-Lore Society.

Herbstritt, M.R. (1973, May). Pennsylvania Housewives Report UFO. *Skylook 66*, p. 14.

Heussler, H., Polnay, L., Marder, E., Standen, P., Lyn U, C., & Butler, N. (2001, September 15). Prevalence of autism in early 1970s may have been underestimated. *British Medical Journal 323*(7313), p. 633.

Hewlett, M. (1913). *Lore of Prosperine*. New York, NY: Charles Scribner's Sons.

Hickey, E.M. (1938). Medical Superstitions in Ireland. *Ulster Medical Journal 7*, pp. 268-270.

Higbee, D. (1995, September). Abductee Brainwashing. *MUFON UFO Journal 329*, pp. 10-12.

Hind, C. (Ed.). (January 1997). The Unexplained! *UFO Afrinews 15*, pp. 28-30.

Hofberg, H. (1893). *Swedish Fairy Tales*. (W.H. Myers, Trans.). Chicago, IL: W.B. Conkey Company.

Holland, E. (2006). *Holland's grimoire of Magickal Correspondences*. Franklin Lakes, NJ: New Page Books.

Holloway, V. (2017, June 15). Fairy Folklore: Come Away, O Human Child. Retrieved December 13, 2017 from http://folklorethursday.com/legends/come-away-o-human-child/#sthash.xXRJkDNb.h2HjS5Lf.dpbs

Holzer, H. (1976). *The UFOnauts*. New York, NY: Fawcett Books.

Hooykaas, J (1960). The Changeling in Balinese Folklore and Religion. *Bijdragen tot de Taal-, Land- en Volkenkunder 116(4)*, pp. 424-426.

Hopkins, B. (1981). *Missing Time*. New York, NY: Richard Marek Publishers.

Hopkins, B. (1981, February). Probable Childhood Abduction. *MUFON UFO Journal 156*, pp. 4-6.

Hopkins, B. (1986, February). A Childhood Abduction? *MUFON UFO Journal 214*, pp. 15-16.

Hopkins, B. (1986, March). A Childhood Abduction? Part II. *MUFON UFO Journal, 215*, pp. 14-15.

Hopkins, B. (1987, March). Intruders: UFO Abductions. *MUFON UFO Journal 227*, pp. 3-4.

Hopkins, B. (1990, March). Thoughts On Psychiatrists & UFO Investigators. *MUFON UFO Journal 263*, pp. 13-14, 17.

Hopkins, B. (1994). The Abduction Experience: Acquisition. In A. Pritchard, D.E. Pritchard, J.E. Mack, P. Kasey, & C. Yapp (Eds.), *Alien Discussions: Proceedings of the Abduction Study Conference* (pp. 49-52). Cambridge, UK: North Cambridge Press.

Hopkins, B. (1994). The Hopkins Image Recognition Test (HIRT) for Children. In A. Pritchard, D.E. Pritchard, J.E. Mack, P. Kasey, & C. Yapp (Eds.), *Alien Discussions: Proceedings of the Abduction Study Conference* (pp. 127-134). Cambridge, UK: North Cambridge Press.

Hopkins, B. (1996, Winter). Abduction and Deception. *Flying Saucer Review 41*(4), pp. 12-15.

Hopkins, B. & Rainey, C. (2003). *Sight Unseen*. New York, NY: Atria Books.

Houlbrook, C. (2017). The Seelie and Unseelie Courts. In S. Young & C. Houlbrook (Eds.), *Magical Folk: British and Irish Fairies: 500 AD to the Present* (Kindle Edition).

House of Commons and Commande. (1863, February 5-July 28). *The Census of Ireland for the Year 1861: Part III – Vital Statistics, Vol. I: Reports and Tables Relating to the Status of Disease*. Dublin, IE: Alexander Thom.

Hunt, B. (1912). *Folk Tales of Breffny*. London, UK: Macmillan.

Hunt, R. (1871). *Popular Romances of the West of England: The Drolls, Traditions, and Superstitions of Old Cornwall*. London, UK: John Camden Hotten (2nd ed.).

Hunt, R. (1903). *Popular Romances of the West of England: The Drolls, Traditions, and Superstitions of Old Cornwall*. London, UK: Chatto and Windus (3rd ed.).

Husband, T., & Gilmore-House, G. (1980). *The Wild Man: Medieval Myth and Symbolism*. New York, NY: The Metropolitan Museum of Art.

Hynek, J.A. (1970, March/April). Commentary on the AAAS Symposium. *Flying Saucer Review 16*(2), pp. 3-5.

Jacobs, D. (1993). *Secret Life.* New York, NY: Simon and Schuster.

Jacobs, D. (1994). Subsequent Procedures. In A. Pritchard, D.E. Pritchard, J.E. Mack, P. Kasey, & C. Yapp (Eds.), *Alien Discussions: Proceedings of the Abduction Study Conference* (pp. 64-68). Cambridge, UK: North Cambridge Press.

Jacobs, D. (1999). *The Threat.* New York, NY: Fireside. (Original work published 1998)

Jacobs, D. (2015). *Walking Among Us: The Alien Plan to Control Humanity.* San Francisco, CA: Disinformation Books.

Jacobs, J. (Ed.). (1892). *Celtic Fairy Tales.* London, UK: David Nutt.

Jacobs, J. (1894). *More English Fairy Tales.* London, UK: G. Putnam's Sons.

Jarvis, S. (Ed.). (1992). *Dark Zones.* New York, NY: Warner Books.

Jasek, M. (n.d.). A Similar Encounter by Jonah. Retrieved August 9, 2017 from http://www.ufobc.ca/Beyond/asimilarencounter.htm

Jeffrey, M. (n.d.). Case 266. In A. Rosales (Ed.), *1995 Humanoid Sighting Reports.* Retrieved February 5, 2014 from http://www.ufoinfo.com/humanoid/humanoid-1995.pdf

Jenkins, R.P. (1997). Witches and Fairies: Supernatural Aggression and Deviance Among the Irish Peasantry. In P. Narváez (Ed.), *The Good People: New Fairylore Essays* (pp. 302-335). Lexington, KY: The University Press of Kentucky.

Jestice, P.G. (2000). *Encyclopedia of Irish Spirituality.* Santa Barabara, CA: ABC-CLIO, Inc.

Jha, A. (2012, October 17). Why Crying Babies are So Hard to Ignore. Retrieved September 5, 2017 from https://www.theguardian.com/science/2012/oct/17/crying-babies-hard-ignore

Johari, H. (2000). *Ayurvedic Healing Cuisine: 200 Vegetarian Recipes for health, Balance, and Longevity.* Rochester, VT: Healing Arts Press. (Original work published in 1994)

Johnson, M.T. (2014). *Seeing Fairies: From the Lost Archives of the Fairy Investigation Society, Authentic Reports of Fairies in Modern Times.* San Antonio, TX: Anomalist Books.

Jones, B. (1977, June). New Ohio Abduction Case. *MUFON UFO Journal 115*, pp. 9-10.

Jozuka, E. (2016, September 22). *Aboriginal Australians are Earth's oldest civilization: DNA study.* Retrieved May 30, 2017 from http://www.cnn.com/2016/09/22/asia/indigenous-australians-earths-oldest-civilization

Kaftal, G. (1943, June). An Apocryphal Legend Relating to the Birth of Several Saints. *Folklore 54(2)*, pp. 308-309.

Kassinger, R. (2003). *Iron and Steel: From Thor's Hammer to the Space Shuttle*. Brookfield, CT: Twenty-First Century Books.

Keel, J. (1971). *Our Haunted Planet*. London, UK: Neville Spearman, Ltd.

Keel, J. (1976). *The Mothman Prophecies*. New York, NY: Signet Books.

Keel, J. (2002). *The Complete Guide to Mysterious Beings*. New York, NY: Tom Doherty Associates, LLC. (Original work published 1970 as *Strange Creatures from Time and Space*)

Keel, J. (2016). *Anomaly: An Irregular Newsletter Edited by John Keel*. Martinez, CA: Paranoia Publishing. (Original works published 1969-1974)

Keightley, T. (1828). *The Fairy Mythology*. London, UK: William Harrison Ainsworth.

Kelleher, C.A. & Knapp, G. (2005). *Hunt for the Skinwalker: Science Confronts the Unexplained at a Remote Ranch*. New York, NY: Paraview Pocket Books.

Kelly. (2015). Weird Spiritual Practices: What's Up With The Red String? Retrieved June 26, 2017 from http://blog.sivanaspirit.com/spiritual-red-string/

Kennedy, P. (1866). *Legendary Fictions of the Irish Celts*. London, UK: Macmillan and Co.

Kenny, A. (2004, June). Western Arrernte Pmere Kwetethe Spirits. *Oceania 74(4)*, pp. 276-288.

Kerner, N. (2010). *Grey Aliens and the Harvesting of Souls*. Rochester, VT: Bear & Company.

Kets de Vries, M.F.R. (2014). *Talking to the Shaman Within: Musings On Hunting*. Bloomington, IN: iUniverse.

Kirby, E.J. (2014, June 20). Why Icelanders are wary of elves living beneath the rocks. Retrieved September 25, 2017 from http://www.bbc.com/news/magazine-27907358

Kirk, R. (1893). *The Secret Commonwealth of Elves, Fauns, & Fairies*. London, UK: D. Nutt.

Klarer, E. (2009). *Beyond the Light Barrier: The Autobiography of Elizabeth Klarer*. Flagstaff, AZ: Light Technology Publishing. (Original work published 1980)

Klintberg, B.A. (1972). *Svenska Folksägner*. Stockholm, SE: Norstedts.

Knapp, G. (2015, September 12). Missing 411: Urban Disappearances. Part 2 of 4. Retrieved September 13, 2017 from https://www.youtube.com/watch?v=2Cs8r8RTrew &feature=youtu.be&t=2234

Kolomiets, I. (2003). Case 326. In A. Rosales (Ed.), *1968 Humanoid Sighting Reports*. Retrieved February 5, 2014 from http://www.ufoinfo.com/humanoid/humanoid-1968. pdf

Koltuv, B.B. (1986). *The Book of Lilith*. York Beach, ME: Nicolas-Hays, Inc.

Kosloski, P. (2017, February 2017). 3 Saints Who May Have Had Autism Spectrum Disorder. Retrieved September 21, 2017 from https://aleteia.org/2017/02/08/3-saints-who-may-have-had-autism-spectrum-disorder/

Kowalewski, D. (2015). *Death Walker: Shamanic Psychopomps, Earthbound Ghosts, and Helping Spirits in the Afterlife Realm*. Bloomington, IN: iUniverse.

Kropej, M. (2012). *Supernatural Beings from Slovenian Myth and Folktales*. Ljubljana, SI: Scientific Research Centre of the Slovenian Academy of Sciences and Arts.

Kroth, J. (2017). *Extraterrestrial Contacts: Roswell Foil, UFOs, and How They Alter Our Understanding of the Modern World*. Santa Clara, CA: Genotype.

Kumar, N. & Vadera, S.R. (2017). Stealth Materials and Technology for Airborne Systems. In N.E. Prasad & R.J.H. Wanhill (Eds.), *Aerospace Materials and Material Technologies – Volume 1: Aerospace Materials* (pp. 519-538). Singapore: Springer Nature.

Kvideland, R., & Sehmsdorf, H.K. (Eds.). (1988). *Scandinavian Folk Belief and Legend*. Minneapolis, MN: University of Minnesota Press.

Lacas, V. (1992, February). Laibow Visits Russia Plans New Treat. *MUFON UFO Journal 286*, p. 14.

Lady Gregory (1920). *Visions and Beliefs in the West of Ireland Collected and Arranged by Lady Gregory, First Series*. New York, NY: The Knickerbocker Press.

Lady Gregory (1920). *Visions and Beliefs in the West of Ireland Collected and Arranged by Lady Gregory, Second Series*. New York, NY: The Knickerbocker Press.

Lagerlöf, S. (1915). *Troll och människor*. Stockholm, SE: Albert Bonniers Boktryckeri.

Lancy, D.F. (2015). *The Anthropology of Childhood*. Cambridge, UK: Cambridge University Press.

Lang, C.R. (2002, October). Psychic/Spiritual Awakenings. *MUFON UFO Journal 414*, pp. 8-10.

Lang, C.R. (2004, February). The Indigo Hypothesis: Is This a Goal of the Visitors' Agenda(s). *MUFON UFO Journal 430*, pp. 9-11.

Latham, M.W. (1930). *The Elizabethan Fairies.* New York, NY: Columbia University Press.

Lawing, S.B. (2013, Summer). The Place of Evil: Infant Abandonment in Old Norse Society. *Scandinavian Studies 85(2),* pp. 133-150.

Lawrence, E. & Ober, M. (2016). *Montana Myths and Legends: The True Stories Behind History's Mysteries.* Helena, MT: Twodot.

Lawrence, R.M. (1898). *The Magic of the Horse-Shoe.* Boston, MA: Houghton, Mifflin, and Company.

Leask, J., Leask, A., & Silove, N. (2005, March) Evidence for Autism in Folklore? *Archives of Disease in Childhood 90*(3), p. 271.

Lebling, R. (2010). *Legends of the Fire Spirits: Jinn and Genies from Arabia to Zanzibar.* New York, NY: I.B. Tauris & Co. Ltd.

Lecouteux, C. (2013). *The Tradition of Household Spirits.* (J.E. Graham, Trans.). Rochester, VT: Inner Traditions. (Original work published 2000)

Lecouteux, C. (2015). *Demons and Spirits of the Land.* (J.E. Graham, Trans.). Rochester, VT: Inner Traditions. (Original work published 1995)

Leland, C.G. (1891). *Gypsy Sorcery and Fortune Telling.* New York, NY: C. Scribner's Sons.

Lenhoff, H.M. (1999). A Real-World Source for the "Little People": A Comparison of Fairies to Individuals with Williams Syndrome. In G. Westfahl & G. Slusser (Eds.), *Nursery Realms: Children in the Worlds of Science Fiction, Fantasy, and Horror* (pp. 150-160). Athens, GA: University of Georgia Press.

Lenin's Way Newspaper. (1990, December 4). Case 552. In A. Rosales (Ed.), *1990 Humanoid Sighting Reports.* Retrieved February 5, 2014 from http://www.ufoinfo.com/humanoid/humanoid-1990.pdf

Levy, I.J., & Zumwalt, R.L. (2013). Folk Belief. In R. Patai & H. Bar-Itzhak (Eds.), *Encyclopedia of Jewish Folklore and Traditions* (pp. 159-161). Abingdon, UK: Routledge.

Lewis, B. (2012). *Angels, Aliens, and Prophecy: The Connection.* Bloomington, IL: AuthorHouse.

Lewis, D.G. (2010). *Welsh-English English-Welsh Dictionary.* Glasgow, UK: The Gresham Publishing Company Ltd.

Lewis, J.R. (2001). *Satanism Today.* Santa Barbara, CA: ABC-CLIO.

Lewis, M.A. (1984, January). 'Earth-Based' UFOs. *MUFON UFO Journal 191,* pp. 16-18.

Lewis, W.J., & Alexander, D.McE. (2008). *Grafting and Budding: A Practical Guide for Fruit and Nut Plants and Ornamentals*. Collingwood, AU: Landlinks Press (2nd ed.).

Lindahl, C. (1986, April). Psychic Ambiguity at the Legend Core. *Journal of Folklore Research 23(1)*, pp. 1-21.

Lindow, J. (1978). *Swedish Legends and Folktales*. Berkeley and Los Angeles, CA: University of California Press.

Lindow, J. (1995, Winter). Supernatural Others and Ethnic Others: A Millennium of World View. *Scandinavian Studies 67(1)*, pp. 8-31.

Locke, J. (1906). *Locke's Essay Concerning Human Understanding: Books II & IV*. M.W. Clakins, Ed. Chicago, IL: The Open Court Publishing Company (2nd ed., original work published 1690)

Lopez, R.A.P. & Bound, R.F. (1974, November). Chaneques: Mexican Gnomes or Interplanetary Visitors? *Fate 27*, pp. 51-57.

Lorgen, E.F. (1999, January). 'The Love Bite': Alien-instigated human bonding dramas, relationship manipulations, and love obsessions. *MUFON UFO Journal 369*, pp. 9-11.

Lorgen, E. (2014, June 17). Evidence for Alien Abduction: Fluorescence Body Marks. Retrieved August 31, 2017 from http://evelorgen.com/wp/news/evidence-for-alien-abduction-fluorescence-body-marks/

Luomala, K. (1983, Fall). Phantom Marchers in the Hawaiian Islands. *Pacific Studies 7*(1), pp. 1-33.

Lvcifer [Screen name]. (2011, February 15). Iron in Folklore – Superstitions Explained. Retrieved June 28, 2017 from https://diabolicalconfusions.wordpress.com/2011/02/15/iron-in-folklore-superstitions-explained/

Lynn, D. (2016). *From Fear to Love*. Huntsville, AR: Ozark Mountain Publishing.

Lysaght, P. (1997). Fairylore from the Midlands of Ireland. In P. Narváez (Ed.), *The Good People: New Fairylore Essays* (pp. 22-46). Lexington, KY: The University Press of Kentucky.

MacDougall, J. (1910). *Folk Tales and Fairy Lore in Gaelic and English*. G. Calder (Ed.). Edinburgh, UK: John Grant.

MacGregor, A. (1901). *Highland Superstitions*. London, UK: Gibbings & Company, Ltd.

MacIsaac, T. (2016, June 18). Retired Police Detective Identifies Mysterious Patterns Across Thousands of Missing Persons Cases. Retrieved September 13, 2017 from http://www.theepochtimes.com/n3/2093486-retired-police-detective-identifies-mysterious-patterns-across-thousands-of-missing-persons-cases/

Mack, C.K., & Mack, D. (1998). *A Field Guide to Demons, Fairies, Fallen Angels, and Other Subversive Spirits.* New York, NY: Henry Holt and Company, LLC.

Mack, J. (1992, March). Secret Life: A Foreward. *MUFON UFO Journal 287*, pp. 8-9.

Mack, J. (1994). *Abduction: Human Encounters with Aliens.* New York, NY: Charles Scribner's Sons.

Mack, J. (1999). *Passport to the Cosmos.* New York, NY: Three Rivers Press.

Mac Suibhné, A. (2017). Páiste Shiobhain Cuimín - A Changeling. Retrieved June 4, 2017 from http://www.duchas.ie/en/cbes/4921674/4889287

MacKinnon, I. (2012, May 18). Briton Arrested with Roasted Human Foetuses fro Use in Black Magic Ritual. Retrieved August 15, 2017 from http://www.telegraph. co.uk/news/worldnews/asia/thailand/9274106/Briton-arrested-with-roasted-human-foetuses-for-use-in-black-magic-ritual.html

Magraner, J. (1991). *Les Hominides reliques d'Asie Centrale.* Valence, FR: Association Troglodytes.

Marden, K. (2012, December). Abduction Study Complete. *MUFON UFO Journal 536*, pp. 1, 4-5, 6.

Marden, K. (2015 ,January). Accidental Awareness or Alien Abduction? *MUFON UFO Journal 561*, pp. 8-9.

Marden, K., & Stoner, D. (2012). The Marden-Stoner Study on Commonalities Among Abduction Experiencers. Retrieved August 24, 2017 from http://www. kathleen-marden.com/commonalities-study-final-report.php

Martin, J. (1994). Case 154. In A. Rosales (Ed.), *1984 Humanoid Sighting Reports.* Retrieved February 5, 2014 from http://www.ufoinfo.com/humanoid/humanoid-1984. pdf

Martin, J. (n.d.). Case 205. In A. Rosales (Ed.), *1991 Humanoid Sighting Reports.* Retrieved February 5, 2014 from http://www.ufoinfo.com/humanoid/humanoid-1991. pdf

Martín, J. (n.d.). Case 318. In A. Rosales (Ed.), *1979 Humanoid Sighting Reports.* Retrieved February 5, 2014 from http://www.ufoinfo.com/humanoid/humanoid-1979. pdf

Martín, J. (1999, Autumn). UFOs and Humanoids in Neighboring Cuba. (G. Creighton, Trans.). *Flying Saucer Review 44*(3), pp. 19-21.

Martin, K., Walker, J. (Producers), & Walker, J. (Director). (2000). *The Fairy Faith* (motion picture). Canada: National Film Board of Canada.

Martin, M. (2000). *A Description of the Western Islands of Scotland.* Edinburgh, UK: Birlinn Ltd. (Original work published 1703)

Mason, T.B.A., Arens, R., Sharman, J., Bintliff-Janisak, B., Schultz, B. Walters, A.S., Cater, J.R., Kaplan, P., Pack, A.I. (2011, October 12). Sleep in Children with Williams Syndrome. *Sleep Medicine 12(9),* pp. 892-897.

Mauro, C. (2015). *Spiritual Telepathy.* Wheaton, IL: Quest Books.

McCabe, D. (2002, Spring). Histories of Errancy: Oral Yoruba Àbíkú Texts and Soyinka's "Abiku." *Research in African Literatures 33(1),* pp. 45-74.

McCauley, R.N. (2017, March 3). An Autistic Saint? Retrieved September 21, 2017 from https://www.psychologytoday.com/blog/why-religion-is-natural-and-science-is-not/201703/autistic-saint

McCutchan, A. (1999). *Muse That Sings: Composers Speak About the Creative Process.* Oxford, UK: Oxford University Press.

McVeigh, J. (2017). The Changeling. Retrieved July 5, 2017 from http://www.duchas.ie/en/cbes/4427871/4352542/4436965

Megargle, A., Morgan, J., Newcomer, N., Taylor, K. (Producers), & Breedlove, S. (Director). (2015). *Minerva Monster* (motion picture). United States of America: Small Town Monsters.

Meldrum, J. (2006). *Sasquatch: Legend Meets Science.* New York, NY: Forge Books.

Menkin, M. (2008). Stop Alien Abductions. Retrieved August 24, 2017 from http://www.stopabductions.com/

Menkin, M. (2013). Aliens and Children. Retrieved September 20, 2017 from http://aliensandchildren.org/

Metzler, I. (2013, October 10). Disability, Witches and the Middle Ages: Some Mythbusting. Retrieved July 11, 2017 from https://irinametzler.org/2013/10/10/disability-witches-and-the-middle-ages-some-mythbusting/

MidWeek Staff. (2010, October 13). Green Lady Lurking in Spooky Wahiawa Park. Retrieved October 17, 2017 from http://archives.midweek.com/content/zones/central_news_article/green_lady_lurking_in_spooky_wahiawa_park/

Millgram, A.E. (1990). *Jerusalem Curiosities.* Philadelphia, PA: The Jewish Publication Society.

Miss Dempster. (1888). The Folk-Lore of Sutherland-Shire [Continued]. *The Folk-Lore Journal 6(4),* pp. 215-252.

M'Manus, L. (1914, September 30). Folk-Tales from Western Ireland. *Folklore 25(3),* pp. 324-341.

Mobolade, T. (1973, Autumn). The Concept of Abiku. *African Arts 7(1)*, pp. 62-64.

Mollon, P. (2000). *Freud and False Memory Syndrome.* London, UK: Icon Books

Monaghan, P. (2004). *The Encyclopedia of Celtic Mythology and Folklore.* New York, NY: Facts on File, Inc.

Monaghan, P. (2014). *Encyclopedia of Goddesses & Heroines: Revised Edition.* Novato, CA: New World Library.

Monaghan, P. (2010). Calamity Meat and Cows of Abundance. *Anthropological Journal of Eurooean Cultures 19*(2), pp. 44-61.

Mooney, J. (1887, January). The Medical Mythology of Ireland. *Proceedings of the American Philosophical Society 24(125)*, pp. 136-166.

Morrison, G. (2000). Grant Morrison Disinfo Con Lecture Magick Terence Mckenna. Retrieved September 21, 2017 from https://www.youtube.com/watch?v=l-cxBuRU09w

Morrison, S. (1911). *Manx Fairy Tales.* London, UK: David Nutt.

Mosier, W.A. (2013). Addressing the Affective Domain: What Neuroscience Says About Social/Emotional Development in Early Childhood. In L.H. Wasserman & D. Zambo (Eds.), *Educating the Young Child 7: Advances in Theory and Research, Implications for Practice - Early Childhood and Neuroscience – Links to Development and Learning* (pp. 77-104). Heidelberg, DE: Springer Science.

Mott, W.M. (2011). *Caverns, Cauldron, and Concealed Creatures* (3rd ed.). Nashville, TN: Grave Distractions Publications.

MUFON CMS. (n.d.) In A. Rosales (Ed.), *1977 Humanoid Sighting Reports.* Retrieved February 5, 2014 from http://www.ufoinfo.com/humanoid/humanoid-1977.pdf

Munro, J.U. (1997). The Invisible Made Visible: The Fairy Changeling as a Folk Articulation of Failure to Thrive in Infants and Children. In P. Narváez (Ed.), *The Good People: New Fairylore Essays* (pp. 251-283). Lexington, KY: The University Press of Kentucky.

Murray, B. (2017). Story – A Changeling. Retrieved July 4, 2017 from http://www.duchas.ie/en/cbes/5009102/4986879/5122047

Murray, U. (2017). Old Stories – A Changeling. Retrieved June 9, 2017 from http://www.duchas.ie/en/cbes/5009032/4979185/5115813

Nagaitis, C., & Mantle, P. (1994). *Without Consent.* Upper Saddle River, NJ: Prentice Hall.

Narváez, P. (1997). Physical Disorders: Changelings and the Blast. In P. Narváez (Ed.), *The Good People: New Fairylore Essays* (pp. 225-226). Lexington, KY: The University Press of Kentucky.

Narváez, P. (1997). Newfoundland Berry Pickers "In the Fairies." In P. Narváez (Ed.), *The Good People: New Fairylore Essays* (pp. 336-368). Lexington, KY: The University Press of Kentucky.

Nazeer, K. (2006). *Send in the Idiots: Stories from the Other Side of Autism.* London, UK: Bloomsbury Publishing.

Newcomb, J., & Geddes-Ward, A. (2007). *A Faerie Treasury.* London, UK: Hay House.

Newman, L.S., & Baumeister, R.F. (1996). Toward and Explanation of the UFO Abduction Phenomenon: Hypnotic Elaboration, Extraterrestrial Sadomasochism, and Spurious Memories. *Psychological Inquiry 7(2),* 99-126.

Nicholas, C. (2015, February). One-on-One: Virginia Chief Investigator Ben Moss. *MUFON UFO Journal 562,* p. 20.

No author. (1889, January-March). Notices of the Folk-Lore of Other Continents. *The Journal of American Folklore 2(4),* pp. 80-82.

No author. (1895, March 30). Black Witchcraft. *The British Medical Journal 1(1,787),* pp. 717-718.

No author. (1937, September 27). Baby Carried on Beam of Light! *The Northern Miner,* p. 2.

No author. (2009, July 10). John Keel (Obituary). Retrieved June 8, 2017 from http://www.telegraph.co.uk/news/obituaries/science-obituaries/5797746/John-Keel.html

Norman, M., & Hickey-Hall, J. (2017). Pixies and Pixy Rocks. In S. Young & C. Houlbrook (Eds.), *Magical Folk: British and Irish Fairies: 500 AD to the Present* (Kindle Edition). London, UK; Gibson Square.

Norman, T. (1999). *Names Through the Ages.* New York, NY: Berkley Books.

NUFORC (n.d.). Case 278. In A. Rosales (Ed.), *1978 Humanoid Sighting Reports.* Retrieved February 5, 2014 from http://www.ufoinfo.com/humanoid/humanoid-1978.pdf

NUFORC (n.d.). Case 281. In A. Rosales (Ed.), *1979 Humanoid Sighting Reports.* Retrieved February 5, 2014 from http://www.ufoinfo.com/humanoid/humanoid-1979.pdf

NUFORC. (n.d.). Case 137. In A. Rosales (Ed.), *1994 Humanoid Sighting Reports.* Retrieved February 5, 2014 from http://www.ufoinfo.com/humanoid/humanoid-1994.pdf

Nunnelly, B.M. (2011). *The Inhumanoids: Real Encounters with Beings That Can't Exist.* Woolsery, UK: CFZ Press.

Nunnelly, B. (2017). *The Inhumanoids: Real Encounters with Beings That Can't Exist!* US: Triangulum Publishing (2nd ed.).

Nyman, J. (1989, March). The Familiar Entity and Dual Reference in the Latent Encounter. *MUFON UFO Journal 251*, pp. 10-12.

Occult Museum. (2017). Missing 411: Why are So Many People Going Missing in America's National Parks? Retrieved September 13, 2017 from http://www.theoccultmuseum.com/missing-411-many-people-going-missing-americas-national-parks/

O'Hanlon, J. (1870). *Irish Folk Lore: Traditions and Superstitions of the Country; with Humorous Tales*. Glasgow, UK: Cameron & Ferguson.

Oker, G. (2014). Recreating Cultural Literacy: A Dane-zaa Knowledge Perspective. *The Canadian Journal For Teacher Research 1*(1), pp. 9-18.

Oldham, B. (2013). *Children of the Greys*. Murfreesboro, TN: House of Halo.

Oldham, B. (2017). *The Baby Takers*. J. Smith (Ed.). Henderson, NV: Halo House Publishing.

Orme, N. (2005). Childhood of Medieval England, *c*. 500-1500. Retrieved August 7, 2017 from http://www.representingchildhood.pitt.edu/medieval_child.htm

Owen, E. (1887). *Welsh Folklore*. Owestry & Wrexham, UK: Woodall, Minshall, and Co.

Paine, R. (1944, Summer). Night Village and the Coming of Men of the Word: The Supernatural as a Source of Meaning among Coastal Saami. *The Journal of American Folklore 107(425)*, pp. 343-363.

Paulides, D. (2011). *Missing 411 – Eastern United States*. Charleston, SC: CreateSpace.

Paulides, D. (2011). *Missing 411 – Western United States and Canada*. Charleston, SC: CreateSpace.

Paulides, D. (2012). *Missing 411 – North America and Beyond*. Charleston, SC: CreateSpace.

Paulides, D. (2013, October). Missing Persons May Be Tied to UFO Cases. *MUFON UFO Journal 546*, pp. 1, 7-9.

Paulides, D. (2015). *Missing 411 – A Sobering Coincidence*. Charleston, SC: CreateSpace.

Paulides, D. (2016). *Missing 411 – Hunters (Volume 1)*. Charleston, SC: CreateSpace.

Parsons, P.T. (1939). *Pueblo Indian Religion, Vol. I*. Chicago, IL: University of Chicago Press.

Pemberton, J. (2013). *Myths and Legends from Cherokee Dances to Voodoo Trances*. Eastbourne, UK: Canary Press.

Pepper, W., & Wilcock, J. (2000). *Magical and Mystical Sites: Europe and the British Isles.* Grand Rapids, MI: Phanes Press.

Persinger, M.A. (1988, August). Possible Increased Cancer and Depression Risk Among UFO Field Researchers and Populations Near "Flap" Areas. *MUFON UFO Journal 244*, pp. 3-6.

Phillips, T. (2005, December). Physical Traces. *MUFON UFO Journal 452*, pp. 18-19.

Pinborg, A. (2017). Vanishing Twin Syndrome and Long-Term Outcome. In R.G. Farquharson & M.D. Stephenson (Eds.), *Early Pregnancy* (pp. 262-271). Cambridge, UK: Cambridge University Press (2nd ed.).

Pontolillo, J. (1993). *INFO Occasional Paper No.2: Demons, Doctors, and Aliens: An Exploration into the Relationships Among Witch Trial Evidence, Sexual-Medical Traditions, and Alien Abductions.* Arlington, VA: RDM Publications.

Powell, D. (2014, Novemeber 25). Telepathy Project with non-verbal autistics children DEBUNKS skeptics. Retrieved September 20, 2017 from https://www.youtube.com/watch?v=BBGwkk8vp3w

Power, M. (2017). A Changeling Story. Retrieved July 2, 2017 from http://www.duchas.ie/en/cbes/5080332/4879042

Pratt, B. (1989, March). An Extraordinary Field-Investigation Trip to Brazil (1986). *Flying Saucer Review 34*(1), pp. 7-12.

Pratt, B. (1996). *UFO Danger Zone: Terror and Death in Brazil – Where Next?* Blue River, WI: Horus House Press.

Pratt, C. (2007). *An Encyclopedia of Shamanism: Volume One – A-M.* New York, NY: The Rosen Publishing Group, Inc.

Puhvel, M. (1978). Snow and Mist in "Sir Gawain and the Green Knight": Portents of the Otherworld? *Folklore 89*(2), pp. 224-228.

Purcell, C. (2005, February 25). Fairytales tell of autistic children. Retrieved July 10, 2017 from http://www.abc.net.au/science/articles/2005/02/25/1309455.htm

Purkiss, D. (2000). *Troublesome Things: A History of Fairies and Fairy Stories.* London, UK: The Penguin Group.

Puthoff, H.A. (1982, January). Mail Bag: Birth of a New Theory? *Flying Saucer Review 27*(4), p. 23.

Quinlan, M. (2017, October 4). Personal communication.

Quinn, R. (2006). *Little People.* Lakeville, MN: Galde Press, Inc.

Rajchel, D. (2016). Crop Lore: When the Plants Talked Back. In E. Day & L. Heineman (Eds.), *Llewellyn's 2017 Herbal Almanac*, pp. 275-280. Woodbury, MN: Llewellyn Worldwide Ltd.

Randles, J. (1977, Winter). Strange Object Near Childrens' Home. *Flying Saucer Review* 23(4), pp. 31-32.

Randles, J. (1981, Spring). Repeater Witnesses. *Flying Saucer Review 26*(6), pp. 26-30.

Randles, J. (1988). *Abduction: Over 200 Documented UFO Kidnappings Exhaustively Investigated.* London, UK: Robert Hale Ltd.

Randles, J. (1994). *Star Children.* London, UK: Robert Hale Limited.

Randles, J. (1997). *Alien Contact: The First Fifty Years.* New York, NY: Barnes & Noble Books.

Raynes, B. (1982, February). UFOs or "Soul Ships?" *MUFON UFO Journal 168*, pp. 15-17.

Redfern, N. (2016). *The Bigfoot Book: The Encyclopedia of Sasquatch, Yeti and Cryptid Primates.* Canton, MI: Visible Ink Press.

Redfern, N. (2017, March 24). The Mystery of the U.K.'s "Phantom" Social Workers. Retrieved September 6, 2017 from http://mysteriousuniverse.org/2017/03/the-mystery-of-the-u-k-s-phantom-social-workers/

Redish, L. (2015). Legendary Native American Figures: Wild People (Mialuka). Retrieved July 18, 2017 from http://www.native-languages.org/morelegends/wild-people.htm

Redish, L. (2015). Legendary Native American Figures: Yehasuri (Wild Indians). Retrieved July 18, 2017 from http://www.native-languages.org/morelegends/yehasuri.htm

Redish, L. (2015). Native American Legends: Big Owl Man. Retrieved July 20, 2017 from http://www.native-languages.org/big-owl.htm

Redish, L. (2015). Native American Legends: Water Babies. Retrieved July 18, 2017 from http://www.native-languages.org/water-babies.htm

Redish, L. (2015). Native Languages of the Americas: Kwakiutl Indian Legends (Kwakwaka'wakw). Retrieved September 11, 2017 from http://www.native-languages.org/kwakiutl-legends.htm

Rees, D. (1979, March). Floating Entity at Reddish. *Flying Saucer Review 25(2)*, pp. 29-31.

Reid, K. (2017). A Funny Story. Retrieved July 5, 2017 from http://www.duchas.ie/en/cbes/5009285/5004673

Rennard, A. (2000, June 18). Pre-Columbian and Early American Legends of Bigfoot-like Beings. Retrieved September 5, 2017 from http://www.bfro.net/legends/salish.htm

Renner, T. (2017). *Bigfoot in Pennsylvania*. Charleston, SC: CreateSpace Independent Publishing Platform.

Renner, T. (2017, June 29). Episode 11: Iron and the Supernatural, part 2: The Blacksmith. Retrieved June 29, 2017 from http://strangefamiliars.darkhollerarts.com/episode-11-iron-supernatural-part-2-blacksmith/

Renner, T. (2018). *Bigfoot: West Coast Wild Men*. Charleston, SC: CreateSpace Independent Publishing Platform.

Rhind, J.P. (2014). *Fragrance and Wellbeing: Plant Aromatics and Their Influence of the Psyche*. London, UK: Singing Dragon.

Rhŷs, J. (1901). *Celtic Folklore: Welsh and Manx, Vol. I*. Oxford, UK: Clarendon Press.

Ribera, A. (1984, August). Do Abductees Fit Into A Certain Pattern? Some Reflections and Findings About an Intriguing Phenomenon. *Flying Saucer Review* *29*(6), pp. 20-21.

Richardson, M.A. (1846). *The Borderer's Table Book: Or, Gatherings of the Local History and Romance of the English and Scottish Border*. Newcastle upon Tyne, UK: Printed for the author.

Rickard, B., & Michell, J. (2000). *Unexplained Phenomena: A Rough Guide Special*. London, UK: Rough Guides, Ltd.

Rickard, B., & Michell, J. (2007). *Unexplained Phenomena: A Rough Guide Special* (2nd ed.). London, UK: Rough Guides, Ltd.

Ring, K. (1992). *The Omega Project*. New York, NY: William Morrow & Co.

Ritzmann, J., Vaeni, J., Tar, D.E.K., Cooper,, K.E., & Kokjohn, T.A. (2014). Project Core Anonymous Survey Synopsis of Results. Retrieved August 8, 2017 from http://paratopiaoculus.com/wp-content/uploads/2016/08/Project-Core-Anonymous-Survey-Synopsis-of-Results.pdf

Roberts, A.L., Lyall, K., Rich-Edwards, J.W., Ascherio, A., & Weisskopf, M.G. (2013, May). Maternal exposure to childhood abuse is associated with elevated risk of autism. *JAMA Psychiatry 70*(5), pp. 508-515.

Roberts, J. (2016). *The Sacred Mythological Centres of Ireland*. IE: Bandia Publishing.

Rodway, A. (1981). *Fairies*. New York, NY: G.P. Putnam's Sons.

Rogerson, P. (1993, June). Fairyland's Hunters: Notes Towards a Revisionist History of Abductions. Part One. Retrieved May 7, 2018 from http://magoniamagazine.blogspot.com/2013/11/notes-towards-revisionist-history-of.html

Rojcewicz, P.M. (1997). Fairies, UFOs, and Problems of Knowledge. In P. Narváez (Ed.), *The Good People: New Fairylore Essays* (pp. 479-514). Lexington, KY: The University Press of Kentucky.

Rolfe, W.J. (Ed.). (1895). *Fairy Tales in Prose and Verse.* New York, NY: Harper & Bros.

Rosales, A. (n.d.). Case 345. In A. Rosales (Ed.), *1996 Humanoid Sighting Reports.* Retrieved February 5, 2014 from http://www.ufoinfo.com/humanoid/humanoid-1996. pdf

Ross, A. (2011). *Folklore of the Scottish Highlands.* Stroud, UK: The History Press. (Original work published in 2000)

Rubtsov, V.V. (1994). Alien Contacts and Abduction Experiences: A Look From the C.I.S. In W.H. Andrus, Jr. (Ed.)., *MUFON 1994 International UFO Symposium Proceedings* (pp. 137-152). Seguin, TX: Mutual UFO Network.

Russell, J.B. (1984). *Lucifer: The Devil in the Middle Ages.* Ithaca, NY: Cornell University Press.

Rutkowski, C. (2008). *A World of UFOs.* Toronto, ON: Dundurn Press.

Rutkowski, C.A. (2009). *I Saw It Too! Real UFO Sightings.* Toronto, ON: Dundurn Press.

Salatun, J. (1982). *UFO: Salah Satu Masalah Dunia Masa Kini.* Jakarta, ID: Yayasan Idayu.

Sandow, G. (1998, April). The UFO Press. *MUFON UFO Journal 360*, pp. 10-12, 13.

Sands, H. (1907). The Woodpecker's Revenge. *The Canadian Magazine of Politics, Science, Art and Literature 28*, pp. 550-552. Toronto, ON: The Ontario Publishing Co., Limited.

Sayce, R.U. (1934, June). The Origins and Development of the Belief in Fairies. *Folklore 45(2)*, pp. 99-143.

Sayne, A. (2017, April 24). Conspirinormal Episode 160 – Joe Jordan (CE4 Research and Stopping Alien Abductions). Retrieved June 27, 2017 from https://www.podomatic.com/podcasts/conspirinormal/episodes/2017-04-23T20_06_18-07_00

Schachter-Shalomi, Z., & Miles-Yepez, N. (2009). *A Heart Afire: Stories and Teachings of the Early Hasidic Masters.* Philadelphia, PA: The Jewish Publication Society.

Schmitt, J.C. (1983). *The Holy Greyhound: Guinefort, Healer of Children Since the Thirteenth Century.* Cambridge, UK: Cambridge University Press (Original work published 1979)

Schwartz, H. (2004). *Tree of Souls: The Mythology of Judaism.* New York, NY: Oxford University Press, Inc.

Schwarz, B.E. (1977, October). Talks with Betty Hill: 2 – The Things That Happen Around Her. *Flying Saucer Review 23*(3), pp. 11-14, 31.

Scutts, J. (2015). *The Pied Piper of Hamelin at the Crossroads of History, Religion, and Literature*. Raleigh, NC: Lulu.

Schuessler, J. (1990, June). The Implant Enigma. *MUFON UFO Journal 266*, pp. 18, 23.

Schmidt, H. (1974). *Psychic Exploration: A Challenge for Science*. New York, NY: G.P. Putnam's Sons.

Schnabel, J. (1994). *Dark White*. London, UK: Hamish Hamilton.

Schreibman, L. (2005). *The Science and Fiction of Autism*. Cambridge, MA: Harvard University Press.

Schwarz, J. (2004, December 9). Imaginary friends: Most kids have one (or more). Retrieved August 10, 2017 from http://www.washington.edu/news/2004/12/09/imaginary-friends-most-kids-have-one-or-more/

Sedlak, A.J., Finkelhor, D., Hammer, H., & Schultz, D.J. (2002, October). *National Estimates of Missing Children: An Overview*. In Flores, J.R. (Ed.), *NISMART: National Incidence Studies of Missing, Abducted, Runaway, and Thrownaway Children*. Washington, DC: U.S. Department of Justice.

Seifert, M. (2002). *Rewriting Newfoundland Mythology: The Works of Tom Dawe*. Glienicke, DE: Galda & Wilch Verlag.

Sharp, A. (1899, May 5). The Design of Wheels and Pulleys. *Practical Engineer and Engineer's Gazette 19-20*, pp. 424-425.

Shiel, L.A. (2012). *Top Secret Sasquatch: Forbidden Bigfoot, Part Two*. USA: Jacobsville Books.

Shiloh, A. (1961, Summer). The System of Medicine in Middle East Culture. *Middle East Journal 15(3)*, pp. 277-288.

Sigismond, R. (1983, December). CE-IIIs: New Dimensions in Investigations. *Flying Saucer Review 29*(2), pp. 21-26.

Sikes, W. (1880). *British Goblins: Welsh Folklore, Fairy Mythology, Legends and Traditions*. London, UK: Sampson Low, Marston, Searle, & Rivington (2nd ed.).

Silva, C. (1993). Case 62. In A. Rosales (Ed.), *1970 Humanoid Sighting Reports*. Retrieved February 5, 2014 from http://www.ufoinfo.com/humanoid/humanoid-1970.pdf

Simpson, J. (2004). *Icelandic Folktales & Legends*. Stroud, UK: The History Press. (Original work published 1972)

Simpson, J. (2011, April). On the Ambiguity of Elves [1]. *Folklore 122(1)*, pp. 76-83.

Simpson, J., & Roud, S. (2000). *A Dictionary of English Folklore*. Oxford, UK: Oxford University Press.

Silver, C.G. (1999). *Strange and Secret Peoples: Fairies and Victorian Consciousness*. New York, NY: Oxford University Press, Inc.

Skjelbred, A.H.B. (1997). Rites of Passage as Meeting Place: Christianity and Fairylore in Connection with the Unclean Woman and the Unchristened Child. In P. Narváez (Ed.), *The Good People: New Fairylore Essays* (pp. 215-223). Lexington, KY: The University Press of Kentucky.

Slemen, T. (2010). The Full Moon Prowler. Retrieved August 3, 2017 from http://www.slemen.com/fullmoonprowler.html

Smith, C. (2005, September). The Land of the Hidden People. *Fortean Times 201*, pp. 42-47.

Smith, W.G. (1883, June). On Fairy Rings. *Transaction of the Essex Field Club III(7)*, pp. 69-73. Buckhurst Hill, UK: Essex Field Club.

Smith, Y.R. (2014). *Coronado: The President, The Secret Service, and Alien Abductions* [Kindle edition].

Sobo, E.J. (1996). Cultural Explanations for Pregnancy Loss in Rural Jamaica. In R. Cecil (Ed.), *The Anthropology of Pregnancy Loss* (pp. 39-58). Oxford, UK: Berg.

Sparks, H.F.D. (Ed.). (1984). *The Apocryphal Old Testament*. Oxford, UK: Oxford University Press.

Spence, L. (1920). *An Encyclopaedia of Occultism*. New York, NY: Dodd, Mead & Company.

Sprenger, J. (2016). *Malleus Maleficarum – The Witch Hammer*. (M. Summers, Trans.). North Charleston, SC: Createspace. (Original work published 1489)

Stacy, D. (1991, February). The UFO Press: Journal of UFO Studies, New Series, Vol. 2. *MUFON UFO Journal*, p. 18.

Stacy, D. (1992, May). Japanese Create Aritifical Womb! *MUFON UFO Journal 289*, p. 5.

Stacy, D. (1994, August). The 1994 MUFON UFO Symposium. *MUFON UFO Journal 316*, pp. 3-10.

Stacy, D. (1996, August). MUFON's 27ᵗʰ Annual Symposium. *MUFON UFO Journal 340*, pp. 3-13.

Stainton, T. (2006). Changeling. In G.L. Abrecht, S.L. Snyder, D.T. Mitchell (Eds.), *Encyclopedia of Disability* (pp. 235-236). Thousand Oaks, CA: SAGE Publications.

Stamp, H. (1915). The Water-Fairies. *The Journal of American Folklore 28(109)*, pp. 310-316.

Sternberg, S. (2003, April 16). Gene found for rapid aging disease in children. Retrieved July 11, 2017 from https://usatoday30.usatoday.com/news/science/2003-04-16-agin-gene_x.htm

Stevenson, I. (2001). *Children Who Remember Previous Lives: A Question of Reincarnation – Revised Edition.* Jefferson, NC: McFarland & Company, Inc.

Stewart, S. (2003, Summer). Genres of Work: The Folktale and "Silas Marner." *New Literary History 34(3)*, pp. 513-533.

Stock. (n.d.). *Oxford Living Dictionaries.* Retrieved June 6, 2017 from https://en.oxforddictionaries.com/definition/stock

Storm, H. (2008). *My Descent Into Death: And the Message of Love Which Brought Me Back.* Forest Row, UK: Clairview Books. (Original work published 2000)

Steiger, B. (1988). *The UFO Abductors.* New York, NY: The Berkley Publishing Group.

Strieber, W. (1987). *Communion.* New York, NY: Avon Books.

Strieber, W. (1997). *Transformation.* New York, NY: Avon Books.

Strieber, W. (2015, January 8). Anne: Lady in Autumn. Retrieved August 3, 2017 from http://www.unknowncountry.com/journal/anne-lady-autumn

Strieber, W., & Kripal, J.J. (2016). *The Super Natural.* New York, NY: Jeremy P. Tarcher.

Stringfield, L.H. (1977, January). The Stanford, Kentucky Abduction. *MUFON UFO Journal 110*, pp. 5-15.

Strong, L. (2016). What is a Psychopomp? Retrieved September 14, 2017 from http://www.psychopomps.org/what-is-a-psychopomp.html

Sugg, R. (2016, May). The Fairy Menace. *BBC History Magazine* pp. 60-63.

Sugg, R. (2017, August 23). Child abduction, poltergeist sightings, crop failure and haunted building sites blamed on sinister work of fairies. Retrieved September 1, 2017 from http://www.mirror.co.uk/news/weird-news/child-abduction-poltergeist-sightings-crop-11036934

Suggett, R. (2017). The Fair Folk and Enchanters. In S. Young & C. Houlbrook (Eds.), *Magical Folk: British and Irish Fairies: 500 AD to the Present* (Kindle Edition). London, UK; Gibson Square.

Sveinsson, E.Ó. (2003). *The Folk-Stories of Iceland.* (B. Benedikz, Trans.). E.G. Pétursson (Ed.). Exeter, UK: Short Run Press Limited.

Swancer, B. (2016, September 23). Truly Strange Cases of People Kidnapped by Bigfoot. Retrieved September 5, 2017 from http://mysteriousuniverse.org/2016/09/truly-strange-cases-of-people-kidnapped-by-bigfoot/

Swancer, B. (2017, June 9). Some Very Strange Information on the Bizarre Vanishing of Dennis Martin. Retrieved September 5, 2017 from http://mysteriousuniverse.org/2017/06/some-very-strange-information-on-the-bizarre-vanishing-of-dennis-martin/

Swancer, B. (2017, June 29). Bizarre Vanishings, Baffling Clues, and Strange Imposters. Retrieved September 13, 2017 from http://mysteriousuniverse.org/2017/06/bizarre-vanishings-baffling-clues-and-strange-imposters/

Swords, M.D. (1984, October). UFO Reports and Dissociative Hysteria. *MUFON UFO Journal 198,* pp. 10-12.

Swords, M.D. (2005). *Grassroots UFOs: Case Reports from the Center for UFO Studies.* San Antonio, TX: Anomalist Books. (Original work published by The Fund for UFO Research)

Tabies, A.C. (1980). *Abordaje al Caleuche.* Santiago, CL: Nascimento.

Taff, B.E. (1991, May). Close, But No Saucer. *MUFON UFO Journal 277,* pp. 3-7.

Tangherlini, T.K. (1995, Winter). From Trolls to Turks: Continuity and Change in Danish Legend Tradition. *Scandinavian Studies 61(1),* pp. 32-62.

Thomas, W.J. (1907). *The Welsh Fairy Book.* London, UK: Fisher Unwin.

Thompson, C.J.S. (1927). *The Mysteries and Secrets of Magic.* London, UK: John Lane, The Bodley Head Ltd.

Topping, A. (2012, March 1). Accusations of witchcraft are part of growing pattern of child abuse in UK. Retrieved July 7, 2017 from https://www.theguardian.com/uk/2012/mar/01/accusations-witchcraft-pattern-child-abuse

Trainor, J. (2001, February). UFO Reportedly Abducts Two in Northern Chile. *MUFON UFO Journal 393,* p. 9.

Tralins, R. (1969). *Children of the Supernatural.* New York, NY: Lancer Books, Inc.

Trei, L. (2004, January 8). Psychologists Offer Proof of Brain's Ability to Suppress Memories. Retrieved August 7, 2017 from http://news.stanford.edu/news/2004/january14/memory-114.html

Trench, B.L.P (1959, September-October). Baby Almost As Forecast. *Flying Saucer Review 5(5),* p. 5.

Trial by fire. (n.d.). Dictionary.com. Retrieved July 7, 2017 from http://www.dictionary.com/browse/trial-by-fire

Truncale, D.B. (1994). Alien/UFO Experiences of Children. In A. Pritchard, D.E. Pritchard, J.E. Mack, P. Kasey, & C. Yapp (Eds.), *Alien Discussions: Proceedings of the Abduction Study Conference* (pp. 116-126). Cambridge, UK: North Cambridge Press.

Tucker, H. (2003). *Pregnant Fictions: Childbirth and the Fairy Tale in Early-Modern France*. Detroit, MI: Wayne State University Press.

Turner, K. (1992). *Into the Fringe*. New York, NY: Berkley Books.

Turner, K. (1994). *Masquerade of Angels*. Roland, AR: Kelt Works.

Turner, K. (1994). *Taken: Inside the Alien-Human Abduction Agenda*. Tallahassee, FL: Rose Printing Company, Inc.

Turner, K. (1994, December). Genetic Agenda A Double-Cross? *MUFON UFO Journal 320*, pp. 13-14.

Turner, K. (1998, Winter). Alien Aftershock: Compulsions in the Aftermath of Alien Abduction Experiences. *Flying Saucer Review 43*(4), pp. 21-24.

TVTropes. (n.d.). Inspirationally Disadvantaged. Retrieved September 19, 2017 from http://tvtropes.org/pmwiki/pmwiki.php/Main/InspirationallyDisadvantaged

UFO Workgroup - The Netherlands. (1995). Case 150. In A. Rosales (Ed.), *1984 Humanoid Sighting Reports*. Retrieved February 5, 2014 from http://www.ufoinfo.com/humanoid/humanoid-1984.pdf

Umbarger, M. (2011). *Harp Song: The Golden Thread with Selected Arrangements for the Folk Harp*. Pacific, MO: Mel Bay Publications.

Vallee, J., & Aubeck, C. (2009). *Wonders in the Sky: Unexplained Aerial Objects from Antiquity to Modern Times*. New York, NY: Jeremy P. Tarcher/Penguin.

Van der Toorn, K., Becking, B., & Van der Horst, P. (1999). *Dictionary of Deities and Demons in the Bible*. Leiden, NL: Koninklijke Brill NV (2nd ed.).

Varner, G.R. (2007). *Creatures in the Mist: Little People, Wild Men, and Spirit Beings Around the World*. New York, NY: Algora Publishing.

Vasey, G.M. (2017). *The Chilling, True Terror of the Black-Eyed Kids*. Asteroth's Books.

Vaughan, J.D. (1879). *The Manners and Customs of the Chinese of the Straits Settlements*. Singapore: Mission Press.

Vendramini, D. (2011). *Them and Us: How Neanderthal Predation Created Modern Humans*. Armidale, AU: Kardoorair Press.

Vicente, X.X.S. & Valle, X.C. (2003). *El Gran Libro de la Mitología Asturiana*. Oviedo, ES: Ediciones Trabe.

Vickery, R. (1988). Linnaeus and the Changeling. *Folklore 99(2)*, p. 250.

Victor, J.S. (1993). *Satanic Panic: The Creation of a Contemporary Legend*. Chicago, IL: Open Court.

Vike, B. (n.d.). Case 43. In A. Rosales (Ed.), *1970 Humanoid Sighting Reports*. Retrieved February 5, 2014 from http://www.ufoinfo.com/humanoid/humanoid-1970.pdf

Virtue, D. (2001). *The Care and Feeding of Indigo Children*. Carlsbad, CA: Hay House, Inc.

Von Sydow, C.W. (1948). The Manhardian Theories about the Last Sheaf and the Fertility Demons from a Modern Critical Point of View. *Selected Papers on Folklore 4*. Copenhagen, DK.

Wahlert, G., & Linwood, R. (2014). *One Shot Kills: A History of Australian Army Sniping*. Sydney, AU: Big Sky Publishing.

Waldron, G. (1744). *The History and Description of the Isle of Man*. London, UK: W. Bickerton (2nd ed.).

Watts, D.C. (2007). *Elsevier's Dictionary of Plant Lore*. Burlington, MA: Academic Press.

Webb, D. (1976). *1973, Year of the Humanoids: An Analysis of the Fall UFO/Humanoid Wave*. Evanston, IL: Center for UFO Studies.

Webb, W.N. (1989, June). The Pelley Time-Lapse UFO Encounter. *MUFON UFO Journal 254*, pp. 11-13.

Westropp, T.J. (1920, June). The Marriages of the Gods at the Sanctuary of Tailltu. *Folklore: A Quarterly Review 31*, pp. 109-141.

Westropp, T.J. (1921). A Study of Folklore on the Coasts of Connacht, Ireland. *Folk-Lore: A Quarterly Review 32*, pp. 103-105.

Weeks, M.E. (1956). *Discovery of the Elements* (6th ed.).. Leicester, H.M., & Dains, F.B. (Eds.). Easton, PA: Journal of Chemical Education.

White, C. (2005). *A History of Irish Fairies*. New York, NY: Carrol & Graf Publishers. (Original work published 1976)

White, G. (January 12, 2017). *Rune Soup: Talking Thai Animism and Sorcery with Jenx*. Retrieved August 15, 2017 from https://runesoup.com/2017/01/talking-thai-animism-and-sorcery-with-jenx/

White, G. (2017, March 1). *Rune Soup: Talking Worldviews, Culture and Comparison with Dr. Jeff Kripal*. Retrieved May 30, 2017 from https://runesoup.com/2017/03/talking-worldviews-culture-and-comparison-with-dr-jeff-kripal

Wilde, J. (1887). *Ancient Legends, Mystic Charms, and Superstitions of Ireland*. London, UK: Ticknor and Co.

Williams Syndrome Association. (2014). Adult Medical Issues. Retrieved July 10, 2017 from https://williams-syndrome.org/doctor/adult-medical-issues

Williamson, R. (2006). The Fisherman's Son and the *Gruagach* of Tricks. On *Four Gruagach Tales* [CD]. Cambridge, UK: Gottdiscs Limited.

Willis, L. (1982, January). Mother and Child Texas Abduction Case. *MUFON UFO Journal 167*, pp. 3-7.

Williston, T.P. (1911). *Japanese Fairy Tales, Second Series*. Chicago, IL: Rand McNally & Co.

Wilson, C. (1998). *Alien Dawn: An Investigation into the Contact Experience*. New York, NY: Fromm International Publishing Corporation.

Wilson, K. (1993). *The Alien Jigsaw*. Portland, OR: Puzzle Publishing.

Wilson, P.A. (2011). *UFOs in Pennsylvania: Encounters with Extraterrestrials in the Keystone State*. Mechanicsburg, PA: Stackpole Books.

Winkvist, A. (1996). Water Spirits, Medicine-men and Witches: Avenues to Successful Reproduction among the Abelam, Papua New Guinea. In R. Cecil (Ed.), *The Anthropology of Pregnancy Loss* (pp. 59-74). Oxford, UK: Berg.

Wood, J. (2005, December). Folk Narrative Research in Wales at the Beginning of the Twentieth Century: The Influence of John Rhᵭrs (1840-1916). *Folklore 116(3)*, pp. 325-341.

Woods, D.L. (2006). *The Philippines: A Global Studies Handbook*. Santa Barbara, CA: ABC CLIO.

Woodyard, C.. (2017). Banshees and Changelings. In S. Young & C. Houlbrook (Eds.), *Magical Folk: British and Irish Fairies: 500 AD to the Present* (Kindle Edition). London, UK; Gibson Square.

Wright, D. (1990, October). Current Case Log. *MUFON UFO Journal 270*, pp. 17-18, 23.

Wright, E.M. (1913). *Rustic Speech and Folk-Lore*. Oxford, UK: Humphrey Milford, Oxford University Press.

Worley, D. (1996, Autumn). Alien Abduction—The Ominous Truth of Our Day. *Flying Saucer Review 41(3)*, pp. 1-4.

Worley, D. (1996, Winter). Examining the Mystery of the "Para-Apes." *Flying Saucer Review 41*(4), pp. 20-22.

Worley, D. (1997, Summer). Some Denizens of the "Black Nether-World" and Their Abductee Victims. *Flying Saucer Review 42*(2), pp. 7-11.

Worley, D. (1999, Spring). A World Under Assault. *Flying Saucer Review 44*(1), pp. 21-22.

Worley, D. (2000, Summer). Researching "Nordic-Type" Alien Experiencer Cases. *Flying Saucer Review 45*(2), pp. 12-15.

Worley, D. (2004, September). While Blue Book Slept. *MUFON UFO Journal 437*, pp. 5-6.

Wright, D. (1996, February). Sexuality, Aliens, Hybrids and Abductions. *MUFON UFO Journal 334*, pp. 11-12.

Wright, D. (1996, June). Sorting Entities. *MUFON UFO Journal 338,* pp. 3-6.

Yeats, W.B. (Ed.). (1890). *Fairy and Folk Tales of the Irish Peasantry.* New York, NY: The Walter Scott Publishing Co., Ltd.

Yeats, W.B. (Ed.). (1892). *Irish Fairy Tales.* London, UK: T. Fisher Unwin.

Young, K. (2004, January). Report of "Screaming Woman" Evolves Into Possible Abduction Case in Ohio. *MUFON UFO Journal* 429, pp. 7-9.

Young, S. (2017). Fairy Bread and Fairy Squalls. In S. Young & C. Houlbrook (Eds.), *Magical Folk: British and Irish Fairies: 500 AD to the Present* (Kindle Edition). London, UK; Gibson Square.

Young, S. (2017, May 10). Personal communication.

Zabava, A. (n.d.). Case 1. In A. Rosales (Ed.), *1910-1919 Humanoid Sighting Reports.* Retrieved February 5, 2014 from http://www.ufoinfo.com/humanoid/humanoid-1919.pdf

Index

abatwa, 144
Abduction (book), 163
Abel (Bible), 13
Abelam, 136-137
abiku, 144-145, 52, 157
Abor (people), 137-138
aborigines (Australian people) (see also *Arrernte*), 6, 162, 186
aborted fetus (see *miscarriage*)
Abu Rigl Maslukha, 143-144
Abu Tor (Israel), 283
Abyssinia (see *Ethiopia*)
Accountant, The (film), 314
acheri, 293
aconite, 135
Adam (see also *Eve*), 7, 13-14, 143
Addingham (England), 291-292
Adelaide (Australia), 219
Adnan, Anita, 139
Afram, Kwane, 145
Africa (see also *Middle East*), 144-145, 154, 172, 197-198, 207, 214, 268
Aichi (Japan), 140
aik (see *oak*)
Akon, 214
al, 143
Alabama (see *United States*)
Alao (Chile), 135
Alaska (see *United States*)
Alaska Dispatch News (publication), 151
Alberta (Canada), 154
alder (wood), 54
Alexander, Victoria, 225
alf, 147
All Hallow's Eve (see *Halloween*)
All Saints Night, 63

Alley, J. Robert, 284
Almqvist, Imelda, 323
Alor Island (Indonesia), 162
Alps (France), 208-209
Alsean (people), 269
Alvarez, Arcadia, 239
Amayersuik, 150
Amazon River, 61, 146, 152
Amazon River Basin (see *Amazon River*)
America (see *United States*)
American Journal of Medical Genetics (publication), 323
amulets, 6, 7, 75, 81, 83, 208
Andreasson Affair, The (book), 182
Andreasson, Betty, 182
Andrew, Jr., Nick, 151
Anglesey (Wales), 14, 305
Anica, 284
Anubis (Egyptian mythology), 294
Antrim (Ireland), 3, 76, 97, 135
Apache (people), 152
apci'lnic, 149
Appalachian Mountains (United States), 155, 228, 273, 317
Appeal to Spiritual Personages (Druffel resistance technique) (see also *prayer*), 230
apples, 35, 186
Appleton, Cynthia, 196
April (month), 66, 76, 169, 204, 302, 307
Aran (Galway), 53,
Archer, Barbara, 247-248
Arctic Circle, 96, 283
Ardennes (Normandy), 94
Argentina, 146, 299
Ariel School (Zimbabwe), 172

Arizona (see *United States*)
Arjuna (Hindu mythology), 258, 316
Armenia, 108, 143
Armstrong, Gerry
Árnason, Jón, 13
Arnhem Land (Australia), 162
Arnoux, Madeleine, 185-186
Arrernte, 6, 137, 157, 204
arrkwetye irrentye (see *pmere kwetethe*)
Asbjørnsen, Peter Christen, 48, 95, 247
ash (wood), 78, 102
Ashliman, D.L., 24, 129, 208
ashthroat, 77
Asia (see also: *Armenia, China, India, Indonesia, Iran, Israel, Japan, Malaysia, Middle East, Mongolia, Nepal, Pakistan, Philippines, Russia, Thailand*), 61, 79, 82, 85, 137-141, 209, 271, 279, 283
asin (see *Sasquatch*)
Aspinall, Kevin, 238
Assisi (Italy), 324
astral realm, 86, 161, 188
aswang, 138
Aubeck, Chris, 238
Aude Valley (France), 76
AUFORN (see *Australian UFO Research Network*)
August (month), 3, 135, 174, 187, 198, 221
Augusta, Isabella (see *Lady Gregory*)
Augustine (Saint), 46
Australia, 6, 123, 130, 137, 138, 140, 162, 186, 189, 191, 198, 204, 205, 218-219, 223, 244, 267, 292
Australian aborigines (see *aborigines*)
Australian Folklore (publication), 138
Australian UFO Research Network, 223
autism (see *autism spectrum disorder*)
autism facilitators, 320, 324

Autism Society, 124
Autism Speaks, 323
autism spectrum disorder, 119, 123-124, 310, 314-315, 319-324, 325
Aveley (England), 212, 300

b'nei temurah, 46
Baba Yaga (see *witch*)
Babalawo (see *faerie man/woman*)
baby farm (see *incubatorium*)
baby presentation (alien), 219-220, 222, 224, 238, 251-252, 256-257, 285
Babylonian Talmud, 46
Bach, Elis (changeling), 117
Bach, Gitto, 20-21, 35
Bacup Echo (publication), 260
badal (see *changeling*)
Badenoch (Scotland), 105
bagpipes, 41, 51, 174, 260
Baile-phuill (Scotland), 58
bald mountains, 155
Bali (Indonesia), 138
Ball, James, 124
Baltic (region), 74, 94
Bamu, Kristy, 110
Bamu, Magalie, 110
Ban-a-teagh, 100
banana, 82
Bangkok (Thailand), 209
banshee, 171, 279
baptism, 26-27, 31, 45, 59, 72, 74, 75, 82-83, 92, 102, 116, 135, 146, 147, 203, 208, 231, 283
barabao, 63
Barrie, J.M., 8
Bartholomew (Saint), 113
Bartholomew, Robert E., 138
Bartlett, Sarah, 140
Bartsch, Karl, 59
Basterfield, Keith, 205
Bean-Sighe (see *banshee*)

bearded vulture (see *lammergeyer*)
Beaver Women, 150
Being There (film), 314
Belfast (Antrim), 3
Belgium, 3
belladonna, 135
Beltane Eve, 76
Benbecula (Hebrides), 51
Benemmerinnen (see *witch*)
Bengal (India), 138
Benin (Africa), 138
Benoni (South Africa), 197-198
Berkshire (England), 293
berries (see *berry-picking*)
berry-picking, 30-31, 75, 76, 77, 78,
    145, 149, 154-155, 185, 186, 225,
    269, 281, 303, 301, 304
Bethel (Minnesota), 201
Bhagavad Gita, 316
Bible, 4, 7, 13-14, 20, 30, 46, 54, 75,
    79, 81, 97-98, 143, 230, 262, 316
Bierce, Ambrose, 297-298
Big Head (see *Bighoots*)
Big Owl Man, 152
Bigfoot (see *Sasquatch*)
Bigfoot: West Coast Wild Men (book),
    273-278
Bighoots, 152-153, 156
Bikubi, Eric, 110
bilberries, 30
bindweed (see *bundweed*)
birch (wood), 104
Birmingham (England), 135, 221
bishopwort, 77
Black Forest (Pennsylvania), 154
black light (see *UV-A light*)
blackberry, 76
Blacker, Carmen, 140-141
Blackfoot (people), 150, 228
blacksmith, 51, 85, 87, 97, 114
Blaxill, Mark F., 322
Blessed Virgin Mary, 5, 29

blighted ovum, 202
Bloecher, Ted, 176
blood, 6, 16, 59-60, 61, 80, 108, 134,
    138, 147, 148, 234
bloodhounds (see *dogs*)
Bloody Bones, 29
Bloody Cap (see *Redcap*)
Bogart, Humphrey, 18
boggarts, 18, 156
bogies (see *boogeyman*)
bogles (see *boogeyman*)
bogs (see *swamps*)
Bohemia (Germany), 104
Boo-Hag (see Old Hag)
booger (see *Sasquatch*)
booger owls (see *Bighoots*)
boogeyman, 18-19, 44, 156
Book of Curses, The (book), 293
Book of the Damned, The (book), 215
Boone, Daniel, 153
Boscobel (Wisconsin), 36
Bourke, Angela, 69, 109
box (wood), 77-78,
Boyne Valley (Ireland), 83
Bradford (Pennsylvania), 272
Bradley, Dora, 272
Brandenburg, John, 216
Brazil, 190, 198, 199, 214, 239
bread, 31, 74-75, 83, 101, 125
Breen, Richard, 106
Brewer, Jack, 163
Briggs, Katharine, 26, 51, 57, 60, 66,
    78, 160, 205, 215
Briggs, Lori, 215
brit milah, 7
British Columbia (Canada), 154, 242,
    290
British Goblins (book), 12
Brittany (France), 63, 93, 117, 307,
    185
Brontë, Emily, 47
Brothers Grimm, 32, 44, 63, 245

Brown dwarfs (see *dwarf*)
Brown, Brian, 286
Brown, Margaret Wiley, 148
brujas (see *witch*)
Bruning, Margaret, 235
British Columbia, 154, 242, 290
Brussels (Belgium), 3
Bryan, C.D.B., 300
Buccola, Regina, 114
Buddhism, 79
Buehring, J. Mark, 304
bugbear (see *boogeyman*)
buk'wus (see *Sasquatch*)
Bullard, Thomas E., 16-17, 173, 183
bundweed, 76
Bunian, 138-139, 157
Burnette, Thomas K., 285-286
Burning of Bridget Cleary, The (book),
    109
Burns, John W., 282
Burtoo, Alfred, 174
Butler, Chris, 238
Butler, Jenny, 14-15
BVM (see *Blessed Virgin Mary*)
bytingr (see *changeling*)

Cadieux, Aaron, 304
Cahuilla (people), 148
Cain (Bible), 13
cairns, 101
Cajabamba (Peru), 172
Calbuyahue, Adolfo, 135, 141
California (see *United States*)
Callan, Mary, 69
calumniated-wife, 208
cambio (see *changeling*)
Cambrensis, Giraldus, 58
Camp Sacramento (California), 301
Campbell, John, 52
Campbell, John Gregorson, 18, 58, 84
Canaanite, 8
Canada, 19, 25, 31, 33, 149, 153, 154,

169, 193, 228, 242, 244, 254, 256,
    260, 271, 281, 290
cancer, 201, 248
Cannibal Babe, 151-152
Canterbury Tales, The (book), 160
Cape Cod (Massachusetts), 253
Capgras Delusion, 125
Capgras, Joseph, 125
carbon black, 234
*Care and Feeding of Indigo Children,
    The* (book), 260
Carnaubinha (Brazil), 199
Carolinas (see *United States*)
Carpenter, John, 170, 175-176, 177,
    189
cats, 7, 50, 107, 125, 279, 294, 302
Catawba (people), 148, 280
Catholicism (see *Christianity*)
cattle, 11, 32, 34, 54, 58, 63, 75, 76,
    78, 84, 85, 143, 147, 164, 206-207,
    250, 267, 274
CDC (see *Centers for Disease Control
    and Prevention*)
Celtic Folklore, Welsh and Manx
    (book), 42-43
Celtic Review (publication), 114
Center for UFO Studies, 2
Centers for Disease Control and
    Prevention, 323
cerebral palsy, 122, 244
Ch'eni (see *Sasquatch*)
Chalaronne River (France), 99
Champ (see *lake monsters*)
Chance the Gardener (see *Being
    There*)
chaneques, 146-147
changelings, 24, 31, 32, 39, 40-55, 57,
    62, 63, 64, 72, 74, 75, 77, 81, 83, 84,
    85, 88, 91-131, 136, 142-143, 144-
    145, 146, 150, 152, 157, 159, 160,
    171, 172, 177, 181, 183, 207, 214,
    234, 235, 237-263, 283-287, 289,

306-307, 310, 313, 314-315, 319
badal, 143
bytingr, 45
cambio, 46
crimbil, 43
divious, 45
dickkopf, 45, 49, 247
kielkropf, 45, 49
killcrop, 45
killkrack, 45
odmieńce, 46
plentyn-newid, 50, 55
podmenek, 45
premien, 45
skiptingr, 45
sibhreach, 85
vixlingr, 45
wechselbalg, 45
wechselkind, 45
wisselkind, 45
Changeling Who Stretched, The
 (story), 53
Charles I (King of England), 289
Charon (Greek mythology), 294
Cheape, Hugh, 55
cheese, 75, 83, 101
Chehalis (people), 282
Cherbourg (France), 307
Chernobrov, Vadim, 240
Cherokee (people), 155, 181
Cherry of Zennor (story), 68
chickens, 73, 80, 93, 97, 100, 261
childbirth, 6, 7, 21, 24, 26-27, 34, 51,
 52, 63, 65, 66, 67, 69, 73-74, 75, 81,
 108, 113, 137, 138, 139, 142, 143,
 147, 159, 196, 203, 205, 221-222,
 243, 249, 253, 284, 285, 298
Children's Crusade, 8
Children's Hospital of Philadelphia,
 204
Childs, Marilyn Henry, 292
Chile, 135, 170, 171, 184

Chilkat Tlingit (people), 150
Chilon, Candelaria, 172
chimley (see *chimney*)
chimney, 26, 43, 62, 92, 94, 95, 106,
 107-108, 156, 246
chimpanzee, 268
China, 79, 82, 85, 271, 279, 283
chlorophyll, 255
Choctaw (people), 149
Christ (see *Jesus of Nazareth*)
christening (see *baptism*)
Christianity, 7, 13-14, 15, 16, 23, 26-
 27, 28, 29, 42, 46-47, 59, 61, 72, 75,
 79, 80-82, 102, 106, 113, 134, 142,
 160, 213, 230-231, 283
 Catholicism, 13, 27, 283, 324
 churches, 8, 15, 18, 20, 47, 81, 82,
 101
 crosses, 14, 43, 50, 52, 54, 77, 78,
 81-82, 84, 107, 108, 193
 crucifixes, 81
 Protestantism, 46, 160
 rosary, 82
Christmas, 110, 194, 255, 298
Chronicon Anglicanum, 23
Chuckchi (people), 283
churches (see *Christianity*)
Cimarron (New Mexico), 192
cinnamon, 200-201
cinquefoil, 135
Ciudad Real (Spain), 168
clairvoyance, 114, 311
Clann Sighe, 100
Clelland, Mike, 147, 225, 313, 316,
 317
clones, 238-241, 256
Clonmel (Tipperary), 109
Cloran the plumber, 65
clover, 68, 77
coast (see shoreline)
cocks (see *chicken*)
coconuts, 138

Coffey, John (see *Green Mile, The*)

cold iron (see *iron*)

Coleman Gray (story), 53, 116

Coleman, Loren, 262

Colorado (see *United States*)

colt (see *horse*)

Columbia University, 177

comparativism, 5, 16, 71, 128, 162, 256

congenital angioma, 211

conger eel (see *eel*)

Conklin (New York), 186

Conspirinormal (podcast), 230

Constantinople (Turkey), 3

consumption, 52, 55, 59, 119, 131, 231

Cooper, Kimbal E., 182

Copycat Effect, The (book), 262

Cordoba (Argentina), 299

Cork (Ireland), 3, 15

Cornwall (England), 25, 35, 68, 100, 103, 104, 249

corp criadh, 55

cow (see *cattle*)

crabapple (see *apples*)

Cranmer, Hiram, 154

crawfish, 205

crimbil (see *changeling*)

Croker, Crofton,

Croker, T.C., 37-38, 43, 49, 79, 215

cromlech (see *megalith*)

Cronin, Emily, 228

crop circles, 17

cropleek, 77

crosses (see *Christianity*)

Crow (people), 298

crucifixes (see *Christianity*)

Cuba, 239

CUFOS (see *Center for UFO Studies*)

Culet, Anthoinette, 271

cumin, 76

cystic fibrosis, 121

d'Aulnoy, Madame, 205

Dagworthy Castle, 23, 174

daisies, 77

Dan, Jefri, 139

dancing, 30, 35, 41, 42, 50, 51, 81, 122, 123, 141, 159, 190, 253-254, 290

Dane-zaa (people), 154

daoine sith (see also *Duiné Sighe*), 59

Dartmoor (Devon), 36

Davies, D.E., 280

Davis (California), 190

Day, John, 300

Dearborn (Michigan), 258

December (month), 170, 172, 174, 249, 285, 291, 303

deer, 167, 188, 294

Delaware (see *United States*)

delivery (see *childbirth*)

Demerest, Janet, 256

demon, 3, 6-7, 13, 15, 29, 33, 34, 46, 49, 59, 67, 72, 74, 82, 85, 108, 112, 113, 114, 126, 129, 136, 137, 149, 213, 284, 294

mazakim/mazikeen, 7, 67

Demon's Rock (Ireland), 33

Denmark, 34, 51, 63, 74, 94, 102, 107

Dennett, Preston, 211-212

Dennis, Caryl, 243

Derbyshire (England), 291

Derdak, Emma, 223

Description of the Isle of Man (book), 95

Deshayes, Catherine, 134

DeSouza, John, 232-233

Dessau (Germany), 46-47

Devil's Children: A History of Childhood and Murder, The (book), 129

devil (see also *Lucifer* and *Satan*), 46-47, 59, 73, 79, 81, 85, 87, 88, 106,

108, 113, 135, 159, 209, 211, 213, 238
Devon (England), 36, 19, 81
dew-rain (see *gwlithlaw*)
Dickens, Charles, 47
dickkopf (see *changeling*)
digitalis (see *foxglove*)
Dima, Noma, 282
diphtheria, 212
Disney, Walt, 281
divious (see *changeling*)
djinn, 85, 141-143, 157, 230
döckalfar, 14
dogs, 36, 99, 113, 137, 164, 189, 190, 242, 271, 278-279, 301, 304, 317, 326
Dogon (people), 145, 311, 325
dolphins, 61
Donegal (Ireland), 30, 35
Donnellan, Anne M., 320
doppelgänger, 55, 307
Doraty, Cindy, 248
Dorset (England), 28
douen, 147
Down's syndrome, 121
Dr. Beachcombing, 95
dracs, 64, 68
drow (see *trow*)
Druffel, Ann, 181, 202, 227-232
Druzhko, Sergey, 159
dsonoqua (see *Sasquatch*)
Dublin (Ireland), 36
Duchesne, Alain, 193
duendes, 111, 146, 157, 184
Duffy, Jimmy, 302
Duffy, Natalie, 302
Dulce (New Mexico), 192
Dumfries (Scotland), 129
Duiné Sighe (see also *daoine sith*), 26
Duine Matha, 100
dún (faerie; see *faerie fort*)
Dunfermline Palace (England), 289

Dunmore (Galway), 109
duodenal perforation, 230
duppies, 76, 147, 157
dust devil (see *whirlwind*)
dwarfs, 13, 15, 18, 37, 43-44, 85, 146, 161, 279
dyn hysvys (see *faerie man/woman*)
dynion hysbys (see *faerie man/woman*)
Dziwozony, 45

Eagle and Child, The (pub), 154
Early, Biddy, 115
Eberhart, George M., 280
Eberly, Susan, 120, 122-123, 124
Ebu Gogo (see *Sasquatch*)
Ecuador, 194
Eden (see also *Adam* and *Eve*), 13-14
Edwards, Kenneth, 302
eels, 31, 68,
eggs
    chicken, 44-45, 92-96, 97, 101, 103, 125, 127, 138, 167, 171, 200, 261-262
    human, 202, 217, 218, 261-262
Egypt (Africa), 142, 143, 208, 283, 294
eidolon, 55
eithin, 76
El Broosha, 294
El Cajon (California), 185
El-Shamy, Hasan M., 142
Elaby Gathan, 73
elves, 13, 15, 21, 27, 29, 36, 43, 44, 45, 49, 50, 58, 67, 77, 81, 95, 115, 116, 133, 160, 215
elf-shot, 32, 149, 267
Elidurus, 58
Elijah (Judaism), 6
Elliot, Renee, 187-188
Elliot, Robert (changeling), 117
Elliott, Megan, 187-888
Ellis, A.B., 145

Ellsworth (Wisconsin), 206
Encyclopedia of Celtic Mythology and Folklore, The (book), 25
Encyclopedia of Fairies, An (book), 57
Encyclopedia of Shamanism, An (book), 324
England, 2, 5, 8, 9, 11, 12, 13, 14, 16, 18, 19, 23, 24, 25, 28, 29, 32, 34, 35, 36, 37, 43, 44, 45, 47, 48, 51, 55, 60, 63, 66, 68, 73, 74, 76, 77, 78, 80, 81, 84, 87, 93, 99, 100, 101, 103, 104, 110, 112, 114, 116, 117, 121, 123, 128, 129, 135, 148, 150, 155, 160, 164, 169, 173, 174, 182, 186, 193, 196, 207, 217, 221, 249, 260, 262, 266, 280, 286, 289, 291-292, 293, 305
epilepsy, 121, 126, 321
equinox, 102, 316
Esau (Bible), 262
Espinoza, Valentina Rojas, 171
Essay Concerning Human Understanding (book), 121
Ethiopia (Africa), 145, 283
Eton (Berkshire), 293
Europe (see also *Baltic, Belgium, Denmark, England, Finland, France, Germany, Greece, Hungary, Iceland, Ireland, Isle of Man, Italy, Lithuania, Netherlands, Norway, Poland, Romania, Scandinavia, Scotland, Slovenia, Spain, Sweden, Switzerland, Ukraine, United Kingdom*), 6, 8, 12, 14, 27, 28, 33, 34, 35, 45, 46, 60, 63, 76, 78, 81, 82, 93, 95, 99, 104, 107, 108, 109, 118, 121, 126, 134, 136, 137, 140, 141, 142, 145, 146, 147, 148, 150, 151, 208, 269, 278, 294, 306
Eve (Bible), 7, 13-14
evil eye, 24, 32, 74, 84, 142
'*Evil Child' in Literature, Film and Popular Culture, The* (book), 129
ewe hop, 77
ex-changeling (see *changeling*)
Exodus (see *Bible*), 316
Expanding Mind (podcast), 322

faerie blast, 54-55, 125, 167
faerie doctor (see *faerie man/woman*)
faerie fort, 14, 16, 17, 28, 37, 53, 66, 67, 69, 77, 85, 92, 94, 97, 105, 106, 109, 160, 171, 186, 205, 245, 278, 292
faerie hill (see *faerie fort*)
faerie man/woman, 30, 37, 99-101, 107, 114, 115, 120, 144, 145, 168, 178
faerie midwife (see *midwife to the faeries*)
faerie ointment (see *ointment*)
faerie ring, 17, 28, 35, 155, 184, 185, 228
faerie thorns, 105, 113, 140
faerie wetnurse (see *wetnurse*)
failure to thrive, 124, 127, 183
Fairies and Folk of Ireland (book), 251
Fairy Bush, 109
Fairy Child of Close Ny Lheiy, The (story), 51
Fairy Hill's Afire, The (story), 92
Fairy Mother of the Sky (story), 207
fairy squall (see also *storm*), 33
fairy stroke, 16, 24, 75, 105, 119, 127, 128
Fairy Tales in Prose and Verse (book), 133
Fairyland, 14, 17, 24, 37-39, 46, 52, 58, 60, 63, 64, 65, 68, 69, 96, 97, 105, 112, 114, 174, 178, 186, 192, 234, 252, 278, 282, 304
false memory syndrome, 163, 175-178, 189
Farrell, Elaine, 109

Fátima (Portugal), 5
fauns, 28, 99
February (month), 173, 191, 202, 214
fennel, 77
feroüers, 142
Ferreira, Antônio Álves, 239
Ferreira, Joana Rodrigues, 199
fetch (see also *stock*), 54-55, 64
Fairy Faith, 13, 16, 27, 32, 37, 42, 46,
    59, 61, 63, 72, 73, 75, 79, 108, 120,
    126, 128, 129, 130, 140, 142, 148,
    156, 160, 187, 203, 217, 229, 231,
    234, 237, 250, 254, 306, 309
Fairy Wife, The (story; see *Lore of*
    Prosperine)
fiddles, 51
Filer, George, 244
filii alieni, 46
Finland, 54
Fionn mac Cumhaill (story), 156
fire, 8, 25, 31, 34, 43, 44, 45, 48, 53,
    54, 62, 64, 73, 74, 76, 77, 78, 79, 80,
    82, 83, 85, 88, 92-93, 94, 100, 101,
    103, 105-108, 109, 111, 113, 136,
    141, 143-144, 145, 150, 151, 153,
    155, 199, 246, 274, 281, 283
Flake, Alan, 205
Flesk River (Ireland), 109
Flores (Indonesia), 281
Florida (see *United States*)
Flying Head (see *Bighoots)*
Flying Saucer Review (publication),
    168, 203, 229, 239, 258, 299
FMS (see *false memory syndrome*)
fog, 25, 36, 37, 153, 165, 272, 285,
    298-300
Folk Tales and Fairy Lore in Gaelic and
    English (book), 44
Folk Tales of Breffny (book), 33
Fort Bragg (North Carolina), 273
Fort, Charles, 2, 215
Fowler, Raymond, 175, 182

foxglove, 104-105, 109
foyson, 252
France, 15, 18, 24, 28, 38, 64, 46, 73,
    76, 77, 82, 85, 94, 96, 99, 117, 125,
    134, 167, 185, 205, 208, 271, 284,
    307, 324
Francis of Assisi (Saint), 324
Francis, Jennet, 32, 87, 113
Frau Holle, 111
Friday, 24, 25, 97
Frost, William Henry, 251
FTT (see *failure to thrive*)
fugue state, 310, 315
furze (see *eithin*)

Galloway (Scotland), 63
Galway (Ireland), 14, 27, 32, 53, 65,
    69, 109, 174
gargoylism (see *Hurler's syndrome,*
    Hunter's syndrome)
garlic, 76, 77
Gauls, 60
Gehenna (see *Valley of Hinnom*)
Geib, Todd, 305
Genesis (Bible), 4, 79
genii loci, 13
Germany, 3, 8, 18, 24, 25, 28, 31, 32,
    37, 43, 44, 45, 46-47, 48, 49, 58, 59,
    60, 63, 74, 76, 78, 79, 88, 94, 96,
    102, 103, 104, 107, 108, 111, 115,
    116, 147, 173, 182, 196, 205, 208,
    247, 301
Germer, Wes, 279, 286
Gervase of Tilbury, 64, 68
Ghengis Khan, 107
Ghillie Dhu, 267
ghillie suit, 267
giant, 12, 37, 134, 145, 150, 152, 156,
    281, 284
Giant's Stairs, 37
Gigantopithecus blacki, 156
Giménez, Graciela del Lourdes, 299

githrife, 77

glamour, 50, 54, 55, 67, 77, 252, 256-257, 287

Glengarry (Scotland), 44

  bug burn (see *bogeyman*)

Glynebwy (Wales), 32

gnome, 12, 37, 79, 85, 290

Goas Al Ludu (Brittany), 307

goblin, 12, 18, 24, 77, 116, 135, 145, 299

Godwin, Francis, 47

gold, 66, 72, 86, 115, 209, 277

Goo-teekhl (see *Sasquatch*)

Goodey, C.F., 127

Gordon, Stan, 266

Gordon, Stuart, 293

Gors Goch Changeling, The (story), 51

Goyozan Mountain (Japan), 281-282

Granchi, Irene, 239

Grange (Sligo), 26, 64

Grant, Biddy, 295

graveyard mold, 82

Great Head (see *Bighoots)*

Great Smoky Mountains (North Carolina & Tennessee), 273

Greece, 18, 28, 50, 78, 87, 101, 134, 258, 294, 316

Green Berets, 273

Green Lady (see *Wahine-oma'o*)

Green Man (see *Woodwose*)

Green Mile, The (film), 314

Green, Andrew, 2, 174

Green, Lawrence, 154

Greenhow Hill (Yorkshire), 66

Gregory, Lady (see *Lady Gregory*)

Greys Have Been Framed, The (book), 163

Grimm (see *Brothers Grimm*)

Grimm, Jacob (see *Brothers Grimm*)

Grimm, Wilhelm (see *Brothers Grimm*)

Grindylow, 29

gruagach, 98

Guatemala, 281

Guibourg, Abbé, 134

Guiley, Rosemary Ellen, 85, 88, 229

Guinefort (Saint), 99

Guiney, Louise, 26, 28, 87

Gutierrez, Arturo, 146-147

Guyana, 147

gwlithlaw, 25

gwyllion, 84

gypsies, 5, 63, 103, 129

Haast eagle, 154

hag stones, 73

Haga Mountain (Norway), 154

Haggerty, Alice, 212

hair, 11, 24, 31, 49, 50, 61, 79, 103, 115, 151, 170, 172, 180, 221, 222, 240, 248, 262, 267, 290

Hall, Mark A., 152-154, 156

Halloween, 25, 35, 76

Hamelin (see *Pied Piper of Hamelin*)

Hancock, Graham, 5, 238

Hansen, Svanhild, 154

Harder, James, 166, 167

Haredi Jews, 324

Hargrove, Rose, 259

Harpur, Patrick, 8, 38, 67, 160

Harrison, Terry and Wally, 270

Hartland, E. Sidney, 67, 79, 105

Harvard University, 163, 182

harwort, 77

Harz Wood (Germany), 43

Haskew, Paul, 320

Hauck, Dennis William, 290

Hawaii (see *United States*)

haws, 30

hawthorn (see *faerie thorns*)

hazel, 69, 275, 276

heathberry, 77

Heaven, 13, 63, 80,

Hebrew (see *Judaism*)
Hebrides Islands (Scotland), 51, 72, 74, 51, 107, 114, 115, 141
hedgerife, 77
Hell, 13, 60, 63, 230
hen (see *chicken*)
henbane, 77
Henson, Jim, 8
Hera (Greek mythology), 316
Heracles, 258
Hermitage Castle (Scotland), 134
Heynist Hill (Scotland), 58
Hickey-Hall, Jo, 19
hidden folk (see *Huldufólk*)
Hieranosos, 121
Higbee, Donna, 257
Highland Superstitions (book), 48
hill (faerie; see *faerie fort*)
Hill, Betty & Barney, 166, 177, 196, 207, 213, 217
Himalayan Mountains, 189, 282
Hinduism, 6, 79, 137, 258, 294, 316, 318
hippopotami, 145
Ho-Chunk (see *Hocąk*)
Hocąk (people), 152
Höðr (Norse mythology), 25
Holland (Netherlands), 45
hollyhock, 69
Holy Water (see also *Baptism*), 26, 65, 77, 82, 83
homocystinuria, 121
Honobia (Oklahoma), 279
Hopkins, Budd, 1, 166-167, 176, 189, 191, 200, 204, 206, 213, 214, 218, 219, 222, 223, 234-235, 239, 252, 256, 257, 260, 261, 262
horehound, 76
horses, 30, 48, 54, 89, 92, 96, 98, 141, 148, 206, 250, 267
Horsley, Jason, 322, 323
Horton, Virginia, 167, 188, 189, 239, 261
Houlbrook, Ceri, 217
How to Defend Yourself Against Alien Abduction (book), 227-232
Hrólf, Güngu, 67
hubrids, 250-251
huckleberries, 186, 269
Hughes, Florence, 272
huldre-folk (see *Huldufólk*)
Huldufólk, 13, 20, 38
Hungary, 73, 97, 122
Hunt, Bampton, 33
Hunt, Robert, 35, 121
Hunter's syndrome, 121
Hurler's syndrome, 121
Husband, Timothy, 283
hybrids, 4, 313
  alien, 159, 203, 206, 207, 211-226, 238, 242, 246-251, 252, 253-254, 254-257, 257-261, 262, 284, 310, 319, 324
  faerie, 21, 26, 59-61, 68, 213, 238, 246-251, 257-261
  Sasquatch, 267, 280-284
hydatidform moles, 202
hydrocephaly, 122
hydrogen sulfide, 200
hymnals, 81

Iberia (see also *Spain* and *Portugal*), 111, 130, 146
Iceland, 13, 21, 36, 38, 45, 53, 59, 60, 63, 67, 81, 95, 144, 219, 249
Icelandic Folktales and Legends (book), 81
Idaho (see *United States*)
Idaho Museum of Natural History, 268
Idaho State University, 268
Igbo (people), 144
Illinois (see *United States*)
implants, 167, 183, 234, 252

incubatorium, 223-224, 255, 256
incubus (see also *succubus*), 46, 49, 61,
    213-214
India, 6, 61, 79, 85, 137, 138, 189,
    241, 258, 281, 293, 294, 316, 318,
    323
Indiana (see *United States*)
Indigo Children (see *Star Children*)
Indo-European language, 8
Indonesia, 138, 162, 281
Inexplicable, Yet a Fact (television
    program), 159
infanticide, 101, 108-110, 120, 128
infantile paralysis, 121
Inhumanoids, The (book), 287
Inishark (Galway), 14, 69
Innocent I (Saint), 113
Innu (people), 149
Inspirationally Disadvantaged
    (trope), 314
Intruders (book), 1, 166, 222
Inverness (Scotland), 105
Iran, 142, 143, 230
ircenrraat, 151
Ireland, 3, 9, 13, 14, 15, 26, 27, 28, 30,
    31, 32, 33, 35, 36, 37, 46, 48, 49, 50,
    52, 53, 60, 64, 65, 69, 73, 74, 75, 76,
    77, 78, 79, 82, 83, 84, 85, 88, 93, 94,
    96, 97, 98, 100, 101, 102, 103, 106,
    107, 108, 109, 115, 119, 120, 123,
    126, 129, 135, 142, 156, 171, 174,
    178, 181, 182, 189, 206, 217, 228,
    231, 239, 246, 251, 262, 268, 279,
    280, 285, 295, 300, 304
Irish Fairy Tales (book), 49
iron, 7, 83-87, 91, 97, 107, 108, 141,
    142, 145, 231-232, 234
Iroquois Confederacy (people), 150,
    153
Islam, 142
Islay (Hebrides), 114
Isle of Man, 31, 43, 50, 51, 54, 59,
    73, 95
Isle of Skye (see *Skye*)
Israel, 74, 258, 283
Italy, 63, 82, 92, 324
Ithaca (New York), 174
ivy, 78

Jacob (Bible), 262
Jacobs, David, 180, 181, 200, 204,
    213, 214, 216, 217, 218, 219, 221,
    222, 223, 247, 248, 250, 251, 252,
    256, 257, 262, 319
Jacobs, Joseph, 93
Jamaica, 76, 79, 147
Jamaludin, Ahman, 138
James (King of England), 289
Jamie Freel & the Young Lady
    (story), 54, 112
January (month), 201, 204, 215, 298
Japan, 135, 140-141, 154, 207, 239,
    245, 281-282
jaracaca, 146, 152
Jeffrey, Martin, 164
Jeffries, Anne, 114, 260
Jenny Greenteeth, 29
Jericho (Israel), 74
Jesus Christ (see *Jesus of Nazareth*)
Jesus of Nazareth, 76, 113, 186, 196,
    230, 258
Jewish (see *Judaism*)
Johns Hopkins University School of
    Medicine, 320
Johnson, Alice, 204
Johnson, Marjorie, 291
Johnson, Pamara, 197
Jones, John, 23
Jones, Sue, 265
Jónsson, Arngrímur, 36
Jordan, Joe, 230
Joseph of Cupertino (Saint), 324
Journal of American Folklore, The
    (publication), 150

Judaism, 6, 7, 8, 16, 46, 61, 67, 73, 142, 147, 284, 324

July (month), 139, 153, 186, 193, 270, 272, 291, 297, 302, 303

June (month), 121, 138, 187, 205, 212, 228, 273

Jungle Book, The (animated film), 281

juniper (plant), 84

Juniper (Brother), 324

Ka-wai-hae (Hawaii), 305

Kamal, Reshma, 181, 253, 256

Kamschtschen Wood (Lithuania), 94

kangaroo, 206

Kangra Valley (India), 189

Kantele Player (story), 54

Kappas, 141

kapu moe, 306

kapu noho, 306

Kathlamet (people), 153

Keble College, 261

Keel, John, 3, 5, 25, 187, 279

Keely, John, 36

Keightley, Thomas, 50, 63, 280

Kelso (Scotland), 129

Kennedy, Patrick, 26, 100, 103

Kensey John Homestead, 290

Kentucky (see *United States*)

Keoki, 305-306

Kephas, Aeolus (see *Horsley, Jason*)

Kerner, Nigel, 215

Kets de Vries, Manfred F.R.W., 283

Kettle Creek (Pennsylvania), 154

Key family, 273

Khumbu Himal (Nepal), 282

kielkropf (see *changeling*)

killcrop (see *kielkropf*)

Kilkenny (Ireland), 102

killkrack (see *changeling*)

Kilyakai, 137

Kingdom of the Netherlands (see *Netherlands*)

King Louie, 281

Kinloch (Missouri), 271

Kipling, Rudyard, 71, 281

Kirk, Robert, 64, 75, 247,

Klarer, Elizabeth, 214, 218

Klemsrud, Daniel, 36-37

Knapp, Tracy, 200

Knockfennel (Limerick), 77

Knockma Woods (Galway), 27

knowe (faerie; see *faerie fort*)

Kokjohn, Tyler A., 182

konakijijii, 239

Koran, 230

Koroška (Slovenia), 282

korrigans, 58, 60

krasue, 140

Kripal, Jeffrey, 5, 313

Krishna (Hindu mythology), 6, 316

Kropej, Monika, 282

Kruckow, Christence, 34

Kuen, Chow Hok, 209

kuman thong, 208-209

Kurz, Shane, 217

kushtakaa (see *Sasquatch*)

Kutty, Fatimah, 139

Kvaloyvik bogs (Norway), 154

Kwakiutl (people), 150, 156, 267, 281

la Lechuza, 147, 152

La Mirada (California), 174

La Razon (publication), 172

labor/labour (see *childbirth*)

Labrador (Canada), 149, 271

Labyrinth (film), 8

   Slender Man, 9

Lady Gregory, 31, 34, 50, 52, 64, 65, 87, 104, 115, 231, 280,

Lady Wilde, 14, 24, 33, 45, 48, 51, 78, 107, 115, 120, 121, 142, 247, 261

lake monsters, 38, 103

Lake Superior (United States), 167

lakes, 12, 29, 38, 94, 103, 104, 150,

151, 167, 187, 300, 302
Lalar, 170
Lamashtu, 6
lammergeyers, 154
Lang, David, 297
Lapp, 13
Larch, Oliver (see *Lang, David*)
Las Vegas (Nevada), 159
Lawndale (Illinois), 153
Lawrence (Saint), 113
Le Verger (Brittany), 185
Leahy, Michael, 109
Leask, Julie, 123
Lecouteux, Claude, 15, 29, 107, 294
Legend of Knockgrafton (story), 126
Legendary Fictions of the Irish Celts
    (book), 26
Leipzig (Germany), 32
Leir, Roger, 255
Leitrim (Ireland), 73
LeMarquands, 228
Lemeignan, 134
Lenihan, Eddie, 13
Leonardi, Richard, 146
Lerch, Oliver (see *Lang, David*)
Lesley, Beatrix, 75
Lessö Forest (Scandinavia), 94
Lewels, Joe, 313
Lewis (Hebrides), 74
Lilith, 6-7, 14, 34, 72, 73, 85, 134,
    143, 147, 269, 290, 294
Lilitu (see *Lilith*)
Limerick (Ireland), 108
liminality, 26-27, 31, 67, 82, 101-102,
    107, 183, 186, 294, 319
Lindahl, Carl, 129
Linn, Lowell, 301
Linnaeus, Carl, 121
Litchfield (New Hampshire), 165
Lithuania, 94
Little *Corrigan* (changeling), 117,
    245, 251

Little Hobbie o' The Castleton (see
    Elliot, Robert)
Littlejohn, Lee, 303
Liverpool (England), 164
Llanfabon Changeling, The (story),
    84
Loach, Loretta, 129
Locke, John, 121
London (England), 110, 207
Long, Serephine, 282, 284
Longford (Ireland), 94
Lord of the Rings, The (book), 160
Lore of Prosperine (book), 34-35
Lorgen, Eve, 181, 255
Lough Gur (Limerick), 60, 77
Loughrea (Galway), 65
Louisiana (Missouri), 270
Louisiana (see *United States*)
Lowe, Marlon, 153
Lucifer (see also *Satan, devil*), 13
lullaby, 73
Lumières Dans La Nuit (publication),
    185
Lund family, 169
Lund, Kyle, 169
Luomala, Katharine, 305-306
lupin, 77
lus-mor (see *foxglove*)
Lusmore, 126
Luther, Martin (see also
    Protestantism), 46-47, 124
lutin, 77
Lyman, Sr., Robert, 154
Lynn, Donna, 319
Lysaght, Patricia, 80

MacDougall, James, 44
MacGregor, Alexander, 48, 82
Mack, John, 163, 166, 169, 182, 183,
    207, 215, 217, 218, 246, 252
Mackenzie, Francis Humberston, 293
MacLeod (Scottish clan), 34

Magical Folk (book), 217

Maine (see *United States*)

Malaysia, 138-140, 281

Malekin (abductee), 23, 59, 174

Mali (Africa), 311

Malleus Maleficarum (book), 49

Man in the Moon: or a Discourse of a Voyage Thither, The (book), 47

Mango (hybrid), 284

Manitoba (Canada), 228

Manx Fairy Tales (book), 51

Maori (people), 61, 154

marasmus, 119

March (month), 78, 139, 196, 291

Marchand, Deborah Goodale, 231

Marden, Kathleen, 199, 232

Mariana Islands, 146

marigold, 69

Marion (North Carolina), 285

marjoram, 76

Markovna, Galina, 240

Marl-Pit (England), 29

Martin, Dennis, 273

Martín, Jorge, 291

Martin, Léonie, 324

Masquerade of Angels (book), 207

Massachusetts (see *United States*)

Matthias (changeling), 116

May (month), 25, 78, 151, 273

May Day, 25

Mayo (Ireland), 304

mazakim/mazikeen (see *demon*)

McDermott Lake (Montana), 150

McIntire, Anne, 35

McKean County (Pennsylvania), 154

McWhorter, L.V. , 269

Mecklenburg (Germany), 74

megalith, 28

Meldrum, Jeffrey, 268

Memorial University of Newfoundland, 19

Mên-an-Tol (Cornwall), 100

menehune, 137, 172, 305

Menger, Howard, 294

menhir (see megalith)

Menkin Helmet, 233-234, 319

Menkin, Michael (see *Menkin Helmet*)

Mental Struggle (Druffel resistance technique), 228

mermaid, 12, 38, 95, 280

merrow-maidens (see *mermaid*)

mesenteric disease, 121

Mesopotamia, 6, 34, 143

Messengers: Owls, Synchronicity, and the UFO Abductee, The (book), 313

metabolic disorders, 121, 123

Metaphysical Methods (Druffel resistance technique), 229-230

Metzler, Irina, 126

Mexico, 146-147, 298

MFS (see *Missing Fetus Syndrome*)

mialuka, 149

mice, 206

Michigan (see *United States*)

Middle East (see also *Egypt, Iran, Israel, Mesopotamia, Sudan, Sumer, Turkey*), 141-144, 285

midwives (see also *midwife to the faeries*), 7, 47, 75, 79 173

midwife to the faeries (motif), 63-69, 240, 251-254

milk, 58, 68, 105, 217, 280

cow, 21, 75, 106, 147, 250, 267

human, 51, 62-63, 97, 152, 220, 252, 311

Millennium Children, The (book), 243

Miller, Lynn, 200

Mind Da Crooked Finger (story), 54, 287

Minerva (Ohio), 156

Minerva Monster (see *Sasquatch*)

Minnesota (see *United States*)

miscarriages, 7, 33-34, 136, 139, 143,

147, 197-204, 205, 206, 242-243, 246, 249
missed abortions, 202
Missing Fetus Syndrome, 195-209, 219, 229
Missing Time (book), 166
Mississippi River, 148
Missoula (Montana), 169
Missouri (see *United States*)
Missouri Monster (see *Momo*)
mist (see *fog*)
Miwok (people), 153
Mobolade, Timothy, 145
Mohammed the Prophet, 230
Mohd, Shuhaimi, 139
Molava, Philip, 207
Moloch (deity), 8
Momo (see *Sasquatch*)
Monaghan, Patricia, 25
Moncrief, Jean, 181
Mongolia, 107
monkey-man (see *Sasquatch*)
Monmouthshire (Wales), 116
Mono Village (California), 302
Montana (see *United States*)
Montauk Project, 5
monument bushes, 27
Mooney, James, 120, 128
Moore, Dinah, 54
Mora (Sweden), 136
Morehead (Kentucky), 170-171
Morris dance, 81
Morrison, Grant, 321, 322
Morrison, Sophia, 51
Moscow (Russia), 298
Mosier, William, 312
Moss, Ben, 189
'Most Diabolical Deed, A' (book), 109
mothan, 75-76
Mother Hulda, 205
Mothman, 5
mound (faerie; see *faerie fort*)

Mount Adams (Washington), 149
Mount Everest (Nepal), 282
Mount Rainier (Washington), 301
Mount Shasta (California), 306
Mowgli (character), 281
MUFON (see *Mutual UFO Network*)
MUFON UFO Journal (publication), 165
multifetal pregnancy (see *Vanishing Twin Syndrome*)
multiple personality disorder, 321
Muñoz, Próspera, 168, 212
Munro, Joyce Underwood, 48, 124-125, 183
Munster (Ireland), 109
Murder (entity), 294
Murphy, Jane, 201
Mutual UFO Network, 165, 199
Mutwa, Credo, 207
Mysterious Creatures (book), 280

näkk, 92
Nalusa Chito, 149
Nampa (Idaho), 187
Nanaimo (people), 284
Nant Gwrtheyrn (Wales), 117
Nantucket (Massachusetts), 153
Narváez, Peter, 19, 31
Nashville (Tennessee), 168
National Centre for Immunisation Research and Surveillance of Vaccine Preventable, 123
National Museums of Scotland, 55
National Folklore Collection of Ireland, 33, 98
National Parks Service (United States), 300
National UFO Recording Center, 190, 196
Naves (France), 271
NAWAC (see *North American Wood Ape Conservancy*)

Naz, Gul, 273
Neanderthal, 269-270
Near Death Experience, 47, 114, 188, 230
Nebraska (see *United States*)
Nepal, 189, 282
Nephilim, 4, 61
Nessie (see *lake monsters*)
Netherlands, 45, 198
Netsilik Inuit (people), 150
Nevada (see *United States*)
New England (see also *United States*), 257
Newfoundland (Canada), 19, 25, 31, 33
New Hampshire (see *United States*)
New Jersey (see *United States*)
New Mexico (see *United States*)
New York (see *United States*)
New Zealand, 61, 154
Newquay (Cornwall), 249
Nez Perce (people), 149
Nicaragua, 146
Nicephorus, 3
Nichols, Sandy, 168
nickert, 49, 103
Nigeria (Africa), 144
night marchers (see also *menehune*), 305-306
ninnimbe, 149
Nisqually (people), 281
Nithsdale (Scotland), 63, 92
nixen, 38
Norman, Mark, 19
Normandy (France), 94
norns, 25
North America (see also *Canada, Cuba, Guatemala, Jamaica, Mexico, Nicaragua, Puerto Rico, United States*), 140, 148, 154, 156, 279, 281, 286
North American Wood Ape

Conservancy, 286
North Carolina (see *United States*)
North Dakota (see *United States*)
Northern Miner, The (publication), 189
Northern Ireland (see *Ireland*)
Northumberland (England), 28
Northumbria (England/Scotland), 78
Norway, 20, 25, 48, 104, 154, 191
Nottinghamshire (England), 169
November (month), 25, 30, 170, 199
Nuer (people), 145
NUFORC (see *National UFO Recording Center*)
Nunnelly, Barton, 149, 287
Nyköping (Sweden), 89
Nyman, Joseph, 290

O'Hanlon, John, 27, 75
oak (wood), 78, 54, 93, 96, 101
Obeah, 147
Obyzouth, 6
October (month), 76, 135, 169, 171, 246, 249, 292, 300, 322
odmieńce (see *changeling*)
ogbanje, 144
ogre, 12
Ohio (see *United States*)
ointment
   faerie, 66, 67-69, 77, 95, 252, 282
   witch, 135-136
Oklahoma (see *United States*)
Öland (Sweden), 121
Old Hag, 73, 293
Oldham, Bret, 175, 179-180, 190, 205, 221, 224, 240, 259
Ole-Higue, 157-148
Olmec (people), 146
Olöf, 21, 219
Omaha (people), 149
Onuphrius (Saint), 283-284
orange (fruit), 250

Orange County (New York), 246
orant (see *horehound*)
Oregon (see *United States*)
Orion, 294
Orkney Islands (Scotland), 18, 80, 97, 216
otkon, 150
Our Haunted Planet (book), 3
Our Lady of Fátima (see *Blessed Virgin Mary*)
Owen, Elias, 53
Owens, Pam, 196
Owl-Woman Monsters (see *Tah-tah-kle'-ah*)
Oxford (Oxfordshire), 280
Oxford English Dictionary (book), 55, 116
Ozark Mountains (United States), 156

Pacific Studies (publication), 305
Padam (people), 138
Pahang River (Malaysia), 138
Paiute (people), 148
Pakistan, 273
Palm Sunday, 77
Pan (see *faun*)
pangkelangke (see *pmere kwetethe*)
panikon, 28
Papua New Guinea, 136-137, 199
Paracelsus, 37
Paraguay, 146
Paraipaba (Brazil), 199
Paramahamsa, Ramakrishna, 323
Paris (France), 46, 134
Parkins, Keith, 302
Passport to Magonia (book), 17, 238
Paulides, David, 235, 300-307
Pçuvus-wives, 63
PDDs (see *Pervasive Developmental Disorders*)
pearlwort (see *mothan*)

Pecém (Brazil), 198
Pelley, David, 184
Penanggalan, 139-140
Pendang (Malaysia), 139
Pennsylvania (see *United States*)
pennyroyal, 231
Penobscot River (Maine), 151
Pereira, Manoel, 194
Persinger, Michael, 201
Peru, 172, 173
Pervasive Developmental Disorders (see *autism spectrum disorder*)
Peter Pan, 8-9
phantom social workers, 8, 176
phenylketonuria, 123
Philadelphia (Pennsylvania), 204
Philippines, 138, 146
Phoenix (Arizona), 259
Physical Struggle (Druffel resistance technique), 87, 228-229
Picard, Pauline, 307
Picts (people), 13, 32, 60
Pied Piper of Hamelin, 8
Pied Pipers, 8, 164
Pikeville (Kentucky), 192
Pilcher Mountain (Alaska), 151
Pilus, Maswati, 138
piskie, 19, 25, 27, 36, 53, 66, 75, 81, 100, 116, 204
Pittsburgh (Pennsylvania), 24
pixie (see *piskie*)
pixie led, 17, 29, 34, 37, 79, 187, 305
PKU (see *phenylketonuria*)
Plaza España (Cordoba), 299
plentyn-newid (see *changeling*)
Pliny the Elder, 87
Plounéventer (Brittany), 117
plums, 30
pmere kwetethe, 6, 137, 157, 140, 204
podmenek (see *changeling*)
Poland, 45
poltergeists, 3, 23, 162, 172, 187, 189,

273

pontianak, 138

pooka, 29, 30

Portas, Hector González, 303

Portugal (see also *Iberia*), 5

Pottstown (Pennsylvania), 271

pouk-ledden (see *pixie led*)

poulpican, 96, 284

Powell, Thom, 272

Powell, Diane, 320-321

Pratt, Bob, 199

Pratt, Christina, 324

prayer (see also *Christianity, Judaism, Hinduism, Islam, Appeal to Spiritual Personages*), 3, 14, 30, 32, 47, 59, 82, 88, 100, 141, 230

prayer book, 81

premien (see *changeling*)

progeria, 122

Project Core, 182

Protective Rage (Druffel resistance technique), 229

Protestantism (see *Christianity*)

Prussia (Germany), 116, 147

Pryor Mountains (Montana), 149

Psalm (see *Bible*)

pseudocyesis, 202

psychic toy theory, 293

psychopomps, 293-294, 306, 315, 318

Public Health Reports (publication), 322

Pueblo (people), 34

Puerto Rico, 190, 212, 291

Puhvel, Martin, 299

pukwudgie, 304

Purkiss, Diane, 261

Putana (demoness), 6

Puthoff, Hal, 203-204

Quail, Salina, 242, 291

Quebec (Canada), 153, 193

Queen of Elfan's Nourice, The (story),

63, 97

Rabbi (see *Judaism*)

rabbits, 207

rain (see also *storms*), 20, 25, 125, 135, 153, 267, 300, 303

Rain Man (film), 314

Ralph of Coggeshall, 23, 59, 64

Ramar, 258

Randles, Jenny, 169, 171, 173, 205, 219, 221, 241, 260, 293

ráth (see *faerie fort*)

Rathlin Island (Antrim), 76, 97, 135

Rawhead, 29

Raynham (Massachusetts), 304

Reboul-Lachaux, Jean, 125

Republic of Ireland (see *Ireland*)

red string, 64, 78-79, 293

Redcap, 80, 134

Redcap Sly (see *Redcap*)

Redcomb (see *Redcap*)

Redding (California), 303

Rees, David, 2

Renner, Karen, J., 129

Renner, Timothy, 273

Repellants (Druffel resistance technique), 231

Reticulian, 216

Reykjavik (Iceland), 38

Rhône River (Switzerland, France), 64

Rhŷs, John, 42, 100, 128, 280

Rhys, Shuï, 11

Rhytherch, Shone Tomos Shone, 20-21

Rice, Ted, 207, 240-241

Richard the Rake (story), 51-52

rickets, 121

Ridge Route (California), 228

Righteous Anger (Druffel resistance technique), 229

Ring, Kenneth, 183

ringfort (see *faerie fort*)

Ritter (Oregon), 302

Ritzmann, Jeffrey, 163, 182

rivers, 20, 44, 58, 61, 64, 98, 99, 101, 102-103, 109, 113, 138, 145, 148, 151, 187, 193, 239, 268, 274, 277, 282, 301

Roggenmutter, 28-29

Rojcewicz, Peter M., 114

Rolfe, William J., 133

Roman (culture), 74, 283, 325

Romania, 147

Rosales, Albert, 292

Rosanoff, Michael, 323

rosary (see *Christianity*)

Rose, Alice, 244

roses, 69

Roskinkrans, 38

Roswell, New Mexico, 21

Rousay Changeling, The (story), 97-98

rowan (wood), 78, 84, 102

Roy, John, 101

Rubtsov, Vladimir, 204, 292

Rueff, Jacob, 47

Rügen (Germany), 18

Rumpelstiltskin, 8

Rusin, Rubén Walter, 299

Russia, 19, 104, 130, 135, 159, 171, 184, 193, 240, 283, 292, 298, 321

Russo, William, 304

Ruwa (Zimbabwe), 172

Rybinsk (Russia), 159

Rye-Mother (see *Roggenmutter*)

Saami (people), 60, 96

sage, 76

Salem (Massachusetts), 136

Salem (Oregon), 190, 273

Salish (people), 269

Salk Institute, 225

sallet oil, 69

salt, 43, 74-75, 82, 99, 104, 108, 232

Salt Lake City (Utah), 187

Samhain (see *Halloween*)

Sami (people) (see *Saami*)

San Antonio (Texas), 192

San Bernardino (California), 181

San Francisco de Chiu-Chiu (Chile), 171, 184

Sandfeldt (Germany), 3

Santa Clara (California), 211

Santa Claus, 107

Sargon, 143

Sark (Galway) (see *Shark*)

Sasquatch, 4, 38, 103, 131, 140, 156-157, 263, 265-287, 303, 318, 326

  Bigfoot, 137, 152, 156, 266, 270, 272, 273, 278, 285

  booger, 156, 268

  buk'wus, 267

  Ch'eni, 156

  dsonoqua, 156, 281

  Ebu Gogo, 281

  Goo-teekhl, 150

  kushtakaa, 279

  Minerva Monster, 156

  Momo, 270

  monkey-man, 268

  Seatco, 281

  Sisemite, 281

  Snanaik, 150

  squee'noos, 284

  Tah-tah-kle'-ah, 269

  tery'ky, 283

  tsiatko, 269

  Woodwose, 267

  yeti, 282

  Yowie, 137, 267

Sasquatch: Legend Meets Science (book), 268

Satan (see also *Lucifer, devil*), 28, 47, 59, 113, 134

Satanic Panic, 5, 176

satyr (see *faun*)

savants, 314, 317, 320

Sayce, R.U., 120

Sayne, Adam, 230

Scandinavia (see also *Denmark, Norway, Sweden, Finland,* and *Iceland*), 14, 27, 37, 45, 60, 73, 78, 85, 94, 95, 96, 104, 109, 115, 116, 127

Scarlet Fever, 293

Schuessler, John, 167

Science of Fairy Tales, The (book), 67

Scotland, 9, 16, 18, 25, 31, 32, 34, 36, 37, 42, 43, 44, 49, 51, 55, 58, 59, 62, 63, 68, 72, 74, 75, 76, 78, 80, 83, 85, 88, 92, 96, 97, 98, 101, 105, 107, 109, 114, 115, 117, 128, 129, 134, 181, 216, 228, 267, 278, 321

Scott, Alvina, 256

Scott, David Allen, 302

Scottish Modern Collections (see *National Museums of Scotland*)

Scranton, Laird, 311

screen memories (see *false memory syndrome*)

Scully, Mary, 135

Seatco (see *Sasquatch*)

Seattle (Washington), 242

secondary amenorrhea, 202

Secret Life (book), 200, 220

seer (see *faerie man/woman*)

Seeress of Prevorst (story), 178

Selma (Alabama), 291

Semele (Greek mythology), 316

Sena, Mr. & Mrs., 159

September (month), 140, 165, 171, 172, 194, 270, 273, 292, 295, 297

Shaanxi (China), 279

Shakespeare, William, 47

shaman sickness (see shamanism)

shamanism, 139, 145, 183, 207, 225, 294, 313-315, 318, 321, 323, 324-

325, 326

shamrock (see *clover*)

Shark (Galway), 69

shoreline, 29, 42, 100, 102, 115, 150, 269, 305-306

Shoshone (people), 149

sibhreach (see *changeling*)

Sicily (Italy),

SIDS (see *sudden infant death syndrome*)

Siege at Honobia (story), 279

Sierra Leone (Africa), 268

Sierra Morena (Spain), 284

Sikes, Wirt, 12, 32, 38, 45, 65, 71, 78, 80

Silbury Hill (Wiltshire), 186

Silent Invasion (book), 266

Silver, Carole, 16, 18, 104, 120, 129, 130

Simon, Benjamin, 166

Simpson, Jacqueline, 81, 116

Simrock, Karl, 58

Sims, Derrel, 255

Sioux (people), 152

Sir Gawain and the Green Knight (story), 299

siren (see *mermaid*)

Sisemite (see *Sasquatch*)

skiptingr (see *changeling*)

Skjelbred, Ann, 27, 127

Skomorowsky, Anne, 177

Skookum impression, 270

Slavic culture, 24, 45, 108, 142

Slemen, Tom, 164

Sligo (Ireland), 26, 64

Slovenia, 282

sluag, 31

smallpox, 128-129

smith (see *blacksmith*)

Smith, Paul, 164

Smith, Yvonne, 167, 170

snake, 92, 99, 145, 146

Snanaik, 150

sneezes, 24, 97, 106, 111

Snöva (Norway), 20

social workers (see *phantom social workers*)

Solomon Islands, 284

Sorbonne (France), 15

Sorkin, Alescha & Karya, 298

Sotuyo, José, 194

Soulis, Lord (134)

souterrain systems, 37, 278

South Africa (Africa), 154, 197-198, 207, 214

South America (see also *Argentina, Brazil, Chile, Columbia, Ecuador, Guyana, Paraguay, Peru, Tobago, Trinidad*), 61, 146, 184

South Carolina (see *Carolinas*)

South Dakota (see *United States*)

Sovereignty (see Righteous Anger)

Spain, 59, 168, 284, 303

Spence Field (North Carolina & Tennessee), 273

spina bifida, 122

Spokane (Washington), 184

spriggans, 103

sprites, 12, 265

squee'noos (see *Sasquatch*)

SRI (see *Stanford Research Institute*)

St. Eustache (Paris), 134

St. John (Newfoundland), 25

St. John's Eve, 25

St. Lawrence River (Quebec), 193

Stacy, Dennis, 224

Stainton, Tim, 127

Stamp, Harley, 151

Stanford Research Institute, 203

Stanford University, 177

Star Children, 221-224, 257-261, 310

Star Children (book), 169, 241

steel, 85, 98

Steiger, Brad, 258

Steiner, Susan, 249

Stemmel, Sharyn, 196

Stephen (Saint), 113

stereotypy, 124

Stevens, Jack, 187

Stevenson, Ian, 174

Stewart, Janet, 201

Stick Indians, 149

Stillman, William, 321

stimming, 323

stock (see also *fetch*), 54-55, 61, 62, 106, 121, 125, 138, 255-256, 286, 287

stone soup, 96

Stoner, Denise, 199, 232

Stories from the Messengers: Owls, UFOs and a Deeper Reality (book), 316

Storm Child (story), 298

Storm, Howard, 230

storms (see also *rain, whirlwind*), 25, 33-34, 84, 153, 154, 185, 186, 190, 241, 298-303

Strain, Bob, 286

strawberries, 225

Strieber, Anne, 188, 198

Strieber, Whitley, 21, 181, 182, 188, 198, 215-216, 241, 256, 313

strigoi, 147, 269

succubus (see also *incubus*), 7, 49, 61, 213

Sudan (Africa), 145

sudden infant death syndrome, 121

Suffolk (England), 23

Suggett, Richard, 32

Sumeria, 6, 143

Sumner County (Tennessee), 297

Sunday, 24, 77, 95, 284

Super Natural, The (book), 241

Supernatural (book), 5

Support from Family Members (Druffel resistance technique), 229

Surrey (England), 16
Surrey Heath (England) 164
swamps, 154, 274, 301
Swancer, Brent, 307
Sweden, 19, 66, 67, 79, 89, 102, 107, 121, 136
Switzerland, 37, 64
Swords, Michael, 176
Sydney (Australia), 292
synchromysticism, 262-263

Taff, Barry, 195
Tah-tah-kle'-ah (see *Sasquatch*)
Tailor and the Changeling, The (story), 41-42, 51, 62, 88, 92, 105
Taken (book), 178
Tam Lin (story), 60
Tang dynasty (China), 283
Tarr, D. Ellen K., 182
Te Hokioi (see *Haast eagle)*
Teleel, 265
telepathy,162, 172, 195, 219, 233, 250, 266, 317
Telltown marriage, 97
Teluke, 365
Temple University, 180
tengu, 141, 154, 157, 245
Tennessee (see *United States)*
tery'ky (see *Sasquatch)*
Testament of Solomon, 6, 294
Texas (see *United States)*
Thailand, 140, 208-209
Them and Us (book), 269-270
Thomas, Larch (see *Lang, David)*
Thomas, Oliver (see *Lang, David)*
Threat, The (book), 180
Thumbeline (story), 35, 85
Thunderbird Steals the Wife of Another Bird (story), 155
Thunderbirds, 153-155
Thunderbirds: America's Living Legends of Giant Birds (book), 153

Thursday, 65, 104
thyme, 69, 76
Tiis Lake (Denmark), 94
timber giants (see *Snanaik)*
Timmerman, John P., 2
tingkah dadi janma, 138
Tipperary (Ireland), 30, 109
Tír na nÓg (see *Fairyland)*
Tiver, Tom, 103
tjolong, 138
tobacco, 77, 153
Tobago, 147
Tolkien, J.R.R., 160
Tomey, Debbie, 222, 249
Tower of Babel, 94
Travers, Marlene, 218-219
Trawsfynydd (Wales), 43
Tres Piedras (New Mexico), 292
Trier (Germany), 196
Trinidad, 147
trolls, 12, 51, 60, 66, 89, 135, 216
Trout, Beverly, 253-254
trow, 16, 80, 216-217
Truncale, Deborah, 175, 185, 229, 312
tsiatko (see *Sasquatch)*
Tubber Rowan (Wicklow), 102
Tuesday, 97
Tunguska (Russia), 321
Turner, Karla, 178, 180-181, 183, 207, 239, 241, 243, 249, 256-257
Tuscarora (people), 153
Two Faces, 152
Tylwyth Teg, 11, 18, 24, 43, 51, 60, 76, 113, 305
Tynset (Norway), 191

Uganda (Africa), 268
Ukraine, 204, 298,
United Kingdom (see also *England, Ireland, Scotland*), 8, 122, 135
United States, 4, 5, 8, 19, 26, 37, 42,

71, 76, 122, 135, 140, 148, 152, 153, 154, 155, 156, 155, 156, 167, 173, 182, 190, 228, 257, 267, 268, 273, 279, 281, 286, 298, 300, 316, 317, 323

Alabama, 297
Alaska, 150-151, 156, 279, 281
Arizona, 259
California, 1, 153, 174, 181, 185, 190, 202, 211, 215, 228, 268, 301, 302, 303, 306
Colorado, 258
Connecticut, 183
Delaware, 290
Florida, 230
Hawaii, 137, 172, 305-306
Idaho, 187, 268
Illinois, 153, 179, 271
Indiana, 197
Kentucky, 170-171, 192
Louisiana, 212
Maine, 151
Massachusetts, 136, 153, 253, 304
Michigan, 258
Minnesota, 36, 201
Missouri, 270, 271, 272
Montana, 149, 150, 151, 169
Nebraska, 151
Nevada, 159
New Hampshire, 165, 166
New Jersey, 184
New Mexico, 21, 153, 192, 292
New York, 36, 109, 174, 186, 232, 246
North Carolina, 148, 273, 285, 316
North Dakota, 151
Ohio, 156, 216, 272
Oklahoma, 278-279
Oregon, 177, 190, 191, 253, 269, 272, 273, 302
Pennsylvania, 24, 154, 196, 204, 270, 271, 272, 319

South Carolina, 148
South Dakota, 151
Tennessee, 168, 196, 232, 273, 297
Texas, 131, 187, 192, 286
Utah, 187
Virginia, 33, 174, 189
Washington, 149, 153, 184, 191, 242, 281, 287, 302
West Virginia, 5, 153
Wisconsin, 9, 36, 206, 258, 271, 290

University College Cork, 15
University of Connecticut, 183
University of Oregon, 177, 191
University of Oxford, 280
University of Pittsburgh, 24
University of Tromsø, 26
University of Virginia School of Medicine, 174
University of Washington, 191
Utah (see *United States*)
UV-A light, 255

Vaeni, Jeremy, 182
Vallee, Jacques, 17, 238
Valley of Hinnom (Israel), 283
vampire, 59, 76, 86, 102, 138, 147-148
Van Klausen, Morgana, 202, 229, 231
Vancouver (Canada), 254, 260, 281
Vanishing Twin Syndrome, 243-244
Vega, Fresia, 171
velostat, 234
Vendramini, Danny, 269-270
Venus, 196
Veracruz (Mexico), 146
Verna (Sweden), 89
Vilas Boas, Antônio, 214, 218
Vingåkir (Sweden), 89
vipers bugloss, 77
Virgin Mary (see *Blessed Virgin Mary*)

virgines silvestres, 25
Virginia (see *United States*)
Virtue, Doreen, 260
Visnudutas, 294
vixlingr (see *changeling*)
von Sydow, Carl Wilhelm, 19-20
Voronezh (Russia), 171, 184, 292
VTS (see *Vanishing Twin Syndrome*)

wachnacht, 7
Wagenvoort, Ine, 198-199
Wahiawa gulch (Hawaii), 137
Wahine-oma'o, 137
wala, 136-137, 199
Waldron, George, 50, 51, 95
Wales (England), 11, 14, 18, 20, 23, 24, 25, 29, 32, 35, 42, 43, 50, 53, 55, 65, 68, 71, 72, 76, 80, 84, 87, 93, 99, 100, 108, 115, 116, 117, 125, 252, 262, 298, 305
Walking Among Us (book), 213
Walter, Abel and Dacey, 32
Wampanoag (people), 304
Wanchun, Yang, 279
warnungmeksooark, 151
Washington (see *United States*)
Washo (people), 148
water babies, 148
water parsley, 135
Waterford (Munster), 109
Watts, D.C., 76
Waukesha (Wisconsin), 9
Wauwatosa (Wisconsin), 290
wechselbalg (see *changeling*)
wechselkind (see *changeling*)
Wednesday, 25
Wednesday Phenomenon, 25
week (see *Tuesday, Wednesday*, etc.)
Weekly Oregon Statesman (publication), 273
Weekly World News (publication), 281
weeping birch (see *birch*)

well, 19, 44, 96, 102, 298
Well of the Ash Tree (see *Tubber Rowan*)
Wenatchee Lake (Washington), 302
Wentz, W.Y. Evans, 13, 18, 23, 24, 25, 27, 30, 37, 38, 42, 47, 48, 51, 52, 54, 58, 72, 76, 86, 88, 111, 112, 113, 117, 125, 178, 204, 228, 241, 245, 251, 295, 305
West Virginia (see *United States*)
Wester Wood (Germany), 45
Westerwald (Germany), 94
Westropp, T.J., 69
whirlwind (see also *storms, rain*), 33-34, 54, 61, 88, 103, 142, 241
whisky/whiskey, 43, 75, 171
White Monkey, The (story), 283
White, Gordon, 87, 108, 326
Whiting (New Jersey), 184
Whitley, Jan, 228
Whitsuntide, 24, 25, 102
whortleberries (see *bilberries*), 30
Wicklow (Ireland), 102
Wienholt, 86
Wild Indians (see *yehasuri*)
Wild Man, The (book), 283
Wilde, Oscar, 14, 120
Wilde, Lady (see *Lady Wilde*)
Wilde, William, 120
Will-O-the-Wisp, 27, 208
William of Auvergne, 46
William, Edmund John, 50, 115
Williams syndrome, 123
Wilson, Katharina, 221, 222-223, 246
Wiltshire (England), 186
Wingate, Patsy, 192, 228
Wisconsin (see *United States*)
wisselkind (see *changeling*)
witch, 19, 32, 34, 75, 78, 81, 82, 84, 85, 97, 103, 104, 110, 126, 133-136, 140, 147, 149, 156, 163, 186, 214, 293, 294, 311

Baba Yaga, 135, 156
Benemmerinnen, 6-7
brujas, 147
Yamamba, 135, 140
Yellow Muitearteach, 134
witch's mark, 136
wolf, 19, 20, 313
Wolff, Christian (see *Accountant, The*), 314
Woodlawn Plantation, 33
Woodwose (see *Sasquatch*)
wooly booger (see *booger*)
Worley, Don, 190, 265
wormwood, 77
Wright State University, 312
Wright, Dan, 175, 199
Wyandot (people), 153

Yallery Brown (story), 103, 116
yama-uba (see *yamaotoko*)
Yamadutas, 294
Yamamba (see *witch*)
yamaotoko, 140
Yankton (Oregon), 272
yarrow, 231
Yasy Yateré, 146
Yeats, W.B., 14, 33, 35, 47, 49, 53, 54, 64, 112, 280
yehasuri, 148, 157, 280
Yel'-lo-kin, 153
Yellow Muitearteach (see *witch*)
yeti (see *Sasquatch*)
Yggdrasil, 78
Yokut (people), 268
Yorkshire (York), 66, 84
   York (England), 66, 84
Yoruba (people), 144, 152
Young, Katie, 280
Young, Simon, 32
Youngstown (Pennsylvania), 270
Yowie (see *Sasquatch*)
Yungay (Peru), 173

Yup'ik (people), 151

Zabava, Andrew, 298
Zanna, 265
Zennor (Cornwall), 68
Zeus (Greek mythology), 316
Zhirkov, Maxim, 193-194
Zimbabwe (Africa), 172
Zimmern Chronicle (publication), 79
zinc, 85, 86
Zohar (book), 6, 46
Zolotaryeva, Inna, 159
Zoroastrianism, 74
Zulu, 144

About the Author

JOSHUA CUTCHIN is an author of speculative nonfiction and a professional tuba player based out of Roswell, Georgia. An alumnus of the Universities of Wisconsin and Georgia, Cutchin is author of two other books: *A Trojan Feast: The Food and Drink Offerings of Aliens, Faeries, and Sasquatch* and *The Brimstone Deceit: An In-Depth Examination of Supernatural Scents, Otherworldly Odors, and Monstrous Miasmas*, both published by Anomalist Books. His writing is also featured in 2017's *UFOs: Reframing the Debate* and 2018's *Wood Knocks, Vol. 3: A Journal of Sasquatch Research*. Cutchin can be heard on the weekly podcast *Where Did the Road Go?* and maintains an online presence at JoshuaCutchin.com.

Lightning Source UK Ltd.
Milton Keynes UK
UKHW02f0627010818
326613UK00011B/679/P